Praise for *The Afghanistan Papers*

"Superb exposé of a war built on lies . . . Whitlock's book is rooted in a database most journalists and historians could only dream of, but it is far more than the sum of its sources. You never feel the weight of the underlying documents because they are so deftly handled . . . [with] many gobsmacking anecdotes and tragic absurdities."
— *The Guardian*

"Craig Whitlock has forged a searing indictment of the deceit, blunders, and hubris of senior military and civilian officials, with the same tragic echoes of the Vietnam conflict. The American dead, wounded, and their families deserved wiser and more honorable leaders."
—Tom Bowman, NPR Pentagon correspondent

"The excellent new book . . . Bombshell revelations . . . [and] damning evidence of things we already intuited."
— *The Washington Post*

"At once page-turning and rigorous, *The Afghanistan Papers* makes a lasting and revelatory contribution to the record of America's tragic management of our longest war. In transparent and nuanced detail, Whitlock chronicles how American leaders and commanders undermined their country's promises to the Afghans who counted on them and to the U.S. troops who made the ultimate sacrifice after 9/11."
—Steve Coll, Pulitzer Prize–winning author of *Ghost Wars* and *Directorate S*

"*The Afghanistan Papers* is a gripping account of why the war in Afghanistan lasted so long. The missed opportunities, the outright mistakes, and more than anything the firsthand accounts from senior commanders who only years later acknowledged they simply did not tell the American people what they knew about how the war was going."

—Barbara Starr, CNN Pentagon correspondent

"Whitlock is unsparing in his assessment of presidents Bush, Obama and Trump, as well as U.S. military leaders, saying all failed to level with the American public."

—NPR

"A hallmark achievement of primary source reporting . . . *The Afghanistan Papers* reminds readers of the power of reportage built on documented evidence with names attached."

—*The Daily Beast*

"A gripping chronicle . . . tenacious."

—*The New York Review of Books*

"A damning account of America's longest war that reveals what top generals and government officials really knew about the cost and futility of the mission. Whitlock puts the pieces together in a way nobody has before, bringing us the most comprehensive, inside story of this conflict ever told."

—Rajiv Chandrasekaran, author of *Little America: The War Within the War for Afghanistan*

"*The Afghanistan Papers* is an autopsy of America's folly into central Asia. It chronicles years of recklessness and bad decision-making that the nation is still grappling with today. This book is one part indictment of mission creep and American hubris, and one part warning to future leaders."

—Kevin Maurer, coauthor of the *New York Times* bestsellers *No Easy Day* and *American Radical*

"Again and again, Whitlock presents the pessimistic assessments and harsh judgments of officials who believed that their remarks would never become public. . . . These files make *The Afghanistan Papers* the most comprehensive American accounting of the conflict."

—*The Intercept*

"Abundant, authoritative, and utterly damning . . . Drawn from unimpeachable sources."

—*The American Conservative*

"Ten, 20, 50 years hence, when a once-again ascendant America is looking to prove itself militarily in a faraway land, *The Afghanistan Papers* will be one of the books that that war's hapless planners will eventually kick themselves for ignoring."

—*PopMatters*

"An unputdownable account of imperial hubris, blundering and deception."

—*The Spectator*

A damning, gut-punch account of a misguided—and misrepresented—military debacle."

—*Washington Independent Review of Books*

"Whitlock's relentless, laser-like focus on the misjudgments and challenges in the early and middle years of the war delivers big-picture clarity. . . . *The Afghanistan Papers* deserves to be counted among the small number of books . . . that will still be read by future generations when they seek to understand America's longest war."

—*The Nation*

THE AFGHANISTAN PAPERS

A SECRET HISTORY
OF THE WAR

* * *

CRAIG WHITLOCK

SIMON & SCHUSTER PAPERBACKS
New York London Toronto Sydney New Delhi

Simon & Schuster Paperbacks
An Imprint of Simon & Schuster, Inc.
1230 Avenue of the Americas
New York, NY 10020

First Simon & Schuster trade paperback edition August 2022

SIMON & SCHUSTER PAPERBACKS and colophon are
registered trademarks of Simon & Schuster, Inc.

For information about special discounts for bulk purchases,
please contact Simon & Schuster Special Sales at 1-866-506-1949
or business@simonandschuster.com.

The Simon & Schuster Speakers Bureau can bring authors to
your live event. For more information or to book an event,
contact the Simon & Schuster Speakers Bureau at 1-866-248-3049
or visit our website at www.simonspeakers.com.

Manufactured in the United States of America

1   3   5   7   9   10   8   6   4   2

The Library of Congress has cataloged the hardcover edition as follows:
Names: Whitlock, Craig, author.
Title: The Afghanistan papers : a secret history of the war / Craig Whitlock.
Description: First Simon & Schuster hardcover edition. | New York :
Simon & Schuster, 2021. | Includes bibliographical references and index.
Identifiers: LCCN 2021016683 | ISBN 9781982159009 (hardcover) |
ISBN 9781982159023 (ebook)
Subjects: LCSH: Afghan War, 2001–
Classification: LCC DS371.412 .W4825 2021 | DDC 958.104/7—dc23
LC record available at https://lccn.loc.gov/2021016683

ISBN 978-1-9821-5900-9
ISBN 978-1-9821-5901-6 (pbk)
ISBN 978-1-9821-5902-3 (ebook)

For Jenny and Kyle,
with love and admiration

Contents

Foreword   xv

PART ONE   **A FALSE TASTE OF VICTORY, 2001-2002**

CHAPTER ONE   A Muddled Mission   3

CHAPTER TWO   "Who Are the Bad Guys?"   17

CHAPTER THREE The Nation-Building Project   29

PART TWO   **THE GREAT DISTRACTION, 2003-2005**

CHAPTER FOUR   Afghanistan Becomes an
               Afterthought   43

CHAPTER FIVE   Raising an Army from the Ashes   55

CHAPTER SIX   Islam for Dummies   67

CHAPTER SEVEN Playing Both Sides   77

PART THREE **THE TALIBAN COMES BACK, 2006-2008**

CHAPTER EIGHT Lies and Spin   91

CHAPTER NINE   An Incoherent Strategy   103

CHAPTER TEN   The Warlords   115

CHAPTER ELEVEN   A War on Opium   129

PART FOUR   **OBAMA'S OVERREACH, 2009–2010**

CHAPTER TWELVE   Doubling Down   145

CHAPTER THIRTEEN "A Dark Pit of Endless Money"   157

CHAPTER FOURTEEN From Friend to Foe   169

CHAPTER FIFTEEN   Consumed by Corruption   183

PART FIVE   **THINGS FALL APART, 2011–2016**

CHAPTER SIXTEEN   At War with the Truth   199

CHAPTER SEVENTEEN The Enemy Within   213

CHAPTER EIGHTEEN The Grand Illusion   227

PART SIX   **STALEMATE, 2017–2021**

CHAPTER NINETEEN   Trump's Turn   241

CHAPTER TWENTY   The Narco-State   253

CHAPTER TWENTY-ONE Talking with the Taliban   263

                  Epilogue   277
                  Acknowledgments   285
                  Note on Sources   291
                  Endnotes   295
                  Bibliography   333
                  Photo Credits   335
                  Index   337

Only a free and unrestrained press can effectively expose deception in government. And paramount among the responsibilities of a free press is the duty to prevent any part of the government from deceiving the people and sending them off to distant lands to die of foreign fevers and foreign shot and shell.

> —Supreme Court Justice Hugo L. Black, in his concurring opinion in *New York Times Co. v. United States*, also known as the Pentagon Papers case, June 30, 1971. In a 6–3 decision, the Court ruled that the U.S. government could not block *The New York Times* or *The Washington Post* from publishing the Defense Department's secret history of the Vietnam War.

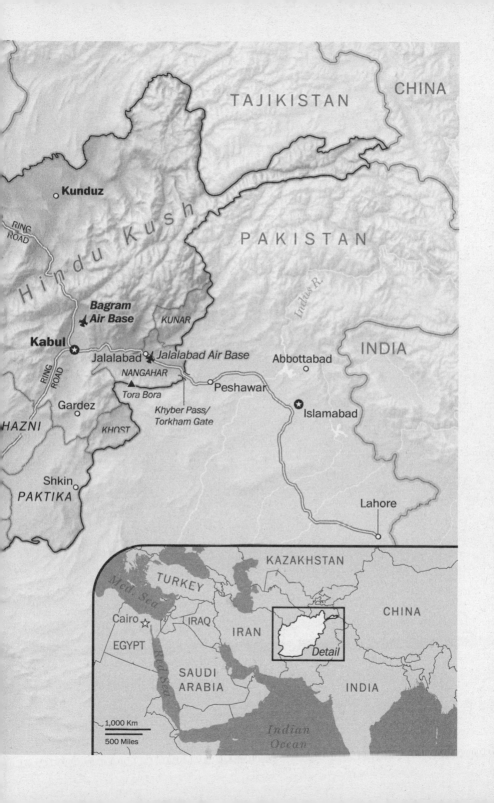

Foreword

Two weeks after the 9/11 attacks, as the United States girded for war in Afghanistan, a reporter asked Defense Secretary Donald Rumsfeld a straightforward question: Would U.S. officials lie to the news media about military operations in order to mislead the enemy?

Rumsfeld stood at the podium in the Pentagon briefing room. The building still smelled of smoke and jet fuel from when American Airlines flight 77 exploded into the west wall, killing 189 people. The defense secretary started to reply by paraphrasing a quotation from British Prime Minister Winston Churchill: "In wartime, truth is so precious that she should always be attended by a bodyguard of lies." Rumsfeld explained how the Allies, prior to D-Day, ran a disinformation campaign called Operation Bodyguard to confuse the Germans about when and where the invasion of western Europe would take place in 1944.

Rumsfeld sounded as if he were justifying the practice of spreading lies during wartime, but then he pivoted and insisted he would never do such a thing. "The answer to your question is, no, I cannot imagine a situation," he said. "I don't recall that I've ever lied to the press. I don't intend to, and it seems to me that there will not be reason for it. There are dozens of ways to avoid having to put yourself in a position where you're lying. And I don't do it."

Asked if the same could be expected of everyone else in the Defense Department, Rumsfeld paused and gave a little smile.

"You've got to be kidding," he said.

The Pentagon press corps laughed. It was classic Rumsfeld: clever, forceful, unscripted, disarming. A former star wrestler at Princeton, he was a master at not getting pinned down.

Twelve days later, on October 7, 2001, when the U.S. military began bombing Afghanistan, no one foresaw that it would turn into the most protracted war in American history—longer than World War I, World War II and Vietnam combined.

Unlike the war in Vietnam, or the one that would erupt in Iraq in 2003, the decision to take military action against Afghanistan was grounded in near-unanimous public support. Shaken and angered by al-Qaeda's devastating terrorist strikes, Americans expected their leaders to defend the homeland with the same resolve as they did after the Japanese attack on Pearl Harbor. Within three days of 9/11, Congress passed legislation authorizing the Bush administration to go to war against al-Qaeda and any country that harbored the network.

For the first time, the North Atlantic Treaty Organization (NATO) invoked Article 5, the alliance's collective commitment to defend any of its member states under attack. The United Nations Security Council unanimously condemned the "horrifying terrorist attacks" and called on all countries to bring the perpetrators to justice. Even hostile powers expressed solidarity with the United States. In Iran, thousands attended candlelight vigils and hardliners stopped shouting "Death to America" at weekly prayers for the first time in twenty-two years.

With such strong backing, U.S. officials had no need to lie or spin to justify the war. Yet leaders at the White House, the Pentagon and the State Department soon began to make false assurances and to paper over setbacks on the battlefield. As months and years passed, the dissembling became more entrenched. Military commanders and diplomats found it harder to acknowledge mistakes and deliver clear-eyed, honest assessments in public.

No one wanted to admit that the war that started as a just cause had deteriorated into a losing one. From Washington to Kabul, an unspoken conspiracy to mask the truth took hold. Omissions inexorably led to deceptions and eventually to outright absurdities. Twice—in 2003 and again in 2014—the U.S. government declared an end to combat operations, episodes of wishful thinking that had no connection to reality on the ground.

*   *   *

President Barack Obama had vowed to end the war and bring all the troops home, but he failed to do so as his second term neared an end in 2016. Americans had grown weary of endless conflict overseas. Disillusioned, many people stopped paying attention.

By then I had logged almost seven years as a beat reporter covering the Pentagon and the U.S. military for *The Washington Post.* I had covered four different secretaries of defense and five war commanders, traveling with senior military officials to Afghanistan and the surrounding region on many occasions. Before that, I had reported overseas for six years as a *Washington Post* foreign correspondent, writing about al-Qaeda and its terrorist affiliates in Afghanistan, Pakistan, the Middle East, North Africa and Europe.

Like many journalists, I knew Afghanistan was a mess. I had grown dismissive of the U.S. military's hollow statements that it was always making progress and on the right track. *The Washington Post* and other news organizations had exposed systemic problems with the war for years. Books and memoirs had delivered insider accounts of pivotal battles in Afghanistan and political infighting in Washington. But I wondered if everyone had missed the big picture.

How had the war degenerated into a stalemate with no realistic prospect for an enduring victory? The United States and its allies had initially crushed the Taliban and al-Qaeda in 2001. What went wrong? No one had conducted a thorough public accounting of the strategic failures or provided an unsparing explanation of how the campaign fell apart.

To this day, there has been no Afghanistan version of the 9/11 Commission, which held the government responsible for its inability to prevent the worst terrorist attack on American soil. Nor has Congress convened an Afghanistan version of the Fulbright Hearings, when senators aggressively questioned the war in Vietnam. With so many people from both parties responsible for a multitude of errors, few political leaders have wanted to assign or accept blame.

In summer 2016, I received a news tip that an obscure federal agency, the Office of the Special Inspector General for Afghanistan Reconstruction, or SIGAR, had interviewed hundreds of participants in the war and that many had unloaded pent-up frustrations. SIGAR had conducted the interviews for a project titled Lessons Learned, which was intended to diagnose policy failures in Afghanistan so the United States would not repeat the mistakes in the future.

That September, SIGAR began to publish a series of Lessons Learned reports that highlighted problems in Afghanistan. But the reports, weighed down with leaden government prose, omitted the harsh criticism and finger-pointing that I heard the interviews contained.

An investigative journalist's mission in life is to find out what truths the government is hiding and reveal them to the public. So I filed Freedom of Information Act requests with SIGAR seeking transcripts, notes and audio recordings of the Lessons Learned interviews. I argued the public had a right to know the government's internal criticisms of the war—the unvarnished truth.

At every turn, SIGAR delayed and resisted the requests—a hypocritical response for an agency that Congress had created to provide accountability for the enormous sums of taxpayer dollars being spent on the war. *The Post* had to file two federal lawsuits to compel SIGAR to release the Lessons Learned documents. After a three-year legal battle, SIGAR finally disclosed more than 2,000 pages of previously unpublished notes of interviews with 428 people who played a direct role in the war, from generals and diplomats to aid workers and Afghan officials.

The agency redacted portions of the documents and concealed the identities of most of the people it interviewed. But the interviews showed that many senior U.S. officials privately viewed the war as an unmitigated disaster, contradicting a chorus of rosy public statements from officials at the White House, the Pentagon and the State

Department, who assured Americans year after year that they were making progress in Afghanistan.

Speaking frankly because they assumed their remarks would not become public, U.S. officials confessed to SIGAR that the war plans had fatal flaws and that Washington had wasted billions of dollars trying to remake Afghanistan into a modern nation. The interviews also exposed the U.S. government's botched attempts to curtail runaway corruption, build a competent Afghan army and police force, and put a dent in Afghanistan's thriving opium trade.

Many of those interviewed described explicit and sustained efforts by the U.S. government to deliberately mislead the public. They said officials at military headquarters in Kabul—and at the White House—routinely distorted statistics to make it appear the United States was winning the war when that was plainly not the case.

Astonishingly, commanding generals admitted that they had tried to fight the war without a functional strategy:

"There was no campaign plan. It just wasn't there," complained Army Gen. Dan McNeill, who twice served as the U.S. commander during the Bush administration.

"There was no coherent long-term strategy," said British Gen. David Richards, who led U.S. and NATO forces from 2006 to 2007. "We were trying to get a single coherent long-term approach—a proper strategy—but instead we got a lot of tactics."

Other officials said the United States flubbed the war from the start, committing missteps on top of miscalculations on top of misjudgments:

"We did not know what we were doing," said Richard Boucher, who served as the Bush administration's top diplomat for South and Central Asia.

"We didn't have the foggiest notion of what we were undertaking," echoed Army Lt. Gen. Douglas Lute, who served as the White House war czar under Bush and Obama.

Lute lamented that so many U.S. troops had lost their lives. But in a shocking departure from convention for a three-star general, he went further and suggested that the government had squandered those sacrifices.

"If the American people knew the magnitude of this dysfunction . . . 2,400 lives lost," Lute said. "Who will say this was in vain?"

Over two decades, more than 775,000 U.S. troops deployed to Afghanistan. Of those, 2,325 died there and 20,712 came home wounded. The U.S. government has not calculated a comprehensive total of how much it spent on war-related expenses, but most estimates exceed $1 trillion.

*   *   *

With their forthright descriptions of how the United States became stuck in a faraway war, as well as the government's determination to conceal them from the public, the Lessons Learned interviews broadly resembled the Pentagon Papers, the Defense Department's top-secret history of the Vietnam War. When they were leaked in 1971, the Pentagon Papers caused a sensation. They revealed that the government had long lied to the public about how the United States came to be embroiled in Vietnam.

Bound into forty-seven volumes, the 7,000-page study was based entirely on internal government documents: diplomatic cables, decision-making memos, intelligence reports. To preserve secrecy Defense Secretary Robert McNamara issued an order prohibiting the authors from interviewing anyone.

The Lessons Learned project faced no such restrictions. SIGAR staffers carried out their interviews between 2014 and 2018, mostly with officials who served during the Bush and Obama years. Unlike the Pentagon Papers, none of the Lessons Learned documents was originally classified as a government secret. Once *The Washington Post* pushed to make them public, however, other federal agencies intervened and classified some material after the fact.

The Lessons Learned interviews contained few revelations about military operations. But running throughout were torrents of criticism that refuted the official narrative of the war, from its earliest days through the start of the Trump administration.

To supplement the Lessons Learned interviews, I obtained hundreds of previously classified memos about the war in Afghanistan that Rumsfeld dictated or received between 2001 and 2006. Dubbed "snowflakes" by Rumsfeld and his staff, the memos are brief instructions or comments that the Pentagon boss dictated to his underlings, often several times a day.

Rumsfeld made a select number of his snowflakes public in 2011, posting them online in conjunction with his memoir, *Known and Unknown*. But most of his snowflake collection—a blizzard of paperwork, composed of an estimated 59,000 pages—remained confidential.

In 2017, in response to a Freedom of Information Act (FOIA) lawsuit filed by the National Security Archive, a nonprofit research institute based at George Washington University, the Defense Department began releasing the remainder of Rumsfeld's snowflakes on a rolling basis. The Archive shared them with me.

Worded in Rumsfeld's brusque style, many of the snowflakes foreshadowed problems that would continue to haunt the U.S. military more than a decade later. "I have no visibility into who the bad guys are in Afghanistan," Rumsfeld complained in a memo to his intelligence chief—almost two years after the war had started.

I also obtained several oral-history interviews that the nonprofit Association for Diplomatic Studies and Training conducted with officials who served in the U.S. embassy in Kabul. Those interviews provided a blunt perspective from Foreign Service officers who vented about Washington's fundamental ignorance of Afghanistan and its mishandling of the war.

As I gradually absorbed all the interviews and memos, it became clear to me that they constituted a secret history of the war—an unflinching appraisal of the never-ending conflict. The documents also showed that U.S. officials had repeatedly lied to the public about what was happening in Afghanistan, just as they had in Vietnam.

Drawing on the talents of a legion of newsroom staffers, *The Washington Post* published a series of articles about the documents in December 2019. Millions of people read the series, which included a database of the interviews and snowflakes that *The Post* published online as a public service.

Congress, which had largely ignored the war for years, held multiple hearings to discuss and debate the findings. In testimony, generals, diplomats and other officials admitted the government had not been honest with the public. Lawmakers of all political persuasions expressed anger and frustration.

"It's a damning record," said Rep. Eliot Engel (D-N.Y.), chairman of the House Foreign Affairs Committee. "It underscores the lack of honest public conversation between the American people and their leaders about what we were doing in Afghanistan." Sen. Rand Paul (R-Ky.) called *The Washington Post*'s series "extraordinarily troubling. It portrays a U.S. war effort severely impaired by mission creep and suffering from a complete absence of clear and achievable objectives."

The revelations touched a nerve. Many Americans had suspected all along that the government had lied to them about the war, and they were angry. The public hungered for more evidence, for more truth-telling about what really happened.

I knew the U.S. Army had conducted some oral-history interviews with soldiers who had served in Afghanistan and had published a few academic monographs about them. But I soon discovered that the Army had a huge trove of these documents.

Between 2005 and 2015, the Army's Operational Leadership Experience project—part of the Combat Studies Institute at Fort Leavenworth, Kansas—interviewed more than 3,000 troops who had served overseas in the "Global War on Terror." Most had fought in Iraq, but a large number had deployed to Afghanistan.

I spent weeks sifting through the unclassified, fully transcribed interviews and set aside more than 600 that featured Afghanistan veterans. The Army oral histories contained vivid, first-hand accounts, mostly from junior officers posted in the field. I also obtained a smaller number of oral-history interviews that were conducted by the U.S Army Center of Military History in Washington, D.C.

Because the Army authorized the interviews for historical research, many of the troops were more open about their experiences than they likely would have been with a journalist working on a news story. Collectively, they presented a raw and honest perspective about the war's faults, the flip side of the talking points peddled by the brass at the Pentagon.

I found another cache of revelatory documents at the University of Virginia. Since 2009, the Miller Center, a nonpartisan affiliate of the university that specializes in political history, has directed an oral-history project of the presidency of George W. Bush. The Miller Center interviewed about a hundred people who worked with Bush, including key administration officials, outside advisers, lawmakers and foreign leaders.

Most consented to the interviews on the condition that the transcripts remain confidential for many years—or until after their deaths. Starting in November 2019, the Miller Center opened portions of its George W. Bush archive to the public. For my purposes, the timing was perfect. I obtained a dozen transcripts of oral-history interviews with military commanders, cabinet members and other senior officials who oversaw the war in Afghanistan.

Once again, the University of Virginia oral-history interviews conveyed an unusual degree of candor. Marine Gen. Peter Pace, who served as chairman and vice-chairman of the Joint Chiefs of Staff under Bush, voiced regret that he had failed to level with the public about how long the wars in Afghanistan and Iraq might last.

"I needed to be saying to the American people that this isn't about months and years, this is about decades," Pace said. "Because I didn't do that, because to my knowledge President Bush didn't do that, the American people I think had a vision of quick-in and quick-out."

*   *   *

This book does not aim to provide an exhaustive record of the U.S. war in Afghanistan. Nor is it a military history that dwells on combat operations. Rather, it is an attempt to explain what went wrong and how three consecutive presidents and their administrations failed to tell the truth.

All told, *The Afghanistan Papers* is based on interviews with more than 1,000 people who played a direct part in the war. The Lessons Learned interviews, oral histories and Rumsfeld snowflakes comprise more than 10,000 pages of documents. Unedited and unfiltered, they reveal the voices of people—from those who made policy in Washington to those who fought in the mountains and deserts of Afghanistan—who knew that the official version of the war being fed to the American people was untrue, or aggressively sanitized at best.

Yet in public, almost no senior government officials had the courage to admit that the United States was slowly losing a war that Americans once overwhelmingly supported. With their complicit silence, military and political leaders avoided accountability and dodged reappraisals that could have changed the outcome or shortened the conflict. Instead, they chose to bury their mistakes and let the war drift.

PART ONE

A FALSE TASTE
OF VICTORY

2001–2002

CHAPTER ONE

A Muddled Mission

Marine One, the white-topped presidential helicopter, made a gentle landing on the perfectly clipped grass of the Virginia Military Institute's Parade Ground around 10 a.m. on April 17, 2002, a hot and sunny spring morning in the Shenandoah Valley. In Cameron Hall, the school's basketball arena, about 2,000 cadets were trying not to sweat in their starched gray-and-white full-dress uniforms as they waited to welcome the commander in chief. When President George W. Bush walked onto the stage a few minutes later, winking and waving and flashing upright thumbs, the audience rose to its feet and gushed with applause.

Bush had reason to smile and bask in the attention. Six months earlier, he had ordered the U.S. military to go to war in Afghanistan to retaliate for the 9/11 terrorist attacks that killed 2,977 people in New York City, northern Virginia and Shanksville, Pennsylvania. Unlike any other war in American history, this one began suddenly and unexpectedly, provoked by a stateless enemy embedded in a landlocked country on the other side of the globe. But the initial success of the military campaign had surpassed the expectations of even the most optimistic field commanders. Victory appeared in hand.

Relying on a combination of punishing airpower, CIA-backed warlords and commando teams on the ground, the United States and its allies toppled the Taliban-led government in Kabul in less than six weeks and killed or captured hundreds of al-Qaeda fighters. The terrorist network's surviving leaders, including Osama bin Laden, went into hiding or fled to other countries.

There had been blessedly few American casualties. By the time of Bush's speech, twenty U.S. troops had died in Afghanistan—one more than had been killed during the four-day U.S. invasion of the Caribbean island of Grenada in 1983. Encounters with hostile forces became so sporadic that some soldiers complained of boredom. Many units had already returned home. About 7,000 U.S. troops remained.

The war transformed Bush's political standing. Although he barely won the presidency in the disputed 2000 election, polls showed 75 percent of Americans now approved of his job performance. In his remarks at the military academy, Bush confidently appraised the months ahead. With the Taliban routed and al-Qaeda on the run, he said the war had moved into a second phase, with the United States focused on eliminating terrorist cells in other countries. He cautioned that violence in Afghanistan could flare up again, but offered reassurances that he had the situation under control.

Alluding to disastrous forays by Britain and the Soviet Union during the past two centuries, Bush promised that the United States would avoid the fate of other great powers that had invaded Afghanistan. "It's been one of initial success, followed by long years of floundering and ultimate failure," he said. "We're not going to repeat that mistake."

Yet Bush's speech masked worries circulating among the top members of his leadership team. As the president flew to southwestern Virginia that morning, his secretary of defense, Donald Rumsfeld, was thinking out loud at the Pentagon, where he worked at a standing desk in a third-floor office in the outer ring of the building. Contrary to the soothing messages he and Bush had delivered in public for months, Rumsfeld very much feared the U.S. military could get stuck in Afghanistan and that it lacked a clear exit strategy.

At 9:15 a.m., he crystallized his thoughts and dictated a brief memo, a longtime habit. He wrote so many that his staff called them snowflakes—white-paper notes from the boss that piled up on their desks. This one was marked classified and addressed to four senior Pentagon officials, including the chairman and vice-chairman of the Joint Chiefs of Staff.

"I may be impatient. In fact I know I'm a bit impatient," Rumsfeld wrote in the single-page memo. "We are never going to get the U.S. military out of Afghanistan unless we take care to see that there is something going on that will provide the stability that will be necessary for us to leave."

"Help!" he added.

Rumsfeld was careful to keep his doubts and misgivings private, just as he had a few weeks earlier when he sat for a long interview with MSNBC. During the March 28 broadcast, he bragged about steamrolling the enemy and said there was no point negotiating with remnants of the Taliban, much less al-Qaeda. "The only thing you can do is to bomb them and try to kill them. And that's what we did, and it worked. They're gone. And the Afghan people are a lot better off."

Like Bush, Rumsfeld cultivated an image as a courageous and decisive leader. MSNBC anchor Brian Williams reinforced it by fawning over the defense secretary, lauding Rumsfeld's "swagger" and suggesting that he was the "most confident man" in America. "He presides over a war like no other, and he has become arguably more than anyone else the public face and voice of that war," Williams told viewers.

The only tough question came when Williams asked Rumsfeld if he was ever tempted to lie about the war during his frequent press conferences at the Pentagon. "How often are you forced to shave the truth in that briefing room, because American lives are at stake?"

"I just don't," Rumsfeld replied. "I think our credibility is so much more important than shaving the truth." He added, "We'll do exactly what we have to do to protect the lives of the men and women in uniform, and to see that our country is successful, but it doesn't involve lying."

By Washington standards, Rumsfeld was not lying—but he wasn't being honest, either. Hours before he taped the MSNBC interview, the defense secretary dictated a snowflake to two staffers with a completely different view of how things were going in Afghanistan.

"I am getting concerned that it is drifting," he wrote in the confidential memo.

At the outset of the war, the mission seemed straightforward and narrow: to defeat al-Qaeda and prevent a repeat of the 9/11 attacks. On September 14, 2001, in a near-unanimous vote, Congress swiftly authorized the use of military force against al-Qaeda and its supporters.*

When the Pentagon launched the first airstrikes against Afghanistan on October 7, no one expected that the bombing would continue unabated for twenty years. In a televised speech that day, Bush said the war had two limited objectives: to disrupt al-Qaeda's use of Afghanistan as a terrorist base of operations and to attack the military capability of the Taliban regime.

The commander in chief also promised the armed forces a clarity of purpose. "To all the men and woman in our military," he declared, "I say this: Your mission is defined. The objectives are clear."

Military strategists are taught never to start a war without having a plan to end it. Yet neither Bush nor anyone else in his administration publicly articulated how or when or under what conditions they intended to bring military operations in Afghanistan to a conclusion.

In the early days of the war, and for the remainder of his presidency, Bush dodged questions about how long U.S. troops would have to fight in Afghanistan. He didn't want to raise expectations or limit his generals' options by committing to a timetable. But he knew Americans had painful memories of the last time the country fought an interminable land war in Asia and tried to assuage concerns that history might repeat itself.

During a prime-time news conference on October 11, 2001, in the East Room of the White House, a reporter asked Bush point-blank: "Can you avoid being drawn into a Vietnam-like quagmire in Afghanistan?"

Bush had a ready answer. "We learned some very important lessons in Vietnam," he said. "Perhaps the most important lesson that I learned

---

* The Senate passed the legislation by a vote of 98–0 and the House of Representatives approved it by a vote of 420–1. Rep. Barbara Lee (D-Calif.) cast the lone dissent.

is that you cannot fight a guerrilla war with conventional forces. That's why I have explained to the American people that we're engaged in a different type of war."

"People often ask me, 'How long will this last?'" he added. "This particular battlefront will last as long as it takes to bring al-Qaeda to justice. It may happen tomorrow, it may happen a month from now, it may take a year or two, but we will prevail."

Speaking confidentially years later to government interviewers, many U.S. officials who played a key role in the war offered harsh judgments about the decision-making during the conflict's early stages. They said the war's goals and objectives soon veered off into directions that had little to do with 9/11. They also admitted that Washington struggled to define with precision what it was hoping to accomplish in a country that most U.S. officials did not understand.

"If I were to write a book, its [message] would be: 'America goes to war without knowing why it does,'" an unnamed former senior State Department official said in a Lessons Learned interview. "We went in reflexively after 9/11 without knowing what we were trying to achieve. I would like to write a book about having a plan and an end game before you go in."

Others said no one bothered to ask, much less answer, many obvious questions.

"What were we actually doing in that country? We went in after 9/11 to defeat al-Qaeda in Afghanistan, but the mission became blurred," an unnamed U.S. official who worked with the NATO Special Civilian Representative to Afghanistan from 2011 to 2013, said in a Lessons Learned interview. "Also blurred were our objectives: what are our objectives? Nation building? Women's rights?"

Richard Boucher, who served as the State Department's chief spokesman at the start of the war and later became the senior U.S. diplomat for South Asia, said the United States foolishly tried to do too much and never settled on a realistic exit strategy.

"If there was ever a notion of mission creep it is Afghanistan," he said in a Lessons Learned interview. "We went from saying we will get rid of al-Qaeda so they can't threaten us anymore to saying we are going to end the Taliban. [Then we said] that we will get rid of all the groups the Taliban works with."

Beyond that, Boucher said, the United States set an "impossible" goal: to create a stable, American-style government in Afghanistan with democratic elections, a functioning Supreme Court, an anti-corruption authority, a women's ministry and thousands of newly constructed public schools with a modernized curriculum. "You are trying to build a systematic government a la Washington, D.C.," he added, "in a country that doesn't operate that way."

With little public discussion, the Bush administration changed its goals and objectives soon after it began bombing Afghanistan in October 2001. Behind the scenes, the military was drawing up its war plans on the fly.

Lt. Cmdr. Philip Kapusta, a Navy officer who served as a planner for Special Operations forces, said the Pentagon's initial orders in fall 2001 were short on specifics. It was unclear, for instance, whether Washington wanted to punish the Taliban or remove it from power. He said many officers at U.S. Central Command—the military headquarters in charge of fighting the war—didn't think the plan would work and viewed it as a placeholder to buy time to develop a more refined strategy.

"We received some general guidance like, 'Hey, we want to go fight the Taliban and al-Qaeda in Afghanistan,'" Kapusta said in an Army oral-history interview. "In fact, in the original plan, regime change wasn't necessarily an objective. It wasn't ruled out but it wasn't primarily what we were actually going to achieve."

On October 16, Bush's National Security Council approved an updated strategy paper. The secret, six-page document—which was attached to one of Rumsfeld's snowflakes and later declassified—called for the elimination of al-Qaeda and the termination of Taliban rule, but listed few concrete objectives beyond that.

The strategy concluded that the United States should "take steps to contribute to a more stable post-Taliban Afghanistan." But it anticipated U.S. troops would not stay for long: "The U.S. should not commit to any post-Taliban military involvement, since the U.S. will be heavily engaged in the anti-terrorism effort worldwide."

Wary of Afghanistan's history of entrapping foreign invaders, the Bush administration wanted to put as few U.S. boots on the ground as possible.

"Rumsfeld said our assumption was that we were going to use a small U.S. force in Afghanistan because we wanted to avoid the big footprint the Soviets had had," Douglas Feith, the Pentagon's undersecretary for policy, said in a University of Virginia oral-history interview. "We didn't want to trigger a xenophobic reaction by the Afghans. The Soviets put 300,000 guys there and failed. We didn't want to re-create that error."

On October 19, the first U.S. Special Operations forces entered Afghanistan, joining a handful of CIA officers already embedded with the Northern Alliance, a coalition of anti-Taliban warlords. U.S. aircraft based in the region brought enormous firepower from the skies. Despite all the U.S. assistance, the ragtag Northern Alliance forces failed to gain much ground against Taliban and al-Qaeda fighters.

On Halloween, during a late-morning meeting with top brass in his Pentagon office, Rumsfeld turned to Feith and Marine Gen. Peter Pace, the vice-chairman of the Joint Chiefs of Staff, and told them they needed to rethink the war strategy. The impatient defense secretary said he wanted a new plan in writing and that Feith and Pace had four hours to get it done, according to Feith's oral-history interview.

Feith and Pace left Rumsfeld's suite and trotted down the Pentagon's outer-ring corridor to Feith's office. They were joined by Air Force Maj. Gen. Michael Dunn, who led the Joint Staff's planning team. With the two generals peering over his shoulders, the 48-year-old Feith sat in front of his computer and drafted a new strategic analysis for Rumsfeld, something that would normally take months and legions of staff to complete.

It was an odd scene in more ways than one. A cerebral Harvard graduate with pursed lips and round spectacles who had never served in uniform, Feith drove many generals batty by presuming to know more about military operations than they did. Army Gen. Tommy Franks, a crusty Oklahoman in charge of the war, would later call Feith "the fucking stupidest guy on the face of the earth." Another four-star Army general, George Casey, described Feith in a University of Virginia oral-history interview as "intransigent" and all-but-impossible to work with, adding: "He was always right and he was so tenacious in his arguments and in his positions that it really became difficult."

Perhaps improbably, Feith got along well with Pace, who had fought in Vietnam as a rifle platoon leader and served in Somalia, Korea and other hotspots during his thirty-four years in the Marines. Together, while keeping a close eye on the clock, they banged out new strategic guidelines for Afghanistan and delivered them to Rumsfeld in time to meet their afternoon deadline. "In the course of this, I turned around to Pace and I said something like, 'This is a little strange, isn't it?'" Feith recalled. "This is like doing an all-nighter in college."

The paper revisited some obvious questions about the military campaign: "Where are we? What are our goals? What are our assumptions? What can we do?" Feith was proud of the final product. In his oral-history interview, he implied his boss approved as well. "It was, in mini-form, a proper strategic analysis from Rumsfeld's point of view. If there's urgency, you can't study a thing to death."

Days later, many U.S. officials were stunned when the tide of battle abruptly shifted in their favor. With U.S. help, Northern Alliance forces seized control of several major cities in short order: Mazar-e-Sharif on November 9, Herat on November 12, Kabul the following day and Jalalabad the day after that.

Kapusta, the Special Operations war planner, sat in a conference room at Central Command headquarters in Tampa with a group of senior officers as they marveled at the progress. "One of the guys actually said—and this was right after Kabul had fallen—'Hey, you didn't believe this shit would work.' And everybody in the room was nodding their heads in agreement."

Leaders in the Pentagon were equally bewildered by the rapid turn of events. "Around November we were wondering, how much of the country can we take back or can we take over before the holidays? Can we carve out enough that we can survive the winter?" Pace, the Marine general, said in a University of Virginia oral history interview. "Now we own the whole country, before Christmas. You go, 'Whoa, that's kind of cool.'"

Having overthrown the Taliban somewhat unexpectedly, U.S. military commanders were unprepared for the aftermath and unsure what to do. They worried Afghanistan would fall into chaos, but they also feared that if they sent more U.S. ground forces to fill the vacuum, they might be saddled with responsibility for the country's many problems. As a result, the Pentagon dispatched a few extra troops to assist with the hunt for bin Laden and other al-Qaeda leaders but limited their visibility and tasks as much as possible.

For the time being, it was enough to keep Afghanistan from tearing itself apart. In public, Rumsfeld acted as if he had never doubted the overall war plan for a minute.

"I think that what was taking place in the earlier phases was exactly as planned. The conditions were being set for what needed to be done," Rumsfeld said during a triumphant November 27 press conference at Central Command headquarters in Tampa. He leveled a sarcastic jab at reporters who had raised the specter of Vietnam. "It looked like nothing was happening. Indeed, it looked like we were in a—all together now!—quagmire."

At first, the U.S. Army was so intent on abbreviating its stay in Afghanistan that it refused to import basic amenities to make the troops more comfortable. Soldiers who wanted fresh clothes had to fly their dirty laundry by helicopter to a temporary support base in neighboring Uzbekistan.

For Thanksgiving, the Army made a small concession to cleanliness and dispatched a two-man team to install the first shower at Bagram Air Base in northern Afghanistan—home at the time to about 200 Special Forces soldiers and scores of allied troops.

"Some of the guys had been there for up to thirty days, so they needed a bath," Maj. Jeremy Smith, the quartermaster who oversaw the laundry unit in Uzbekistan, said in an Army oral-history interview. His superiors didn't want to send any extra personnel or equipment to Bagram but finally relented.

"Eventually they said, 'Okay, let's go ahead and do this,'" Smith recalled. "But it was, 'We're not sure how long we're going to be here, we're not sure about a whole lot of things, so our presence here is going to be as small as possible. How few people can you send?' The smallest number I could send was two. 'What's the smallest shower configuration you can send?' 'Well, it's designed for twelve, but the smallest we can realistically send is a six-head shower unit.' The mixer and the boiler and the pumps were all designed for a twelve-head shower, so a twelve-head shower only going through six heads had some really good water pressure. Everybody liked that."

Over time, Bagram would balloon in size to become one of the largest U.S. military bases overseas. When Smith returned to Bagram a decade later for a second tour of duty, he was greeted by a fully functioning city with a shopping mall, a Harley-Davidson dealer and about 30,000 troops, civilians and contractors. "Even before the plane stopped," Smith said, "I instantly recognized the mountains and after that I noticed it was the same smell. Then getting off, it was like, 'Holy cow! I don't recognize hardly anything.'"

In December 2001, however, only 2,500 American troops were on the ground in all of Afghanistan. Rumsfeld allowed the number to rise slowly but imposed strict limits. By the end of January, more U.S. military personnel were guarding the 2002 Winter Olympics in Salt Lake City (4,369) than serving in Afghanistan (4,003).

Many of the troops in southern Afghanistan stayed at an airstrip near Kandahar, where the conditions were even more primitive than at Bagram, about 300 miles away. "There was one shower point in the whole place," Maj. David King of the 160th Special Operations Aviation Regiment said in an Army oral-history interview. "You have to go in planning on using a piss tube and you're going to be crapping in a barrel and burning it with diesel fuel . . . There wasn't any honey wagon or porta potties or that stuff, at least at that point."

When Maj. Glen Helberg, an infantry officer, arrived at Kandahar Air Field in January 2002, he spent the night in a sleeping bag in the desert dirt. "It was moon dust and it rained that night and water was flowing under the tent flaps. I woke up and some of my stuff was floating," he said in an Army oral-history interview.

By the time Helberg's unit departed six months later, soldiers slept on cots instead of the ground. No one imagined that the dusty camp at Kandahar was destined to become a giant combat hub on a similar scale to Bagram. At times, it would become the busiest airfield between Delhi and Dubai, handling 5,000 takeoffs and landings each week.

Rather, in the moment, it felt as if the war had already crested and reached the mop-up stage. In an Army oral-history interview, Maj. Lance Baker, an intelligence officer, said rumors circulated that his unit, the 10th Mountain Division, didn't "have anything else to do, there's no more fighting, Afghanistan's done. We're going home."

In June 2002, Army Maj. Andrew Steadman and his paratrooper battalion landed in Kandahar all gung-ho to hunt al-Qaeda—only to end up sitting on their hands. "The guys just played video games," he said in an Army oral-history interview. "They worked out in the morning and did some training in the afternoon."

In eastern Afghanistan, near the Pakistani border, Army Maj. Steven Wallace's rifle platoon also had a hard time finding anyone to battle. "We were there for eight weeks and didn't have one single firefight," he told Army historians. "It was actually very boring."

On the surface, Afghanistan looked like it was stabilizing. The United Nations hosted a conference in Bonn, Germany, that set up a governance plan for Afghanistan in December 2001. Hamid Karzai, a Pashtun tribal leader and CIA asset who spoke fluent English, was chosen as interim leader. Humanitarian groups and dozens of donor countries delivered much-needed aid.

The Bush administration was still leery of getting bogged down. But the swift and decisive military victories boosted U.S. officials' confidence and they tacked on new goals.

Stephen Hadley, the White House's deputy national security adviser at the time, said the war shifted into "an ideological phase" in which the United States decided to introduce freedom and democracy to Afghanistan as an alternative to terrorism. To make that happen, U.S. troops needed to prolong their stay.

"We originally said that we don't do nation-building but there is no way to ensure that al-Qaeda won't come back without it," Hadley said in a Lessons Learned interview. "[We] did not want to become occupiers or to overwhelm the Afghans. But once the Taliban was flushed, we did not want to throw that progress away."

By the time Bush gave his speech to the Virginia Military Institute cadets in April 2002, he had settled on a much more ambitious set of objectives for the war. The United States, he said, was obligated to help Afghanistan build a country free of terrorism, with a stable government, a new national army and an education system for boys and girls alike. "True peace will only be achieved when we give the Afghan people the means to achieve their own aspirations," he added.

Bush was now promising that the United States would transform an impoverished country that had been traumatized by warfare and ethnic strife for the past quarter-century. The goals were noble and high-minded, but Bush offered no specifics or benchmarks for achieving them. In his VMI speech, he also dodged the issue of how much it would all cost or how long it might take, saying only: "We'll stay until the mission is done."

It was a classic mistake of failing to adhere to a clear strategy with concise, attainable objectives. Still, few people expressed concern that the United States had committed to an open-ended mission. Those who raised doubts were ignored. "When we went to Afghanistan everybody was talking about a year or two, and I said to them that we would be lucky if we were out of here in twenty years," Robert Finn, the U.S. ambassador to Afghanistan from 2002 to 2003, said in a Lessons Learned interview.

For years, senior military commanders were reluctant to acknowledge that they had committed fundamental strategic errors. Tommy Franks, the Army general who oversaw the start of the war, believed he had done his duty: to defeat al-Qaeda and knock out the Taliban.

"How many more attacks have there been on U.S. soil sponsored out of Afghanistan?" Franks said in a University of Virginia oral-history interview. "Give me a break, guys. We solved a problem."

As for sorting out the future of Afghanistan, Franks thought that was somebody else's responsibility: "Now, we created other problems and we have not taken care of the centuries if not thousands of years of poverty and all the problems that go on in Afghanistan," he said. "Should we have outlined that as an objective? That's not for me to say. I was glad many times that the president never asked me, 'Well, should we do this?' Because I would have said, 'That's your job, not mine.'"

It wasn't the last time Franks would lead an invasion but fail to plan adequately for the post-war occupation.

Six months after the war began, the United States made the hubristic mistake of assuming the conflict had ended successfully, on American terms. Bin Laden was still on the loose, but otherwise people in Washington stopped paying much attention to Afghanistan and became preoccupied with another country in the region: Iraq.

In May 2002, a new three-star Army general arrived in Afghanistan to take command of U.S. forces. Dan McNeill, a 54-year-old North Carolinian and a veteran of Vietnam, said the Pentagon was already so focused on Iraq that it gave him little guidance.

"There was no campaign plan in the early days," McNeill said in a Lessons Learned interview. "Rumsfeld would get excited if there was any increase in the number of boots on the ground."

By the time fall arrived, even the commander in chief had become distracted and had forgotten key details about the war.

On the afternoon of October 21, Bush was working in the Oval Office when Rumsfeld walked in with a quick question: Did the president want to meet that week with General Franks and General McNeill?

Bush seemed perplexed, according to a snowflake that Rumsfeld wrote later that day.

"He said, 'Who is General McNeill?'" Rumsfeld recalled. "I said he is the general in charge of Afghanistan. He said, 'Well, I don't need to meet with him.'"

CHAPTER TWO

"Who Are the Bad Guys?"

In August 2002, an unusual report from the war zone caught the attention of Rumsfeld and other senior officials at the Pentagon. Written by a member of a team of allied commandos hunting for high-value targets, the fourteen-page email provided an unfiltered, firsthand account of conditions in southern Afghanistan.

"Greetings from scenic Kandahar," it began. "Formerly known as 'Home of the Taliban.' Now known as 'Miserable Rat-Fuck Shithole.'"

Part intelligence brief and part tongue-in-cheek travelogue, the unclassified email was authored by Roger Pardo-Maurer, a 38-year-old Green Beret with atypical credentials. A Connecticut native, the Yale graduate joined the Nicaraguan contras in the 1980s and worked as a trade and investment consultant during the 1990s. He was serving in the Defense Department as a deputy assistant secretary for Western Hemisphere affairs—the civilian equivalent of a three-star general—when his Army Reserve unit was activated after the 9/11 attacks.

Known for his sense of humor at the office, Pardo-Maurer's observations from the front became a must-read for his colleagues back at the Pentagon. He memorably described Kandahar's suffocating summertime as "a quasi-Venusian sub-Martian environment of heat, dust, and parched air that stuns you, rasps your corneas, produces constant sinus-clogging migraines and nosebleeds, and crackles your skin in weird tender places."

"If there is a landscape less welcoming to humans anywhere on earth, apart from the Sahara, the Poles, and the cauldrons of Kilauea, I cannot imagine it, and I certainly don't intend to go there," he added.

In the email, Pardo-Maurer unsparingly portrayed other actors on the wartime stage. His unit stayed in what was known as the Special Forces Village at Kandahar Air Field, a shantytown of tents and plywood shacks that housed "a formidable pack" of bearded commandos from the United States and allied nations.

Pardo-Maurer depicted Navy SEALs as "louts" known for their "rowdy conceits," including the time they trashed the courtyard of the New Zealand special forces unit and let the commander's pet snakes loose. He dismissed CIA operatives as "crude vainglorious chumps" who wasted hours shopping for Afghan handicrafts.

He spoke respectfully of the commandos from Canada, calling them "quite likely the deadliest bunch in town, but also the friendliest," known for sharing deep-dish pizza and maintaining an Elvis shrine in their compound. As for the Afghans, he mocked Kandaharis as "a crusty lot of downtrodden moochers."

That summer in Washington, Pentagon officials repeatedly told Congress and the public that the Taliban had been destroyed, al-Qaeda dispersed and Afghanistan's terrorist training camps shut down. But Pardo-Maurer warned his colleagues the war was far from over and that the enemy was unvanquished.

"Time is of the essence here," he noted in the email, which he wrote during five days in mid-August. "The situation we're in now is that Al Qaeda have licked their wounds and are regrouping in the Southeast, with the connivance of a few disgruntled junior warlords and the double-dealing Pakistanis. The shooting match is still very much on. Along the border provinces, you can't kick a stone over without Bad Guys swarming out like ants and snakes and scorpions."

Pardo-Maurer's colorful descriptions aside, U.S. troops struggled to distinguish the bad guys from everybody else in Afghanistan. Taliban and al-Qaeda regulars moved around in small groups and wore the same headwear and baggy trousers as local civilians, blending into the population. Just because someone carried an AK-47 didn't automatically make them a combatant. Firearms had poured into the country since the Soviet invasion of 1979 and Afghans hoarded them for self-protection.

On a broader level, the United States had jumped into the war with only a hazy idea of whom it was fighting—a fundamental blunder from which it would never recover.

Although bin Laden and al-Qaeda had declared war against the United States in 1996, bombed two U.S. embassies in East Africa in 1998 and nearly sank the USS *Cole* in Yemen in 2000, U.S. national-security agencies had paid limited attention to the terrorist network and failed to see it as a threat to the continental United States.

"The reality is that on 9/11 we didn't know jack shit about al-Qaeda," Robert Gates, who served as director of the CIA in the early 1990s and later replaced Rumsfeld as defense secretary, said in a University of Virginia oral-history interview. "If we'd had a great database and knew exactly what al-Qaeda was all about, what their capabilities were and stuff like that, some of these measures wouldn't have been necessary. But the fact is that we'd just been attacked by a group we didn't know anything about."

The Bush administration made another basic mistake by blurring the line between al-Qaeda and the Taliban. The two groups shared an extremist religious ideology and a mutual support pact, but pursued different goals and objectives.

Al-Qaeda was primarily a network of Arabs, not Afghans, with a global presence and outlook; bin Laden spent his days plotting to overthrow the Saudi royal family and other Middle East autocrats allied with the United States. The al-Qaeda leader was living in Afghanistan only because he had been expelled from his previous refuge, in Sudan.

In contrast, the Taliban's preoccupations were entirely local. Most of its followers belonged to the Pashtun tribes in southern and eastern Afghanistan that had been warring for years with other ethnic groups and power brokers for control of the country. The Taliban protected bin Laden and built a strong alliance with al-Qaeda, but Afghans did not play a role in the 9/11 hijackings and there is no evidence they had advance knowledge of the attacks.

The Bush administration targeted the Taliban because its leader, Mullah Mohammed Omar, refused to hand over bin Laden after 9/11. In practice, however, the U.S. military drew little distinction between the Taliban and al-Qaeda, categorizing them all as bad guys.

By 2002, few al-Qaeda followers remained in Afghanistan. Hundreds had been killed or captured, while the rest fled to Pakistan, Iran and other countries.

The United States and its allies were left fighting the Taliban and other militants from the region—Uzbeks, Pakistanis, Chechens. So for the next two decades, the war in Afghanistan was waged against people who had nothing to do with 9/11.

Jeffrey Eggers, a Navy SEAL who served in Afghanistan and worked on the National Security Council staff under Bush and Obama, said most of the world felt the United States was justified in taking military action in Afghanistan in response to the 9/11 attacks. But once al-Qaeda's presence in Afghanistan shriveled up, U.S. officials failed to step back and reassess who else they were fighting or why.

"The complexities will take a long time to unravel. Our entire post–9/11 response is all subject to question because of this increasing complexity. Why did we make the Taliban the enemy when we were attacked by al-Qaeda? Why did we want to defeat the Taliban? Why did we think it was necessary to build a hyper-function[ing] state to forgo the return of the Taliban?" Eggers said in a Lessons Learned interview.

"Why, if we were focused on al-Qaeda, were we talking about the Taliban? Why were we talking about the Taliban all the time instead of focusing our strategy on al-Qaeda?"

One reason the war dragged on for so long was because the United States never really understood what motivated its enemies to fight. At the war's outset, scarcely any U.S. officials possessed an elementary understanding of Afghan society or had visited the country since the American embassy in Kabul closed in 1989. To an ignorant foreigner, Afghanistan's history, complex tribal dynamics, and ethnic and religious fault lines felt bewildering. It was much easier to divide the country into two camps: good guys and bad guys.

Anybody willing to help the United States fight al-Qaeda and the Taliban qualified as a good guy—morals notwithstanding. Dangling bags of cash as a lure, the CIA recruited war criminals, drug traffickers, smugglers and ex-communists. While such people could be useful, they often found the Americans easy to manipulate.

One of the few Americans who possessed more than a passing familiarity with Afghan culture was Michael Metrinko, a legendary Foreign Service officer. He first visited Afghanistan in 1970 when he was in the Peace Corps, "basically getting stoned at the time as a hippie," as he described it in a diplomatic oral-history interview. He served for several years as a political officer in neighboring Iran, and he was posted to the U.S. embassy in Tehran in 1979 when he and dozens of other Americans were taken hostage by revolutionaries.

In January 2002, the State Department sent the 55-year-old Metrinko to Kabul to help reopen the U.S. embassy there and serve as head of the political section. Fluent in Farsi—similar to Dari, one of Afghanistan's national languages—from his service in Iran, he was the rare American diplomat who could converse with Afghans in their native tongue.

Metrinko said Afghans learned that if they wanted to eliminate a personal rival in a power struggle, land grab or commercial dispute, all they had to do was tell the Americans that their foe belonged to the Taliban.

"Much of what we call Taliban activity was really tribal or it was rivalry or it was old feuding," he said. "I'd had this explained to me over and over and over again by tribal elders, you know, the old men who had come in with their long white beards and would sit and talk for an hour or two. They would laugh about some of the things that were happening. What they always said was you American soldiers don't understand this, but you know, what they think is a Taliban act is really a feud going back more than one hundred years in that particular family."

Metrinko especially disdained CIA operatives who flooded into the country and tried to blend in. "They had a lot of people who couldn't speak a word of the language and ran around in beards and funny clothes and thought they had a grasp of what was happening. I would dismiss all—99 percent—of them as amateurs," said Metrinko, who served two separate tours in Afghanistan in 2002 and 2003. "As far as any real knowledge of what was happening, where they were, what they were trying to get done, the past, the present, the future, [it] was zero."

In the field, U.S. troops often couldn't tell friend from foe either. In Army oral-history interviews, they said defining and identifying the enemy was a problem that persisted for the entirety of the conflict.

Maj. Stuart Farris, an officer with the 3rd Special Forces Group who served in Helmand province in 2003, said his unit's mission was to capture and kill "anti-coalition militia," a vague, catchall description for the enemy. But his soldiers often could not tell who qualified for the label.

"There was a lot of crime. It was hard to determine if folks were actually no-joke Taliban or just criminals," he said. "That's where a lot of the problems were. We had to figure out who the bad guys were, whether they were in the scope of our mission and who we were there to target versus just being criminals and thugs."

Maj. Thomas Clinton Jr., a Marine officer who served in Kandahar, guessed that he probably spoke with a dozen or so Afghans every week without realizing they were Taliban fighters.

"At any given moment you could find yourself in the middle of the Wild West," he said. "Guys would say that the Taliban were shooting at us. Well, how the hell do you know it's the Taliban? It could just be some pissed-off local, for all you know."

Maj. Gen. Eric Olson, who deployed to southern Afghanistan as commander of the 25th Infantry Division, said many of the hostile forces his troops encountered were really just "hillbillies" from small towns and villages. "I'm not sure they were Taliban," he said. "These people had spent their whole lives, I think, opposing the central government and protecting their turf."

In a Lessons Learned interview, an unnamed combat adviser to an Army Special Forces team said even elite soldiers, who were supposed to have a nuanced understanding of the battlefield, were unsure who to fight.

"They thought I was going to come to them with a map to show them where the good guys and the bad guys live," the combat adviser said. "It took several conversations for them to understand that I did not have that information in my hands. At first, they just kept asking: 'But who are the bad guys, where are they?'"

The view was no clearer from the Pentagon.

"I have no visibility into who the bad guys are," Rumsfeld complained in a snowflake almost two years after the war started. "We are woefully deficient in human intelligence."

*   *   *

In December 2001, the United States bungled two golden opportunities that might have brought the war to a quick and favorable end.

At the start of the month, a critical mass of intelligence reports indicated that Public Enemy Number One—bin Laden—had sought refuge with an estimated 500 to 2,000 al-Qaeda fighters in a large complex of fortified tunnels and caves at Tora Bora, about thirty miles southeast of the city of Jalalabad.

The mountainous district near the Pakistani border was a natural and obvious hideout for the al-Qaeda leader. Bin Laden had financed the construction of roads and bunkers at Tora Bora during the 1980's war against the Soviets, and he spent time there after he returned to Afghanistan in 1996.

On December 3, Army Gen. Tommy Franks, the head of U.S. Central Command, ordered a bombing campaign against the al-Qaeda fighters in Tora Bora that continued around the clock for two weeks. A small force of about one hundred U.S. commandos and CIA operatives guided the airstrikes from the ground and recruited two Afghan warlords and their militias to pursue the al-Qaeda force on foot.

The Afghan hired guns proved unreliable and reluctant to fight, however, and the bombs failed to find their most-wanted target. Fearing that bin Laden might escape over the unguarded border to Pakistan, CIA and Army Delta Force commanders pleaded with Central Command to send reinforcements.

Insistent on sticking with his light-footprint war strategy, Franks refused. "You say, 'Why didn't you?' Look at the political context in America at that time. What was the appetite to have positioned . . . another 15,000 or 20,000 Americans in Afghanistan? Why would we do that?" he said in a University of Virginia oral-history interview.

Yet nobody had asked for that many troops. CIA and Delta Force commanders said they were hoping for 800 to 2,000 Army Rangers, Marines and other personnel. Regardless, help of that magnitude never arrived and bin Laden and his surviving al-Qaeda confederates slipped away.

During the apex of the fighting at Tora Bora, Army Maj. William Rodebaugh, a logistics officer with the 10th Mountain Division, was about one hundred miles away at Bagram Air Base monitoring radio traffic of the battle. On December 11, he heard radio chatter about a major development—a reported sighting of bin Laden—and became surprised when his unit wasn't called upon to rush to the scene.

"We were ready if they asked us," he said in an Army oral-history interview. "I always wonder what would have happened if they had found him that night or if they had asked our battalion to go and help, which never happened."

There is no guarantee that more U.S. forces at Tora Bora would have led to bin Laden's death or capture. The altitude and terrain made maneuvering difficult and a large-scale ground assault posed many risks. But there is also no question that his escape prolonged the war in Afghanistan. Politically, it was impossible for the United States to bring its troops home as long as the mastermind of the 9/11 attacks roamed the region.

In response to criticism that they had blown their best chance to get bin Laden, Franks and Rumsfeld tried to sow doubt with the public that the al-Qaeda leader had actually been at Tora Bora in December 2001—despite later, conclusive findings to the contrary by the U.S. Special Operations Command, the CIA and the Senate Foreign Relations Committee.

When the issue arose as a vulnerability for Bush during his 2004 reelection campaign, Franks wrote an op-ed in *The New York Times* declaring that "Mr. bin Laden was never within our grasp." Eight days later, with Rumsfeld's blessing, the Pentagon distributed a dubious set of talking points, claiming that "the allegation that the U.S. military allowed Osama bin Laden to escape Tora Bora in December 2001 is utterly false and has been refuted by the commanders of that operation."

Years later, in his oral-history interview, Franks continued to dismiss evidence that bin Laden had been at Tora Bora.

"On the day that someone first told me, 'Tora Bora is the deal, Franks. He's in Tora Bora.' Literally on that same day I had an intelligence report that bin Laden had been seen yesterday at a recreational lake northwest of Kandahar and that bin Laden had been positively identified someplace in the ungoverned western areas of Pakistan," he said.

After the Battle of Tora Bora, it would take a decade before the United States could pinpoint bin Laden's location again. By then, the number of U.S. troops in Afghanistan had soared to 100,000—forty times the number in December 2001.

Early on, the United States also missed a diplomatic opportunity to end the war. While bin Laden burrowed into the mountains at Tora Bora, an eclectic assortment of Afghan power brokers met in Bonn, Germany, to haggle over the future of their country with diplomats from the United States, Central Asia and Europe. Led by the United Nations, the gathering took place at the Petersberg, a hotel and conference center owned by the German government that was perched on a forested ridge overlooking the Rhine River.

The Petersberg served as the headquarters of the Allied High Commission for Germany after World War II and hosted numerous summits, including talks in 1999 to end the war in Kosovo. The United Nations invited the Afghans to Bonn to discuss an interim power-sharing agreement. The idea was to end Afghanistan's long-running civil war by bringing all potential troublemakers, internal and external, to the table.

Attending were two dozen delegates from four different Afghan factions—a mix of warlords, expatriates, monarchists and former communists—plus their aides and hangers-on. Officials from Iran, Pakistan, Russia, India and other countries in the region also participated.

Because the conference was held during the Muslim holy month of Ramadan, most delegates fasted during the day and negotiated late into the night. The hotel assured its guests that it had removed pork from the menu, though alcohol was still available upon request.

On December 5, the delegates reached an accord that was hailed as a diplomatic triumph. It named Hamid Karzai as Afghanistan's interim leader and laid out the process for writing a new constitution and holding national elections. But the Bonn Agreement had a fatal flaw that was overlooked at the time: It excluded the Taliban.

At that point in the war, most U.S. officials saw the Taliban as a vanquished foe, a misjudgment they would come to regret. Some Taliban leaders had indicated a willingness to surrender and engage in the discussions about Afghanistan's future. But the Bush administration and its warlord partners in the Northern Alliance refused to negotiate, labeling the Taliban as terrorists who deserved death or prison.

"A major mistake we made was treating the Taliban the same as al-Qaeda," Barnett Rubin, an American academic expert on Afghanistan who served as an adviser to the United Nations during the Bonn conference, said in a Lessons Learned interview. "Key Taliban leaders were interested in giving the new system a chance, but we didn't give them a chance."

While the Taliban was easy to demonize because of its brutality and religious fanaticism, it proved too large and ingrained in Afghan society to eradicate. The movement emerged in Kandahar in 1994 and drew support, especially from Pashtuns, for restoring a measure of order to Afghanistan and marginalizing hated warlords who had torn apart the country for the sake of preserving their own power and fiefdoms.

"Everyone wanted the Taliban to disappear," Rubin said in a second Lessons Learned interview. "There was not much appetite for what we called threat reduction, for regional diplomacy and bringing the Taliban into the peace process."

Todd Greentree, a Foreign Service officer who spent years in Afghanistan, said it was another example of the United States' ignorance of the country. "One of the unfortunate errors that took place after 9/11 was in our eagerness to get revenge we violated the Afghan way of war. That is when one side wins, the other side puts down their arms and reconciles with the side that won. And this is what the Taliban wanted to do," he said in a diplomatic oral-history interview. "Our insistence on hunting them down as if they were all criminals, rather than just adversaries who had lost, was what provoked the rise of the insurgency more than anything else."

Lakhdar Brahimi, an Algerian diplomat who served as the chief U.N. representative during the Bonn conference, admitted later that it had been a major blunder to shut out the Taliban from the negotiations, calling it "the original sin."

James Dobbins, a veteran U.S. diplomat who guided the Bonn talks with Brahimi, acknowledged in a Lessons Learned interview that Washington failed to realize the gravity of the error. "I think there was a missed opportunity in the subsequent months when a number of Taliban leaders and influential figures either did surrender or offered to surrender including, according to one account, Mullah Omar himself," Dobbins said. He added that he was among those who erroneously assumed that the Taliban "had been heavily discredited and was unlikely to make a comeback."

Another opportunity for reconciliation wouldn't present itself for years. It would take more than a decade of deadlocked warfare before the United States and the Taliban would finally agree to hold face-to-face talks.

For the man who would lead those negotiations, the war had come full circle. An Afghan-American, Zalmay Khalilzad was born in Mazar-e-Sharif and grew up in Kabul before arriving in the United States as a teenager. He served as a National Security Council staffer in the Bush White House during the Bonn conference and as U.S. ambassador to Afghanistan from 2003 to 2005. Thirteen years later, the Trump administration called him back into government service, appointing him as special envoy for talks with the Taliban. All told, he would spend more time in the presence of the Taliban than any other U.S. official.

In a Lessons Learned interview, Khalilzad said America's longest war might have instead gone down in history as one of its shortest had the United States been willing to talk to the Taliban in December 2001. "Maybe we were not agile or wise enough to reach out to the Taliban early on, that we thought they were defeated and that they needed to be brought to justice, rather than that they should be accommodated or some reconciliation be done," he said.

CHAPTER THREE

The Nation-Building Project

When U.S. dignitaries visited Kabul in late December 2001 for the inauguration of Afghanistan's interim government, they found overflowing toilets in the presidential palace. Outside, a thick haze of smoke hung over the ruins of the capital; most Afghans burned wood or charcoal to stay warm. The few public buildings still standing had been stripped of their window glass, copper wiring, telephone cables and lightbulbs. Not that it mattered much. Phone and electrical service in Kabul had not worked in years.

Ryan Crocker, a 52-year-old Arabist in the Foreign Service, arrived days later to help reopen the long-shuttered U.S. embassy and serve as acting ambassador. Because Kabul lacked a functioning airport, he landed at the U.S. military air base in Bagram, thirty miles away.

Crocker rode into Kabul, "driving through mile after mile of basically lifeless lug" and fording a river because the bridge was out. The scenes reminded him of photographs depicting the rubble-strewn boulevards of Berlin, circa 1945. He discovered the U.S. embassy compound had survived years of shelling in Kabul, though its broken plumbing was in no better shape than the clogged pipes at the presidential palace. In one building, about a hundred Marine guards had to share a single toilet. In another part of the compound, fifty civilians had to make do with one working shower.

When Crocker sat down for a series of introductory meetings with Hamid Karzai, he realized Afghanistan faced bigger challenges than repairing the physical devastation inflicted by years of war. "Here was a leader of the interim authority, who had no real authority and nothing to work with, no military, no police, no civil service, no functioning society," Crocker said in a Lessons Learned interview.

After the United States invaded Afghanistan, President George W. Bush told the American people that they would not get stuck with the burden and expense of "nation-building." But that presidential promise, repeated by his two successors, turned out to be one of the biggest falsehoods uttered about the war.

Nation-building is exactly what the United States tried to do in war-battered Afghanistan—and on a colossal scale. Between 2001 and 2020, Washington spent more on nation-building in Afghanistan than in any country ever, allocating $143 billion for reconstruction, aid programs and Afghan security forces. Adjusted for inflation, that is more than the United States spent in Western Europe with the Marshall Plan after World War II.

Unlike the Marshall Plan, the nation-building project for Afghanistan went astray from the start and spun further out of control as the war persisted. Instead of bringing stability and peace, the United States inadvertently built a corrupt, dysfunctional Afghan government that depended on U.S. military power for its survival. Even under best-case scenarios, U.S. officials projected Afghanistan would need billions more dollars in aid, annually, for decades.

During two decades of American patronage, the star-crossed campaign to transform Afghanistan into a modern nation swung from extreme to extreme in terms of funding. At the beginning, when Afghans most needed help, the Bush administration insisted on a miserly approach even as it pushed Afghanistan to build a democracy and national institutions from scratch. Later, the Obama administration overcompensated by flooding the country with more aid than it could possibly absorb, creating a new set of insolvable problems. Throughout, the endeavor was hobbled by hubris, incompetence, bureaucratic infighting and haphazard planning.

"I mean, the writing is on the wall now. We spent so much money and there is so little to show for it," Michael Callen, an economist with the University of California San Diego who specialized in the Afghan public sector, said in a Lessons Learned interview. "What is a counterfactual if we had spent no money? I don't know. Maybe it would be worse. Probably it would be worse but how much worse?"

No nation needed more building than Afghanistan in 2001. Historically poor, it had been consumed by constant warfare since the Soviet invasion two decades earlier. Out of a population of about 22 million, an estimated 3 million had fled the country as refugees. Illiteracy and malnourishment plagued most who remained. As winter descended, aid agencies warned that one out of every three Afghans was at risk of starvation.

At that point, however, the Bush administration still had not decided whether it wanted to commit to a long-term nation-building campaign or leave Afghanistan's problems for others to deal with.

In 2000, Bush had arrived at the White House professing an aversion for costly foreign entanglements. During the presidential campaign, he had ripped the Clinton administration for committing the armed forces to "nation-building exercises" in Somalia, Haiti and the Balkans. "I don't think our troops ought to be used for what's called nation-building," he said during a debate with his Democratic opponent, Al Gore. "I think our troops ought to be used to fight and win war." When the plainspoken Texan ordered the U.S. military to start bombing Afghanistan, he reassured Americans that the United Nations—not Washington— would "take over the so-called nation-building."

When Crocker arrived in Afghanistan in January 2002, he thought leaving its problems to others "would have been pretty hard to justify and defend, given the extraordinary conditions in the country and the suffering of the Afghan people." But he wasn't authorized to make any grand promises during his brief, three-month stint in Kabul.

In reports back to Washington, officials with the U.S. Agency for International Development (USAID) delivered bleak assessments about the Afghans' ability to stabilize their country without massive help. A senior USAID official who was advising the Afghan government noted that the country had no banks and no legal tender; warlords had printed their own, largely worthless, currency. A Finance Ministry existed, but 80 percent of the staff could not read or write.

"It's hard to explain to people just how bad Afghanistan was in the early years," the unnamed USAID official said in a Lessons Learned interview. "It would have been easier if they had nothing. We had to destroy what was there to start building."

Richard Boucher, the State Department's chief spokesman, visited Kabul in January 2002 with Secretary of State Colin Powell. Karzai invited the U.S. diplomats to the stone-walled presidential palace to attend a meeting of his new cabinet, which felt like a hollow movie-set version of the American one back in Washington. Thirty people crowded around the table, including the minister for women's affairs, a brand-new post the Americans had insisted upon for the new Afghan government.

"It was just like the American cabinet. They were sitting around but they had nothing," Boucher said in a Lessons Learned interview. "The central bank governor was telling us how he went and opened the vaults and there was nothing inside. There was no money, no currency, no gold and none of what you would expect."

But Karzai and his cabinet maintained their manners, insisting on a traditional display of Afghan hospitality. "Somehow the Afghans managed to put on this amazing lunch. This huge banquet with piles of rice and dead goats," Boucher said. "They were capable people but they didn't [have] anything to run a government with so it really was from scratch both organizationally and materially."

As Afghanistan's desperation became plain for the world to see, Bush softened his stance on nation-building. During his January 2002 State of the Union Address to Congress, the president praised the spirit of the Afghan people and promised: "We'll be partners in rebuilding that country."

The words brought a smile to Karzai's bearded face. He had been invited to the speech as an honored guest and assigned a coveted seat next to the first lady, Laura Bush. Karzai clutched his lamb's wool hat and bowed slightly when lawmakers gave him a standing ovation. Joining him in the first lady's box was a bespectacled woman in a white headscarf: Sima Samar, the new Afghan minister of women's affairs.

Despite his new rhetoric about partnering with the Afghans, Bush clung to his tightwad inclinations. At an international donors' conference for Afghanistan prior to the president's State of the Union speech, the United States pledged $296 million in reconstruction aid and extended a $50 million line of credit. Combined, the amount was less than one-half of one percent of what Washington would end up spending to rebuild Afghanistan during the next two decades.

Bush also refused to contribute U.S. troops to an international peacekeeping force in Kabul because he didn't want the Pentagon to stray from its mission of chasing al-Qaeda and the Taliban. The Pentagon agreed to take responsibility for training a new Afghan army, but only as part of a nation-building division of labor among U.S. allies.

Under the arrangement, the Germans accepted the task of creating a new Afghan police force, the Italians agreed to help the Afghans overhaul their justice system and the British volunteered to discourage Afghan farmers from growing opium—historically, the country's leading cash crop. In the years to come, each of the allies muffed their assignments.

In Lessons Learned interviews, several Bush administration officials said nobody wanted to draw attention to the fact that the president was gradually breaking his campaign vows about nation-building. But they said Bush and others in the White House feared repeating the mistake Washington made during the 1990s, when it stopped paying attention to Afghanistan after U.S.-backed rebels forced the Soviet Army to withdraw—leaving chaos in its wake.

"We released the furies and then went home," said Stephen Hadley, who served as Bush's deputy national security adviser during his first term in the White House. Hadley and many other officials feared the country would again erupt in civil war and al-Qaeda would return if the United States failed to stabilize Afghanistan this time around.

"Nation-building was not high on the agenda. But we got there and realized we couldn't walk away," one unnamed U.S. official said. Another unidentified U.S. official said that while it was clear to insiders that the policy had "changed from anti– to pro–nation-building," the shift was never spelled out in strategy documents.

Still, expectations remained low. Richard Haass, a senior diplomat who served as the Bush administration's special coordinator for Afghanistan after the 9/11 attacks, said, "There was a profound sense of a lack of possibility in Afghanistan" and the U.S. government was "not willing to make a significant investment."

Haass recalled giving a briefing during fall 2001 to Bush, Powell, Rumsfeld and National Security Adviser Condoleezza Rice, with Vice President Dick Cheney patched in by video from an undisclosed location.

"There was just not any appetite for what you might call an ambitious policy," Haass said. "The feeling was that you could put a lot into it and you wouldn't get a lot out of it. I would not call it cynical, I would call it pessimistic about what the relationship between investment and return in Afghanistan [might be]."

Like the overall war strategy, the nation-building campaign suffered from a lack of clear goals and benchmarks. "When we're doing reconstruction, what is our theory and objectives?" an unnamed senior Bush administration official said in a Lessons Learned interview. "We need a theory, instead of just sending someone like me and saying, go help President Karzai."

Internal divisions hardened. At the State Department, diplomats and USAID officials fought to do more, arguing that only the United States had the resources and influence to get Afghanistan on the right track. At the Pentagon, Rumsfeld and his aides pushed back, countering that it would be a mistake to take ownership of all of Afghanistan's problems.

Crocker, who would later serve as U.S. ambassador to Baghdad, said Rumsfeld and other neoconservatives approached the wars in Afghanistan and in Iraq in the same manner. He summarized Rumsfeld's mindset this way: "'Our job is about killing bad guys, so we will have killed the bad guys, who cares what happens next. That's their problem. And if in a decade and a half, we have to go in and kill more bad guys, we can do that too, but we're not going to get involved in nation-building.'"

James Dobbins, the diplomat who helped organize the Bonn Conference in 2001, said the outcome of such philosophical disputes was rarely in doubt. The Pentagon, which had all the guns and unrivaled political clout, got its way.

"There was no way the State Department was going to get the Defense Department or Don Rumsfeld to do what it wanted. It was hard enough for the White House to do that and virtually impossible for the State Department," Dobbins said in a Lessons Learned interview.

While many Foreign Service officers portrayed Rumsfeld as an uncompromising bogeyman, other officials called the critique overly simplistic. They said Rumsfeld had no problems with reconstruction. He just didn't want the military to get saddled with a job that he thought civilians were supposed to do.

After years of budget cuts, however, USAID was a diminished agency and depended on contractors to perform its work. The rest of the State Department and other arms of the government also lacked the capacity to put a dent in Afghanistan's long list of problems. That made it easy for Rumsfeld to blame other agencies for a lack of progress.

In an August 20, 2002, memo to Bush, Rumsfeld argued that "the critical problem in Afghanistan is not really a security problem. Rather, the problem that needs to be addressed is the slow progress that is being made on the civil side." He agreed that Karzai's fledgling government needed more help—financially and otherwise—but he warned that sending more U.S. troops to stabilize and rebuild Afghanistan could backfire.

"The result would be that U.S. and coalition forces would grow in number and we could run the risk of ending up being as hated as the Soviets were," Rumsfeld wrote. "In any event, without successful reconstruction, no amount of added security forces would be enough. The Soviets had over 100,000 troops and failed."

Marin Strmecki, a civilian adviser to Rumsfeld, called the Pentagon chief "a misunderstood figure." He said Rumsfeld believed it was essential to strengthen Afghan government institutions, but didn't want the Afghans to become perpetually dependent on Washington. "It is often easier to do stuff ourselves than to coach people along to do it, given the very low level of human capital after twenty-five years of war," Strmecki said in a Lessons Learned interview. He added that Rumsfeld's concern was that the United States would entangle itself so deeply in Afghanistan's basic functions that it could never extricate itself.

But did the United States ever have a plan for how to pull that off? In his Lessons Learned interview, Stephen Hadley admitted that the Bush White House labored to devise an effective model for nation-building in Afghanistan. Even in retrospect, he said it was difficult to envision an approach that would have succeeded.

"We originally said that we won't do nation-building but there is no way to ensure that al-Qaeda won't come back without it," he said. "We just don't have a post-conflict stabilization model that works. Every time we have one of these things, it is a pickup game. I don't have any confidence that if we did it again, we would do any better."

It didn't take an Ivy League political scientist or a member of the Council on Foreign Relations to see that Afghanistan needed a better system of government. Riven by feuding tribes and implacable warlords, the country had a volatile history of coups, assassinations and civil wars.

The 2001 Bonn Agreement laid out a timeline for the Afghans to agree on a new political framework. A *loya jirga*—a traditional assembly of elders and leaders—was supposed to write a constitution within two years. Technically, it was up to the Afghans to decide how they wanted to govern their country. But the Bush administration persuaded them to adopt a made-in-America solution: a constitutional democracy under a president elected by popular vote.

In many ways, the new government resembled a rudimentary version of Washington. Power was concentrated in the capital, Kabul. A federal bureaucracy began to sprout in all directions, cultivated by dollars and legions of Western advisers.

Yet there was a key difference. The Bush administration pushed the Afghans to consolidate power in the hands of their president, with few checks or balances. Part of the reason was to curtail the influence of Afghanistan's many regional warlords. But more importantly, Washington thought it had the perfect man to install as Afghanistan's ruler: Karzai, an English-speaking tribal leader whom the Americans had taken under their wing.

In Lessons Learned interviews, numerous U.S. and European officials who were directly involved in the nation-building deliberations admitted that the decision to put so much power in the hands of one man was a disastrous miscalculation. The rigid system conflicted with Afghan tradition, typified by a mix of decentralized authority and tribal customs. And while the Americans got along blissfully with Karzai at first, the relationship would crash and burn at critical times.

"In hindsight the worst decision was to centralize power," said an unnamed European Union official. An unidentified senior German official added that it would have made more sense to slowly build a democracy from the ground up, starting at the municipal level: "After the fall of the Taliban, it was thought that we needed a president right away, but that was wrong."

An unidentified senior U.S. official said he was astounded that the State Department thought an American-style presidency would work in Afghanistan. "You'd think they've never worked overseas," he said. "Why did we create centralized government in a place that has never had one?"

Even some State Department officials said they were baffled. "In Afghanistan our policy was to create a strong central government, which was idiotic because Afghanistan does not have a history of a strong central government," said an unnamed senior U.S. diplomat. "The time frame for creating a strong central government is one hundred years, which we didn't have."

"We did not know what we were doing," added Richard Boucher, the former State Department chief spokesman. "The only time this country has worked properly was when it was a floating pool of tribes and warlords presided over by someone who had a certain eminence who was able to centralize them to the extent that they didn't fight each other too much. I think this idea that we went in with, that this was going to become a state government like a U.S. state or something like that, was just wrong and is what condemned us to fifteen years of war instead of two or three."

Even American soldiers who had no familiarity with Afghan history and culture before they arrived said it became obvious that trying to impose a strong, centralized government was foolish. In Army oral-history interviews, they described Afghans as instinctually hostile toward national power brokers, with little concept of what a bureaucracy in Kabul might actually do.

"You had to prove to a lot of people why government mattered to them at all, because you know, they're remote people," said Col. Terry Sellers, who served as a battalion commander in Uruzgan province. "The central government, at least to this point, in a lot of locations, had not been a provider to them, and they didn't really understand or see a benefit to having a centralized government: 'I've raised my sheep and goats and vegetables on this piece of land for hundreds of years and not had a central government. Why do I need one now?'"

Other Army officers said it often fell to them to try to explain to the Afghans what a government did and how a democracy worked. Col. David Paschal, an infantry officer who served for six months in Ghazni province in eastern Afghanistan, said his unit handed out posters of Karzai to villagers who had never seen an image of their president before.

A veteran of the Balkan Wars in the 1990s, Paschal said when the U.S. military and its NATO allies established democracy in Bosnia and Kosovo, they started with elections for district chiefs and worked their way up to regional and national voting. "We did it the exact opposite in Afghanistan, though. We had them voting for the president first—and most of these people didn't even know what it meant to vote. Yeah, they had the purple ink on their fingers," but they didn't understand the sig-nificance of casting a ballot, he said. "I think it's very challenging in the rural environment. I remember one time we had a unit on patrol and people asked, 'What are the Russians doing back here?' These people didn't even know the Americans had been there for a couple years."

Maj. Thomas Clinton Jr., a Marine officer, said the Afghan soldiers he trained were no different than average Americans: They wanted access to roads, schools, water and other basic services. But he said it was hard to explain to them how the American system of government paid for such things.

"The Afghans think Americans have money coming out of their butts," Clinton said. "I talked about taxation and all this stuff . . . They asked what taxes were. I started explaining that it was much like your warlords who used to tax people. 'Oh no, that's just stealing.' Then I had to explain the whole tax thing. The officers were enthralled because they didn't have any concept of taxes."

"There's no real concept of a central government that has all this overarching power from Asadabad to Herat in the west down to Kalat and Kandahar in the south and Spin Boldak, and Mazar-e-Sharif to the north," he added. "So that's an education."

Lt. Col. Todd Guggisberg, an Army officer who was detailed to NATO headquarters in Kabul, said he was dubious that the Afghans would ever embrace a modern, centralized government. "They have a very long history of being loyal to their family and their tribe, so the guy sitting out in Chaghcharan couldn't really care less who President Hamid Karzai is and the fact that he's in charge of Kabul," he said. "It reminds me of a Monty Python movie where the king goes riding by some peasant in the dirt and the king rides up and says, 'I'm the king,' and the peasant turns around and says, 'What's a king?'"

PART TWO

THE GREAT DISTRACTION

2003—2005

CHAPTER FOUR

Afghanistan Becomes an Afterthought

Six weeks after the invasion of Iraq, on May 1, 2003, the commander in chief boarded another flight to deliver another victorious speech with a military audience as the backdrop. Unlike his visit to the Virginia Military Institute one year earlier, this address would be broadcast live by the networks during prime time.

Instead of taking the usual presidential aircraft, Bush zipped himself into a green flight suit, donned a white helmet and climbed into a Navy S-3B Viking warplane waiting to transport him to a rendezvous thirty miles off the coast of San Diego. The back of the jet was marked "Navy 1." It had been more than three decades since Bush had flown with the Texas Air National Guard, but the Navy flight crew let him take a brief turn at the cockpit controls before landing at sea on the USS *Abraham Lincoln,* a nuclear-powered aircraft carrier returning from the war in the Persian Gulf.

Thousands of sailors cheered as Bush stepped off the plane and exchanged salutes with crew members on the flight deck. The president mingled and posed for photos before changing into a civilian business suit to give his speech as the sun dipped over the Pacific Ocean. Standing in front of a billowing red-white-and-blue banner proclaiming "Mission Accomplished," Bush announced that "major combat operations have ended" and thanked the U.S. military for "a job well done" in Operation Iraqi Freedom.

In fact, the worst in Iraq was yet to come and Bush's visit to the aircraft carrier would haunt him as the biggest public-relations blunder of his presidency. It also overshadowed an equally nonsensical claim that his defense secretary had made hours earlier about the war in Afghanistan.

Traveling in a bulky, gray C-17 military transport plane, Rumsfeld landed in Kabul on the afternoon of May 1 for a four-hour visit that attracted far less attention than Bush's stage-managed trip to the aircraft carrier. Rumsfeld's convoy rolled through the capital's decrepit streets to the presidential palace, where he met with Karzai and his cabinet.

Afterward, they held a joint news conference in a wood-paneled reception room that looked like it had not been remodeled in decades. The Afghan president opened by saying he was surprised to see so many international journalists. "I thought you had all gone to Iraq," Karzai joked in English. "Still here. Good. That means the world is interested in Afghanistan."

When his turn came, Rumsfeld read from a script similar to Bush's and declared that major combat operations had also ended in Afghanistan. "The bulk of this country today is permissive, it's secure," he said.

The defense secretary qualified his statement by adding that "pockets of resistance" and other dangers still existed—a hedge that Bush repeated about Iraq. But as in Iraq, the fighting in Afghanistan was far from over. Combat operations would re-intensify and turn much more deadly. More than 95 percent of U.S. casualties in America's longest war had yet to occur.

In oral-history interviews, Army officers who served in Afghanistan in 2003 said Rumsfeld's assertion that combat had ended was absurd. "We used to laugh," said Lt. Col. Mark Schmidt, a Special Forces officer with a background in psychological operations. "There was still plenty of fighting going on . . . Quite frankly, we were just going around killing people. We'd fly in, do a mission for a few weeks, then we'd fly out—and of course the Taliban would just flow right back in."

At his press conference in Kabul, Rumsfeld said the mission in Afghanistan would shift from combat to "stability operations"—military jargon for peacekeeping and nation-building. But Army officers said nothing on the ground really changed.

"Essentially, there was no written order, there was nothing else that came out about it," said Col. Thomas Snukis, who arrived that summer to serve as a staff officer at military headquarters in Bagram. "There was still a lot of combat action going on."

Others suggested that Rumsfeld's remarks were a combination of wishful thinking and a desire to move on. "I think Washington had probably lost a little bit of interest in Afghanistan," said Col. Tucker Mansager, another staff officer who arrived in July 2003 after serving as a military attaché in Warsaw. "That is not to say we were neglected, but clearly, people had their eyes on Iraq a lot."

It soon became apparent that Bush's decision to invade Iraq was a titanic mistake—not just for Iraq, but for Afghanistan.

The Iraq War was a far bigger undertaking at first. It required an invasion force of 120,000 U.S. troops, about thirteen times the number deployed to Afghanistan. Lulled into overconfidence by its rapid defeat of the Taliban, the Bush administration figured it could handle two wars at once. It was a rash assumption that defied history and common sense.

"There are certain sorts of basic policy conclusions that are hard to legislate. First, you know, sort of just invade only one country at a time. I mean that seriously," James Dobbins, the U.S. diplomat who helped negotiate the Bonn Agreement, said in a Lessons Learned interview.

During the 1990s, Dobbins was dispatched as a special envoy to one trouble spot after another: Somalia, Haiti, Bosnia and Kosovo. He wrote several books about his experiences, including *The Beginner's Guide to Nation-Building*. Although Bush had bashed Clinton for sending the U.S. military to war-torn countries on nation-building missions, at least Clinton didn't try to tackle two at a time, Dobbins said.

"If you look at the Clinton administration it very consciously did not invade Haiti until it had withdrawn from Somalia. It did not do anything about the Balkans until it had withdrawn from Haiti. And it didn't do anything about Kosovo until Bosnia had been stabilized," Dobbins said. "They take a lot of high-level time and attention and we'll overload the system if we do more than one of these at a time."

Iraq posed an enormous distraction from the start. The U.S. military began making plans to take Baghdad in December 2001, while bin Laden was escaping from Tora Bora. On the day after Christmas, General Tommy Franks was working at Central Command headquarters in Tampa when Rumsfeld called from the Pentagon and summoned him to a secret meeting at Bush's secluded ranch in central Texas, according to Franks' University of Virginia oral-history interview.

"The president wants to see you in Crawford," Rumsfeld told Franks on the phone. "Be ready to talk to the president about what you're thinking about Iraq."

Within forty-eight hours, the general departed for the small town of Crawford to brief the president on military options for Iraq. Among other questions, Bush and Rumsfeld asked Franks if he thought it was too much for a single commander to oversee a war in Iraq—if it came to that—and the war in Afghanistan at the same time. Franks persuaded them he could handle both operations from his Central Command post in Tampa.

In his oral history, Franks defended the decision to allow him to manage both wars. He said he never neglected Afghanistan and noted that troop levels there actually increased as the Iraq War got underway. "So this idea of people taking their eye off the ball in Afghanistan is simply not true," he said. "That's not to say we did everything right, but what we didn't do right wasn't because of an absence of attention."

But other U.S. officials said there was no question that the Bush administration looked away from Afghanistan. Many at the White House and the Pentagon thought there was nothing left to accomplish other than catching bin Laden and tying up a few loose ends.

By August 2002, "for lots of reasons, the Bush administration had already concluded Afghanistan was done," Philip Zelikow, a member of Bush's foreign intelligence advisory board, said in a University of Virginia oral-history interview.

Most U.S. officials wrongly assumed the Taliban would never pose a serious threat again. In his Mission Accomplished speech, Bush declared flatly: "We destroyed the Taliban." Robert Finn, who served as U.S. ambassador to Afghanistan from 2002 to 2003, said in a Lessons Learned interview that he figured remnants of the Taliban might survive, "but basically would be nuisance bandits up in the mountains."

That strategic miscalculation reverberated down the chain of command. With the Pentagon preoccupied by Iraq, the already blurry mission in Afghanistan grew even hazier for units in the field.

Maj. Gregory Trahan, an 82nd Airborne Division officer, said troops were unsure of their objectives. "Before we left, my soldiers wanted to know if we were going there for humanitarian assistance, or were we going there to—in the soldier's vernacular—kill people," he recalled in an Army oral-history interview.

Maj. Phil Bergeron, an artillery officer who deployed to Kandahar in 2003, said he never got a handle on the big picture. "We had Iraq going on at the time so that just pulled all the focus," he told Army historians.

In a Lessons Learned interview, an unnamed U.S. official who worked at the White House and the Pentagon during the Bush administration, said work on Afghanistan took a back seat to Iraq starting in spring 2002. At that point, Americans serving at all levels in Afghanistan recalibrated their expectations; their job was to simply avoid defeat.

"Either materially or politically, it all seemed to be about Iraq," the U.S. official said. "It was hard to come to terms with the reality that your whole portfolio is a secondary effort or, at worst, an 'economy of force' mission. Your job was not to win, it was to not lose. Emotionally and psychologically, this is hard."

During summer 2003, the U.S. military rapidly lost its grip on the war in Iraq. Fifty American troops died there in the six weeks following Bush's Mission Accomplished speech and nobody could find the weapons of mass destruction that Saddam Hussein supposedly had been hiding.

Still, the Bush administration reassured the public it had everything under control. At a June 18 press conference at the Pentagon, Rumsfeld belittled the Iraqi insurgency as "pockets of dead-enders." He also said the U.S.-led military coalition was "making good progress"—a dubious phrase he and other Pentagon officials would repeat countless times about both wars in the years ahead.

Meanwhile, the dead-enders grew stronger. In August, insurgents blew up the Jordanian embassy and the United Nations headquarters in Baghdad. U.N. workers and relief organizations fled the country. In October, al-Qaeda piled insult on injury by circulating a video of bin Laden. From his undisclosed location, the 9/11 mastermind mocked the Americans for getting "mired in the swamps of the Tigris and Euphrates."

That same month, a new Army general arrived to take charge of the increasingly overlooked war in Afghanistan. Lt. Gen. David Barno was a native of Endicott, New York, a small town in the state's Southern Tier. After graduating from West Point, he led a company of Army Rangers that invaded Grenada in 1983 and a battalion that parachuted into Panama during the 1989 invasion of that country.

Barno landed in Afghanistan at a turbulent time. The Pentagon had downsized the military headquarters at Bagram and, due to unexpected turnover, Barno was the fourth commanding general in six months. Operations were equally unstable on the diplomatic side, where the U.S. embassy had lacked a permanent ambassador for an extended period.

"The whole effort in Afghanistan was in a bit of a sideways drift," Barno said in an Army oral-history interview. "There was a tremendous, in my view, dysfunctionality in unity of command inside of Afghanistan, inside the military."

Barno stood up a new headquarters—the Combined Forces Command–Afghanistan—and moved it from Bagram Air Base to the embassy compound in Kabul so he could work more closely with the diplomats. For his quarters, he occupied a half-trailer located just fifty feet away from the double-wide trailer reserved for the ambassador.

Cramped conditions aside, Barno had trouble building his staff. Military personnel commands back in the United States said there was a shortage of available officers because of Iraq. But Barno said it was clear they saw the war in Afghanistan as a backwater and didn't want to send their best people. It infuriated him.

"None of the people the Army sent me were people who would ever grow up to be generals," he said. "The Army was unhelpful, to be generous . . . They clearly had Iraq on their minds, but there was no interest whatsoever in providing us with anything but the absolute minimum level of support."

At first, Barno had to make do with staff officers of unusually low rank. When he pushed for upgrades, the services sent reservists who had been out of uniform for years; "an extraordinary array of people who were kind of at the end of the pipeline," as Barno put it. Many were older than the three-star general—he was 49—and the staff jokingly called itself the world's most forward-deployed chapter of the American Association of Retired People.

Although Afghanistan was nowhere as violent as Iraq, the nature of the conflict was changing and growing more worrisome. Days after Barno's arrival, United Nations officials based in Kabul gave him an earful about worsening security in the south and east of the country and challenged him to do something.

The general ordered his skeleton headquarters staff to review the war strategy. They concluded that—as in Iraq—a popular rebellion was taking root. The military would need to shift from a narrow focus on hunting terrorists to "a classic counterinsurgency campaign," aimed at winning the support of Afghan civilians caught in the middle of the conflict.

The problem was that the military had not run a counterinsurgency campaign since the Vietnam War. To figure out what to do, Barno scrounged up three textbooks on counterrevolutionary warfare he had read as a West Point cadet more than twenty-five years earlier. "We had no U.S. military doctrine whatsoever at that point in time by which to guide us," he said. "None of us really had much of any training on the counterinsurgency business, so we were kind of scraping on how to think about this."

Meanwhile, other intrinsic doubts arose in the executive suites at the Pentagon. On October 16, 2003, Rumsfeld dictated a snowflake to a handful of generals and aides with a provocative question: "Are we winning or losing the Global War on Terror?"

Rumsfeld was pessimistic. "It is pretty clear that the coalition can win in Afghanistan and Iraq in one way or another, but it will be a long, hard slog," he concluded in the two-page memo.

Someone leaked the snowflake to *USA Today*, which triggered a cascade of news coverage about whether the defense secretary had been lying to the public about the wars. Rumsfeld was forced to hold a press conference to address the controversy. At first, he tried to joke about it, saying that his wife, Joyce, had asked him if "slog" was actually a word; then he jousted with reporters over the dictionary definition. He denied the Bush administration had been "putting a happy face" on the wars in public. "What we have done is we've put out a very straightforward, accurate, to the best of our ability, and balanced view of what we see happening," he said.

Defying Rumsfeld's declaration about the end of combat, the Taliban slowly regrouped. During the latter half of 2003, the U.S. military found it necessary to launch three major offensives: Operation Mountain Viper, Operation Mountain Resolve and Operation Avalanche. Sticking with the alpine theme, U.S. forces kicked off Operation Mountain Blizzard and Operation Mountain Storm in early 2004.

But with the Iraq War sliding downhill, the Bush administration decided it was more important than ever to minimize the fighting and showcase Afghanistan as a success. In December 2003, Rumsfeld visited Kabul and made a side trip to the northern city of Mazar-e-Sharif. Asked by a reporter if he was afraid the Taliban was mounting a comeback, he dismissively said no. "They will not have that opportunity," he said. "To the extent that they assemble in anything more than ones and twos . . . they'll be killed or captured." Upon his return to Washington, Rumsfeld told the board of trustees at the American Enterprise Institute, a conservative think tank, that "signs of progress are everywhere" and that "Afghanistan has turned a corner."

In January 2004, Zalmay Khalilzad, the Afghan-American diplomat who had taken up residence in the embassy's double-wide trailer as the new U.S. ambassador, wrote an op-ed in *The Washington Post* praising the Afghans for holding a *loya jirga*, a traditional assembly, to draft a new constitution that embraced democracy and women's rights. At the end of the column, Khalilzad mentioned as an aside that U.S. troops might have to stay in Afghanistan for several years. "Given the stakes involved, we must remain committed for as long as it takes to succeed," he wrote.

The op-ed prompted eye-rolling among other diplomats in Kabul who thought it put the most positive spin possible on what was happening in Afghanistan. Thomas Hutson, a political officer, said he bumped into a public-relations strategist in the U.S. embassy cafeteria who told him twenty people had teamed up to write Khalilzad's column. He wondered why the government was paying the salaries of so many people to draft glowing press releases about the war.

Hutson grew up in tiny Red Cloud, Nebraska, before embarking on a Foreign Service career that took him to Iran, Russia, the Balkans, Nigeria, Taiwan, Kyrgyzstan and Barbados. Having seen much of the world, he held few illusions about what it would take to transform Afghanistan into a stable country.

A few days after the op-ed appeared, Hutson was chatting with a British military officer when a journalist asked them how long they thought U.S. and British troops might need to stay. "We answered almost simultaneously," Hutson recalled in a diplomatic oral-history interview. "The colonel said, 'forty years' and I said, 'check with my grandson.'"

As Afghanistan drifted and Iraq burned, simmering rivalries inside Bush's war cabinet grew more heated. The biggest spats usually involved Rumsfeld and Powell. Both men were strong-willed with self-assured personalities and had contemplated running for president.

The only two-time defense secretary in history, Rumsfeld wrestled at Princeton, flew fighter jets in the Navy, ran Fortune 500 companies and showed few signs of mellowing in his 70s. A retired four-star general, Powell was a hero of the first Iraq War, the only African-American to serve as chairman of the Joint Chiefs of Staff and by some measures the most popular political figure in America.

Each blamed the other and their staffs for fiascoes in the war zones. Rumsfeld complained that the State Department and USAID had bungled reconstruction and stabilization programs. Powell viewed

Rumsfeld and his civilian aides as neoconservative ideologues who abused the military.

Their feud sometimes bubbled to the surface and turned petty during meetings at the White House, according to Pace, the Marine general.

"The two secretaries would kind of get nipping at each other's shorts. Secretary Powell might say 'Kabul' and Secretary Rumsfeld would say, 'Is it Kabaaal or Kabuuul?' just to pimp him a little bit," said Pace, who served as vice-chairman of the Joint Chiefs from 2001 to 2005.

From the head of the table, National Security Adviser Condoleezza Rice would have to step into the fray. "She would say, 'Now Don, now Colin,'" Pace recalled in his University of Virginia oral-history interview. "Condi, God bless her, would just kind of get in the locker room saying, 'Okay, boys, break.'"

Rumsfeld promoted his reputation as a taskmaster who thrived on a relentless schedule, but there were signs that stress from the wars was affecting his health. Though the defense secretary kept it a secret, in December 2003 he became "very ill" for about three months, according to Pace. Asked in the oral-history interview if he meant Rumsfeld was suffering from nervous exhaustion, Pace replied: "I don't know. He was very sick. He tried to cover that up and did cover it up I think, but it was during that time when he basically said—Pete Pace's words, not his—'Screw it. If Condi and Colin want to run the show, let them.'"*

Rumsfeld's leadership traits—he often ruled by fear—generated resentment among the generals. In a University of Virginia oral-history interview, Army Lt. Gen. Douglas Lute said Rumsfeld was dismissive of people in uniform and not a team player. "When you see leadership that is divisive and caustic and that is disrespectful, it grinds on you," he said.

Tommy Franks, another hard-headed leader, couldn't stand Rumsfeld at first and resented him for questioning his war plans for Afghanistan, though he later came to admire the defense secretary for his

---

* Rumsfeld did not publicly disclose any serious health problems during this period or in his 2011 memoir, *Known and Unknown*. He did not respond to requests for comment on Pace's assertion.

patriotism. "Don Rumsfeld is not the easiest guy in the world for military leaders to get along with," Franks said in his University of Virginia oral-history interview. "Being the contrarian guy that he is—keep in mind the personality issue—he automatically didn't like anything, ever."

Military officials in Kabul enjoyed a relative reprieve while Rumsfeld was fixated on Iraq from 2002 through the first half of 2004. In June 2004, however, he told his commanders he wanted to hold weekly video conferences about Afghanistan. The country's first-ever presidential election was coming up in October—a major step in the nation-building campaign—and Rumsfeld wanted to ensure everything was on the right track.

Word of the defense secretary's renewed interest ignited panic at Barno's headquarters. Staff officers fretted so much about triggering Rumsfeld's wrath that they spent most of their workweek prepping for a video conference that usually lasted less than an hour.

Maj. Gen. Peter Gilchrist, a British Army officer who served as Barno's deputy commander, said he was astonished by how much Rumsfeld intimidated his American counterparts. "This was a real cultural shock for me," Gilchrist said in an oral-history interview. "You should see these guys—and they're great men, grown up, intelligent, sensible, but like the jellies when it came to going in front of the SecDef."

Joining Rumsfeld in the meetings from the Pentagon was an imposing assortment of senior brass and deputy secretaries. In Kabul, the staff fielded their questions through a tiny video monitor propped up in the back of an interpreter's trailer at the embassy. Barno called the sessions "very contentious, painful, difficult and tribulating" and said they required a "backbreaking effort" that "about brought us to our knees." Eventually, he persuaded the Pentagon to scale back the conferences to twice a month, which he said was still "barely sustainable."

Part of the reason the meetings were so painful is because Rumsfeld asked smart questions that exposed core problems. Col. Tucker Mansager said the staff could not prove that the war strategy was working. Although they collected all sorts of statistics, it was hard to know what conclusions to draw.

"The secretary was beating us up. Secretary Rumsfeld was always asking, 'Where are your measures of effectiveness? How can you make progress?' " Mansager said in an Army oral-history interview. "I was working long hours, doing lots of stuff, and even a couple of times in my journals, I said, 'Are we making progress?' So the frustration there is, how do you know?"

Despite its internal misgivings about the war, the Bush administration maintained its happy face in public. In August 2004, Rumsfeld delivered a speech in Phoenix and cited indicator after indicator of progress in Afghanistan: a boom in highway construction, a spike in voter registrations, more energy in the streets. He swatted away evidence that the insurgency was spreading. "There is absolutely no way in the world that we can be militarily defeated in Afghanistan," he said. The following month, while campaigning for a second term in the White House, Bush went even further and falsely declared that the Taliban "no longer is in existence."

In October 2004, the Afghan presidential election went off largely without a hitch. Karzai won convincingly and secured another five years in the palace. It was a slice of good news for the U.S. government, especially compared to Iraq, where the Pentagon was still reeling from the Abu Ghraib prison torture scandal and a sectarian bloodbath.

In a Pentagon press briefing, Rumsfeld hailed the vote as the clearest sign yet of progress in Afghanistan. He also seized the opportunity to mock the skeptics. "Everyone said that it wouldn't work in Afghanistan. 'They've never done it in 500 years, and the Taliban are reorganizing; they're going to go in there and kill everybody. And we're in a quagmire.' And lo and behold, Afghanistan had an election. Amazing."

Three years in, it was the high point of the war.

CHAPTER FIVE

Raising an Army from the Ashes

In 2003, the United States pinned its hopes for ending the war on a washed-out tract of land next to a Soviet tank graveyard on the eastern edge of the capital. Known as the Kabul Military Training Center, the rundown site functioned as a boot camp for the new Afghan national army. Each morning, drill instructors rousted Afghan volunteers from their stone-cold barracks to teach them the art of soldiering. If recruits survived the horrible sanitation conditions and dodged the old land mines buried around the property, they could earn about $2.50 a day to defend the Afghan government.

The road leading from Kabul to the boot camp was so riddled with potholes that the driver for Maj. Gen. Karl Eikenberry had to zigzag along at five to ten miles an hour. As head of the Office of Military Cooperation at the U.S. embassy, Eikenberry's job was to create, from scratch, a 70,000-man indigenous army to protect the weak Afghan government from an array of enemies: the Taliban, al-Qaeda, other insurgents, renegade warlords.

A Mandarin-speaking scholar-general, Eikenberry had recorded two tours of duty as a military attaché in Beijing. On 9/11, he narrowly escaped death when American Airlines flight 77 crashed into the Pentagon and the shock waves threw him against the wall of his outer-ring office; two people working nearby were killed. When he arrived at the Kabul Military Training Center, the hardscrabble scene reminded him of the suffering that George Washington's Continental Army endured at Valley Forge during the winter of 1777.

"Everyone was having some pretty rough nights," Eikenberry said in an Army oral-history interview. "It was just an extraordinary set of challenges."

Because the Afghans had no money, it fell to the United States and its allies to pay for the new army and supply the trainers and equipment. NATO ally Germany, with help from the State Department and other countries, agreed to oversee a parallel program to recruit and train 62,000 officers for an Afghan national police force.

In spring 2003, Eikenberry set up a new command to oversee the massive training effort for the Afghan army. He named it Task Force Phoenix to symbolize the rebirth of the Afghan state from, as he put it, "the ashes of thirty years of very brutal warfare." The entire U.S. war strategy hinged on the program. As soon as the Afghans could field competent security forces to secure their own territory, the U.S. military and its allies could go home.

Year after year, U.S. officials reassured the American public that the plan was working and gave the Afghan forces rave reviews. In June 2004, Lt. Gen. David Barno, the commander of U.S. forces in Afghanistan, boasted to reporters that the Taliban and al-Qaeda were scared of fighting the Afghan army "because when they do, the terrorists come out second best."

Three months later, Army Lt. Gen. Walter Sharp, director of strategic plans and policy for the Joint Staff at the Pentagon, testified before Congress that the Afghan army was "performing admirably" and called it "the principal pillar" of the country's security. In a set of talking points released at the same time, the Pentagon bragged that the Afghan army had become "a highly professional, multi-ethnic force."

In reality, the project flopped from the start and would defy all attempts to make it work. Washington wildly underestimated how much the Afghan security forces would cost, how long it would take to train them and how many soldiers and police would be needed to battle the country's rising insurgency.

The Bush administration compounded the miscalculations by moving too slowly to strengthen the Afghan security forces during the first few years of the war when the Taliban presented a minimal threat. Then, after the Taliban rebounded, the U.S. government tried to train too many Afghans too quickly.

"We got the [Afghan forces] we deserve," Douglas Lute, an Army lieutenant general who served as the White House's Afghanistan war czar under Bush and Obama, said in a Lessons Learned interview. If the U.S. government had ramped up training "when the Taliban was weak and disorganized, things may have been different," Lute added. "Instead, we went to Iraq. If we committed money deliberately and sooner, we could have a different outcome."

The Pentagon also committed a fundamental mistake by designing the Afghan army as a facsimile of the U.S. military, forcing it to adopt similar rules, customs and structures in spite of vast differences in culture and knowledge.

Almost all Afghan recruits had been deprived of a basic education during their country's decades of turmoil. An estimated 80 to 90 percent could not read or write. Some could not count or did not know their colors. Yet the Americans expected them to embrace PowerPoint presentations and operate complex weapons systems.

Even simple communications posed a challenge. U.S. trainers and combat advisers needed a cluster of interpreters who could translate between English and three separate Afghan languages: Dari, Pashto and Uzbek. When words failed, the troops did a lot of talking with their hands or drawing in the dirt.

Maj. Bradd Schultz, who served with Task Force Phoenix in 2003 and 2004, recalled trying to explain to newly minted Afghan soldiers what it would be like to board a military aircraft. "When you get down there, there's going to be a thing there called a helicopter," he said in an Army oral-history interview. "It was like, 'This is an airplane. Touch it.'"

In another Army oral-history interview, Maj. Brian Doyle, a geography instructor from the U.S. Military Academy at West Point, recounted tutoring a class of young Afghan officers in Kabul. As he explained the significance of high tide and low tide during the D-Day invasion at Normandy, his interpreter, a trained medical doctor whom Doyle described as "a very smart man," interrupted and said, "Tides? What are tides?" Doyle explained to the landlocked Afghans that it was when ocean waters rise and fall. "Well, you would have thought I'd just told him that the world was round and he'd been thinking it was flat. He was like, 'What do you mean the water comes up and down?'"

Robert Gates, who later served as defense secretary under Bush and Obama, said U.S. goals for the Afghan security forces were "ludicrously modest" during the early years of the war and that the Pentagon and State Department never settled on a consistent approach.

"We kept changing guys who were in charge of training the Afghan forces, and every time a new guy came in he changed the way that they were being trained," Gates said in a University of Virginia oral-history interview. "The one thing they all had in common was they were all trying to train a Western army instead of figuring out the strengths of the Afghans as a fighting people and then building on that."

In the beginning, the Pentagon underscored its minimalist expectations for the Afghan army by trying to build it on the cheap. In a January 2002 snowflake, Rumsfeld blasted as "crazy" a request from the Afghan interim government for $466 million a year to train and equip 200,000 soldiers. Three months later, he sent an angry memo to Colin Powell upon learning the State Department had committed the United States to cover 20 percent of the Afghan Army's expenses. Rumsfeld thought allies should foot the bill instead.

"The U.S. spent billions of dollars freeing Afghanistan and providing security. We are spending a fortune every day," Rumsfeld wrote. "The U.S. position should be zero. We are already doing more than anyone."

Powell responded in a memo that he was "naturally sympathetic" to Rumsfeld's argument, but he didn't back down: "Recognizing that others are unlikely to shoulder these burdens adequately unless the United States leads the way, we have pledged to do our fair share."

Over the next two decades, Washington would spend exponentially more on security assistance to the Afghan government: more than

$85 billion, the single biggest expense of the entire nation-building extravaganza.

During the Bush administration, the debate festered about how big the Afghan security forces should be and who should pay for them. "The way it gets resolved is the way everything gets resolved in Washington— by not getting resolved," Marin Strmecki, an influential civilian adviser to Rumsfeld, said in a Lessons Learned interview.

Zalmay Khalilzad, a Bush White House staffer before he served as U.S. ambassador to Kabul from 2003 to 2005, said the Afghan government scaled back its original request and asked Washington to pay for security forces with 100,000 to 120,000 armed personnel. But he said in a Lessons Learned interview that Rumsfeld demanded further cuts and held the training program "hostage" until the Afghans agreed to cap the number at 50,000.

Over the years, as the Taliban grew stronger, the Americans and Afghans would be forced to lift the cap again and again to avoid losing the war. Eventually, the United States paid to train and maintain 352,000 Afghan security forces, with about 227,000 enlisted in the army and 125,000 belonging to the national police. "So we were fighting in 2002, 2003 about those sort of numbers," Khalilzad said, referring to Rumsfeld's 50,000 cap. "Now we're talking about God knows what, 300,000 or whatever."

Policy bickering about the size of the Afghan security forces was exacerbated by another shortcoming: the U.S. government lacked the ability and capacity to create foreign armies from whole cloth. Just as it had forgotten how to fight an insurgency since Vietnam, the U.S. military had not built anything on the scale of the Afghan army in decades. Green Berets specialized in training small units from other countries, not entire armies. The Pentagon tried to figure it out on the fly and the lack of preparation showed.

"You wouldn't invent how to do infantry operations at the start of a war. You wouldn't invent how to do artillery at the start of a war," Strmecki said. "Right now, it is all ad hoc. There is no doctrine, no science to it. It gets done very unevenly. When you are creating security forces for another society, it is the most important political act you will ever do. That requires an awful lot of thought and sophistication."

Initially, in 2003, the Pentagon assigned an active-duty Army brigade from the 10th Mountain Division to run Task Force Phoenix. Just as it was getting established, however, the Bush administration decided to go to war in Iraq, placing an immediate strain on military units worldwide. The brigade at Task Force Phoenix pulled out and was replaced by a motley, undermanned collection of National Guard troops and Army reservists. "Our inability to keep up . . . became a very acute challenge," Eikenberry said.

Many had no experience training foreign soldiers and did not know what they were supposed to be doing in Afghanistan until they got there. Staff Sgt. Anton Berendsen said he was preparing to deploy to Iraq in 2003 when he received last-minute orders to divert to Afghanistan and join Task Force Phoenix instead. "You're in country and like, 'What do we do now?'" he said in an Army oral-history interview. "There was a lot of growing pains."

Maj. Rick Rabe, an engineer with the California National Guard, arrived at the Kabul Military Training Center in the summer of 2004 to oversee basic training. Under pressure to produce more Afghan soldiers, he tripled the number of enlisted recruits in the twelve-week program. But standards suffered. In fact, there were few standards at all. Recruits could flunk certification tests or go AWOL, yet not get kicked out of boot camp.

"You couldn't fail basic training," Rabe said in an Army oral-history interview. Weak qualifications became an open joke. "As long as they could pull the trigger fifty times, it didn't matter if they hit anything. As long as the bullet went in the right direction, they were good."

Even under ideal conditions, the U.S. military projected it would take several years before the Afghan army could operate on its own. In the field, Afghan battalions partnered with U.S. troops, but the Americans did most of the fighting. U.S. combat advisers and mentors embedded with Afghan units to provide guidance, but often found that the Afghans lacked basic combat skills and needed constant retraining.

Maj. Christopher Plummer, an infantry officer, arrived at U.S. head-quarters in Kabul in 2005 to coordinate training and fielding for the Afghan army. After hearing frequent complaints about the Afghan troops' poor marksmanship, he visited the Kabul Military Training Center to observe recruits on the firing range.

"Of course, it was no surprise to anybody that I came back with a report which said that these guys couldn't hit the broad side of a barn at ten meters," Plummer said in an Army oral-history interview. Out of 800 recruits in basic training at the time, only eighty passed the marksmanship test—yet they were all permitted to graduate anyway. "They were just going through the motions," he said.

At first, the Pentagon outfitted the Afghan army with Russian-made AK-47s: a simple, easy-to-use and largely indestructible rifle. Many Afghans were familiar with the weapon, but instead of taking careful aim they used a method that U.S. military advisers ridiculed as "spray and pray." Afghan soldiers often wasted all their ammunition during a firefight without killing anyone, forcing U.S. troops to come to their rescue, according to Maj. Gerd Schroeder, a roving firearms instructor who deployed to Afghanistan in 2005.

Schroeder once took an Afghan battalion to a firing range near Kandahar for remedial work. A believer in teaching by example, he stabbed a watermelon with a long stick and jammed it in the ground. "You say, 'Okay, Mr. Afghan Soldier, shoot that watermelon,' and he'd just shoot from the hip at it," leaving the fruit unscathed, Schroeder said in an Army oral-history interview.

Then Schroeder asked a U.S. soldier to demonstrate. "And he'd put a bullet right through the watermelon—one round." The lessons gradually sunk in. "Before that they had no comprehension of marksmanship at all," he said. "They'd just throw as many rounds as they could downrange and see if they hit something."

Some Afghan soldiers were veteran fighters who performed well in battle. But when bullets started to fly, many Afghans got caught up in the moment and forgot their training, said Lt. Col. Michael Slusher, a Kansas National Guard officer who embedded with an Afghan unit.

"They go out and they run right into the fire," he said in an Army oral-history interview. "It's kind of crazy because the [enemy] will sit in those defensive positions and just let these guys run right up on them. They'll run right up the side of the mountain after them, shooting all the way and yelling. They're brave little dudes but that's not the way we want to do business."

Maj. John Bates, another National Guardsman who served as an embedded trainer, praised his Afghan company as a "crack outfit" that had fought cohesively for three years. But some basics were hard to learn. Bates said U.S. advisers had to teach Afghans the concept of taking care of their own weapon instead of just grabbing one that was handy.

"We actually wrote their names on the weapons so the first sergeant could walk down the row and see that that was their name on the weapon," he said in an Army oral-history interview. Another revelation for the Afghans was that uniforms came in a variety of sizes, and left shoes were shaped differently from right shoes. "We'd get a shipment of boots in and these guys had never had their feet measured so they didn't know what size boot they were," Bates said.

Not that it mattered with the defective footwear they often received. "The first day, halfway through the mission, the sole of the boots come completely off," he said.

Teaching the Afghans to drive military vehicles was another adventure. "It was all either full gas or full brake, one or the other," said Command Master Sgt. Jeff Janke, a trainer with the Wisconsin National Guard. "If they crashed something, there wasn't any responsibility for it. Their thinking was, 'the [trainer] should bring me a new one. This one is broke.'"

During spring 2004, Maj. Dan Williamson, a trainer with Task Force Phoenix, needed to show Afghan soldiers how to operate a 2.5-ton cargo truck with a six-speed manual transmission. He found an out-of-the-way spot on a military base near Kabul where nothing could be sideswiped. First, the Afghans tried to learn how to drive a straight line forward and a straight line back, with U.S. instructors in the passenger's seat and interpreters clinging to the sideboards. Then they practiced turns on an oval dirt track.

"These guys were a menace to society," Williamson said in an Army oral-history interview. "They'd let go of the steering wheel, grab the gear shift with both hands and look at the gear shift, not the road. They couldn't seem to get it into gear and the trucks would be going all over the place." The sideboard-riding interpreters, he added, had to be "stout of heart."

As the Afghan army expanded, the United States went on a building spree to construct bases and barracks for their partners. Projects adhered to U.S. specifications, but the Western designs often left the Afghans bewildered.

One U.S. military official said in a Lessons Learned interview that the Afghans mistook urinals as drinking fountains. Sit-down toilets were another hazardous novelty. "[We] realized that the commodes were being broken because the soldiers were trying to squat on them like they usually do, or the soldiers were getting hurt as they slipped off and whacked their knee into the wall," Maj. Kevin Lovell, an officer with the Army Corps of Engineers, said in an oral-history interview.

Towel racks didn't last long either. The Afghans tied and twisted their wet laundry around the towel rod to wring out the water, ripping the racks out of the wall. They draped soggy clothes over electric heaters, causing them to short-circuit. Such problems could have been averted, Lovell said, "if we would have had a little bit less hubris, thought how these guys normally live and provided a construction to that standard."

The American-designed kitchens and chow halls also didn't translate well. Afghans preferred to cook communal meals in a huge pot over an open flame, boiling rice, meat and other ingredients in a single stew. "They stand there in their bare feet and they use a giant spoon to move the rice around. It wasn't very clean," Maj. Matthew Little, another Army Corps of Engineers officer, said in an Army oral-history interview.

On one base, Afghan cooks relocated their indoor fire away from contractor-installed air vents without realizing what the vents were for.

"The entire kitchen would fill up with smoke. It would spill out into the dining area and the beige walls would turn black," Little said. "You'd walk in there and you had to wash your uniform after."

In another instance, he said an Afghan army leader asked to dig an open trench along the kitchen floor so the cooks could throw their waste into it and "just have it wash downstream into the drainage system. Kind of like a river, I guess, or a small creek that might be in the West in the olden days."

U.S. combat advisers and trainers gave Afghan soldiers mixed reviews on the most important issue: their willingness to fight. Some praised their dedication and determination, while others complained of laziness and indifference. Given that the U.S. war strategy depended on the Afghan army's performance, however, the Pentagon paid surprisingly little attention to the question of whether Afghans were willing to die for their government.

Absenteeism was a chronic problem. After boot camp, soldiers usually received several days off before they had to report for duty at a new location. Many collected their first paycheck and disappeared. Others showed up, but without their uniform, gear or weapon, having sold them for extra cash. Large numbers of soldiers reported sporadically or late. No Afghan battalion operated anywhere near full strength, which only intensified the pressure to recruit and train replacements.

Maj. Charles Abeyawardena, a strategic planning officer with the Army's Center for Lessons Learned at Fort Leavenworth, Kansas, arrived in Afghanistan in 2005 to interview U.S. combat advisers and senior Afghan officials about their experiences. As an aside, he decided to ask low-ranking Afghan soldiers why they had enlisted. He said their responses echoed those usually given by American troops: it's a solid paycheck, I want to serve my country, it's an opportunity to do something new with my life.

But when he followed up by asking whether they would stay in the Afghan army after the United States left, the answers startled him. "The majority, almost everyone I talked to, said, 'No,'" Abeyawardena said in an Army oral-history interview. "They were going to go back and grow opium or marijuana or something like that, because that's where the money is. That threw me for a complete loop."

As difficult as it was to train the Afghan army, the attempts to create a national police force produced an even bigger debacle. Germany agreed to oversee police training in early 2002, but quickly became overwhelmed. The German government invested insufficient money in the program, struggled to find German cops willing to go to Afghanistan to serve as trainers and confined those who did to a peaceful zone in the north. Eventually, the United States intervened and took over the bulk of the responsibility.

From 2002 to 2006, the Americans spent ten times as much on police training as the Germans but performed no better. The State Department outsourced the program to private contractors, who collected big fees but delivered poor results. Training for police recruits was brief—often just two to three weeks—and their pay was abysmal.

Partly because they earned so little, many police officers morphed into shakedown artists who extorted bribes from the people they were supposed to protect. "They're so corrupt that if your house gets robbed and you call the police . . . the police will show up and rob your house a second time," Maj. Del Saam, a National Guardsman who worked with the Afghan security forces, said in an Army oral-history interview.

Pentagon officials complained that the State Department's dismal police training program was undermining the war strategy. In February 2005, Rumsfeld forwarded a confidential report to Secretary of State Condoleezza Rice about the Afghan National Police, or ANP. The report was titled, "ANP Horror Stories" and described how most of the police were illiterate, underequipped and unprepared.

"Please take a look," Rumsfeld wrote in a snowflake accompanying the report. "This is the Afghanistan National Police situation. It is a serious problem. My impression is that these two pages were written in as graceful and noninflammatory a way as is humanly possible."

By summer 2005, the U.S. military took over most of the responsibility for training the police. While the Pentagon had more resources and personnel to throw at the problem than the State Department, it couldn't untangle the knot of expectations that Washington had created.

On one hand, the United States and its allies wanted to impose a Western-style system of law enforcement to maintain stability and order. On the other, the Pentagon wanted the Afghan police to fight insurgents, much as the army did, and trained the police as a paramilitary force. Either way, the notion of a uniformed police officer carrying a badge and a gun to enforce the laws of the state was a foreign concept to most Afghans, especially in rural areas.

Major Saam of the National Guard said Afghans were accustomed to settling disputes differently. "If you have a problem, you don't go to the police. You go to the village elder," he said. "He makes up the rules as he goes. There's no rule of law. If he likes you, he's going to say, 'Hey, this is really good.' If he doesn't like you, he's going to say, 'Give me some goats or sheep or we'll have you shot on sight.'"

In such situations, tribal or religious codes of conduct that had been in place for generations usually determined the outcomes. Inserting police officers into the equation stirred disruption and trouble.

"They have a hard time picturing what we're trying to do with the police forces. They don't understand how it fits into their culture," Saam said. "Americans are trying to force something on them that we understand, but that they can't visualize."

It was a mistake the United States would repeat again and again.

CHAPTER SIX

Islam for Dummies

As the U.S. military settled into Afghanistan, it mobilized Special Forces teams to carry out operations to influence the emotions, thinking and behavior of ordinary Afghans and their leaders. Known as psychological operations, or psy-ops, the tactics were a longstanding form of unconventional warfare to shape popular opinion in favor of American objectives and sap the enemy's will to fight. Green Berets and military contractors on psy-op teams studied foreign cultures so they could exploit religious, linguistic and social nuances to their advantage.

But the psy-op specialists and other soldiers who parachuted into Afghanistan were operating in the dark. Years after the war started, the U.S. military still had almost no uniformed personnel who could speak Dari or Pashto fluently. Few troops possessed even a remote grasp of Afghanistan's history, its religious customs or tribal dynamics.

When Maj. Louis Frias, an officer with the 8th PSYOP Battalion from Fort Bragg, North Carolina, deployed to Afghanistan in July 2003, he prepared by reading the paperback *Islam For Dummies* on the plane ride over. He taught himself a couple phrases in Dari but garbled them so badly that Afghans pleaded with him to stick to English. "I felt like a dork," he said in an Army oral-history interview.

Frias led a small psy-ops team that worked out of the U.S. embassy and distributed radio scripts and posters to build support for democratic principles and the Afghan security forces. But the team's biggest project was developing a comic book. The idea came from a soldier Frias met in the chow hall who suggested it as a way to manipulate the minds of Afghan youth. So the psy-ops team decided to design a comic book about the importance of voting, centered around a story about kids playing soccer because, as Frias put it, "soccer is such a big thing in Afghanistan."

In the comic, a bunch of kids from different tribes and ethnic groups are kicking the ball around when a wise old man appears with a rule book. A symbol of the new Afghan constitution, the rule book not only dictated how children were supposed to play the game, but also laid out a novel process for picking a team captain—by voting.

"We had all the kids saying they would be the leader and the wise old man would come in and say, 'You need to vote for one person to be the leader of the soccer team,'" Frias said. "That was the story of our comic book." The team showed drafts of the comics to children hanging out at bazaars and the kids provided "good feedback," according to Frias.

But the project ran into bureaucratic hurdles and delays. Diplomats at the U.S. embassy and military commanders in Kabul and Bagram all insisted on reviewing the illustrations. "Everybody wanted to have their say in it," Frias said. By the time his six-month tour of duty ended and he returned to Fort Bragg, the comic book still hadn't been printed and he never got to see the final version. "I was told it went into production," he said. "What I don't know is what type of effect it had."

A second psy-ops team based at Bagram also seized on soccer as a propaganda medium. Starting in 2002, the Bagram team distributed more than 1,000 soccer balls featuring the black-red-and-green Afghan flag and the phrase "peace and unity" in Dari and Pashto. The balls became a hit with youth around the country and the psy-ops team judged the program a huge success.

Others had their doubts. Army Maj. Gen. Jason Kamiya, the commander of U.S. forces at Bagram from 2005 to 2006, came across the soccer balls one day and decided to conduct an experiment. He took a couple of balls on a trip to Paktika province in eastern Afghanistan. When a crowd of kids gathered around his Humvee, he rolled out one of the soccer balls. As the children happily kicked it around, Kamiya noticed that none of them bothered to look at the flag or the "peace and unity" phrase etched on the balls.

Upon his return to Bagram, he advised the psy-ops crew to rethink their tactics and use common sense. "I said, 'Look, guys. Our job in Afghanistan is not to train the next Afghan Olympic soccer team, okay?'" he said in an Army oral-history interview. "The soccer ball is a means to convey the message. It is not *the* message."

But instead of abandoning soccer propaganda, the psy-ops warriors recommitted to it. They designed another ball featuring the flags of several countries, including Saudi Arabia, whose flag depicts the Koranic declaration of faith in Arabic script. Expecting the new items to be highly popular, psy-ops teams distributed the soccer balls widely and even dropped them from helicopters—only to trigger public protests from angry Afghans who thought putting holy words on a ball was sacrilegious.

"To have a verse of the Koran on something you kick with your foot would be an insult in any Muslim country," Mirwais Yasini, an Afghan member of parliament, told the BBC. The U.S. military was forced to issue a public apology.

The psy-ops teams were not the only ones who struggled to comprehend Afghanistan. Cultural ignorance and misunderstandings vexed U.S. military units for the entirety of the war, hampering their ability to conduct operations, collect intelligence and make tactical judgments. Most troops deployed to the war zone for six to twelve months. By the time they started to become comfortable in their surroundings, it was usually time to go home. Their untutored replacements repeated the cycle, year after year.

Troops were supposed to receive a smattering of instruction in Afghan languages, customs and cultural dos and don'ts before they left the United States. But at many military installations, officers said such training was worthless or tailored for the larger masses of troops headed for Iraq, based on the misguided assumption that people in all faraway Muslim countries were the same.

In 2005, Maj. Daniel Lovett, a field artillery officer with the Tennessee National Guard, reported for pre-deployment training at Camp Shelby, a sprawling base in southern Mississippi that dated to World War I. During cultural awareness class, the instructor opened the PowerPoint presentation by saying, "All right, when you get to Iraq." Lovett interrupted to say his unit was headed to the other war, but the instructor responded: "Oh, Iraq, Afghanistan. It's the same thing."

The indifference exasperated Lovett, who had been assigned to serve as an adviser to the Afghan army and hungered for insights. "Our mission was all about cultural awareness," he said in an Army oral-history interview. "Our mission was all about developing personal relationships . . . so we have legitimacy and credibility with the people we were trying to work with. I'll tell you that was tough. It was a tough job. Were we prepared to go and do that? I'd have to say that at the time, absolutely not."

Training at other bases usually was no better. Army Maj. James Reese, tapped to serve with a Special Operations task force in Afghanistan, said instructors at Fort Benning, Georgia, tried to teach his class Arabic—widely spoken in Iraq, but a foreign tongue in Afghanistan—instead of Dari or Pashto. "The training overall," he said, "was a waste."

Maj. Christian Anderson said the training at Fort Riley, an Army post on the plains of Kansas, "was horrible" and did nothing to prepare him for the task of advising an Afghan border police unit. Just from a geographic perspective, he thought the pre-deployment tactical training was foolish.

"I would say actually train your personnel as they're going to fight. Afghanistan has a lot of mountains, right? Tora Bora, Hindu Kush, all this stuff—mountains," Anderson said in an Army oral-history interview. "Afghanistan doesn't have swamps so why are we training [units] at Fort Polk, Louisiana? Why were we training . . . at Fort Riley where it's as flat as a dinner table?"

The lessons that did address the cultural peculiarities of Afghanistan, as opposed to Iraq, were often outdated or downright laughable.

Maj. Brent Novak, a West Point faculty member who served as a guest instructor at a military academy in Kabul, attended pre-deployment training at Fort Benning in 2005. He had to sit through classes on surviving nuclear, chemical and biological attacks—even though such threats were nonexistent in Afghanistan. Afghan culture received only a cursory mention.

One PowerPoint slide at Fort Benning warned against giving anyone a thumbs-up sign because Afghans regarded it as a rude gesture. "When I got there, though, kids were giving me the thumbs-up and I was like, 'Geez, are these kids flipping me off?'" Novak recalled in an Army oral-history interview. After enduring a flurry of upright thumbs, the clueless American asked an interpreter what he had done to cause offense. The translator patiently explained that a thumbs-up meant "good job" or "way to go."

In retrospect, officers said they wished someone had just taught them good Afghan manners: build personal relationships, learn a few words of the language, resist yelling or blowing your stack and accept offers to drink tea.

Army Maj. Rich Garey, who led a company of soldiers in eastern Afghanistan in 2003 and 2004, said it took him a while to learn to slow down. "We'd come in like gangbusters, track down the village elder and ask him where the bad guys were. We were always told there weren't any bad guys there, even though we were very close to the Pakistan border," he said. "There were obviously bad guys out there, but we didn't go about it the right way to get that information."

In another Army oral-history interview, Maj. Nikolai Andresky said he regretted not learning more about the basic rhythms of Afghan society before he deployed in 2003 to train Afghan soldiers. It finally occurred to him that he needed to work at the Afghans' pace instead of expecting them to adapt to American ways of doing business.

"If you would have told me that there wasn't such a thing as a one-hour meeting in Afghanistan, I wouldn't have believed you. After having been there, I know that's true. There is no such thing. If you have a meeting, it has to be at least three hours," Andresky said. "They start off by thanking Allah and then they basically thank everyone between Allah and them in the chain of command. Every speaker does that, so if you cut that out you'd probably save two hours. I just wished I had a better understanding of the culture."

U.S. troops, usually in a hurry, found it challenging to suppress their impatience and bite their tongues. "Time to Americans is very important," Maj. William Woodring, an officer with the Alaska National Guard, said in an Army oral-history interview. "Time over there, though, means nothing. We're trying to force them to do things on our time which to them, they don't understand. A lot of them don't have watches and can't even tell time. We're trying to force them to leave for a mission at a certain time and they can't understand why. 'Why do we have to leave at that time?'"

As an institution, the U.S. military stressed the importance of showing respect for Islam, the official state religion of Afghanistan, where about 85 percent of the population was Sunni Muslim. But the systemic lack of cultural and religious education meant some U.S. soldiers held stereotypical or prejudicial views of the Afghans.

"Theirs is a culture of dishonesty and corruption that seems prevalent in Muslim cultures going back thousands of years," Maj. Christopher Plummer, who served in 2005 as the training and fielding officer for the Afghan army, said in an Army oral-history interview.

Others saw Islam as intolerant and concluded it was impossible to bridge differences. "In the Islamic world, it's either my way or death. Everybody that's not a Muslim is an infidel, according to their Mohammed," John Davis, a retired Army officer who served as a mentor to the Afghan Defense Ministry, said in an Army oral-history interview. "We have to overcome the religious aspect of that, but the religious aspect is tied into the Taliban, who say they are trying to maintain a purist, fundamentalist Islam approach and control of the country, and they want to get rid of the infidels."

Yet many troops developed a more nuanced outlook. While Afghans strongly identified as Muslim, Thomas Clinton, a Marine major, noticed that did not necessarily mean they were deeply devout. "They're just like any other religion in America," he said in an Army oral-history interview. "You have ultra-extreme Catholics, Baptists, Protestants,

TO: Steve Cambone

FROM: Donald Rumsfeld

DATE: September 8, 2003

I have no visibility into who the bad guys are in Afghanistan or Iraq. I read all the intel from the community and it sounds as though we know a great deal but in fact, when you push at it, you find out we haven't got anything that is actionable. We are woefully deficient in human intelligence.

Let's discuss it.

DHR/azn
090803.26b

Please respond by: _____ 9/18

Response attached
V/r CDR Nosenzo
9/15

11-L-0559/OSD/18828

Defense Secretary Donald Rumsfeld dictated thousands of succinct memos between 2001 and 2006 that his staff referred to as "snowflakes." Worded in Rumsfeld's brusque style, many of the snowflakes about Afghanistan foreshadowed problems that would haunt the U.S. military for years.

Vice President Dick Cheney and Defense Secretary Donald Rumsfeld confer in Washington on October 6, 2001, the day before the U.S. military began bombing.

Soldiers from the 82nd Airborne Division looking for a weapons cache prepare to enter a housing compound during an early morning raid in southeastern Afghanistan in October 2002. About 9,000 U.S. troops remained in Afghanistan to hunt for al-Qaeda targets even though the vast majority of the network's leaders had fled the country or had been killed or captured.

Northern Alliance fighters take positions in a frontline trench during a skirmish with Taliban forces on November 7, 2001. During the next several days, the Northern Alliance—with the help of the U.S. military—seized control of several major cities, including Mazar-e-Sharif, Herat, Kabul and Jalalabad.

Afghan fighters allied with the U.S. military maneuver tanks near the White Mountains during the battle of Tora Bora in December 2001. Al-Qaeda leader Osama bin Laden escapes the region after several days of heavy fighting.

Army Gen. Tommy Franks, left, and senior military officers at U.S. Central Command headquarters in Tampa, Florida, conduct a daily conference via satellite with U.S. forces in Afghanistan in February 2002.

At the Pentagon, Defense Secretary Donald Rumsfeld records a video message for U.S. troops on March 21, 2003, after the U.S. military launched its invasion of Iraq. The Bush administration shifted almost all of its attention to Iraq and the war in Afghanistan became an afterthought.

Girls from a remote Afghan village in Badakhshan province near the border with Tajikistan watch U.N. workers unload ballots before the October 2004 presidential election. The vote went smoothly and Hamid Karzai won a five-year term in office. The outcome was welcome news for the Bush administration, which was grappling with a rising insurgency and sectarian bloodbath in Iraq.

Afghan women wearing veils walk past a portrait of Karzai in Kabul in October 2004. An elegantly dressed and highly educated Pashtun tribal leader, Karzai built a close rapport with the Bush administration. U.S. officials, however, gradually soured on him and the relationship turned dysfunctional.

10

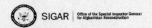SIGAR | Office of the Special Inspector General for Afghanistan Reconstruction

LESSONS LEARNED RECORD OF INTERVIEW

| Project Title and Code: |
| LL-01 – Strategy and Planning |

| Interview Title: |
| Interview Ambassador Richard Boucher, former Assistant Secretary of State for South and Central Asian Affairs. |

| Interview Code: |
| LL-01-b9 |

| Date/Time: |
| 10/15/2015; 15:10-16:45 |

| Location: |
| Providence, RI |

| Purpose: |
| To elicit his officials from his time serving as Assistant Secretary of State for South and Central Asian Affairs. |

| Interviewees:(Either list interviewees below, attach sign-in sheet to this document or hyperlink to a file) |

| SIGAR Attendees: |
| Matthew Sternenberger, Candace Rondeaux |

| Sourcing Conditions (On the Record/On Background/etc.): | On the record. |

| Recorded: | Yes | x | No | | |

| Recording File Record Number (if recorded): |

| Prepared By: (Name, title and date) |
| Matthew Sternenberger |

| Reviewed By: (Name, title and date) |

| Key Topics: |

- General Observations
- The State and DOD Struggle
- Building Security Forces
- Governance Expectations and Karzai

- Capable Actors
- Regional Economics and Cooperation
- General Comments on Syria & Iraq
- Lessons Learned

General Observations

Let me approach this from two directions. The first question of did we know what we were doing? The second is what was wrong with how we did it? The first question of did we know what we were doing – I think the answer is no. First, we went in to get al-Qaeda, and to get al-Qaeda out of Afghanistan, and even without killing Bin Laden we did that. The Taliban was shooting back at us so we started shooting at them and they became the enemy. Ultimately, we kept expanding the mission. George W. [Bush], when he was running for president, said that the military should not be involved in nation building. In the end, I think he was right. **If there was ever a notion of mission creep it is Afghanistan.** We went from saying we will get rid of al-Qaeda so they can't threaten us

For its Lessons Learned project, the Special Inspector General for Afghanistan Reconstruction (SIGAR) interviewed hundreds of people who played a key role in the war in Afghanistan. SIGAR tried to keep the interview notes and transcripts a secret, but *The Washington Post* sued the agency and obtained the documents under the Freedom of Information Act.

and then you have other guys who say they were raised a certain religion but don't go to church anymore." Of the young Afghan soldiers he trained, he said only a few prayed five times a day or went to the mosque regularly.

With the notable exception of Zalmay Khalilzad, the Afghan-American who served as ambassador for almost two years, most U.S. diplomats were also in unfamiliar territory. Because the U.S. embassy was shuttered from 1989 until 2002, hardly any had visited Afghanistan before the U.S. invasion.

The State Department counted numerous regional experts in its ranks who had served in other parts of South and Central Asia, but not many volunteered to go to Kabul. To fill the void, the post was backfilled by a combination of Foreign Service rookies and oldsters lured out of retirement.

"The embassy itself was a very, very small, very junior organization with an extraordinarily limited number of people who did not have a tremendous amount of experience," Lt. Gen. David Barno, the U.S. military commander from 2003 to 2005, said in an Army oral-history interview. Like the troops, diplomats typically served short rotations of six to twelve months before moving on. As a result, veteran wisdom at the embassy was perpetually in short supply.

Many Afghans found the cultural disconnect just as jarring, especially those from rural areas who rarely glimpsed the outside world and never watched American television or Hollywood movies. The sight of armor-plated U.S. troops dressed in camouflage, with reflective eyewear wrapped around their faces and wires protruding from their heads, could evoke the extraterrestrial.

"For probably 90 to 95 percent of the Afghans that I interfaced with, we might as well have been aliens," said Maj. Clint Cox, an Army officer who served in Kandahar. "They thought we could see through walls with our sunglasses."

Maj. Keller Durkin, who deployed twice to Afghanistan with the 82nd Airborne Division, said it was tough to make a good first impression with the Afghans. "One of the things I firmly believe is that if you look at an American all kitted-up for war, we look astonishingly like the stormtroopers from Star Wars, and those might not be the best people to go try and win hearts and minds," he said in an Army oral-history interview.

Maj. Alvin Tilley, an African-American soldier, recalled passing through villages where people had never encountered a person with black skin before. "The kids looked at me like, 'Oh my God. What is that?' They're rubbing their faces and I asked my interpreter what the kids were doing and he said, 'Oh, they think your color comes off.'"

A city dweller back in the United States, Tilley said he was just as stunned by the sight of so many primitive mud huts without power or water. "You go there and you think you're going to see Moses walking down the street," he said. "That was more of a culture shock than anything."

Among the places that conjured Old Testament imagery for U.S. soldiers was Uruzgan province in south-central Afghanistan. Ringed by mountain ranges and desiccated terrain, Uruzgan blazed hot in summer and froze over in winter. Farmers eked out a living by tending plots of drought-tolerant opium. Home to conservative Pashtun tribes, the province's most famous son was Mullah Mohammed Omar, the Taliban's one-eyed spiritual leader.

Army Maj. William Burley, a civil-affairs team leader, delivered humanitarian aid to Uruzgan's rural Shin Kay region in 2005. He said destitute villagers there had few water sources and were so isolated that it was common for young people to marry their first cousins.

"I hate to say it, but there was a lot of inbreeding. The district chief had three thumbs," he said in an Army oral-history interview.

As a Special Forces officer, Burley was exempt from the Army's normal grooming standards, so he grew as much facial hair as possible to fit in with the locals. "It would have been a serious cultural faux pas for me not to have had a beard," he added. "They were able to grab my chin, and in their culture, if you can grab the beard you can trust the guy."

Other trust-building exercises were harder for the Americans to embrace. Throughout the country, tribal elders and Afghan military officers demonstrated their friendship and fidelity by walking around, hand-in-hand, with other men. U.S. troops had to accept the gesture when offered or risk offending their hosts.

"For an American male, walking through town holding the hand of another man? Yeah, it's—" said Army Maj. Christian Anderson, the officer who trained the Afghan border police, pausing for the right word before trailing off. "But I did it because it's kind of insulting not to do it."

From an American perspective, it could be hard to tell when the practice was platonic or when it might represent something else. Homosexuality was banned by the Taliban and considered taboo among adults, but it was not uncommon for Afghan men of means to commit a form of sexual abuse known as *bacha bazi,* or boy play.

Afghan military officers, warlords and other power brokers proclaimed their status by keeping tea boys or other adolescent male servants as sex slaves. U.S. troops referred to the practice as "man-love Thursday" because Afghan pederasts would force boys to dress up or dance on Thursday evenings before the start of the Afghan weekend. Although American soldiers were sickened by the abuse, their commanders instructed them to look the other way because they didn't want to alienate allies in the fight against the Taliban.

Major Woodring, the Alaska National Guard officer, said man-love Thursday came as a shock when he embedded with the Afghan army for a year as a trainer. "Just understanding the whole lifestyle of the Afghans" was a challenge, he said. U.S. soldiers had a hard time reconciling how Afghan men could hold extremely conservative views about women, yet flirt with other men and flaunt having sex with boys.

"You really have to put your feelings aside and understand that this is not your country," Woodring said. "You have to accept what they do and don't interject your personal feelings about their culture. Looking at women is forbidden. Even if a young 17-year-old stares at a woman he can be killed for that. We weren't taught any of that, though, in any of our training. You need to understand that people might hit on you."

When it came to being propositioned, risk factors included a youth-ful appearance and a clean shave—traits that applied to most U.S. troops (nearly 90 percent were men).*

Maj. Randy James, an aviation intelligence officer, recalled a tense encounter in 2003 when an Afghan man approached a baby-faced male American soldier in his unit and declared, "You're my wife." Luckily, the incident didn't erupt into violence.

"It didn't get out of hand; nothing bad happened," James said in an Army oral-history interview. "But it just wasn't a happy moment for him or anybody else around."

---

* Women played a critical role in the war, with many serving in combat roles. As of August 2020, fifty-five female U.S. troops had been killed in Afghanistan and more than 400 wounded, according to the Defense Department.

CHAPTER SEVEN

Playing Both Sides

By 2003, as the Taliban and al-Qaeda escalated their hit-and-run attacks on U.S. and allied forces, there was no mystery about where the guerrillas were coming from. They had regrouped on the other side of Afghanistan's 1,500-mile border with Pakistan.

Most hid in Pakistan's remote Pashtun tribal areas that historically had resisted the authority of government officials in Islamabad and, before them, British colonial viceroys. For insurgents, it was the perfect refuge, walled off by mountains and deserts. It was also beyond the reach of the U.S. troops, who were forbidden from crossing into sovereign Pakistani territory.

For U.S. forces stationed along the border, the restrictions tied their hands in a never-ending game of cat and mouse. But there was a more fundamental problem: Whose side were the Pakistanis on, anyway?

The answer became abundantly clear on April 25, 2003, a sunny spring day, when a dozen heavily armed men dressed in black walked past the Pakistani town of Angur Ada, altitude 7,400 feet. The gunmen disappeared into the scrub pines along a ridge on the Afghan side of the border. About four miles away, at a tiny U.S. Army outpost called Firebase Shkin, then-Capt. Gregory Trahan, a company commander with the 82nd Airborne Division, was reading a book in his hooch.

It had been a quiet day at Shkin, named after a nearby Afghan village and positioned strategically near a border checkpoint in Paktika province. The firebase was perched on a hillside so the roughly one hundred U.S. troops stationed there could look out for Taliban infiltrators sneaking over from South Waziristan. The square-shaped firebase covered a dirt patch half the size of a football field. Along with watchtowers on each corner, the compound was protected by three-foot-thick ramparts of dried mud, triple-strand concertina wire and rock-filled blast walls known as HESCO barriers.

Trahan and his soldiers from Bravo Company, 3rd Battalion had been at Shkin for six weeks and had settled into a routine of conducting patrols. After lunch, a soldier ducked into Trahan's quarters to say he was needed in the tactical operations center. The captain put his book down to find out what was going on.

A CIA Predator drone orbiting overhead had glimpsed the gunmen dressed in black. Intelligence analysts presumed they were hostile. Trahan figured they might be the same guerrillas who had fired 107mm rockets at Shkin several days earlier from a hilltop hugging the Afghan side of the border. The rockets had come close enough to shatter windows, though no one was hurt. He knew the insurgents would be difficult to catch but decided to try anyway.

Trahan organized a patrol of about twenty U.S. soldiers and twenty allied fighters from a local Afghan militia and rolled out in a convoy of Humvees and trucks. They checked in at the border-control station and stopped at a few nearby homes, but none of the locals reported seeing anything.

"From the time we left until the time we searched these few homes, about an hour and a half had passed—and I was ready to pack it in, thinking this was all a dry well," Trahan said in an Army oral-history interview. Dusk was approaching, but he decided the patrol should scout out the spot where insurgents had launched rockets from the last time. "It was on some hilly terrain but we could get vehicles up there," he said.

As the patrol climbed the winding dirt track up the hill, one of the trucks broke down. The other three vehicles kept going to the top. The patrol dismounted and moved out slowly in three directions. Scrub vegetation and dips in the terrain obscured their fields of vision. Leading one group, Trahan spied a campsite with canteens of water, burlap bags and a cache of 107mm rockets. Suddenly, the air erupted in a fusillade of small-arms fire. "It seemed that we were completely encircled by it and I had no idea where it was coming from," he said.

As the Americans and their Afghan allies scrambled for cover, the enemy pinned them down from several directions with AK-47s, grenades and at least one heavy machine gun. Trahan dodged a grenade, but AK-47 rounds hit him once in the helmet, grazing his skull; twice in the right leg; and once in the left leg. As he was struck, other soldiers saw a red mist spray out from behind his body.

The U.S. troops radioed for help and requested howitzer fire from the base at Shkin so they could try to escape the ambush. It was risky given that enemy fighters had closed to within thirty feet of their vehicles.

The shelling worked, forcing the attackers to back off and giving the patrol a chance to regroup. By the time they gathered the fallen and rolled back down the hill to safety, seven Americans had been badly wounded.

Trahan survived, but two would later die: Private Jerod Dennis, a 19-year-old from Antlers, Oklahoma, a one-stoplight town where he had graduated from high school ten months earlier; and Airman First Class Raymond Losano, a tactical air controller from Del Rio, Texas, who had just celebrated his 24th birthday at Shkin and left behind a pregnant wife and two-year-old daughter.

Helicopters evacuated Trahan and the other wounded from Shkin. Trahan endured multiple surgeries, but one painful memory from the ambush stayed with him long after the fighting ended: Pakistan's unofficial hostile role in the war.

When all hell broke loose on the hilltop, the Pakistani border guards positioned at the checkpoint a mile away jumped into the fight by firing rocket-propelled grenades, treating the insurgents as friends and the U.S. forces as foes. "I think the Pakistanis thought we were shooting at them—and they started firing into our formation," Trahan said.

The question of whose side Pakistan was on would bedevil the Americans for two decades. No matter how many troops the Pentagon sent to Afghanistan, or how many firebases it built, the flow of insurgents and weapons from Pakistan into the war zone kept rising. The Af-Pak border, which stretched as far as the distance from Washington, D.C., to Denver, was impossible to seal off. The terrain was a smuggler's paradise, with the Hindu Kush mountains soaring higher than the Rockies.

Beyond the geographic challenges, U.S. military analysts and the CIA had great difficulty discerning the organizational roots of the insurgency inside Pakistan and determining who, exactly, was providing the Taliban with money, weapons and training. But the supply of fighters crossing the border never dried up and the Pakistani government was unable—or unwilling—to stop it.

"If we were there to kill or capture remnants of the Taliban regime and al-Qaeda, then the biggest challenge was getting timely, accurate intelligence," Trahan said. Intelligence reports from military headquarters, he added, "inevitably said that they thought there was an area where guys were coming back and forth across the border. Well, guys don't just do that. They're funded in some way, they get equipment somehow, they have to eat. In other words, it's a system. How are we going to attack that system? I don't think we ever got answers to those questions."

In the case of the April 2003 firefight that wounded Trahan and killed two U.S. troops, answers about who was responsible took nearly a decade to emerge, and then only by happenstance.

In 2011, Italian authorities arrested a refugee from North Africa with a peripatetic past who admitted that he was an al-Qaeda operative. Ibrahim Suleiman Adnan Harun, 40, had traveled to Afghanistan before the 9/11 attacks and passed through a chain of al-Qaeda training camps. After the American invasion, he moved across the Pakistani border into Waziristan, where he reported to Abdul Hadi al-Iraqi, a senior deputy to bin Laden, and helped lead the ambush against the U.S. troops near Shkin. Harun was wounded in the attack and escaped back to Pakistan. But he abandoned a pocket-sized Koran and a journal on the hilltop. Investigators later confirmed that fingerprints on the holy book matched his.

Italy extradited Harun to the United States in 2012. His federal trial in New York City in 2017 revealed fresh details about how al-Qaeda's core leadership had taken refuge in Pakistan and rebuilt their operations there. Jurors heard testimony about how al-Qaeda commanders rewarded Harun for the success of the Shkin ambush by giving him a more ambitious mission: to build al-Qaeda's network in West Africa and bomb the U.S. embassy in Nigeria. The embassy plot failed, but the jury convicted Harun of several terrorism-related crimes, including conspiring to murder Americans at Shkin. He was sentenced to life in prison.*

Along the border, suspicions about Pakistan's role in the insurgency intensified after Trahan's company and other units with the 82nd Airborne Division rotated out of Afghanistan in 2003 and were replaced by the 10th Mountain Division.

In August 2003, two more U.S. soldiers were killed near Shkin during a gun battle with insurgents who had slipped across the border. In September, another U.S. soldier was killed during a twelve-hour firefight with dozens of al-Qaeda and Taliban guerrillas; once again, Pakistani government forces guarding the border jumped into the fray by firing rockets at the Americans. In October, two contractors working for the CIA were killed in an ambush near Shkin by yet another group of fighters that had crossed over from Pakistan.

Pakistan's military and its powerful spy agency—the Inter-Services Intelligence, or ISI—had an extensive history of supporting insurgents in Afghanistan.

During the 1980s, the ISI teamed up with the CIA on the covert operation that funneled weapons to Afghan rebels fighting the Soviet Army. After the Russians withdrew in defeat, the ISI continued to

---

* The trial also highlighted the strain on U.S. troops who served multiple combat tours. The Army sent Trahan to Iraq just five months after he was wounded at Shkin. Sgt. First Class Conrad Reed, who survived a direct hit from a grenade at Shkin, later deployed three times to Iraq and told jurors he was preparing to return to Afghanistan in 2018. According to Pentagon statistics, more than 28,000 troops deployed to Afghanistan five or more times.

back many of the same guerrillas during Afghanistan's civil war and helped lift the Taliban into power. By the time of the 9/11 hijackings, Pakistan was one of only three countries—along with Saudi Arabia and the United Arab Emirates—that maintained diplomatic relations with the Taliban-led government in Kabul.

After the terrorist attacks on the United States, Washington coerced Pakistan's military ruler, Gen. Pervez Musharraf, to sever ties with the Taliban. On the surface, Musharraf pirouetted swiftly and became a critical ally to the Bush administration.

He permitted the U.S. military to use Pakistani seaports, land routes and airspace to reach Afghanistan. Under his direction, the ISI worked hand-in-glove with the CIA to apprehend several al-Qaeda leaders in Pakistan, including 9/11 plotters Ramzi Binalshibh and Khalid Sheikh Mohammed. In exchange for U.S. bounties, Pakistan also detained and handed over hundreds of suspected Taliban members. Though many had been rounded up for dubious reasons, the Americans transported them en masse to the U.S. naval prison at Guantanamo Bay, Cuba.

U.S. officials knew Musharraf was facing pressures at home to limit his cooperation but thought they could sway him with money. "If we are going to get the Paks to really fight the war on terror where it is, which is in their country, don't you think we ought to get a chunk of money, so that we can ease Musharraf's transition from where he is to where we need him," Rumsfeld wrote in a June 25, 2002, snowflake to Doug Feith, the Pentagon policy chief.

To Islamabad's delight, the chunk of money turned out to be generous: about $10 billion in aid over six years, much of it in the form of military and counterterrorism assistance.

Yet the Bush administration was slow to recognize that Musharraf and the ISI were playing both sides. In Lessons Learned interviews, U.S. officials said Bush invested too much personal trust in Musharraf. They said Bush glossed over persistent evidence that the Pakistani military under Musharraf still supported the Taliban, using the same covert channels and tactics it had developed to help anti-Soviet guerrillas during the 1980s.

While Pakistan did not want to alienate Washington, its military establishment was determined to influence Afghanistan over the long term and—because of regional politics and ethnic factors—saw the Taliban as its best vehicle to exert control.

The Taliban was comprised mostly of Afghan Pashtuns who shared cultural, religious and economic ties with 28 million fellow Pashtuns living in the tribal areas of Pakistan. In contrast, Islamabad distrusted the Uzbek, Tajik and Hazara warlords who composed Afghanistan's Northern Alliance because of their tight relationship with archrival India.

"Because of people's personal confidence in Musharraf and because of things he was continuing to do in helping police up a bunch of the al-Qaeda in Pakistan, there was a failure to perceive the double game that he starts to play by late 2002, early 2003," Marin Strmecki, the civilian adviser to Rumsfeld, said in a Lessons Learned interview. "You are seeing the security incidents start to go up and it is out of the safe havens. I think that the Afghans, and Karzai himself, are bringing this up constantly even in the earlier parts of 2002. They are meeting unsympathetic ears because of the belief that Pakistan was helping us so much on al-Qaeda."

Other U.S. officials admitted they were blind to Pakistani intentions because they mistakenly assumed the Taliban had been defeated for good. "That turned out to be wrong largely because it discounted the likelihood that Pakistan would continue to see the Taliban as a useful surrogate and would essentially help resuscitate it," said James Dobbins, the U.S. diplomat who helped organize the Bonn conference in 2001. "I think that wasn't spotted by anybody at the time. The Pakistani role wasn't really recognized in Washington for seven or eight years."

Pakistani officials argued that they were making great sacrifices on behalf of Washington and putting the stability of their country at risk to do so. In December 2003, Musharraf dodged two assassination attempts that Pakistan blamed on al-Qaeda. Around the same time, bowing to American pressure, he sent 80,000 troops into the tribal areas to guard the border. Hundreds of Pakistani soldiers were killed in clashes with militants, triggering a domestic political backlash. While Musharraf's sacrifices and challenges were real, they also made it easy for him and his military leadership to swat away suggestions that they were being duplicitous or not providing enough help to the United States.

Everybody had a theory about who was to blame for the cross-border insurgency. Maj. Gen. Eric Olson served in Afghanistan from 2004 to 2005 as the commanding general of the 25th Infantry Division. In an Army oral-history interview, he explained that there were two "schools of thought." One, he said, "was that all problems in Afghanistan are linked to Pakistan and their inability to control the frontier provinces. The other is that all the problems in Pakistan originate with the Taliban that we allowed to get out of Afghanistan."

Maj. Stuart Farris, a Special Forces officer who deployed three times to Afghanistan during the 2000s, regularly attended tripartite talks with American, Afghan and Pakistani military officials to discuss security problems along the border.

"The American and Afghan perception was that the Pakistanis weren't doing enough in their country to go after and attack these terrorists—the Taliban and al-Qaeda who we claim are over there," Farris said in an Army oral-history interview. In response, "the Pakistanis would say, 'They're not hiding in our country. They're hiding in Afghanistan.' I think we all know the truth about that. That was a challenge."

The Pakistani commanders were career military men whose professional bearing and manner usually gave them an air of believability. Many had attended military exchange programs in the United States and spoke British-accented English that, to American ears, sounded suave and sophisticated. In that regard, they were a contrast to the unschooled, inexperienced Afghan officers whom the Americans partnered with on a daily basis.

"You'd have these well-educated Pakistani generals who were nicely dressed and very articulate, and then you'd have his [Afghan] counterpart in a uniform that was three sizes too big, a pair of boots that were too big and gloves that didn't fit," Farris said. "We used to get together once a month. There would be this feeling that we were all great friends and everyone would be patting each other on the back, telling each other that we were really going to make things happen. After everyone left, though, it would just go back to the status quo and it would never happen. It left me feeling like the whole process was just a waste of time and a lot of cheap talk with no action."

Despite doubts from their troops in the field, senior U.S. military commanders lavished praise on the Pakistanis in public. "I would give a strong commendation to the ongoing aggressive efforts of the Pakistani government and military to eliminate terrorist sanctuaries," General Barno, the commander of U.S. forces in Afghanistan, told reporters in June 2004.

Seven months later, in an interview with National Public Radio, Barno downplayed the possibility that bin Laden was hiding in Pakistan, let alone that officials there might be sheltering him. "I think that's pretty speculative in terms of estimating where he might be, but I can tell you that the Pakistani government has proven to be great allies here," he said.

Rumsfeld was even more effusive. In an August 2004 speech in Phoenix, the defense secretary lauded Musharraf, calling the military dictator "courageous," "thoughtful" and "a superb partner in this global war on terror." He said Washington was "so fortunate" and "so grateful" that Musharraf was in power, adding: "He has, without question, one of the most difficult tasks of any governmental leader that I can think of."

In private, Rumsfeld's advisers cautioned him to be less credulous. In June 2006, the defense secretary received a memo from retired Army Gen. Barry McCaffrey, who had just returned from a fact-finding trip to Afghanistan and Pakistan. McCaffrey reported that intrigue over Islamabad's true motives was running wild.

"The central question seems to be—are the Pakistanis playing a giant double-cross in which they absorb one billion dollars a year from the U.S. while pretending to support U.S. objectives to create a stable Afghanistan—while in fact actively supporting cross-border operations of the Taliban (that they created)," McCaffrey wrote in the memo.

The general failed to definitively answer his own question. But he indicated that he was inclined to give the benefit of the doubt to

Musharraf. "The web of paranoia and innuendo on both sides of the border is difficult to assess," McCaffrey added. "However, I do not believe that President Musharaff [sic] is playing a deliberate double-game."

Others disagreed. Two months after McCaffrey's report, Rumsfeld received a forty-page classified memo from Strmecki, who had just returned from his own visit to Afghanistan to assess the state of the war. In his report, Strmecki pulled fewer punches about Pakistan.

"President Pervez Musharraf has not made the strategic choice to cooperate fully with the United States and Afghanistan to suppress the Taliban," he wrote. "Since 2002, the Taliban has enjoyed a sanctuary in Pakistan that has enabled recruitment, training, finance, equipping, and infiltrating of fighters. Pakistan's ISI provides some operational support to the Taliban, though the level at which this assistance is authorized within the Pakistani government remains unclear."

In most official meetings, Pakistan continued to deny complicity with the Taliban. But occasionally, some Pakistani leaders let their mask slip.

Ryan Crocker, who had served briefly as the top U.S. diplomat in Afghanistan in 2002, returned to the region two years later to become ambassador to Pakistan. In a Lessons Learned interview, he said his Pakistani interlocutors habitually complained that Washington had abandoned the region after the Soviet withdrawal from Afghanistan in 1989, leaving Islamabad to deal with the civil war that broke out next door. That history, they told Crocker, explained why Pakistan had backed the Taliban in the past, though they reassured him those days were over.

But on one occasion, Crocker had an unusually frank conversation with the head of the ISI: Lt. Gen. Ashfaq Kayani. A chain-smoker with dark, hooded eyes who tended to mumble, the Pakistani spymaster had been well-known to the Americans since early in his career, when he attended the U.S. Army's infantry school at Fort Benning, Georgia, and its staff college at Fort Leavenworth, Kansas, as an exchange officer.

Crocker recalled prodding Kayani, as he often did, to crack down against Taliban leaders who were believed to have taken refuge in Pakistan. Instead of denying their presence, Kayani for once gave an unvarnished reply.

"He says, 'You know, I know you think we're hedging our bets, you're right, we are because one day you'll be gone again, it'll be like Afghanistan the first time, you'll be done with us, but we're still going to be here because we can't actually move the country. And the last thing we want with all of our other problems is to have turned the Taliban into a mortal enemy, so, yes, we're hedging our bets.'"

PART THREE

THE TALIBAN COMES BACK

2006—2008

CHAPTER EIGHT

Lies and Spin

The suicide bomber arrived at Bagram Air Base in a Toyota Corolla late in the morning on February 27, 2007. He maneuvered past the Afghan police at the first checkpoint. The bomber continued a quarter mile down the road toward the main gate and approached the second checkpoint, this one staffed by U.S. soldiers. Amid mud puddles and a jumble of pedestrians and vehicle traffic, he triggered his vest of explosives.

The blast killed two Americans and a South Korean assigned to the international military coalition: U.S. Army Private First Class Daniel Zizumbo, a 27-year-old from Chicago with a fondness for lollipops; Staff Sgt. Yoon Jang-Ho, the first South Korean soldier to die in a foreign conflict since Vietnam; and Geraldine Marquez, an American contractor for Lockheed Martin who had just celebrated her 31st birthday. The explosion also claimed the lives of twenty Afghan laborers who came to the base that day looking for work.

Unharmed in the explosion was a VIP guest at Bagram who had been trying to keep a low profile—Vice President Dick Cheney.

Cheney had slipped into the war zone the day before on an unannounced trip to the region. Arriving on Air Force Two from Islamabad, he intended to spend only a few hours in Afghanistan to see President Hamid Karzai. But bad weather prevented him from reaching Kabul so he spent the night at Bagram, about thirty miles from the capital.

The base itself illustrated his administration's deepening footprint in Afghanistan: Since 2001, it had mushroomed into a major installation with 9,000 troops, contractors and other personnel.

Within hours of the bombing, the Taliban called journalists to claim responsibility and to say Cheney was the target. U.S. military officials scoffed and accused the insurgents of spreading lies as part of a psychological warfare campaign. The vice president, they said, was a mile away at the other end of the base and never in danger. They insisted the Taliban could not have planned an attack against Cheney on short notice, given that his visit was not publicized in advance and his travel plans had changed at the last minute.

"The Taliban's claims that they were going after the vice president were absurd," Army Col. Tom Collins, a spokesman for U.S. and NATO forces, told reporters.

But the U.S. military officials were the ones hiding the truth.

In an Army oral-history interview, then-Capt. Shawn Dalrymple, a company commander with the 82nd Airborne Division who was responsible for security at Bagram, said word had leaked out about Cheney's presence. The suicide bomber, he added, saw a convoy of vehicles coming out of the front gate and blew himself up because he mistakenly thought Cheney was a passenger.

The bomber wasn't far off the mark. The vice president was supposed to depart for Kabul in a different convoy about thirty minutes later, according to Dalrymple, who had worked with the Secret Service to plan Cheney's movements.

"The insurgents knew this, it was all over the news no matter how much it was tried to keep secret," Dalrymple said. "They caught a convoy going out the gate with an up-armored sport-utility vehicle and thought it was him . . . That opened up a lot of eyes into the fact that Bagram was not a safe place. There was a direct link with the insurgencies."

Their public statements notwithstanding, U.S. military officials had been so worried the Taliban might target Cheney on the drive to Kabul that they originally set up a ruse. Their plan was to depart Bagram from a rarely used gate. Members of Cheney's traveling party would ride as decoys in the SUVs normally reserved for senior officials. Cheney would ride with Dalrymple in a lumbering military vehicle equipped with a machine gun. "You'd never expect him to ride in the gun truck," Dalrymple said.*

That plan was scrapped after the suicide attack. Military officials decided it was too dangerous for Cheney to travel by road. He waited for the weather to clear and instead flew to Kabul to meet with Karzai. Cheney finally left Afghanistan that afternoon on a C-17 military aircraft without further incident.

But the episode marked an escalation in the war on two fronts. By targeting the vice president at the heavily fortified base at Bagram, the Taliban demonstrated an ability to inflict high-profile, mass-casualty attacks far from the insurgents' strongholds in southern and eastern Afghanistan.

And by lying about how close the insurgents had come to harming Cheney, the U.S. military sank deeper into a pattern of deceiving the public about many facets of the war, from discrete events to the big picture. What began as selective, self-serving disclosures hardened into willful distortions and, eventually, flat-out fabrications.

For the United States and its NATO and Afghan allies, the previous year had been awful by any measure. During 2006, the number of suicide attacks increased almost fivefold and the number of roadside bombs doubled compared to 2005. The Taliban's cross-border sanctuaries in Pakistan were fueling the problem, and Washington could do little about it. Before his arrival at Bagram, Cheney met with Pakistan's president, Pervez Musharraf, to urge him to crack down. The Pakistani strongman offered no help, saying his government had already "done the maximum."

---

* One year after the failed attack on Cheney, Captain Dalrymple would help rescue the man destined to become the next vice president of the United States: Joseph Biden. In February 2008, two Black Hawk helicopters carrying three members of the Senate Foreign Relations Committee—Biden, John Kerry and Chuck Hagel—and other personnel were forced to make an emergency landing in a snowstorm about twelve miles from Bagram. Dalrymple led a ground convoy to rescue the senators, who had been touring the war zone with Army Maj. Gen. David Rodriguez. The convoy returned safely with the VIPs to Bagram five hours later.

At the same time, the United States was faring even worse with its much-larger war in Iraq, where 150,000 U.S. troops were bogged down—about six times as many as the number deployed in Afghanistan. In January 2007, Bush announced he would send a surge force of 21,500 additional troops to Iraq and asked Congress to approve $94 billion in emergency war spending. Given the calamity in Iraq, the Bush administration badly wanted to avoid the perception it was losing in Afghanistan as well.

Consequently, as the new year got underway, American commanders in Afghanistan expressed new levels of optimism in public that were so unwarranted and baseless that their statements amounted to a disinformation campaign.

"We are prevailing," Army Maj. Gen. Robert Durbin, the commander in charge of training the Afghan security forces, told reporters on January 9, 2007. He added that the Afghan army and police "continue to show great progress each day."

Army Maj. Gen. Benjamin Freakley, commander of the 10th Mountain Division, gave an even sunnier assessment a few weeks later. "We're winning," he said during a January 27 news conference. Despite the surge in bombings the year before, he declared that U.S. and Afghan forces had made "great progress" and "defeated the Taliban and the terrorists that oppose this nation at every turn." As for the insurgents, Freakley said the rebels "achieved none of their objectives" and were "quickly running out of time." He dismissed the increase in suicide attacks as a sign of the Taliban's "desperation."

Three days later, Karl Eikenberry, now a three-star general on his second tour of duty in Afghanistan, visited Berlin to shore up European public support for NATO forces. As the U.S. war commander, he said the allies were "postured well for success" in 2007 and suggested the Taliban was panicking. "Our assessment is that they actually look at time working against them," Eikenberry added.

The generals' chorus of happy talk defied a yearlong stream of intelligence assessments that the insurgency had gained strength. The refrain about the Taliban's desperation wholly contradicted classified reports that the guerrillas believed momentum and time were firmly on their side.

In February 2006, Ronald Neumann, the U.S. ambassador to Afghanistan, told officials in Washington in a classified diplomatic cable that a confident Taliban leader had warned, "You have all the clocks but we have all the time."

The flood of suicide attacks and roadside bombs—insurgent tactics imported from Iraq—stoked fear among U.S. officials in Afghanistan of a potential "Tet Offensive in Kandahar," an unnamed Bush administration official said in a Lessons Learned interview, referring to the bloody 1968 military campaign by North Vietnamese forces that undermined public support for the Vietnam War. "The turning point came at the end of 2005, beginning of 2006 when we finally woke up to the fact that there was an insurgency that could actually make us fail," the official said. "Everything was turning the wrong way at the end of 2005."

Neumann arrived in Kabul as the top U.S. diplomat in July 2005. The son of a former U.S. ambassador to Afghanistan, he had spent a pleasant summer there as a young newlywed in 1967, traveling cross-country, camping and riding horses and yaks during a time of peace. When he returned thirty-eight years later, Afghanistan had been continuously at war for a quarter century. Right away, he told his superiors in Washington it was obvious the violence was about to escalate further.

"By the fall of 2005, I had reported, in combination with General Eikenberry, that we were going to face a vastly increased insurgency in the next year, in 2006, and that it was going to get much bloodier, much worse," Neumann said in a diplomatic oral-history interview. Despite his dire forecast, Washington balked at sending more troops and extra resources. Neumann said he requested $600 million in additional economic aid for the Afghan government, but the Bush administration approved only $43 million.

"Nobody ever said to me, 'You can't have the money because we need it for Iraq,'" Neumann said. "But in fact, that's what happened."

At first, many officials in Washington found it hard to believe the Taliban could present a serious danger. Even some military leaders in the field underestimated the Taliban and thought that, while it might control pockets of rural territory, it posed no threat to the government in Kabul. "We thought the Taliban's capability was greatly reduced," Brig. Gen. Bernard Champoux, deputy commander of a U.S. military task force from 2004 to 2005, said in an Army oral-history interview.

Paul Toolan, a Special Forces captain who served in Helmand province in 2005, said many U.S. officials mistakenly viewed the war as a peacekeeping and reconstruction mission. He tried to explain to anyone who would listen that the fighting had intensified and the Taliban had bolstered its firepower. "If we don't do this right, we're going to allow these guys to keep us languishing here for a lot of years," he cautioned.

But the Bush administration suppressed the internal warnings and put a shine on the war in public. In a December 2005 interview with CNN talk show host Larry King, Rumsfeld said things were going so well that the Pentagon would soon bring home 2,000 to 3,000 U.S. troops, or roughly 10 percent of its forces in Afghanistan.

"It's a direct result of the progress that's being made in the country," Rumsfeld declared.

Two months later, however, Rumsfeld's office and other officials in Washington received another classified warning from their ambassador in Kabul. In a gloomy February 21, 2006, cable, Neumann predicted that "violence will rise through the next several months," with more suicide bombings in Kabul and other major cities. He blamed the Taliban's sanctuaries in Pakistan and warned that, if left unaddressed, they could "lead to the re-emergence of the same strategic threat to the United States that prompted our . . . intervention over 4 years ago"—in other words, another 9/11.

In the dispatch, Neumann expressed fear that popular support would wane if expectations weren't managed. "I thought it was important to try to prepare the American public for that so that they wouldn't be surprised and see everything as a reverse," he said in his diplomatic oral-history interview.

But the public heard no such straight talk from the Bush administration. In a presidential visit to Afghanistan shortly after the ambassador sent his cable, Bush did not mention rising violence levels or the resurgent Taliban. Instead, he touted improvements such as the establishment of democracy and a free press, schools for girls and a growing entrepreneurial class.

"We're impressed by the progress your country is making," Bush told Karzai at a March 1 news conference.

Two weeks later, in a briefing with the Pentagon press corps via teleconference from Bagram Air Base, Major General Freakley denied that the Taliban and al-Qaeda were getting stronger. The reasons for the spikes in violence, the general said, were because the weather was getting warmer and his forces were going on the offensive.

"We're taking the fight to the enemy," the 10th Mountain Division commander said. "If you see an increase in violence here in the coming weeks and months, it's probably driven by offensive operations that the Afghan National Army, Afghan National Police and coalition forces are taking." He added, "I'll tell you that progress in Afghanistan is steady and you can really see it."

In another Pentagon press briefing in May, Major General Durbin presented a rosy report on the state of the Afghan security forces. He said they had been "effective at disrupting and destroying" their enemies and that the Afghan army had made "remarkable" progress in recruiting.

The two-star general closed on a high note by praising the Afghan security forces and inviting journalists to visit the country and judge for themselves. "I think if you do, you'll be as impressed as I am with their progress," Durbin said.

Later that May, someone did come see for himself. Retired Army Gen. Barry McCaffrey was a hero of the first Persian Gulf war and served as the national drug czar in the Clinton administration. It had been a decade since he had been on active duty, but the U.S. military asked him to visit Afghanistan and Pakistan and conduct an independent assessment. The mission was not publicized.

McCaffrey interviewed about fifty high-ranking officials over the course of a week. In his nine-page report, he lauded U.S. commanders and highlighted several successes, but he didn't sugarcoat his verdict:

the Taliban was nowhere near defeated and the war was "deteriorating." He judged the Taliban as well-trained, "very aggressive and smart
in their tactics," as well as armed with "excellent weapons." Far from
panicking or feeling the pressure of time, the insurgents would "soon
adopt a strategy of 'waiting us out,'" he added.

In contrast, McCaffrey said the Afghan army was "miserably under-
resourced" and that its soldiers had little ammunition and shoddier weapons than the Taliban. He blasted the Afghan police as worthless. "They
are in a disastrous condition: badly equipped, corrupt, incompetent,
poorly led and trained, riddled by drug use." Even under a best-case scenario, McCaffrey predicted, it would take another fourteen years—until
2020—before the Afghan security forces could operate without U.S. help.

The report was passed up the chain of command to Rumsfeld and
the Joint Chiefs of Staff. "We will encounter some very unpleasant
surprises in the coming twenty-four months," McCaffrey warned. "The
Afghan national leadership are collectively terrified that we will tip-toe
out of Afghanistan in the coming years—leaving NATO holding the
bag—and the whole thing will again collapse into mayhem."

If McCaffrey's conclusions weren't sobering enough, Rumsfeld soon
received another harsh dose of reality. On August 17, 2006, Marin
Strmecki, the defense secretary's trusted civilian adviser, delivered a
forty-page classified report titled, "Afghanistan at a Crossroads." Strmecki
made a separate fact-finding trip to the war zone after McCaffrey and
arrived at many of the same conclusions. But he cast further doubt on
the reliability and viability of Washington's allies in Kabul.

The Afghan government, he said, was crooked and feckless and had
left a power vacuum in many parts of the country for the Taliban to
exploit. "It is not that the enemy is so strong but that the Afghan government is so weak," Strmecki added, repeating a comment he heard
often during his visit.

Meanwhile, the U.S. embassy in Kabul grappled with a fresh wave
of internal pessimism. Neumann, the ambassador, sent another dour
classified cable to Washington on August 29, which began with this
declaration: "We are not winning in Afghanistan."

Two weeks after the ambassador's warning, Eikenberry sat down for an interview with ABC News on the fifth anniversary of the 9/11 attacks and offered the flip version for public consumption. "We are winning," the general said, adding, "but I also say we have not yet won." Asked if the United States could lose, Eikenberry responded: "Losing is not an option in Afghanistan."

That fall, Rumsfeld's speechwriters revved up the spin campaign with a new set of talking points titled, "Afghanistan: Five Years Later." Brimming with optimism, it highlighted more than fifty promising facts and figures, from the number of Afghan women trained in "improved poultry management" (more than 19,000) to "the average speed on most roads" (up 300 percent).

"Five years on, there is a multitude of good news," the talking points asserted. "While it has become fashionable in some circles to call Afghanistan a forgotten war, or to say the United States has lost its focus, the facts belie the myths."

Rumsfeld thought it was brilliant. "This paper," he wrote in an October 16 snowflake, "is an excellent piece. How do we use it? Should it be an article? An Op-ed piece? A handout? A press briefing? All of the above? I think it ought to get to a lot of people." He shared a copy with the White House, while his staffers sent a version to reporters and posted it on the Pentagon's website.

If leaders at the Pentagon or the generals in Kabul and at Bagram had listened to their soldiers in the field, they would have heard a very different message. Staff Sgt. John Bickford, a 26-year-old soldier from Lake Placid, New York, spent much of 2006 in Paktika province in eastern Afghanistan. He was stationed with other 10th Mountain Division soldiers at Firebase Tillman, named after Pat Tillman, the NFL football player who enlisted in the Army after 9/11 and was killed by friendly fire two years later. Located about forty miles north of Shkin, on a little finger of rugged Afghan territory that poked into Pakistan, the isolated firebase sat a mile from the border between two enemy infiltration routes from North Waziristan.

Bickford said the fighting was "about ten times worse" than his first deployment to eastern Afghanistan three years earlier. His unit clashed with insurgents four or five times a week during summer 2006. The enemy massed as many as 200 fighters to try to overrun U.S. observation posts.

"We said that we defeated the Taliban, but they were always in Pakistan and regrouping and planning and now they're back stronger than they have ever been," he said in an Army oral-history interview. "Anytime that they did an assault or an ambush it was well-organized, and they knew what they were doing."

In August 2006, Bickford was leading a patrol in an armored Humvee when insurgents ambushed his convoy with rocket-propelled grenades. One RPG blew some of the armor off Bickford's vehicle. Another hit the same spot and penetrated the interior of the Humvee. Shrapnel tore up Bickford's right thigh, calf, ankle and foot. His team fended off the assault, but his days as an infantryman were over.

Bickford spent three months in a wheelchair and on crutches while he recovered at Walter Reed Army Medical Center in Washington. While convalescing, he reflected on what the United States faced in Afghanistan. "These are very smart people, and they're the enemy but they deserve tons of respect and they should never, never, never be underestimated," he said.

Five years into the war, however, the U.S. military still lacked an understanding of its enemies and what motivated them to fight.

Paul Toolan, the Special Forces captain who served in Helmand province, said U.S. troops often puzzled over who was shooting at them and why. In one area, it might be narcotics traffickers protecting their turf. In another, it might be "hardcore ideologues who were really anti-government and that was their only focus." In yet another locale, it might be a hostile militia taking orders from a corrupt local official. "That's a big question in Afghanistan: Who are you fighting and are you fighting the right guys?" he said.

Some attacks were rooted in grievances that had simmered for generations or centuries. Maj. Darryl Schroeder, a psy-ops officer from Redding, California, served as an adviser to the Afghan police in 2006. He said his forces could drive through parts of Kandahar without taking any fire. But when British troops followed closely behind on the same route they would get attacked.

"We'd ask the Afghans why and they'd say, 'Because the British came and they killed my grandfather and my great-grandfather,'" he said in an Army oral-history interview. "There are so many reasons why people fight over there."

*   *   *

Even when they had it explained to them, however, the Americans still failed to grasp the forces behind the insurgency. More than anything, that inability condemned them to year after year of repetitive warfare.

When Brig. Gen. James Terry, the deputy commander of the 10th Mountain Division, deployed to Afghanistan in 2006, he thought his personal background would help him comprehend the complexities of rural Afghanistan. A native of the mountains of north Georgia, he told people his great-grandmother was a Cherokee, that one of his grandfathers was a farmer and the other a bootlegger. When he grew up during the tumultuous 1960s and 1970s, Lester Maddox, a populist demagogue, was governor of Georgia, and George Wallace, another strident racist, governed the state of Alabama.

"So you'd think that I'd have an appreciation of clans, tribes, illegal substance trafficking and corruption," Terry said in an Army oral-history interview.

Still, Terry saw the enemy as an enigma. One day, he sat down with an Afghan army general and pleaded for enlightenment. "I said, 'Tell me about the Taliban,'" Terry recalled. "And he looked at me and through an interpreter said, 'Which Taliban are you talking about?'"

"The Taliban, tell me about the Taliban," Terry repeated.

"There are three kinds, tell me what kind you want to hear about," the Afghan general said.

"Tell me about all three," Terry said. "Tell me what they are."

The Afghan general explained to his American ally that one type of Taliban were "radical terrorists." Another group was "in it just for themselves." The rest were "the poor and the ignorant, who are simply influenced by the other two groups."

"If you want to do something significant, you separate the two groups from the poor and the ignorant," the Afghan general said, "and you'll have stability and prosperity in Afghanistan."

It was an oversimplified explanation, but Terry thought it made more sense than anything else he had heard. "Pretty insightful guy," he said.

CHAPTER NINE

An Incoherent Strategy

The veteran Cold Warrior woke up before 5 a.m. on a Sunday—November 5, 2006—to begin his clandestine mission. Robert Gates, the 63-year-old president of Texas A&M University, hadn't worked for the government since his term as director of the CIA ended thirteen years earlier. But the White House had asked for him personally and he felt obligated to help.

An inscrutable Midwesterner with a doctorate in Russian and Soviet history, Gates took care to leave his brick home on the College Station campus without drawing attention. He drove northwest for two hours through central Texas to the nondescript town of McGregor. As instructed, he pulled into the parking lot of a Brookshire Brothers grocery store. His contact was waiting in a white Dodge Durango with tinted windows. Gates climbed in and they headed north another fifteen miles to the Prairie Chapel Ranch for the rendezvous with the man who had summoned him: President Bush.

The Durango passed the security checkpoints and dropped Gates off at a one-story building away from the main residence on the ranch. Bush wanted to hide his visitor from the other ranch guests present for his wife's 60th birthday. The November 2006 congressional elections were in two days. The president worried that if word of Gates's presence leaked, people might realize he was planning to shake up his Cabinet. Voters might see it as an admission that the wars were going badly.

Bush had secretly decided to sack Donald Rumsfeld as defense secretary and needed a replacement. Rumsfeld had alienated Congress and NATO allies by mishandling Iraq, and his combative personality had worn thin with the public. Bush had heard good things about Gates, who worked for his father's administration, and he wanted to hear his ideas about how to fix the wars in Iraq and Afghanistan.

They chatted for an hour, mainly about Iraq. Gates said he supported Bush's undisclosed plan to send a surge force of 25,000 to 40,000 more troops to Iraq, even though an expansion of the war would buck public sentiment. But Gates also told the president he had overreached in Afghanistan and needed a new strategy there.

"I thought that our goals were too ambitious in Afghanistan, that it was being neglected and that we needed to narrow those goals," Gates said in a University of Virginia oral-history interview. He thought the Bush administration's democratic aspirations and nation-building agenda for Afghanistan "were a pipe dream" that would take generations to fulfill.

He favored a scaled-back strategy to "crush the Taliban, weaken them to the extent you possibly can, strengthen the Afghan security forces so that they can keep the Taliban out or down on their own, and prevent anybody from ever using the country as a launch pad against us again, period."

Gates caught a ride back to the grocery store, then drove himself to College Station. Late that afternoon, he received a call from Joshua Bolten, the White House chief of staff, asking him to fly to Washington. The president wanted to hold a news conference the day after the election to introduce Gates as the new boss at the Pentagon.

The taciturn former spymaster represented fresh leadership and a change in temperament from the brash, polarizing Rumsfeld. Yet Gates would find it just as difficult to extricate the U.S. military from Afghanistan. In fact, he would send far more troops to fight and die in the war than Rumsfeld ever contemplated.

Despite their reassuring talk of progress in public, Bush and his national-security team knew their strategy in Afghanistan was not working. Nobody had a clear idea of what they were trying to accomplish, let alone a timetable or benchmarks for achieving it.

With its hands full in Iraq, the United States leaned on its NATO allies in 2006 to accept more responsibility in Afghanistan. The U.S. military retained control of operations in eastern Afghanistan along the Pakistani border, but NATO agreed to take a lead role in the south where the Taliban was gaining strength. The British moved forces into the deserts of Helmand province, the Dutch sent troops to Uruzgan and the Canadians took over in Kandahar, the Taliban's birthplace.

In May, British Lt. Gen. David Richards arrived in Kabul to take charge of NATO forces. A few months later, he also assumed command of U.S. troops in the east—the first time the Americans and their NATO allies served under the same banner in Afghanistan. A veteran of far-flung conflicts in Sierra Leone, East Timor and Northern Ireland, he oversaw a combined force of 35,000 troops from thirty-seven countries, a formidable presence on paper.

In public, Richards embraced his role as the commander of NATO's first combat mission outside Europe. But in private, he was appalled by the coalition's absence of strategic thinking and its inability to agree on the war's objectives.

"There was no coherent long-term strategy," he said in a Lessons Learned interview. "We were trying to get a single coherent long-term approach—a proper strategy—but instead we got a lot of tactics."

The 54-year-old Richards wanted to pursue a counterinsurgency strategy to build popular support for the Afghan government. Under that approach, NATO would target specific districts, clear out the guerrillas and help the Afghans stabilize the area with reconstruction projects. But it all proved harder than NATO expected.

In September 2006, on Richards's orders, Canadian and allied forces launched Operation Medusa, an offensive to seize control of Panjwai district, a Taliban stronghold in the province of Kandahar. The operation quickly veered off course.

On the first day, the Taliban ambushed the Canadians and forced them to retreat. The next day, a U.S. Air Force A-10 Warthog—a low-flying attack aircraft with fearsome teeth painted on the nose cone—mistakenly strafed a Canadian platoon with cannon fire and "just completely knocked the stuffing out of them," according to Richards. The Canadians wanted to call off the operation, but Richards told them that would humiliate NATO and persuaded them to stick with it.

After two weeks, the Canadian-led force finally won the battle, killing an estimated several hundred Taliban fighters. But the allies suffered unusually heavy losses: Nineteen Canadian and British troops died and scores were wounded. Making matters worse, the allies failed to maintain security in Panjwai and insurgents gradually returned. Richards said the Canadians "were knackered" and short on forces because they also needed to secure the city of Kandahar, a higher priority. The "Canadians fought a tough battle and nearly were beaten, so they were collectively exhausted," Richards said.

For the counterinsurgency strategy to succeed, Richards said he needed more troops as well as financial support and manpower for reconstruction. But the alliance did not furnish enough of either.

In his Lessons Learned interview, Richards recalled a tense encounter with an unsympathetic Rumsfeld around the time of the Panjwai debacle. The Pentagon chief asked why the war was deteriorating in the south. Richards replied that he lacked money and personnel. "And Rummy said, 'General what do you mean?' I said, 'We don't have enough troops and resources and we've raised expectations.' He said, 'General, I don't agree. Move on.'"

Washington bore plenty of frustrations with its allies. Each NATO member imposed different restrictions on its troops as a condition for joining the coalition in Afghanistan. Some bordered on the ridiculous.

Germany would not allow its soldiers to join combat missions, patrol at night, or leave mostly peaceful northern Afghanistan. Yet it permitted them to enjoy copious amounts of alcohol. In 2007, the German government shipped 260,000 gallons of home-brewed beer and 18,000 gallons of wine to the war zone for its 3,500 troops.

In contrast, U.S. troops did most of the fighting and hardly any of the drinking. General Order Number 1—the U.S. military's biggest restriction—prohibited the consumption of alcohol on U.S. bases to avoid offending Afghanistan's teetotaling Muslims.

"We felt that we were giving it our all, and we didn't always feel that way about some of the other allies," Nicholas Burns, the U.S. ambassador to NATO under Bush, said in a Lessons Learned interview. "So, it was a tough issue in NATO."

The NATO-led coalition—formally known as the International Security Assistance Force, or ISAF—located its headquarters in a large yellow building adjacent to the U.S. embassy in the Wazir Akbar Khan quarter of Kabul. Behind its tall concrete blast walls, the ISAF compound stood out as a pleasant oasis in the capital and featured a well-tended garden.

Inside the headquarters building, however, the coalition battled bureaucratic dysfunction. Representatives from the thirty-seven countries had to coordinate operations, make staffing decisions and iron out political conflicts. Constant turnover made things harder. Coalition members limited their personnel to short tours of duty, usually three to six months. By the time new arrivals got up to speed, they had to train a replacement.

Maj. Brian Patterson, a U.S. Air Force fighter pilot, spent four months in 2007 at ISAF headquarters running the air-support operations center at night. He could call on British Harriers, Dutch F-16s, French Mirages and Rafales, as well as U.S. fighter jets and bombers. But juggling the patchwork of capabilities and restrictions took nerve and patience. German Tornado fighter-bomber aircraft, for example, could only be used in certain emergencies.

Patterson likened the headquarters to "a Frankenstein organization" that emphasized inclusion over efficiency. "We like straight lines, but if you go to a NATO headquarters, it's going to look like spaghetti. It's going to be very convoluted," he said in an Army oral-history interview. "It's kind of like kindergarten where everybody gets to play, everybody gets a speaking part." (Working for NATO did have an upside: The Americans could drink. "There were several bars that were located on the base, which was a pretty nice situation," Patterson conceded.)

While the Americans had legitimate complaints about the coalition, the other partners nursed their own resentments about the United States. After 9/11, Canada and European members of NATO deployed troops to Afghanistan to show solidarity. But the alliance members felt Washington took them for granted and disparaged their contributions, especially as the war morphed into an open-ended mission and the Pentagon grew preoccupied with Iraq.

In December 2006, British Defense Secretary Desmond Browne sent a letter to Rumsfeld that highlighted the lack of a war strategy and asked for a meeting of allied ministers "to give better political shape" to the military mission. Rumsfeld, by then a lame duck, called it a "commendable" idea but said he would defer to Gates, who was still awaiting Senate confirmation. The NATO ministers met two months later, but nothing changed. As Gates later recalled, he had three priorities: "Iraq, Iraq and Iraq." Without U.S. leadership, the Afghan mission stagnated. "There was no center. There was no sense of common purpose," an unidentified NATO official said in a Lessons Learned interview. "In reality, strategy wasn't treated urgently."

U.S. leaders braced for a rough year in 2007, knowing it would be difficult to contain the spreading insurgency. Reinforcements were in short supply. NATO allies had brushed off requests for extra troops. The Pentagon was tapped out because of Iraq. "As the military saying at the time went, at that point I was 'out of Schlitz.' I had nothing more to send," Gates said in his oral-history interview.

In public, however, U.S. leaders expressed complete confidence in their approach. In a February 2007 address to the American Enterprise Institute, the conservative think tank, Bush reported that his administration had completed "a top to bottom review of our strategy" and he announced a fresh "strategy for success."

Other than a commitment to expand the size of the Afghan army and police, however, the new strategy was really more of the old. Bush gave no indication that he had taken Gates's advice from their meeting at the ranch three months earlier to truncate the war's objectives. Instead, he declared that his ambitious goal was not just to "defeat the terrorists," but to transform Afghanistan into "a stable, moderate, democratic state that respects the rights of its citizens."

"For some, that may seem like an impossible task. But it's not impossible," Bush said. "Over the past five years, we've made real progress."

Yet even the president's new war commander had a hard time making sense of the so-called "strategy for success."

Army Gen. Dan McNeill arrived in Kabul to take charge of U.S. and NATO forces a few days before Bush's think-tank speech. It was the second command tour in Afghanistan for the silver-haired soldier from eastern North Carolina. Like Richards, his British predecessor, McNeill quickly judged that the United States and NATO didn't have a coherent war strategy. Instead, the conflict had shifted into automatic cruise control, without a roadmap or a destination.

"In 2007, there was no NATO campaign plan, a lot of verbiage and talk, but no plan," McNeill said in a Lessons Learned interview. "The instructions were kill terrorists and build the [Afghan army]. Also, don't fracture the alliance, and that was it."

Six years into the conflict, there was still no consensus on the war's aims. Some officials thought the goals should include tackling poverty and child mortality. Others, like Bush, talked about freedom and democracy. The high-mindedness and lack of clarity baffled the four-star general. "I tried to get someone to define for me what winning meant, even before I went over, and nobody could," McNeill said.

Lower-ranking soldiers in the field also sensed that no strategy existed. The unofficial mission, they said, was to keep a lid on Afghanistan and not let things spiral out of control while the U.S. military surged into Iraq. "Iraq was sucking up all the resources and all the time and attention," Lt. Col. Richard Phillips, who ran a combat support hospital in eastern Afghanistan in 2007, said in an Army oral-history interview, "Afghanistan was nothing . . . It was a backwater second effort for everybody."

Maj. Stephen Boesen, an officer with the Iowa National Guard, described the U.S. war effort as "just spinning our wheels" and lacking "any kind of strategy" when he served in 2007 as a combat adviser to

Afghan infantry forces. Senior commanders, he said, failed to articulate expectations or benchmarks.

When he returned home, he predicted—accurately—that the war would muddle along aimlessly for years to come. "I'm sad to say that my children will probably be doing the same mission I did when they're old enough, if we don't get our act together," Boesen told Army historians.

In spring 2007, the White House recognized that it needed better strategic advice. National Security Adviser Stephen Hadley persuaded Bush to appoint a White House "war czar" to coordinate strategy and policy for Iraq and Afghanistan. Bush selected Army Lt. Gen. Douglas Lute, the director of operations for the Joint Staff at the Pentagon, an Indiana native and West Point graduate who had served in in Kosovo and the first Iraq War.

In a reflection of the Bush administration's focus, Lute estimated that he spent 85 percent of his time in his new job on Iraq and just 15 percent on Afghanistan. At his Senate confirmation hearing, lawmakers asked him only a single question about the war in Afghanistan, a query about the Taliban's sanctuaries in Pakistan. Despite Bush's public pronouncements about his "strategy for success," Lute found that few people at the White House had done any real strategic thinking about Afghanistan.

"We were devoid of a fundamental understanding of Afghanistan—we didn't know what we were doing," Lute recalled in a Lessons Learned interview. "What are we trying to do here? We didn't have the foggiest notion of what we were undertaking." Lute insisted he wasn't being hyperbolic. "It's really much worse than you think. There is a fundamental gap of understanding on the front end, overstated objectives, an overreliance on the military, and a lack of understanding of the resources necessary."

As 2007 came to a close, news from the front grew bleaker. U.S. military deaths reached a new annual high. Civilian casualties from suicide bombings increased by 50 percent. Opium production set a record, with Afghanistan generating about 90 percent of the world's supply.

Yet with lawmakers, the White House, journalists and other Americans fixated on Iraq, the war in Afghanistan drifted along with little scrutiny. When Afghanistan did come up in public, military commanders downplayed the Taliban's resurgence to an almost laughable extent.

In a December 2007 television appearance on PBS, General McNeill dusted off the old military talking point that violence was getting worse not because the Taliban was growing stronger, but because U.S. and NATO forces were aggressively pursuing the enemy. "We just felt we wouldn't wait on them and we'd go out after them," he said.

The PBS interviewer, Gwen Ifill, was skeptical. "But the Taliban, we thought at one point, we were told at one point, was vanquished, had been wiped out," she said. "Is it alive and well now?"

"Well, that statement didn't come from me," McNeill replied. "They had scattered to some areas where we could not get to them, and now we are getting into those areas."

*   *   *

Though the war in Iraq had depleted the available supply of U.S. forces, in January 2008 the Pentagon scrounged up a little more Schlitz. It announced 3,000 additional troops would go to Afghanistan, for a total U.S. force of 28,000.

In a February news conference, McNeill put a spin on the grim conditions from the front. He told Pentagon reporters that the decision to send more troops showed the United States and NATO were winning, not losing.

"There's a basic military adage that says reinforce where you're having some success," he said. "We are looking to have more success in 2008." He insisted the insurgency had stalled, though military intelligence assessments uniformly reported that it was metastasizing.

The commander in chief reinforced the message in a political speech two days later. Speaking to the Conservative Political Action Conference, Bush again scoffed at critics who said Afghanistan had devolved into a quagmire. "We stood our ground—and we have seen the results," he said. "The Taliban, al-Qaeda and their allies are on the run."

In private, however, Bush was concerned. Though he had less than a year remaining in his second term, he decided it was time to review the war strategy yet again. Lute, his war czar, and a team of aides traveled to Afghanistan in May 2008 to conduct an assessment for the White House. Meanwhile, the State Department and the Joint Staff at the Pentagon carried out their own strategy reviews.

None of the agencies thought the U.S. military was on the verge of defeat. The Taliban, while on the rebound, was still too weak to seize a major city or march on Kabul. But to Lute, it was apparent conditions did not favor the United States and were spiraling downward. The scale of attacks by insurgents, their geographic dispersion and overall levels of violence had risen for three straight years.

In a report compiled after his trip, Lute attributed many failings to the spaghetti-like chains-of-command that had taken root among the allies. One PowerPoint slide illustrated what he called "the 10-war problem." Lute's team had visited Kandahar—a Taliban hub—and found a host of different coalition forces working at cross-purposes: U.S. and NATO conventional troops, the CIA, Special Operations forces, the Afghan army, the Afghan police, combat advisers and trainers, and an assortment of others.

"The tally was ten, and the problem was that nobody was talking to all the others," Lute said in a University of Virginia oral-history interview. "The left hand was not talking to the right hand."

As an example, he said commandos from the Navy SEALs or the Army's Delta Force "would come in, raid a compound overnight, and the conventional Army would not know [if] it was coming or going. The sun would come up and there would be a burning compound. And a conventional infantry unit would have to go and figure out what happened, make amends with the locals, and it just went on and on."

More broadly, the war-strategy reviews in 2008 arrived at many of the same conclusions reached during previous reviews in 2003, 2006 and 2007. All found the conflict had been neglected because of Iraq and recommended that the U.S. government dedicate more time, money and other resources to Afghanistan.

While the strategy reviews were underway, the generals continued to deliver soothing reports in public. As his sixteen-month tour as war commander came to an end in June 2008, McNeill sounded upbeat notes about everything that the United States and NATO had accomplished on his watch. He cited "many signs of visible progress"—new roads, improved health care, better and bigger schools.

"I'm simply trying to make a statement that there has been progress there. There's certainly progress in the security sector. There is progress in reconstruction," he said in a farewell news conference at the Pentagon. "So, again, I see that the prospects are good and that progress there will continue."

Yet as the months passed, the war strategy remained undefined. The contradictions between the generals' happy talk and the discouraging reality on the ground became harder to ignore.

By summer 2008, U.S. commanders in the field decided the 3,000 extra troops that had arrived earlier in the year were insufficient. They asked the Pentagon for even more reinforcements. With a presidential election coming up, the Bush administration decided to leave the request for the next occupant of the White House.

Still, no general wanted to admit he couldn't defeat the Taliban.

In September, Army Maj. Gen. Jeffrey Schloesser, the commander of U.S. forces in eastern Afghanistan, held a press conference to underscore the "steady progress" his troops were making. Choosing his words with care, he said he needed more soldiers "if we're going to continue to make good progress in a timely way."

Asked point-blank by a reporter if he was winning the war, Schloesser hesitated. "Look, you know, the truth is—is that I—I feel like, you know we're making some steady progress," he said. "It's a slow win, I guess."

Later that month, Gates, the defense secretary, visited Kabul to meet with Army Gen. David McKiernan, the new 57-year-old commander of U.S. and NATO forces. A Georgia native, McKiernan had served as the commander of U.S. ground forces during the invasion of Iraq five years earlier. Now he, too, was pressing for more troops in Afghanistan.

At a press conference, McKiernan said the Taliban was incapable of winning the war. But with unusual candor, he said the United States was not assured of victory, either. "We are not losing, but we are winning slower in some places than others," he said.

Within weeks, his public remarks turned even more pessimistic. "In large parts of Afghanistan, we don't see progress," he told reporters during a visit to Washington in October. "I won't say that things are all on the right track . . . We are in a tough fight. So the idea that it might get worse before it gets better is certainly a possibility."

McKiernan's shift in tone spoke volumes. For the first time an Afghanistan war commander had given the public a frank and honest account of how the tide of battle had shifted.

He would not last in the job for long.

CHAPTER TEN

The Warlords

In December 2006, the advocacy group Human Rights Watch publicly urged Afghanistan to confront its tumultuous past by creating a special court to investigate warlords suspected of committing atrocities during the country's civil war in the 1990s. The New York–based organization named and shamed a list of ten alleged war criminals who were still at large.

The plea for justice and accountability highlighted a wound that Washington had long tried to ignore. Several warlords on the list held senior posts in the Afghan government and enjoyed close relations with the U.S. government. Their brutal records were common knowledge in Afghanistan, but the list embarrassed the Bush administration and served as a reminder that it had teamed with an ugly cast of characters to fight the Taliban and al-Qaeda.

Rather than distance themselves from the warlords because of the bad publicity, however, U.S. officials reached out to console them. Two days before Christmas, Richard Norland, the number-two diplomat at the U.S. embassy in Kabul, paid a private visit to one of the most notorious figures on the list, Gen. Abdul Rashid Dostum, to reassure him that the United States still valued his friendship.

A merciless strongman with a passion for whiskey, Dostum commanded an Uzbek militia that shelled and looted Kabul in the early 1990s, leaving the capital in ruins. In 2001, his fighters killed hundreds of Taliban prisoners by suffocating them in shipping containers.

Dostum stood personally accused of kidnapping and sexually assaulting political rivals. But he also did the bidding of the CIA and the Pentagon, so U.S. officials wanted to preserve the alliance.

When Norland and other U.S. diplomats arrived at Dostum's marbled new mansion in the capital's Sherpur district—a nouveau riche neighborhood popular with war profiteers—they found the warlord in a melancholy mood. Stung by the Human Rights Watch criticism, the 52-year-old Dostum complained his opponents were also spreading gossip that he was plotting a coup against the central government and secretly scheming with the Taliban.

"I've been called so many names, there are no names left," Dostum said, according to a classified diplomatic cable that Norland wrote summarizing the visit. "My sin was to fight for my country."

Norland, a career Foreign Service officer, settled into an overstuffed chair and did his best to calm Dostum's "quasi-paranoia," telling the warlord "it would be a good idea for him to have a positive role in shaping current events." In the cable, however, Norland told officials in Washington that Dostum remained as odious as ever, recounting rumors that he had recently raped a young house servant and ordered his guards to beat and rape a member of the Afghan parliament. "Stories about his drunkenness are constant fare," the diplomat added.

While Dostum denied the allegations, the episode represented yet another awkward turn in the lengthy, toxic and codependent relationship between Afghanistan's warlords and the U.S. government.

The partnership dated to the 1980s, when the CIA covertly delivered weapons and supplies to commanders of the mujahedin—the Islamist guerrillas fighting the Red Army and the communist Afghan regime. The CIA–mujahedin alliance pressured the Soviets into withdrawing in 1989. Afterward, in 1992, the Afghan state collapsed and the country plunged into civil war.

Mujahedin leaders turned on one another and the armed factions further tore the country apart in a free for all. Commanders of the various groups—which were usually based on tribe and ethnicity— became known as warlords and ruled as regional dictators. Though the

CIA curtailed its contacts with the warlords during the 1990s, the U.S. government re-embraced many of them after 9/11 to fight the Taliban.

After driving the Taliban from power, the Bush administration wanted the warlords to support the new Afghan government, so it swallowed concerns about their human-rights records. But Washington's tolerance of their behavior alienated and angered many Afghans who saw the warlords as corrupt, incorrigible and the root of the country's problems.

The Taliban were just as cruel and oppressive. The group massacred thousands, treated women as chattel and beheaded people in public spectacles during their rule from 1996 to 2001. But compared to the warlords, a substantial number of Afghans viewed the Taliban as the lesser of two evils and credited them for their religious devotion and consistent, if harsh, administration of justice based on Islamic law.

Sarah Chayes, a journalist who lived in Kandahar during the 2000s and later served as a civilian adviser to the U.S. military, said the United States was so "obsessed with chasing" the Taliban after 9/11 that it failed to grasp the downside of partnering with thugs like Dostum. "On the basis of the enemy of my enemy is my friend, we relied on the warlords" and helped them grab power, she said in a Lessons Learned interview. "We didn't know the population was thrilled with the Taliban kicking the warlords out."

Within the Bush administration, opinions about the warlords diverged greatly. Many diplomats—though not all—held their noses when they had to engage with them. The CIA, which placed a lower priority on personal morality and human rights, treated warlords as vital partners and cemented their loyalty with gifts of cash. Some U.S. military commanders admired the most egregious warlords for their ability to impose order in their home regions. Others argued that they deserved imprisonment or death.

Andre Hollis, who served as the Pentagon's senior official for drug policy under Bush, said the U.S. government took a "schizophrenic" approach with the warlords from the start and never straightened it out. "It was inconsistent across agencies and within agencies," he said in a Lessons Learned interview.

Dostum filled a special niche in the warlords' pantheon. A burly former wrestler with fierce eyebrows and a thick mustache, he fought alongside the Soviets and Afghan communists against the mujahedin during the 1980s. After the Russians left, he retained command of tens of thousands of Uzbek fighters, buttressed by tanks and a small fleet of aircraft. He expanded his power base in the northern cities of Sheberghan and Mazar-e-Sharif, nurturing a cult of personality by splashing his image on billboards.

During the civil war in the 1990s, he allied himself with—and double-crossed—just about every other faction at one time or another. Twice, he fled the country to avoid capture by the Taliban. In May 2001, he returned to join the coalition of warlords known as the Northern Alliance in a last-ditch attempt to prevent the Taliban from seizing the few parts of Afghanistan it did not already control.

Dostum's timing proved lucky. A few months later, small teams of CIA paramilitary operatives and Special Forces soldiers arrived in northern Afghanistan seeking vengeance for the 9/11 hijackings in the United States. They embedded with Dostum's besieged forces as combat advisers and—backed by overwhelming U.S. airpower—orchestrated an offensive that forced the Taliban to abandon Mazar-e-Sharif and Kunduz, another key city in the north.

Thousands of Taliban fighters surrendered to Dostum's militia in late November 2001, but that triggered another set of problems. Several hundred Taliban, whom Dostum had imprisoned in a decrepit fort near Mazar-e-Sharif, staged a bloody revolt that lasted several days. Dozens of Dostum's men and a CIA officer—Johnny Micheal Spann—were killed in the uprising, along with at least 200 Taliban.

As the revolt unfolded, Dostum's commanders packed about 2,000 other Taliban captives who had been apprehended near Kunduz into tightly sealed shipping containers. A convoy drove them 200 miles to another prison in Sheberghan. By the time the containers arrived, most of the prisoners had suffocated or been shot by Dostum's forces. Their deaths remained a secret until early 2002, when journalists and human-rights groups discovered evidence that the prisoners had been buried in mass graves in the desert near Sheberghan. Advocacy organizations urged the Afghan and U.S. governments to conduct war-crimes investigations. The U.S. government opened an inquiry after Bush left office, but no one was ever held accountable.

U.S. officials said publicly that they were unaware of the convoy deaths until the news media broke the story, despite the close relationship CIA and Special Forces personnel had with Dostum and his staff. But documents show the Bush administration and Dostum went to great lengths to maintain lines of communication at the highest levels. A few weeks after the prisoner deaths, Dostum dispatched a warm holiday letter from his command post to the White House.

"Dear U.S. president, George W. Bush!" Dostum wrote in the typed note, which listed a U.S. military postal code as the return address. "Please accept my cardinal greetings on New Year's Day! Afghan people, experiencing peace after a long period of sufferings are grateful for your efforts in this regard."

"I wish your Excellency good health, great successes and the best of luck," he added.

Rather than intercept the warlord's missive, the Pentagon took special care to deliver it. On January 9, Gen. Tommy Franks, the head of U.S. Central Command, faxed the letter directly to Donald Rumsfeld, who in turn dictated a snowflake ordering his staff to ensure that Dostum's greetings reached Bush's desk. "Dostum is one of the Northern Alliance commanders," one of Rumsfeld's aides scribbled on the snowflake. "He turned out to be quite a warfighter—and our forces worked very well with him."

As Afghans tried to solidify their new government in 2002 and 2003, however, Dostum worked against them. His forces battled rival militias as they competed for supremacy in the northern provinces. He resisted international calls to demobilize his troops and surrender his heavy weaponry to the government in Kabul.

U.S. support for Dostum remained steadfast despite his disruptive ways. In April 2003, Rep. Dana Rohrabacher, a Republican congressman from southern California, visited Hamid Karzai in the presidential palace and urged him to give Dostum more power in the new government. Oddly, the U.S. lawmaker also asked Karzai to stop calling Dostum and his ilk "warlords," suggesting that he use a less pejorative term such as "ethnic leader" instead, according to a classified U.S. diplomatic cable describing the meeting.

Karzai was incredulous. He called Dostum an "outlaw" and pointed out that his fighters had gotten into a shootout just a few days earlier, killing seventeen people. He warned that if Dostum and other warlords didn't stop killing, raping and looting, Afghans would wish for the return of the Taliban. "Karzai noted that what the people really want is to live under law, and people are starting to complain that under the Taliban at least there was law and order," the cable concluded.

Other U.S. diplomats tried but failed to persuade Dostum to become less belligerent. Thomas Hutson, a Dari speaker who served as a political officer in Mazar-e-Sharif in 2003 and 2004, made a point of seeing Dostum every two weeks. He brought cigars to build a rapport with the man he described as "a babyface Stalinesque Tito."

Hutson hoped he could entice Dostum to leave Afghanistan voluntarily and floated an assortment of half-baked ideas. He offered to hire him as the executive producer for a couple of movies the diplomat was involved in. When that didn't fly, he suggested that Dostum—a noted hypochondriac—travel to the island of Grenada for medical treatment, hoping the warlord would find the Caribbean climate to his liking and never come back.

On other occasions, Hutson took a harder line and told Dostum he needed to think realistically about what happened to others like him who had once been allies of the United States, such as the Shah of Iran and the president of Haiti, Jean-Bertrand Aristide.

"Dostum had never heard of Aristide, or Haiti for that matter. I pointed out that he had made a deal with the U.S., which enabled him to survive. I would then suggest that he, Dostum, also consider making a deal which would enable him to leave the warlord business," Hutson recalled in a diplomatic oral-history interview. "I don't think he considered any of my suggestions very seriously, but I kept telling the embassy people and to some degree the people in Washington to make Dostum an offer he could not refuse."

In April 2004, U.S. officials lost patience with Dostum when his militia defied the government in Kabul and briefly took control of the northern province of Faryab, forcing Karzai's appointed governor to flee. U.S. military commanders ordered a B-1 bomber to make several low passes over Dostum's home in Sheberghan, a warning that he had crossed a line.

Still, several months later, the Americans couldn't resist throwing a lifeline to their old friend. In winter 2004, one of the warlord's aides placed a panicky phone call to Army Col. David Lamm, the chief of staff at U.S. military headquarters in Kabul. Dostum was very sick and his doctors thought he was dying. Could the Americans help?

Lamm thought about saying no. He knew Dostum's death might solve a lot of problems. Instead, he agreed to fly Dostum from Mazar-e-Sharif to the U.S. medical trauma center at Bagram Air Base for tests. A colonel at Bagram called Lamm with the results: The warlord's heavy drinking had damaged his liver. He was dying. The only hope was to transport him to an advanced hospital. The colonel at Bagram recommended Walter Reed Army Medical Center in Washington.

"And I said, 'He's going to Washington? We've got to treat a warlord at Walter Reed? The ambassador isn't going to go for that,'" Lamm said in an Army oral-history interview. They settled on an alternative: Landstuhl Regional Medical Center, a premier U.S. Army hospital in Germany. "And so we sent Dostum to Landstuhl, and they cured him. They fixed him, and they worked out the equipment he would need to stay alive."

When Dostum returned home, he invited Lamm and other U.S. officials to his Kabul home for a celebratory banquet and thanked them for saving his life. But he reverted to his troublemaking ways before long and remained a destabilizing force in Afghan politics for years to come.*

---

* In 2014, *The Washington Post* reported that Dostum had been receiving about $70,000 a month in CIA funds routed through the Afghan presidential palace. In an interview with *Post* reporter Joshua Partlow, Dostum denied receiving such payouts, as well as a variety of other allegations against him. "This is just propaganda against me," he said.

In Lessons Learned interviews, senior Bush administration officials defended their warlord policy and said they played a difficult hand as best they could.

After defeating the Taliban in 2001, they said their toughest task was to persuade the warlords to disband their militias and pledge allegiance to the new government headed by Karzai. The warlords' armies and arsenals were their source of power and key to their personal survival.

The disarmament campaign largely succeeded but took years of cajoling. The Bush administration did not want to forcibly disarm the warlords because it would have required a huge influx of U.S. troops and torn Afghanistan further apart.

The warlords "had thirty years of civil war behind them. They were not about to turn everything in because the Americans said that this would be a good idea," said Robert Finn, the U.S. ambassador from 2002 to 2003.

The approach carried a stark downside. In exchange for disarmament, the United States and Karzai had to guarantee the warlords a role in the new government and give them political legitimacy.

Marin Strmecki, the civilian adviser to Rumsfeld, said the Pentagon and State Department held no illusions about how awful the warlords could be and recognized that they posed "a mortal threat to the legitimacy of the regime that we were helping to establish."

"I think people who diminish what was achieved in this phase are a little unfair. The elimination of private armies was an important political milestone to normalizing the country's politics," Strmecki said. Dostum and other warlords, he noted, had "serious armories of stuff," including Soviet-built short-range missiles. "When they don't have their private armies that is good in and of itself. You can then deal with them if they continue to misbehave."

But by welcoming them into the government, the Americans made the warlords a permanent fixture of the new political system—as well as a perpetual problem. Many warlords generated huge streams of revenue by illicit means, such as drug trafficking and collecting bribes, which escalated as they became high-ranking officials. As a result, corruption soon became a defining feature of the government.

By 2005, some U.S. officials started to realize that they had helped to create a Frankenstein monster. In September, Ronald Neumann, the U.S. ambassador, sent a classified cable to Washington warning that Afghanistan faced a "corruption crisis" that posed "a major threat to the country's future." Neumann admitted the U.S. government was partly to blame because of its "engagement with some unsavory figures," but he wanted Karzai to "take the moral high ground" and fire "some of his government's most notoriously corrupt officials."

Topping Neumann's most-notorious list were Ahmed Wali Karzai, a Kandahar power broker who happened to be the president's half-brother, and Gul Agha Sherzai, a former mujahedin commander known as "the Bulldozer."

Both men, however, were politically untouchable. Besides being the president's sibling, Ahmed Wali Karzai worked closely with the CIA and received lucrative contracts from the U.S. military.*

Sherzai helped U.S. forces capture Kandahar in 2001 and later served as governor of Nangahar, an eastern province that included the key city of Jalalabad. As governor, he amassed a fortune by skimming taxes and receiving kickbacks, but he also maintained a network of boosters within the U.S. government.

His supporters included Neumann's boss at the State Department: Richard Boucher, the former chief spokesman who had become assistant secretary of state for South and Central Asia. Boucher admired Sherzai for the way he kept the peace in his province by doling out patronage jobs and government contracts. He recalled visiting Jalalabad once and asking Sherzai whether he needed more aid for construction projects.

"He said, 'I need five schools, five colleges, five dams, and five highways,'" Boucher said in a Lessons Learned interview. "I said, well, okay, but why five? He said, 'I got this tribe, this tribe, this tribe, this tribe, and one for everybody else.' I thought that was one of the funniest things I ever heard and now I think it is one of the smartest things I ever heard."

---

* In July 2011, Ahmed Wali Karzai was assassinated by a member of his security detail in Kandahar.

Boucher said it was better to funnel contracts to Afghans who "would probably take 20 percent for personal use or for their extended families and friends" than give the money to "a bunch of expensive American experts" who would waste 80 to 90 percent of the funds on overhead and profit. "I want it to disappear in Afghanistan, rather than in the Beltway," he said. "Probably in the end it is going to make sure that more of the money gets to some villager, maybe through five layers of corrupt officials, but still gets to some villager."

But others said the United States and its allies were foolish to lionize warlords like Sherzai and encourage corrupt behavior. In a Lessons Learned interview, Nils Taxell, a Swedish anti-corruption expert who served in Afghanistan, mocked foreign officials for justifying Sherzai as "a benevolent asshole" because "he didn't take or keep everything for himself, he left a little for others."*

Like they did with Sherzai, U.S. officials had a love-hate relationship with another warlord: Sher Mohammad Akhundzada, the governor of Helmand province from 2001 to 2005. Dubbed "SMA" by Americans, he was renowned for ruthlessly enforcing order, but equally famous for his role in Helmand's thriving opium industry.

Marine Lt. Col. Eugene Augustine, who served in Helmand in 2004 and 2005, said suspicions about whether SMA and his top security aides were involved in drug trafficking made it difficult for U.S.-sponsored reconstruction projects to move forward. "There was always a question of corruption, and with all of the drugs and poppy production going on in Helmand, these guys always had that in there as a question mark behind them, not just from me but from higher headquarters, intel," Augustine said in an Army oral-history interview. "Everybody else was always like, 'Are these guys involved in drugs?' That was always the thing behind every conversation— this ongoing chess game of corruption, who's making money."

---

* Sherzai remained active in Afghan politics and denied allegations of wrongdoing when he ran, unsuccessfully, for president in 2014. "There is no evidence against me," he told NBC News. "If I was involved in corruption, I would have high-rise buildings in Dubai and would have millions of dollars in foreign banks!"

In 2005, U.S. and Afghan narcotics agents raided Akhundzada's offices and found an enormous stash—nine tons—of opium. He denied wrongdoing. But under international pressure, Karzai removed him as governor. In the absence of SMA's iron hand, the province quickly became a magnet for insurgents, and its drug-trafficking problem exploded. Some U.S. officials came to regret his departure.

McNeill, the two-time U.S. military commander in Afghanistan, described SMA as "a simple-minded tyrant" but said he was effective as governor because he "kept other bad guys at bay." In a Lessons Learned interview, he called Akhundzada's removal a "huge mistake." He said the British demanded SMA's removal before they took over responsibility for security in Helmand as part of a new NATO command structure.

"SMA was dirty but he kept stability because people were afraid of him," McNeill said. "It's not good and I'm not advocating dancing with the devil, but maybe one of his disciples, and that was SMA."*

Perhaps the most powerful and challenging warlord for the Americans to deal with was Mohammed Qasim Fahim Khan, a Tajik militia commander. As the senior general in the Northern Alliance, Fahim Khan played a critical role in helping the U.S. military overthrow the Taliban in 2001. Afterward, he secured the job of defense minister in Afghanistan's new government.

In public, the Bush administration treated Fahim Khan as a VIP and welcomed him to the Pentagon with an honor cordon. In private, U.S. officials saw him as a corrupt, destabilizing presence and feared he would try to launch a violent coup.

The black-bearded warlord had a tense history with Karzai. In 1994, Fahim Khan oversaw the Afghan government's secret police and ordered the arrest of Karzai—the deputy foreign minister at the time—on suspicion of spying. Karzai was captured and interrogated,

---

* Akhundzada, who went on to become a provincial senator, was unapologetic about his ruthless tactics. In an interview with the British news outlet the *Telegraph*, he said that after he was fired as governor, 3,000 of his followers switched sides and joined the Taliban "because they had lost respect for the government."

and his fate looked grim. But in a providential moment, a rocket crashed into the building where he was detained, enabling his escape.

As defense minister from 2001 to 2004, Fahim Khan installed his loyalists in the Afghan army and controlled security forces in Kabul. U.S. officials were so worried that he might try to knock off Karzai, who had no militia of his own to protect him, that they supplied the Afghan leader with American bodyguards.

*   *   *

Fahim Khan enjoyed his fearsome reputation and did little to hide his involvement in drug trafficking. Russell Thaden, a retired U.S. Army colonel who served as intelligence chief for NATO forces in Kabul from 2003 to 2004, said the defense minister once blew his stack upon learning U.S. and British forces had jointly bombed a large drug lab in northern Afghanistan.

"Fahim Khan was really upset about it until he learned which drug lab," Thaden said in an Army oral-history interview. "It wasn't one of his, so he was okay with it."

Ryan Crocker, who served as acting U.S. ambassador to Afghanistan in early 2002, recalled a bloodcurdling encounter when Fahim Khan nonchalantly informed him that another Afghan government minister had been murdered by a mob at the Kabul airport.

"He giggled while he related this," Crocker said in a Lessons Learned interview. "Later, much later, it emerged, I don't know if it was ever verified or not, it emerged that Khan himself had the minister killed. But I certainly came out of those opening months with the feeling that even by Afghan standards, I was in the presence of a totally evil person."

Crocker returned to Afghanistan years later to serve a second stint as ambassador during the Obama administration. By then, Fahim Khan had returned to power as Afghanistan's vice president—and he still made Crocker's skin crawl. "When I came back, my sense of him was that he was not directly involved in major strategy or operational deci- sions, that he was more interested in making even more illicit millions, but that Karzai had to handle him with real care, because he could be dangerous and no question in my mind, he could be dangerous," Crocker said. "I would have considered him capable of any iniquity."

Fahim Khan died of natural causes in 2014. But in his Lessons Learned interview two years later, the ambassador said he was still haunted by memories of the warlord.

"I check just about every other day, and as far as I know, he is still dead," Crocker said.

CHAPTER ELEVEN

A War on Opium

In March 2006, a fleet of Massey Ferguson farm tractors fanned out across the arid plains of Helmand province, home of the most fertile opium poppy fields in the world. Dragging heavy metal sleds, the tractors crushed rows of tender green poppy plants that had grown calf-high but were still weeks away from harvest. A small army of stick-wielding laborers covered terrain the Massey Fergusons couldn't reach, trudging through canal-irrigated fields and whacking poppy stems one by one.

The invasion of the poppy fields marked the start of Operation River Dance, touted by the United States as a major escalation in its war on opium. On paper, the two-month eradication campaign was a joint mission by the U.S. and Afghan governments. But the work and costs were not equally divided. Afghan security forces and private contractors attacked the poppies and dirtied their boots while U.S. military advisers and agents from the State Department and Drug Enforcement Administration stood watch and provided guidance. U.S. taxpayers, meanwhile, covered the operational expenses.

Afghan poppies—the plant from which opium is extracted to make heroin—had dominated global drug markets for decades. But production reached new heights after the U.S.-led invasion in 2001. Hardscrabble farmers took advantage of the collapse of Taliban rule and sowed as much of the cash crop as they could. By 2006, U.S. officials estimated that poppies were powering one-third of Afghanistan's entire economic output and supplying 80 to 90 percent of the world's opium.

The drug boom paralleled the Taliban's revival and the Bush administration concluded that narcotics revenue was underpinning the insurgency's comeback. As a result, the administration pushed for an opium crackdown in Helmand, the southern province where farmers grew most of Afghanistan's poppies.

As soon as Operation River Dance started, U.S. and Afghan officials publicly proclaimed it a tremendous success. Mohammed Daud, the newly installed governor of Helmand, promised that within two months "there will be no opium in this province." Maj. Gen. Benjamin Freakley, the 10th Mountain Division commander, called River Dance "very encouraging" and said "this bodes well for the future."

John Walters, the Bush administration's drug czar, visited Afghanistan while Operation River Dance was underway. Upon his return to Washington, he told reporters at the State Department that the country was "making enormous progress" and that "the scene there is getting better every day." He lauded Helmand's governor for being "in the forefront" of the war on opium and claimed that all farmers, religious leaders and local officials in the province supported the eradication campaign.

None of it was true.

Operation River Dance backfired in every regard. In diplomatic cables and Army oral-history interviews, U.S. officials described it as a poorly planned calamity that faltered from the start. "They say it was very successful. I think that's just plain B.S.," said Lt. Col. Michael Slusher, an officer with the Kentucky National Guard who advised Afghan soldiers during the campaign. The whole operation, he added, was not "worth a damn."

Tractors got stuck in ditches and mired in fields. Bulldozers and military vehicles frequently broke down. The stick-whacking approach proved so inefficient that leaders soon wrote it off as a useless exercise.

On April 24, the campaign suffered another blow when a State Department–leased aircraft with sixteen people on board—most of them U.S. drug-enforcement officials—crashed into a row of mud-brick houses in Helmand. At the time, U.S. and NATO officials said only that the two Ukrainian pilots were killed while news reports added that two Afghan girls on the ground also died.

But Mike Winstead, a U.S. Army colonel who helped to coordinate Operation River Dance, said the devastation was far worse. In an Army oral-history interview, he said he rushed to the scene and helped remove the bodies of about fifteen Afghans from their wrecked homes. He also recovered a briefcase of classified documents from the demolished aircraft and a bag with $250,000 in cash that the State Department had sent to pay for the anti-poppy exercise.

The crash underlined the futility of the campaign. "I'm not sure that we were doing much good by the end of it," Winstead said. "We were really struggling."

Making matters worse, as the growing season unfolded and the poppies bloomed into spectacular displays of pink-and-white flowers, many Afghans on the eradication teams went AWOL.

According to a U.S. diplomatic cable, most of the stick-swingers "deserted their posts" once they discovered they could earn far more harvesting opium for the farmers than killing the plants for the Afghan government. The farmers offered wages five times higher than the government rate, payable in cash or drugs. By the end of Operation River Dance, the ranks of the eradicators had dwindled from 500 to fewer than 100.

To cover up the debacle, Afghan officials lied in their public reports about how many acres of poppies they flattened, exaggerating the results by severalfold. In a pair of diplomatic cables sent to Washington in May, the U.S. embassy in Kabul admitted that only "a modest amount" of the poppy crop was destroyed and cast doubt on the official Afghan statistics. Yet the State Department certified the false numbers as accurate to Congress, citing them as evidence of a successful mission.

Operation River Dance did succeed in infuriating Helmand's poppy farmers. To sabotage the eradicators, they planted homemade bombs and other booby-traps in the soil and flooded their fields to bog down the tractors. Many blamed the Americans for ruining their livelihood. They were especially indignant that the Americans were destroying a product consumed mostly in the West. "I had a number of villagers ask me, 'Colonel, why are you eradicating something that your folks use and want?' They could not understand that," Winstead said.

U.S. officials cringed as it became evident their Afghan government allies were pocketing much of the profit from Helmand's opium and using Operation River Dance to punish their competitors in the drug trade. It dawned on the Americans well into the operation that they were being used.

A May 3 diplomatic cable signed by U.S. Ambassador Ronald Neumann singled out Helmand's deputy governor and police chief as "very corrupt individuals." The cable admitted that the province's main poppy belt had gone largely unscathed because land there was under the control of "powerful tribal leaders" and officials with "significant interests and influence." Afghan police also solicited bribes from farmers in exchange for sparing their fields from eradication. This put U.S. officials at risk of being seen as complicit in a major shake-down.

Maj. Douglas Ross, a U.S. military adviser embedded with a unit of Afghan soldiers, called River Dance an "illegal operation" and worried it would trigger a mass revolt against U.S. and Afghan forces. "If somebody's in there fleecing the people and we're providing security, then we're sending the wrong message," he said in an Army oral-history interview. "Believe me, my hair turned white by the end of this operation."

The eradication campaign primarily hurt poor farmers who lacked political connections or money to pay bribes. Alienated and destitute, they became perfect recruits for the Taliban.

"Ninety percent of the people's income of the Helmand province comes from selling poppy. Now we're taking it away," Col. Dominic Cariello, a Wisconsin National Guard officer who advised an Afghan army unit during the operation, said in an Army oral-history interview. "Yeah, of course they're going to take up weapons and shoot at you. You just took away their livelihood. They have a family to feed."

Farmers who didn't volunteer to join the insurgency were often conscripted anyway. Prior to planting, many farmers had signed deals with drug traffickers promising to deliver a fixed quantity of dried opium resin, or "poppy gum," at the end of the season. With their crops razed, they were hard-pressed to pay their debt.

"That drug dealer doesn't care where he gets the poppy gum but [says], 'I gave you $2,000 last winter and you owe me eighteen kilos; and if you can't give me the poppy gum, then I'll either kill you, kill your wife, kill your kids, or you can pick up this gun and help me fight the Americans,'" Maj. John Bates, an aide-de-camp to the deputy commander of U.S. forces in Afghanistan, said in an Army oral-history interview. "We were disgruntling the whole province," he added. "Helmand exploded."

Prior to Operation River Dance, Helmand presented a relatively quiet sector in the war with the Taliban. But after the operation kicked off, insurgents poured in. "The eradication campaign also appears to have attracted more Taliban to fight in Helmand, perhaps in an effort to protect their own financial interest and to win favor with the local population by 'protecting' their poppy crops," Neumann reported in the May 3 cable. Two weeks later, another U.S. embassy cable reported that security in Lashkar Gah, the provincial capital, was "very bad and continuing to deteriorate."

The spike in violence coincided with the arrival of British troops in Helmand in May as part of a previously planned reshuffling of NATO forces. The British found themselves underprepared and overwhelmed. "As soon as we handed it off to the British within a week they were taking numerous KIAs and WIAs pretty bad," said Slusher, the Kentucky National Guardsman, referring to troops killed in action and wounded in action. "The drug lords weighed in and the Taliban weighed in and it got real tough."

Despite the public accolades from U.S. and Afghan officials, Operation River Dance had turned into one of the biggest strategic blunders of the war. Instead of building confidence in the Afghan government and starving the Taliban of revenue, the 2006 Helmand campaign helped to transform the region into a lethal stronghold for the insurgency.

U.S., NATO and Afghan forces would pay dearly for the mistake for the remainder of the war.

*   *   *

Afghan farmers have tended varieties of the opium poppy—*Papaver somniferum*—for generations. With a little irrigation, the plants thrive in warm, dry climates. They grow especially well in the Helmand River valley, thanks to an extensive network of canals financed by American taxpayers. In the 1960s, the U.S. Agency for International Development built the canals to stimulate the production of cotton and other crops in southern Afghanistan during the Cold War.

In full bloom, poppy flowers look majestic in incandescent shades of white, pink, red or purple. After the petals fall away, the stem is capped by a seedpod the size of an egg. At harvest, farmworkers slice open the pods to drain a milky white sap that is dried into a resin. For Afghanistan, it is an ideal cash crop. Unlike fruits, vegetables and grains, the resin doesn't rot or attract pests. It can be easily stored and transported over long distances.

Traffickers take the opium resin to drug labs or refineries, where it is processed into morphine and heroin. Afghan opium feeds the demand for heroin in Europe, Iran and other parts of Asia. One of the few markets it does not dominate is the United States, which gets most of its heroin from Mexico.

Ironically, the only power that has been able to curtail the Afghan drug industry is the Taliban.

In July 2000, when the Taliban controlled most of the country, its reclusive one-eyed leader, Mullah Mohammad Omar, declared that opium was un-Islamic and imposed a ban on growing poppies. Much to the surprise of the rest of the world, the ban worked. Afraid to cross the Taliban, Afghan farmers immediately ceased planting poppies. The United Nations estimated that poppy cultivation plunged by 90 percent from 2000 to 2001.

The edict stirred tumult in global heroin markets and disrupted the Afghan economy. Years later, Afghans recalled the moment with awe and said it showed the comparative haplessness of the United States and their Afghan government allies in the opium battles.

"When [the] Taliban ordered to stop poppy cultivation, Mullah Omar could enforce it with his blind eye. No one cultivated poppy after the order was passed," Tooryalai Wesa, a former governor of Kandahar province, said in a Lessons Learned interview. "Now, billions of dollars came and were given to the Ministry of Counternarcotics. It actually didn't decrease [anything]. The poppy even increased."

The Taliban had hoped the 2000 opium ban would win favor in Washington and entice the United States to provide humanitarian aid. But those hopes vanished when al-Qaeda—which had been given sanctuary by the Taliban—launched the 9/11 attacks.

As soon as the U.S. military invaded and removed the Taliban from power in 2001, Afghan farmers resumed sowing their poppy seeds. U.S. officials and their allies recognized the problem would likely snowball but couldn't agree what to do.

The U.S. military was focused on hunting for al-Qaeda leaders. The State Department had its hands full trying to solidify the new Afghan state. Though poppies had nothing to do with why the United States had declared war, members of Congress pressed the Bush administration to prioritize the issue.

Michael Metrinko, the U.S. diplomat who survived captivity during the Iranian hostage crisis, said, "Everyone from Congress brought it up immediately," when they visited the mothballed U.S. embassy compound in Kabul in 2002. In a diplomatic oral-history interview, he recalled an exchange with one unnamed lawmaker who refused to drop the issue. "I looked at the congressman and I said, "Congressman, we don't have a functioning toilet here in the embassy yet. I share one with about a hundred other men. How far do you want me to go trying to eradicate the poppy production on the other side of the country?"

President Bush persuaded the United Nations and European allies to devise a strategy for tackling opium poppies. In spring 2002, British officials, who had agreed to take charge, floated an irresistible offer. They agreed to pay Afghan poppy farmers $700 an acre—a fortune in the impoverished, war-ravaged country—to destroy their crops.

Word of the $30 million program ignited a poppy-growing frenzy. Farmers planted as many poppies as they could, offering part of their crop to the British for destruction while selling the rest on the open market. Others harvested the opium sap right before destroying their plants and got paid anyway. "Afghans, like most other people, are quite willing to accept large sums of money and promise anything knowing that you will go away," Metrinko said. "The British would come and hand out sums of money and the Afghans would say, 'Yes, yes, yes, we're going to burn it right now,' and the Brits would leave. They would then get two sources of income from the same crop."

In a Lessons Learned interview, Anthony Fitzherbert, a British agricultural expert, called the cash-for-poppies program "an appalling piece of complete raw naivete," saying that the people in charge had "no knowledge of nuances and [I] don't know they really cared."

In 2004, as Afghan farmers tilled more soil to grow poppies and the British struggled to cope, the Bush administration started to reconsider whether it should become involved. But the U.S. bureaucracy lacked consensus and direction on how to address the problem. The State Department's Bureau of International Narcotics and Law Enforcement Affairs, or INL, was supposed to oversee the U.S. policy. But INL posted just one employee to the U.S. embassy in Kabul at the time, according to Lt. Gen. David Barno, the commander of U.S. forces from 2003 to 2005.

The U.S. military possessed exponentially more resources than the State Department but commanders hesitated to touch the issue. They did not see fighting drug traffickers as part of their mission and worried that targeting farmers would put their troops at risk. The CIA was reluctant to jeopardize its relationships with warlords over drugs. NATO allies couldn't agree what to do, either.

"There was literally no coordination and a lot of interagency fighting—not only between your agencies, but between your agencies and our agencies, British agencies," British Maj. Gen. Peter Gilchrist, who served as Barno's deputy commander from 2004 to 2005, said in an Army oral-history interview. "So it was just dysfunctional. It just wasn't working. We weren't getting any traction at all."

In November 2004, Defense Secretary Donald Rumsfeld sent a snowflake to Doug Feith, the Pentagon's policy chief, to complain about the Bush administration's aimless approach. "With respect to the drug strategy for Afghanistan, it appears not to be synchronized—no one's in charge," he wrote.

As the number of suicide bombings and other attacks rose from 2004 to 2006, members of Congress and agents from the DEA and INL argued that opium profits were fueling the insurgency. Other U.S. officials countered that the funding sources and motivations behind the insurgency were more complex, but lost the debate. The Bush administration decided to take a harder line with Afghan poppy growers and set aside $1 billion a year for programs like Operation River Dance.

By declaring opium an enemy, the United States effectively opened a second front in the war in Afghanistan.

Barnett Rubin, the academic expert on Afghanistan and former U.N. adviser, said the Bush administration misunderstood the factors behind the Taliban's resurgence. "We somehow came up with the explanation that it was drugs: the Taliban profit from drugs, and therefore drugs cause the Taliban," he said in a Lessons Learned interview.

At the same time, people besides the Taliban were getting rich from the drug trade. Governors, warlords and other senior Afghan officials who were supposedly allies of Washington became hooked on opium profits, collecting a cut from farmers and traffickers operating in their areas of influence. U.S. and NATO officials belatedly recognized that drug-related corruption was undermining the broader war and threatening to turn Afghanistan into what they called a "narco-state."

In an October 2004 snowflake, Rumsfeld reported to several senior Pentagon officials that the French defense minister, Michèle Alliot-Marie, was worried the opium industry could weaken President Hamid Karzai's grip on power. "She thinks it is important to act soon, to avoid having a situation where drug money elects the Afghan Parliament, and the Afghan Parliament then opposes Karzai and corrupts the government," Rumsfeld wrote.

A year later, Neumann sounded a similar alarm. "Many of our contacts correctly fear that the burgeoning narcotics sector could spin Afghan corruption out of anyone's control," Neumann wrote in a classified September 2005 cable to officials in Washington. "They fear that the sheer mass of illegal money from growing, processing, and trafficking opium could strangle the legitimate Afghanistan state in its cradle."

But U.S. officials remained at odds about what to do.

After Operation River Dance demonstrated the folly of attacking poppy fields with tractors and sticks, some Bush administration officials and members of Congress pushed to adopt a more aggressive approach that Washington had backed in Colombia to combat cocaine trafficking. A core part of that program, known as Plan Colombia, was the aerial spraying of herbicides to eradicate coca plants. The Bush administration hailed Plan Colombia as a success, despite concerns that the herbicides could cause cancer.

Some U.S. officials doubted it would work in Afghanistan for those and other reasons. John Wood, a National Security Council staffer in the Bush White House, said in a Lessons Learned interview that Colombia's then-president, Álvaro Uribe, was a reliable ally who supported aerial spraying: "Uribe was a credible leader and linked insurgency and drugs. The Colombian military was competent."

In contrast, the Afghan security forces were much weaker and Karzai, the Afghan president, was less committed. In public, Karzai declared a "holy war" against poppies and called the business "more dangerous than terrorism." But in private, he had serious doubts.

Karzai and his cabinet ministers resisted the U.S. spraying proposal. They feared the herbicides could poison water and food supplies, and that rural Afghans would rebel if their government allowed foreigners to unleash strange substances from the sky. "Karzai thought this would be seen by Afghans as chemical warfare against them," Zalmay Khalilzad,

the U.S. ambassador to Kabul from 2003 to 2005, said in a Lessons
Learned interview.

On another level, Afghan officials knew that if the spraying worked,
it would crush the one part of the national economy that was thriving.
And that would alienate rural Afghans even more.

"Urging Karzai to mount an effective counternarcotics campaign
was like asking an American president to halt all U.S. economic activity
west of the Mississippi," Ronald McMullen, who served as director of
INL's Afghanistan-Pakistan office, said in a diplomatic oral-history
interview. "That was the magnitude of what we were asking the Afghans
to do."

U.S. military leaders were equally leery of spraying, despite the
Bush administration's support for it. Most commanders saw opium as
a law-enforcement problem. They also worried about potential health
risks to their troops and had flashbacks to the Vietnam War, when U.S.
forces sprayed Agent Orange—a toxic defoliant—over tropical jungles.

The military's reticence irritated members of Congress. Politically,
it was hard to explain to voters why Americans were fighting a war
to rescue a country that produced more opium than any other in the
world. It didn't help when newspapers published photos of U.S. soldiers
patrolling on foot through poppy fields in full bloom (most U.S. units
were under orders not to interfere with the farming).

Shortly after Operation River Dance commenced in March 2006, a
congressional delegation led by Rep. Peter Hoekstra (R-Mich.) visited
Afghanistan to discuss eradication efforts with U.S., Afghan and British officials. INL arranged for some of the lawmakers to tour central
Helmand by helicopter.

Wide-eyed congressmen saw poppies growing everywhere: near
homesteads, inside mud-walled compounds, even all around the provincial capital of Lashkar Gah, according to a classified diplomatic
cable summarizing the visit. "Poppy fields were truly ubiquitous. Hundreds of large fields of poppy could be seen easily from the helicopters
in varying stages of growth. Many fields were in full bloom," the cable
read.

Yet some senior U.S. diplomats said they understood the military's reluctance to turn farmers and field hands into enemies. "I sympathize with the troops. If I was in my flak jacket and there was poppy—I would just say they were pretty flowers," said Richard Boucher, who oversaw South Asia policy for the State Department from 2004 to 2008. "They were not there to start chopping flowers and then have someone start shooting at you."

During Neumann's stint as ambassador from 2005 to 2007, he and other officials in the U.S. embassy in Kabul tried to persuade visiting members of Congress that the United States needed to take a long-term approach. He thought it would take many years for the Afghans to transform their rural economy and find realistic alternatives to growing poppies.

In a Lessons Learned interview, Neumann said there was "desperate pressure for short-term results." Ground eradication and aerial spraying were "driven by Congress wanting to see something tangible," he added, even though it was clear there was no simple solution. "Washington did not understand that a successful counternarcotics effort was going to be a function of a massive rural development effort."

By the end of 2006, it was clear Operation River Dance had accomplished little. That year, Afghanistan reaped a record opium harvest, with the number of acres under cultivation up by 59 percent, according to U.N. estimates. The next year proved even more bountiful, as cultivation increased by another 16 percent.

In 2007, the White House named a new U.S. ambassador to Afghanistan: William Wood, formerly the top U.S. diplomat in Colombia and a strong advocate of aerial spraying. Nicknamed "Chemical Bill," Wood pressed Karzai to accept a major spraying campaign. But by then the Afghan leader had grown distrustful and doubted Washington's assurances that the herbicides were safe. Even after receiving a personal appeal from Bush, Karzai said no. It was his final answer.

In January 2008, Richard Holbrooke, a former U.S. ambassador to the United Nations, trashed the Bush administration's war on opium in an opinion column in *The Washington Post*. He said the emphasis on eradication "may be the single most ineffective program in the history of American foreign policy"

"It's not just a waste of money. It actually strengthens the Taliban and al-Qaeda," Holbrooke wrote. He called for a reexamination of the U.S. government's "disastrous drug policies" in Afghanistan.

He would soon get to try it his way.

PART FOUR

OBAMA'S OVERREACH

2009—2010

CHAPTER TWELVE

Doubling Down

Wearing his habitual poker face, Robert Gates strode purposefully into the Pentagon briefing room on May 11, 2009, for a hastily arranged news conference. In his left hand, he clutched a four-page statement, folded over so no one could peek. He sat down at a table next to Adm. Mike Mullen, the chairman of the Joint Chiefs of Staff, to face about three dozen journalists who had no inkling why they had been summoned. Except for the clicking of cameras, the room fell silent.

The defense secretary, never one for small talk, got right down to business. He briefly addressed the news of the day: a U.S. Army sergeant had inexplicably gunned down five fellow service members at a health clinic in Iraq. Remaining somber, Gates began reading from his statement. After a careful review of operations in Afghanistan, he had concluded the U.S. military "can and must do better" and that the war required "new thinking and new approaches."

Then he dropped the big news: Five days earlier, he had sacked Army Gen. David McKiernan, the commander of U.S. and NATO troops in Afghanistan. Though the Pentagon was notoriously prone to leaks, Gates had kept the bombshell under wraps. Even the reporters who had just traveled with Gates to Afghanistan the week before and met with McKiernan had no clue.

Two and a half years into his tenure at the Pentagon, Gates had earned a reputation as an unsentimental boss who held the brass accountable. But dismissing a war commander was another thing entirely. The last notable instance occurred in 1951 when President Truman relieved General Douglas MacArthur for insubordination during the Korean War.

Yet Gates was better at safeguarding his secret than he was at explaining why he had taken such drastic action. He said McKiernan had refused no order, nor done anything wrong. "It was nothing specific," he said, just "time for new leadership and fresh eyes."

Admiral Mullen was equally cryptic. He said he was "very encouraged by the progress being made" in parts of Afghanistan, but nevertheless thought "it was time for a change."

The press corps looked at Gates and Mullen skeptically. Barbara Starr, a hard-nosed CNN correspondent and a fixture inside the Pentagon's corridors, prodded them for a fuller answer. "Is it just loss of confidence?" she asked. "I haven't heard anything yet—I'm so sorry— about why you both think he couldn't do the job."

Gates repeated the line that it was just time for a change. He noted that President Barack Obama, the new commander in chief, had unveiled his "comprehensive strategy" for the war six weeks earlier and agreed to send 21,000 more troops to Afghanistan, bringing the U.S. total to about 60,000. Given all the changes, Gates said that he and Mullen wanted a new war commander: Army Gen. Stanley McChrystal, a Special Operations warrior who worked for Mullen on the Joint Staff.

On the surface, McKiernan's abrupt removal made little sense. Gates and Mullen were the ones who had put him in the job eleven months earlier. McKiernan had been pleading for more troops and equipment ever since he landed in Afghanistan. Now, with reinforcements finally on the way, he was getting the ax.

But McKiernan had violated an unspoken rule. In the waning days of the Bush administration, he became the first general in Afghanistan to admit the war was going poorly. Unlike other commanding officers, he did not deceive the public with specious language. He told it straight until the end.

In what turned out to be his final press conference in Kabul on May 6, 2009, McKiernan described the war as "stalemated" in the south and "a very tough fight" in the east. Hours later, at a private dinner at military headquarters, Gates told him he was done.

Whether Gates or Mullen intended it or not, they had sent a message to the rest of the U.S. armed forces: They were cashiering the commanding general for telling the truth.

Days prior his firing, McKiernan confided to other officers in Afghanistan that his candid assessments and repeated requests for more troops had upset senior officials at the Pentagon. In a meeting with Army Brig. Gen. John Nicholson, the regional commander in Kandahar, McKiernan said: "We may have done too good of a job explaining how bad it is over here," according to Maj. Fred Tanner, Nicholson's military assistant.

In retrospect, McKiernan must have already known his fate, Tanner said in an Army oral-history interview. "He said it very professionally. He wasn't angry. But now I can look back and reflect that he had just gotten the word."

The change at the top made headlines. But it failed to solve the underlying problems. Instead, it led to more doubt and uncertainty about the erratic U.S. war strategy.

Obama won the election in 2008 after he promised to end the unpopular war in Iraq and pay more attention to the one in Afghanistan. Most Americans at the time still viewed the war in Afghanistan as a just cause because of 9/11.

After he took office, Obama retained Gates—a Republican—as defense secretary and put him in charge of what the president called a new "comprehensive strategy" for Afghanistan. Obama said he would emphasize more diplomacy with Pakistan, where Taliban and al-Qaeda leaders had found sanctuary and rejuvenated their networks. But the new strategy largely resembled the old one. Obama stuck with Bush's plan to contain the insurgency and strengthen the Afghan government until it could fend for itself.

In the field, U.S. troops continued to wrestle with many of the same basic questions that had gone unanswered since 2001. What were their specific goals, benchmarks and objectives? In other words, to what end were they fighting?

By 2009, many soldiers, airmen, sailors and Marines had logged multiple tours of duty in Afghanistan. The war made less sense each time they went back. Years of hunting suspected terrorists had gotten them nowhere. The Taliban kept holding their ground.

"At the time, I was looking at Afghanistan and I was thinking that there has to be more to solving this problem than killing people, because that's what we were doing and every time I went back security was worse," Army Maj. Gen. Edward Reeder, Jr., a Special Operations commander who served six combat tours in Afghanistan, said in a Lessons Learned interview.

Maj. George Lachicotte, born in Caribou, Maine, first deployed to Afghanistan in 2004 as an infantry officer. Five years later, he returned as a team leader with the 7th Special Forces Group, serving under Reeder.

"It was a lot more convoluted. It was a lot harder to tell who was the enemy and who was not," he said in an Army oral-history interview. "Even the guys who were the enemy one day, were not the next."

Partway through his 2009 deployment, as the U.S. military moved troops to reinforce beleaguered NATO forces in southern Afghanistan, Lachicotte's Special Forces team was suddenly reassigned from Helmand province to neighboring Kandahar without much explanation. "There wasn't a clear strategy," he said.

When Alabama native Joseph Claburn first deployed to the war zone in 2001, he was a young Army first lieutenant with the 101st Airborne Division. His unit fought in Operation Anaconda, the last major battle with al-Qaeda forces, in March 2002. By the time he returned to Afghanistan six years later, he had been promoted to major. As a brigade-level staff officer with British forces in Kandahar, he found it hard to visualize how, or when, the fighting might end.

"What does it look like when it comes time for us to leave?" Claburn asked in an Army oral-history interview. "If I was to give you a piece of paper right now and say, 'In order for us to leave, this is what it has to look like,' we could be there for an extremely long time."

Obama's new strategy lasted only a few months. As soon as McChrystal took over as the war commander in June 2009, he ordered yet another review of the war strategy—a clear signal that the conflict had deteriorated further and that he did not think the president's plan would work.

The son of a two-star Army general, McChrystal had served previously in Afghanistan but made his mark in Iraq, where he led a Special Operations task force that hunted down and killed hundreds of insurgent leaders. He had grown close to Army Gen. David Petraeus, the commander of U.S. troops in Iraq and the architect of the Pentagon's counterinsurgency strategy in that country. Petraeus had since been promoted to head of U.S. Central Command, overseeing military operations in the Middle East and Afghanistan. He had recommended McChrystal for the war commander job in Afghanistan.

Both generals nourished public images as cerebral, multitasking, workaholic supermen.

The 56-year-old Petraeus held a doctorate from Princeton and liked to challenge reporters to push-up contests. He answered their questions if they could keep up during his daily five-mile runs.

The 54-year-old McChrystal portrayed himself as an ascetic taskmaster who absorbed audio books while running eight-mile circuits. He had no time for breakfast or lunch. "He pushes himself mercilessly, sleeping four or five hours a night, eating one meal a day," *The New York Times Magazine* gushed in a profile.

Fresh off their experience in Iraq, McChrystal and Petraeus wanted to adopt a counterinsurgency strategy in Afghanistan. Other generals had tried a similar approach in Afghanistan since 2004, but with only a fraction of the troops that McChrystal and Petraeus thought were necessary.

Some Army officers with experience in Afghanistan thought McChrystal, Petraeus and their aides arrogantly assumed they could make their version of counterinsurgency work while ignoring the lessons learned by previous commanders. "It was disappointing to come back in 2009 and hear people, primarily drunk on their Iraq experience, talk about, 'Now I'm going to fix things here in Afghanistan,'" Maj. John Popiak, an intelligence officer with the National Security Agency who deployed three times to Afghanistan between 2005 and 2010, said in an Army oral-history interview. "I personally believe there is sort of a misnomer that good counterinsurgency began somewhere around the time when General McChrystal arrived in Afghanistan."

McChrystal finished his strategy review in August 2009. His classified sixty-six-page report called for a "properly resourced" counterinsurgency campaign. As part of that, he wanted as many as 60,000 more troops—almost double the number he already had. The new war commander also wanted a massive infusion of aid to build up the Afghan government and expand the size of its army and police force. At the same time, he pushed to restrict the U.S. military's rules of engagement to limit civilian casualties in airstrikes and raids, a recurring problem that enraged many Afghans.

But McChrystal's new strategy failed to address other basic flaws that undermined the effort in Afghanistan. In a jarring disconnect, the United States and its allies could not agree whether they were actually fighting a war in Afghanistan, engaged in a peacekeeping operation, leading a training mission, or doing something else. The distinctions were important because some NATO allies were only authorized to engage in combat in self-defense.

"There are big implications with calling this a war," an unnamed senior NATO official who assisted with McChrystal's review said in a Lessons Learned interview. "Legally under international law that has serious implications. So we checked with the legal team and they agree it's not a war." To paper over the problem, McChrystal added a line in his report that described the conflict as "not a war in the conventional sense."

The official U.S. and NATO mission statement was even more convoluted. It said the objective was to "reduce the capability and will of the insurgency, support the growth in capacity and capability of the Afghan National Security Forces (ANSF), and facilitate improvements in governance and socio-economic development, in order to provide a secure environment for sustainable stability that is observable to the population."

McChrystal's strategy glossed over another fundamental question: Who was the enemy?

The first draft of McChrystal's report did not mention al-Qaeda because the group had all but disappeared from Afghanistan, according to the NATO official who helped with the review. "In 2009, the perception was that al-Qaeda was no longer a problem," the NATO official said. "But the entire reason for being in Afghanistan was al-Qaeda. So then the second draft included them."

Even Afghan leaders had a hard time following the logic behind the ever-changing U.S. war strategies.

"I'm confused," Hamid Karzai told Secretary of State Hillary Clinton during a 2009 meeting in Kabul. "I understand what we were supposed to be doing from '01 to '05. It was the war on terror. And then all of a sudden I started hearing people in your government saying that we didn't need to kill bin Laden and Mullah Omar. And I didn't know what that meant."

McChrystal based his new counterinsurgency strategy on some questionable assumptions. It presumed that most Afghans saw the Taliban as oppressors and would side with the Afghan government if it could provide security and reliable public services.

But a substantial number of Afghans, especially in the Pashtun regions in the south and east, sympathized with the Taliban. Many joined the insurgency because they saw the Americans as infidel invaders and the Afghan government as a foreign puppet.

"Taliban presence was a symptom, but we rarely tried to understand what the disease was," an unnamed USAID official said in a Lessons Learned interview. When U.S. and Afghan forces tried to take over insurgent strongholds, they sometimes just made "the cancer worse because we didn't know why the Taliban was there."

In his strategic review, McChrystal also minimized Pakistan's critical influence on the war. His report acknowledged the presence of the Taliban's safe havens in Pakistan but concluded that the United States and NATO could win the war despite the protection and aid the Taliban received from the Pakistani intelligence services.

That judgment put McChrystal at loggerheads with other senior U.S. officials. Among them was Richard Holbrooke, the longtime diplomat who had trashed the Bush administration's war on opium. After the election, Obama named Holbrooke as his special representative for Afghanistan and Pakistan.

Holbrooke had served as a civilian in Vietnam and saw parallels between that war and the one in Afghanistan. "The most important similarity is the fact that in both cases, the enemy had a safe sanctuary in a neighboring country," he told NPR.

Pakistan aside, Holbrooke doubted McChrystal's strategy would work. "He didn't believe in [counterinsurgency], but he knew he would get in trouble if he said that," Barnett Rubin, the Afghan expert who joined Holbrooke's team at the State Department, said in a Lessons Learned interview.

The new U.S. ambassador to Afghanistan also held strong doubts about the merits of McChrystal's plan. Karl Eikenberry, the Mandarin-speaking general, had retired from the Army in spring 2009 to become Obama's top diplomat in Afghanistan. After serving two tours of duty in the war zone, he had grown pessimistic about what he thought the United States could achieve.

In November 2009, Eikenberry sent two classified cables urging the Obama administration to reject McChrystal's counterinsurgency plan. In the cables, Eikenberry warned that "Pakistan will remain the single greatest source of Afghan instability so long as the border sanctuaries remain." He also predicted that if Obama approved McChrystal's request for tens of thousands of additional troops, it would only lead to more violence and "dig us in more deeply."

Faced with dissension in the ranks, the commander in chief tried to thread the needle. In a December 2009 speech at the U.S. Military Academy at West Point, Obama announced he would deploy 30,000 more troops to Afghanistan. With all the forces he and Bush had already authorized, that meant McChrystal would have 100,000 U.S. troops under his command. In addition, NATO members and other allies agreed to increase their forces to 50,000.

But Obama added a wrinkle. He imposed a strict timeline on the mission and said the extra troops would start to come home in eighteen months. The timetable stunned many senior leaders in the Pentagon and the State Department. They thought it was a serious strategic error to commit to a withdrawal schedule in advance and make it public. The Taliban just had to lie low until the U.S. and NATO surge forces left

"The timeline was just sprung on us," Petraeus said in a Lessons Learned interview. "Two days before the president made the speech, on a Sunday, we all got called and were told to be in the Oval Office that night for the president to lay out what he would announce two evenings later. And he laid it out, there it is." Petraeus added, "None of us had heard that before."

"And we were then asked, are you all okay with that? He went around the room and everyone said yes. And it was take it or leave it."

Barnett Rubin, the Afghanistan expert working for Holbrooke, didn't see eye-to-eye with the generals on much. But like Petraeus, he said he was "stupefied" when he heard Obama reveal his timeline during the West Point speech. Rubin understood that Obama wanted to put the Afghan government and the Pentagon on notice that the United States wouldn't fight the war forever. "But there was a mismatch between deadline and strategy," Rubin said in a Lessons Learned interview. "With that deadline, you can't use that strategy."

Instead of resolving the inherent contradictions, Obama administration officials set aside their qualms and presented a unified front in public. They promised the United States would not get bogged down in Afghanistan. Some pledged outright victory.

"The next eighteen months will likely be decisive and ultimately enable success," McChrystal testified at a Senate hearing in December 2009. "In fact, we are going to win. We and the Afghan government are going to win."

But doubts persisted among the troops on the front lines.

Maj. Jeremy Smith, the Army quartermaster whose unit installed the first showerheads at Bagram Air Base shortly after the war began, returned in February 2010 for a year-long tour of duty. He barely recognized Bagram, which had transformed into a medium-sized city, though it emitted the same "unique" smell. "I can't describe the smell other than you'd know it if you were there," he said in an Army oral-history interview.

But Smith saw no strategic accomplishments after nearly a decade of war. "Been there, done that," he said he thought to himself. "I was there at the beginning. I'm here now. Wow. This whole situation should be a lot further along on the road than it is."

Maj. Jason Liddell, an Army intelligence officer who served at Bagram from November 2009 until June 2010, said he and his soldiers followed orders and did their jobs without flinching. But he said neither he nor senior U.S. commanders could explain to anyone's satisfaction why they were putting American lives at risk and what they were trying to achieve.

"I have had the pleasure of working with a bunch of soldiers, great Americans, and the biggest questions these young soldiers ask: 'Hey sir, why the hell are we doing this?'" Liddell said in an Army oral-history interview.

"I have a difficult time answering this because I can give them the written answer, but when I go back and look at it myself and do a sanity check on it, it doesn't always make sense," he added. "If I can't make sense of it as a leader after some 'no kidding' soul searching and doing some good logical critical thinking, then I have to question if our leaders are doing some logical critical thinking."

At first, Obama administration officials counseled patience and said it would take at least a year to determine whether the troop surge and McChrystal's strategy were working. But after a few months, they couldn't resist proclaiming success.

"The evidence suggests that our shift in approach is beginning to produce results," Michèle Flournoy, Obama's under secretary of defense for policy, told the House Armed Services Committee in May 2010. She cited "signs of progress" with the Afghan security forces and said she was "cautiously optimistic." The insurgency, she added, was "losing momentum."

"When do we declare victory?" asked Rep. Ike Skelton (D-Mo.), the committee chairman.

"I believe we are achieving success," Flournoy replied. "We are on the right road for the first time in a long time."

The upbeat declarations were premature. U.S. casualties soared and would soon reach a peak, with 496 U.S. troops dying in 2010—more than the previous two years combined.

Meanwhile, a major offensive that spring by 15,000 U.S., NATO and Afghan troops to seize control of the city of Marja, a drug-smuggling hub in Helmand province, hit unexpectedly ferocious resistance from a much smaller force of Taliban fighters. McChrystal called the drawn-out campaign "a bleeding ulcer." Plans to secure Kandahar province—the Taliban's historical stronghold—ran into repeated delays.

In June 2010, Flournoy returned to Congress to testify before the Senate Armed Services Committee. She acknowledged "challenges" in the war but remained steadfastly positive. "We believe we have been making gradual but important progress," she said.

Also testifying at the Senate hearing was Petraeus. The committee's vice chairman, Sen. John McCain (R-Ariz.), grilled the general about whether he concurred with Obama's eighteen-month timetable for withdrawing troops. Petraeus started to answer, but suddenly slumped forward and collapsed head-first onto the witness table.

"Oh my God," McCain gasped.

Petraeus passed out briefly but recovered after a few moments. He said he was just dehydrated and returned the next day to resume his testimony. But it seemed like a metaphor for how the war was really going.

A week later, another general fell flat on his face.

Rolling Stone magazine published a long profile of McChrystal titled "The Runaway General" and quoted the commander and his staff making a string of backbiting, catty remarks about Obama, Holbrooke and other senior administration officials. One anonymous McChrystal aide mocked Vice President Joseph Biden by referring to him as "Bite Me." Obama fired McChrystal for insubordination, making him the second war commander in thirteen months to lose the job.

The president replaced him with Petraeus. For the third time in two weeks, Petraeus stood before the Senate Armed Services Committee to answer questions about the war, this time for his confirmation hearing as the new commander of U.S. and NATO forces in Afghanistan.

Petraeus said he still believed they were making progress. But he sounded subdued as he acknowledged the recent setbacks. "It is a roller-coaster existence," he said.

CHAPTER THIRTEEN

"A Dark Pit of Endless Money"

Barack Obama knew his December 1, 2009, speech about Afghanistan would be one of the most important of his presidency. After months of agonizing deliberations, he had decided to boost the number of U.S. troops in the war zone to 100,000, triple the number from when he took office. He needed a solemn backdrop to deliver his remarks and chose the Military Academy at West Point, the 207-year-old training ground for Army officers in upstate New York.

After supper, about 4,000 cadets in their gray-wool uniforms filed into dimly lit Eisenhower Hall, the performing arts center on the west bank of the Hudson River, to hear what their commander in chief had in store for them. In his thirty-three-minute address, Obama announced the troop surge and tried to be frank without sounding hopeless.

"Afghanistan is not lost, but for several years it has moved backwards," he told the cadets. "I know that this decision asks even more of you—a military that, along with your families, has already borne the heaviest of all burdens."

At the same time, Obama had another message for a different audience: the tens of millions of Americans who were watching his speech live on national television. Economically frail, the United States was recovering from its most brutal recession since the 1930s. The unemployment rate had peaked that fall at 10 percent. Obama was expanding the war, but he tried to reassure the public that he was mindful of the cost.

"We can't simply afford to ignore the price of these wars," he said, noting that the Bush administration had spent $1 trillion in Iraq and Afghanistan. "The American people are understandably focused on rebuilding our economy and putting people to work here at home."

Obama said he opposed a drawn-out "nation-building project" in Afghanistan and promised to cap the gusher of war spending as soon as possible. "The days of providing a blank check are over," he declared. "Our troop commitment in Afghanistan cannot be open-ended, because the nation that I'm most interested in building is our own."

But the United States would keep signing one blank check after another.

The cornerstone of the Obama administration's counterinsurgency strategy was to strengthen the Afghan government and economy. Obama and his generals hoped the Afghan people would choke off popular support for the Taliban if they believed Hamid Karzai's government could protect them and deliver basic services.

Yet there were two big hurdles. First, eighteen months was not much time for the counterinsurgency strategy to succeed. Second, the Afghan government still had no presence in much of the country. As a result, the Obama administration and Congress ordered the military, the State Department, USAID and their contractors to bolster and expand the reach of the Afghan government as quickly as possible. Troops and aid workers constructed schools, hospitals, roads, soccer fields—anything that might win loyalty from the populace, with little concern for expense.

Spending in the destitute country skyrocketed to unimaginable heights. In two years, annual U.S. reconstruction aid to Afghanistan nearly tripled, from $6 billion in 2008 to $17 billion in 2010. At that point, the U.S. government was pumping roughly as much money into Afghanistan as the undeveloped country's economy produced on its own.

In retrospect, aid workers and military officials said it was a colossal misjudgment. In its rush to spend, the U.S. government drenched Afghanistan with far more money than it could absorb.

"During the surge there were massive amounts of people and money going into Afghanistan," David Marsden, a former USAID official, said in a Lessons Learned interview. "It's like pouring a lot of water into a funnel; if you pour it too fast, the water overflows the funnel onto the ground. We were flooding the ground."

U.S. officials wasted huge sums on projects that Afghans did not need or did not want. Much of the money ended up in the pockets of overpriced contractors or corrupt Afghan officials, while U.S.-financed schools, clinics and roads fell into disrepair due to poor construction or maintenance—if they were built at all.

One unnamed USAID official estimated that 90 percent of what they spent was overkill. "We lost objectivity. We were given money, told to spend it and we did, without reason," he said in a Lessons Learned interview.

Another aid contractor said officials in Washington expected him to dole out roughly $3 million daily for projects in a single Afghan district roughly the size of a U.S. county. In a Lessons Learned interview, he recalled once asking a visiting congressman whether the lawmaker could responsibly spend that kind of money back home. "He said hell no. 'Well, sir, that's what you just obligated us to spend and I'm doing it for communities that live in mud huts with no windows.'"

Lt. Gen. Douglas Lute, who served in the White House as Obama's war policy czar, said the United States lavished money on dams and highways just "to show we could spend it," fully aware that the Afghans, among the poorest and least educated people in the world, could not maintain the massive projects once they were completed.

"Once in a while, okay, we can overspend," Lute said in a Lessons Learned interview. "We are a rich country and can pour money down a hole and it doesn't bust the bank. But should we? Can't we get a bit more rational about this?"

He recalled attending a ribbon-cutting ceremony—complete with a giant scissors—for a fancy new district police headquarters that the United States built "in some God-forsaken province." The U.S. Army Corps of Engineers oversaw the construction of the building, which featured a glass façade and an atrium. But it immediately became apparent that the Americans hadn't bothered to ask the Afghans what they thought of the design.

"The police chief couldn't even open the door," Lute said. "He had never seen a doorknob like this. To me, this encapsulates the whole experience in Afghanistan."

The U.S. government approved so many projects that it could not keep track of them all. Turnover among USAID staff and its contractors was so high that the people who drew up the plans rarely stuck around to see them through to completion. Follow-up inspections were sporadic, in part because civilian aid workers needed military escorts to move around the country.

When it came to economics, the United States often treated Afghanistan like a theoretical case study instead of applying common sense. Government donors insisted that a large portion of aid be spent on education even though Afghanistan—a nation of subsistence farmers— had few jobs for graduates.

"We were building schools next to empty schools, and it just didn't make sense," an unnamed adviser to a Special Forces team said in a Lessons Learned interview. He said local Afghans made clear "they didn't really want schools. They said they wanted their kids out herding goats."

In some cases, U.S. agencies wasted money on phantom projects.

In October 2009, Tim Graczewski, a lieutenant in the Navy Reserve, took leave from his full-time civilian job with Intuit, a Silicon Valley business-software firm, and deployed to Kandahar Air Field to oversee economic development projects in southern Afghanistan. One of his tasks was to hunt for a thirty-seven-acre project that appeared only on paper.

Before his arrival, the U.S. government had signed about $8 million in contracts to build an industrial park for forty-eight businesses near Kandahar. But after reviewing the files, Graczewski could not figure out where the industrial park was, or if it even existed.

"It blew my mind how much we didn't know about the park in the first place when we embarked on this project," he said in a Lessons

Learned interview. "It was impossible to get info on it, even where it was located. It was that much of a blank spot. Nobody knew anything." It took him a few months to finally pinpoint the property and arrange a visit. There were no buildings—only some empty streets and sewer pipes.

"Don't know who did it, but figured it was there, so let's try to use it," Graczewski recalled. Despite efforts to revive the project, it "fell apart" after he left in 2010. U.S. auditors visited the site four years later and found it largely deserted. A single company, an ice cream packing outfit, was open for business.

The U.S. government had intended for the industrial park to benefit from an even more ambitious nation-building project—the electrification of Kandahar, Afghanistan's second-biggest city, and its surrounding areas.

Because of a primitive electrical grid, Kandahar suffered from a scarcity of power. U.S. military commanders saw an opportunity. If they could generate a reliable flow of electricity, the theory went, grateful Kandaharis would support the Afghan government and turn against the Taliban.

To do that, the U.S. military wanted to rebuild the aging hydroelectric power station at the Kajaki Dam, about 100 miles north of Kandahar. USAID had built the dam in the 1950s and installed turbines in the 1970s, but the power station crumbled from years of war and neglect.

Since 2004, the U.S. government had been trying to jump-start the project and add capacity but had made little progress. The Taliban controlled the area surrounding the dam, as well as some transmission lines. Repair crews needed armed convoys or helicopters to access the site.

Despite the risks, by 2010, U.S. generals were lobbying to invest hundreds of millions of additional dollars into the project, calling it a critical part of their counterinsurgency strategy. Some development experts argued that it made no sense to finance a giant construction project in enemy territory. They noted that the Afghans lacked the technical expertise to maintain it in the long run. They also questioned whether it would really help win the hearts and minds of Afghans accustomed to life without central power.

"Why did we think providing electricity to communities in Kandahar, who had no concept of what to do with it, would convince them to abandon the Taliban?" a senior USAID official said in a Lessons Learned interview.

In the end, the generals won the argument. Ryan Crocker, who had served briefly in Afghanistan at the start of the Bush administration, returned in 2011 to become the U.S. ambassador. He had deep misgivings about the dam project but approved a portion of it anyway. "I made the decision to go ahead with it, but I was sure it was never going to work," Crocker said in a Lessons Learned interview. "The biggest lesson learned for me is, don't do major infrastructure projects."

That was not a lesson the generals wanted to learn. In fact, the dam project was just the beginning.

The turbines and power station at the dam would take years to fix. With the clock ticking on their counterinsurgency strategy, U.S. military commanders wanted to supply electricity to the Kandaharis right away. So they drew up a temporary plan to buy giant diesel-fueled generators that could start humming in a matter of months, not years. It was a horribly inefficient and costly way to generate electricity for an entire city. Expenses would run to $256 million over five years, mostly for fuel. Again, critics complained that the plan defied logic.

In a Lessons Learned interview, an unidentified NATO official said he was given the task of trying to secure financing for the generators from international donors but got nowhere. "Anyone who looked at this more closely could see that the math didn't add up, that it was all nonsense," he said. "We went to the World Bank [and] they didn't want to touch it . . . People look at it and they think it's crazy."

By December 2018, the U.S. government had spent $775 million on the dam, the diesel generators and other electrical projects in Kandahar and neighboring Helmand province, according to a federal audit.

Power generation at the dam nearly tripled, but the project never made sense economically. In 2018, USAID admitted that the Afghan public utility for Kandahar would always need foreign subsidies.

Jeffrey Eggers, a Navy SEAL who served in Afghanistan and worked as a White House staffer for Bush and Obama, said that such projects failed to achieve their objective. In a Lessons Learned interview, he raised what he called the "bigger" question: "Why does the U.S. undertake actions that are beyond its abilities?" he said. "This question gets at strategy and human psychology, and it is a hard question to answer."

Under both Bush and Obama, U.S. officials steadfastly avoided the term "nation-building." Everybody knew they were doing it, but there was an unspoken rule against admitting it in public.

One of the few who did was Gen. David Petraeus.

Six months after Obama's West Point speech, Petraeus appeared before the House Armed Services Committee to answer questions about how the war was going. Rep. Carol Shea-Porter, a Democrat from New Hampshire, asked the general point-blank whether the United States was nation-building in Afghanistan.

"We are indeed," Petraeus replied.

The congresswoman sounded taken aback by the confession. "Well, let me just say that I've heard over and over again that we are not nation-building, that we are here, you know, in Afghanistan for a different reason," she said.

But Petraeus stood his ground. He said a key part of the strategy "clearly can be described as nation-building. I'm just not going to evade it and play rhetorical games."

The U.S. military's counterinsurgency doctrine treated money—the most important ingredient in nation-building—as a powerful weapon of war. Battlefield commanders thought they could win support from Afghans by funding public-works projects or hiring locals through cash-for-labor programs.

In 2009, the Army published a handbook titled, *Commander's Guide to Money as a Weapons System*. The introduction quoted a remark by Petraeus when he was a two-star general fighting in Iraq: "Money is my most important ammunition in this war."

From a commander's perspective, it was better to spend that ammunition quickly than wisely. Normally, USAID studied project proposals for months or years to ensure they would bring long-lasting benefits. But the U.S. military could not afford to wait that long. It was trying to win the war. "Petraeus was hell-bent on throwing money at the problem," an unnamed U.S. military officer said in a Lessons Learned interview. "When Petraeus was around, all that mattered was spending. He wanted to put Afghans to work."

In a Lessons Learned interview, Petraeus acknowledged the spend-thrift strategy. But he said the U.S. military had no choice given Obama's order to start reversing the troop surge after eighteen months.

"What drove spending was the need to solidify gains as quickly as we could knowing that we had a tight drawdown timeline," he said. "And we wound up spending faster than we would have if we felt we had forces longer than we did."

The nation-building campaign depended on military and civilian personnel from the U.S. government, as well as private subcontractors, working together to coordinate projects. In practice, the different groups clashed constantly.

The Pentagon's insistence on speed put it at odds with USAID and others in the State Department, which struggled to find enough staffers willing to go to Afghanistan. In the field, military commanders often viewed USAID personnel and contractors as slow-moving bureaucrats who were content to collect a paycheck while the troops did most of the work.

In Khost province in eastern Afghanistan, Army Col. Brian Copes led a team of Indiana National Guardsmen that worked on agribusiness projects and taught villagers modern techniques for pruning their fruit trees. He said the Afghan farmers were a century behind the times but that the pushback, resistance and criticism he received from U.S. civilian aid workers frustrated him more than anything.

"Some of them just had a certain elitist bias, really looked down their noses at people in uniform as a bunch of knuckle-dragging Neanderthals," he said in an Army oral-history interview.

The civilians complained that the military stereotyped them as timid paper pushers who didn't understand the urgency of the mission. "We were always chasing the dragon—always behind, never good enough in the military's eyes," an unidentified senior USAID official said in a Lessons Learned interview.

They also grumbled that people in uniform dismissed their views about the value of specific projects. An unnamed former State Department official said he got "the shit kicked out of me" by military officials after he questioned the wisdom of building a highway in a hostile district in Kandahar. "So we'd go see it and we'd fly in and get shot at," he said in a Lessons Learned interview. "Think about that. We were supposed to build roads in an area so dangerous that armed U.S. military helicopters could not even land near it."

Afghan officials said they were also baffled by military commanders' insistence on building projects in hard-to-reach areas that remained under Taliban influence.

Barna Karimi, a former Afghan deputy minister for local governance, said the Americans badgered him to send teams of Afghan civil servants to Garmsir, a district in Helmand, after U.S. Marines cleared the area of insurgents. He said the Marines didn't care that the Taliban still controlled the main roads leading into the district.

"They started shouting, 'We have cleared Garmsir, come here and establish the government administration,'" Karimi said in a Lessons Learned interview. "I used to tell them that I am not coming, because I cannot travel there by road. You are going there by helicopters. I cannot take all my staff there by plane. How is my clerk able to go [there]? He will be kidnapped on his way in."

Safiullah Baran, an Afghan who worked for USAID as a project manager, said the Americans were so intent on building things that they paid little attention to who was benefiting. He said the Taliban once sabotaged a bridge in Laghman, a rural province in eastern Afghanistan. U.S. officials were eager to replace it. Within a week they hired an Afghan construction firm to erect another one.

It turned out that the owner of the construction firm had a brother who was in the local wing of the Taliban. Together, they had built a thriving business: the Taliban brother blew up U.S. projects, and then the unwitting Americans paid his sibling to rebuild them.

USAID officials blamed the U.S. military for being in a rush and said its whole approach was backward. They said it would have made more sense to focus first on projects in peaceful provinces to solidify their allegiance to the central government, and then gradually expand the work into more turbulent areas.

"Why not make an example of stable areas to make others envious?" one unidentified U.S. official asked in a Lessons Learned interview. "Afghans are some of the most jealous people I've ever met, but we didn't take advantage of that or leverage it. Instead, we built schools in areas that are too dangerous for kids to leave the house."

Mammoth civic works contributed to the failure of the nation-building campaign. But smaller projects also fueled the frenzy of spending. Many originated with a military program called the Commanders' Emergency Response Program, or CERP.

Authorized by Congress, CERP allowed military commanders in the field to bypass normal contracting rules and spend up to $1 million on infrastructure projects, though the cost of most projects was less than $50,000 each.

Commanders were under so much pressure to spend that they blindly copied CERP paperwork from past projects, knowing that it was unlikely anyone would notice. One military officer said a photo of the same health clinic appeared in about a hundred different project reports for clinics around the country.

An Army civil-affairs officer who served in eastern Afghanistan said in a Lessons Learned interview that he often saw CERP proposals that referred to "sheikhs"—a giveaway that they were cut-and-pasted from reconstruction projects in Iraq. "Sheikh" is an Arabic title of respect but is generally not used in Afghanistan.

At one point, the Army officer recalled telling soldiers in his brigade that if they could not show that a CERP project would be beneficial, "then the smartest thing to do is nothing." In response, he said: "I got crickets. 'We can't build nothing,' they said. I told them we might as well throw our money away."

Copes, the Indiana National Guard officer who served as a civil-affairs commander in Khost province in eastern Afghanistan, likened the flood of aid to "crack cocaine," calling it "an addiction that affected every agency." In a Lessons Learned interview, he said he came across a U.S.-built greenhouse that cost $30,000 and had fallen into disuse because the Afghans could not maintain it. His unit built a replacement greenhouse out of iron rebar that worked better and cost only $55—despite pressure to spend far more.

"Congress gives us money to spend and expects us to spend all of it," Copes said. "The attitude became, 'We don't care what you do with the money as long as you spend it.'"

Despite its best efforts, the U.S. military spent only two-thirds of the $3.7 billion that Congress funded for CERP, according to Defense Department figures. Of the $2.3 billion it did spend, the Pentagon was able to provide financial details for only about $890 million worth of projects, according to a 2015 audit.

In Lessons Learned interviews, officials from other agencies were appalled by the waste and mismanagement. "CERP was nothing but walking-around money," said Ken Yamashita, the USAID mission director for Afghanistan from 2011 to 2014, likening the payments to cash handouts for votes. An unidentified NATO official called the program "a dark pit of endless money for anything with no accountability."

Of all the flaws with the Afghanistan nation-building campaign—the waste, the inefficiency, the half-baked ideas—nothing confounded U.S. officials more than the fact that they could never tell whether any of it was actually helping them win the war.

An Army officer assigned to U.S. military headquarters in Kabul during the surge said it was hard enough to track whether CERP projects were really built. "We wanted hard quantitative metrics that would tell us that X project is producing the desired outcomes, but we had a hard time defining those metrics," he said in a Lessons Learned interview. "We had no idea how to measure if [a] hospital's existence was reducing support for the Taliban. That was always the last ten yards that we couldn't run."

The U.S. government's unfamiliarity with Afghan culture doomed even the most well-intentioned projects. Tooryalai Wesa, who served as governor of Kandahar province from 2008 to 2015, said U.S. aid workers once insisted on carrying out a public-health project to teach Afghans how to wash their hands. "It was an insult to the people. Here people wash their hands five times a day for prayers," Wesa said in a Lessons Learned interview. "Moreover, hand wash project is not needed."

He said a better program would have provided jobs or a skill to earn money. But those kinds of projects could backfire too. For one project in Kandahar, U.S. and Canadian troops paid villagers $90 to $100 a month to clear irrigation canals, according to Thomas Johnson, a specialist on Afghanistan and a professor at the Naval Postgraduate School who served as a counterinsurgency adviser to the Canadians.

Eventually, the troops realized their program was indirectly disrupting local schools. Teachers in the area earned much less, only $60 to $80 a month. "So initially all the schoolteachers quit their jobs and joined the ditch diggers," Johnson said in a Lessons Learned interview.

In eastern Afghanistan, one gung-ho Army brigade was so determined to improve public education that it promised to build fifty schools—but inadvertently ended up helping the Taliban, according to an officer involved in the project. "There weren't enough teachers to fill them, so buildings languished," the unnamed U.S. military officer said in a Lessons Learned interview, "and some of them even became bomb-making factories."

A girl plays with a clothesline in the ruins of a Soviet-built theater in 2005. Desperately poor and its infrastructure in tatters, Afghanistan had been consumed by continuous warfare since the Soviet invasion in 1979.

Afghan police trainees walk to their rooms at a police academy in Kabul in May 2004. The United States and NATO bungled early attempts to create a national police force. In a 2005 memo, Rumsfeld called the training program a mess and said he was "ready to toss in the towel."

A helicopter used by an Afghan drug interdiction team lands during an operation in Nangahar province in eastern Afghanistan in May 2006. Opium production soared after the war began in 2001. The United States spent $9 billion on a dizzying array of programs in a futile attempt to deter Afghanistan from supplying the world with heroin.

British Marines take cover while blasting a hole in a wall during an assault on a Taliban-held village near the Kajaki Dam in March 2007. The United States and its NATO allies spent hundreds of millions of dollars to fix and upgrade the hydroelectric dam in an ill-fated attempt to supply electricity to Helmand and Kandahar provinces.

A farmer watches as Afghan police eradicate poppy fields in Badakhshan province in June 2006. The United States and its NATO ally, Britain, tried a range of strategies to curtail opium production. They paid farmers to stop cultivating poppies, hired mercenaries to destroy crops and drew up plans to spray defoliants from the sky. None of it worked.

Army Spec. Brandon Olson leans against an embankment in a bunker at Outpost Restrepo in the Korengal Valley in eastern Afghanistan in September 2007. U.S. soldiers arrived in the Korengal in 2005 to clear out al-Qaeda and Taliban fighters. The small stretch of land generated some of the deadliest firefights and ambushes of the war.

Afghan security forces carry a wounded soldier to a U.S. medevac helicopter after a Taliban ambush near the village of Tsunek in Kunar province in March 2010. U.S. casualties peaked in 2010, when 496 troops lost their lives.

Cadets at the U.S. Military Academy at West Point listen as President Barack Obama announces his plan to expand the war in a December 1, 2009, speech in Eisenhower Hall. Obama ordered the deployment of 30,000 more troops, boosting the size of the U.S. force to 100,000.

Campaign leaflets dropped from a helicopter flutter to the ground as supporters of Afghan presidential candidate Abdullah Abdullah cheer during a political rally at a Kabul stadium in August 2009. Hamid Karzai won reelection but the vote was discredited by massive fraud. A U.N.-backed investigative panel determined that Karzai received about 1 million illegal votes, a quarter of all that were cast.

Hagi Zahir, an official in the town of Marja in Helmand province, meets with local elders in March 2010 after U.S. Marines seized control of the area from the Taliban. Initially hailed as a success, the military operation and subsequent efforts by the Afghan government failed to stabilize the region. Large parts of Helmand were reclaimed by insurgent forces.

Afghan currency traders exchange piles of cash in a money market in Kabul in May 2009. The Obama administration flooded Afghanistan with tens of billions of dollars in aid and defense contracts, which exacerbated already staggering levels of corruption.

The remains of Army Specialist Christopher Griffin of Kincheloe, Michigan, arrive in a transfer case at Dover Air Force Base in Delaware in October 2009. Griffin, 24, was one of eight soldiers killed when a large force of Taliban fighters attacked Combat Outpost Keating in Nuristan province.

CHAPTER FOURTEEN

From Friend to Foe

Wearing a green-and-blue silk Uzbek cape and a gray lambskin hat, Hamid Karzai looked splendid as usual for his November 19, 2009, inauguration at the presidential palace in Kabul. His closely trimmed beard had gone wholly gray since his last swearing-in, five years earlier. But the 51-year-old sounded like the same model statesman in his acceptance speech as he extolled good governance, women's rights and his country's friendship with the United States.

"The people of Afghanistan will never forget the sacrifices made by American soldiers to bring peace to Afghanistan," he said. "With the help of the Almighty God, Afghanistan will be in the possession of a strong democratic order for the next five years."

About 800 diplomats and other VIPs gathered in the palace to applaud the historic moment. Once again, millions of Afghans had defied the threat of violence to cast ballots for a democratic government.

In the front row, Secretary of State Hillary Clinton looked elegant herself, wrapped in an embroidered black-and-red floral coat she had purchased in Afghanistan. Beaming, she nodded in approval when Karzai bowed toward her at the close of his speech. Afterward, Clinton told reporters she was "heartened" by Karzai's remarks. "So many brave Americans are serving here because we believe that we can make progress," she said.

But the smiles and good feelings were all a show. Behind the scenes, Karzai and the Americans had angrily turned on one another.

As everyone attending his inauguration knew, Karzai had stolen the election three months earlier. Though Washington once celebrated him as a paragon of liberty and freedom, his supporters had committed fraud on an epic scale by stuffing ballot boxes and fixing vote totals. A U.N.-backed investigative panel determined that Karzai had received about one million illegal votes, a quarter of all those cast.

The rupture between Karzai and the United States jeopardized the alliance and came at the worst possible time in the war: just as Obama prepared to send 30,000 more U.S. troops to Afghanistan.

After eight years of fighting, it was difficult enough to justify an expansion of the conflict. Now Obama wanted U.S. troops and American taxpayers to make further sacrifices for a resentful foreign leader who had cheated his way to reelection.

But Obama and his administration had helped create the election debacle.

By the time Obama took office in January 2009, many U.S. officials from both parties had soured on Karzai. They faulted the Afghan leader for allowing corruption to fester and belittled him as weak and indecisive.

Richard Holbrooke, Obama's special envoy for Afghanistan and Pakistan, particularly disliked Karzai and barely concealed his contempt from the start. "Richard Holbrooke hated Hamid Karzai. He thought he was corrupt as hell," Barnett Rubin, the Afghan academic expert whom Holbrooke had hired as an adviser, said in a Lessons Learned interview.

Karzai retained broad popular appeal in Afghanistan and was favored to win reelection. But Holbrooke and other U.S. officials stirred things up by openly meeting with Karzai's rivals and encouraging them to run for president as well. Holbrooke hoped a large field would prevent Karzai from winning a majority and force him into a runoff, where he would be more vulnerable against a single challenger.

The U.S. scheming galled Karzai, who saw it as treachery. Realizing he could no longer trust the Americans, he scrambled to expand his political base and cut deals with old foes from different ethnic groups.

Much to the dismay of human-rights groups, Karzai tapped Gen. Mohammed Fahim Khan, the giggling Tajik warlord, as his vice-presidential running mate. He negotiated an endorsement from Gen. Abdul Rashid Dostum, the accused war criminal, who controlled a large bloc of Uzbek votes. As further insurance of victory, Karzai stacked Afghanistan's election oversight commission with his cronies.

Some U.S. officials said the Obama administration should have realized that its gamesmanship with Karzai would backfire. "The reason Karzai made deals with the warlords and engaged in fraud in the election was that, unlike the previous election, when we had supported him, he knew we'd walked away from him, so he basically said the hell with you," Robert Gates, the defense secretary, said in his University of Virginia oral-history interview.

One month after Karzai's inauguration, Gates attended a meeting of NATO defense ministers in Brussels. He sat next to Kai Eide, a Norwegian diplomat who served as the U.N. Secretary-General's special representative to Afghanistan. The pair were friendly and had known each other for years. Before Eide delivered his status report on Afghanistan, he leaned over and whispered a message to Gates: "I am going to tell the ministers that there was blatant foreign interference in the Afghan election," Eide said. "What I will not say is it was the United States and Richard Holbrooke."

*   *   *

In the beginning, Washington's affinity for Karzai seemed limitless.

The son of an Afghan parliamentarian, Karzai belonged to the Popalzai tribe, a clan from the scrublands in Kandahar province. He attended high school in Kabul with other Afghan elites in the 1970s and furthered his education in India, where he polished his English. He became involved in politics and served briefly as a deputy foreign minister during the early 1990s, but the slight, balding, poetry-loving intellectual largely avoided the battlefield during Afghanistan's civil wars.

On 9/11, Karzai was living in exile in Pakistan. The CIA had previously cultivated a limited relationship with him because of his opposition to the Taliban and their bond soon intensified.

Though Karzai lacked credentials as a guerrilla, the spy agency encouraged him to cross into southern Afghanistan in October 2001 to lead an uprising against the Taliban as the U.S. Air Force began dropping bombs. Weeks later, the CIA dispatched a helicopter to rescue Karzai when he became pinned down in a skirmish. A CIA paramilitary officer and a Special Forces team stayed by his side after that.

After the fall of the Taliban that winter, Afghanistan desperately needed a leader who could unite its belligerent factions. Karzai emerged as the consensus choice inside and outside the country. He was a Pashtun yet acceptable to the Tajik, Uzbek and Hazara strongmen who led the Northern Alliance.

He also drew support from all the foreign powers that gathered in Germany at the Bonn conference to help the Afghans plot their future. James Dobbins, the U.S. diplomat who guided the summit, said Pakistan's ISI spy agency first floated Karzai's name as a potential leader. Russia, Iran and the United States also approved—a rare moment of agreement among historic rivals.

"Karzai was telegenic and cooperative and moderate and broadly popular," Dobbins said in a diplomatic oral-history interview. "So he had an unusual ability to win the confidence of a wide variety of disparate governments and individuals."

He also grew increasingly beholden to the Americans. While the Bonn conference unfolded, Karzai remained in southern Afghanistan to help with mop-up operations against the Taliban. On December 5, 2001, a U.S. Air Force B-52 mistakenly dropped a bomb on his camp in Kandahar.

A CIA officer, Greg "Spider" Vogle, dove on top of Karzai to shield him from the explosion. Both men survived, though three U.S. soldiers and five Afghans were killed.

Hours after the blast, Karzai's satellite phone rang. It was Lyse Doucet, a BBC journalist in Kabul whom he had known for years. The

BBC had broadcast a news bulletin that the Bonn delegates had named Karzai as the interim head of Afghanistan's government.

"Hamid, what's your reaction to being chosen as the new leader?" she shouted over the static-filled connection.

This was news to Karzai. "Are you sure?" he asked. Doucet assured him she was.

"That's nice," Karzai replied. He did not mention that he had just narrowly escaped death.

A few weeks later, Karzai moved into the presidential palace. He knew he was entirely dependent on the Americans. In charge of a country in ruins, he had no security forces, no bureaucracy and no resources.

"Just a cold, drafty palace to try and preside over," Ryan Crocker, who served as acting U.S. ambassador in early 2002, said in a University of Virginia oral-history interview.

Karzai invited Crocker to breakfast at the palace almost every day, offering a spread of freshly baked bread, cheese, honey and olives. Crocker jumped at the chance for a homemade meal; the U.S. embassy only had packets of nonperishable military rations. But he also knew that Karzai faced thousands of decisions—big and small—and hungered for guidance.

One morning, Karzai brought up something unexpectedly.

"We need a flag," he said. "What do you think it should look like?"

"That's up to you," Crocker replied.

Karzai took out a napkin and started sketching a black, red and green flag with the national emblem—an image of a mosque—in the center.

"The traditional colors, that means something to people," Karzai explained as he drew. "We got to accept that we are the Islamic Republic of Afghanistan, so we need to work in God somewhere."

Presto! A new flag for a reborn country—doodled on a napkin.

Crocker admired Karzai for his personal courage and his determination to govern Afghanistan as a nation instead of as a feuding collection of tribes. But he questioned whether Karzai had the political instincts and capacity to rule effectively.

Among his many duties, Karzai needed to handpick new governors for each of the country's thirty-four provinces. "And he would ask me,

'Who should be governor of Ghazni?' Like I had a clue," Crocker said. "And he made some really bad choices."

Karzai entrusted his life to the Americans. Taliban gunmen had assassinated his father in 1999 outside a mosque in Quetta, Pakistan. He knew the Taliban would redouble its efforts to kill him, too, but he lacked a reliable security force of his own. For his first few years in office, the U.S. government assigned a security detail to guard him around the clock.

His enemies constantly had him in their sights. In September 2002, a Taliban infiltrator wearing an Afghan police uniform took aim at Karzai as he leaned out of a vehicle to greet supporters in Kandahar. The would-be assassin squeezed off four rounds before he was killed by U.S. Special Forces. Karzai avoided injury. But it was another close call.

By October 2004, Afghanistan had stabilized enough to hold its first national election to choose a head of state. More than eight million people braved threats from the Taliban and a giant sandstorm in Kabul to cast ballots. Karzai won easily with 55 percent of the vote, beating a crowded field of seventeen other candidates.

International observers judged the election free and fair. From the U.S. perspective, the Bush administration could not have hoped for a better political outcome to the war it had launched three years earlier. Hard-luck Afghanistan, once a communist vassal state, had transformed into a democracy and its grateful leader felt indebted to the United States.

In December 2004, Rumsfeld and Cheney flew to Kabul to attend Karzai's inaugural ceremony. Afterward, Rumsfeld raved about the event in a snowflake to Bush. "It was a day I will never forget," Rumsfeld wrote, recapping how he and Cheney met with a rhapsodic Karzai right before the swearing-in. "He said, 'Now life is working. Before the U.S. came to Afghanistan, we were like a still-life picture; when you arrived, everything came to life. With your help, we have come so far.'"

The Bush administration designated Zalmay Khalilzad, the Afghan-American diplomat, as its primary Karzai-charmer. Like Karzai, he was a Pashtun and the pair had known each other since the 1990s. The relationship intensified when Bush appointed Khalilzad as his special envoy to Afghanistan in 2002 and named him as U.S. ambassador one year later.

Khalilzad spoke with Karzai multiple times a day and dined with him at the palace almost every evening. Unlike most Afghans, Karzai was punctual. Supper started precisely at 7:30 p.m. and he expected his guests to arrive thirty minutes early. The menu rarely changed: either chicken or lamb with rice, plus two vegetables. Afterward, they chatted for hours. By the time Khalilzad got back to the embassy, it was often past midnight.

In 2005, the Bush administration decided to send Khalilzad to Baghdad to deal with the turmoil there as U.S. ambassador to Iraq. Karzai personally pleaded with White House officials to allow Khalilzad to remain in his post in Afghanistan, to no avail. At that point, U.S. officials had plenty of confidence in Karzai and saw him as an archetypal leader.

"When I went to Iraq, Karzai was so popular," Khalilzad recalled in a Lessons Learned interview. He said White House officials half-jokingly asked him, "'Why can't you try to find a Karzai-type figure in Iraq?'"

But Karzai felt abandoned. He was accustomed to unceasing reassurance from the Americans. The Bush administration, for its part, wanted to normalize the relationship with an ambassador who would not have to dine with Karzai every day. Both sides struggled to adjust.

Marin Strmecki, the Pentagon adviser, said Karzai needed to spend hours talking through his leadership dilemmas before he felt comfortable making tough decisions. It required a lot of hand-holding.

Khalilzad's successors lacked his patient touch and sometimes made ill-considered demands. When Ronald Neumann arrived as U.S. ambassador in 2005, he prodded Karzai to remove corrupt officials—including his half-brother, Ahmed Wali Karzai, the chief of the Kandahar provincial council.

In January 2006, *Newsweek* published a story accusing Ahmed Wali Karzai of controlling the drug trade in southern Afghanistan. Enraged, Hamid Karzai summoned Neumann and the British ambassador to the palace. He threatened to file a libel suit and demanded to know if U.S. or British officials had any hard evidence against his brother.

"We all said that we had numerous rumors and allegations to that effect that his brother is corrupt and a narco-trafficker but that we have never had clear evidence that one could take to court," Richard Norland, the U.S. embassy's deputy chief of mission, reported to Washington in a classified cable. The Americans didn't back down. They told Karzai that perception was reality and he needed to deal with the problem.

But the U.S. government was asking Karzai to clean up a mess of its own making. Behind the scenes, the CIA worked closely with Ahmed Wali Karzai and had helped turn him into a regional power broker. For years, the agency paid him to recruit and support a secretive paramilitary strike force, almost certainly with Hamid Karzai's knowledge. Given that ongoing relationship, it took chutzpah for U.S. embassy officials to urge the Afghan president to punish his brother based on vague allegations of wrongdoing. Karzai never forgot it.

"By targeting him, we were damaging our relations," Todd Greentree, a Foreign Service officer who served for several years in Afghanistan, said in a diplomatic oral-history interview. "The wisdom of that was always pretty questionable."

As the insurgency worsened, Bush administration officials grew critical of Karzai's ad hoc governing style. They groused that he acted more like a tribal leader than the president of a modern nation. They also worried that the Taliban was exploiting popular dissatisfaction with his government's corruption and incompetence.

U.S. officials had worked hard with Karzai to marginalize the influence of Afghanistan's warlords, so they became exasperated when he brought the strongmen back in from the cold to forge alliances. To the White House, the one-time poster boy for democracy was losing his sheen.

"Karzai was never sold on democracy and did not rely on democratic institutions, but instead relied on patronage," Stephen Hadley, Bush's national security adviser during his second term, said in a Lessons Learned interview. "My impression was that the warlords were back because Karzai wanted them back."

Yet Karzai held legitimate grievances of his own against the United States.

The U.S. military controlled the skies of Afghanistan with squadrons of fighter aircraft, attack helicopters and armed drones. Even with advanced cameras and sensors, however, pinpointing individual targets on the ground was inherently difficult. Insurgents disguised their presence by moving in small groups and hiding in villages.

As fighting with the Taliban escalated, so did the number of U.S. airstrikes that killed or wounded innocent civilians. U.S. commanders often worsened matters by reflexively branding civilians as terrorists when there was clear evidence to the contrary. Karzai had protested for years about errant airstrikes. But his objections grew louder and more public in 2008 when the United States tried to cover up a string of catastrophes.

On July 6, Afghan witnesses reported that U.S. warplanes had mistakenly bombed a wedding party near a remote village in Nangahar province in eastern Afghanistan, killing dozens of women and children. The U.S. military issued a swift public denial, stating that it had struck "a large group of enemy fighters" on a mountain range in a "precision" attack.

"Whenever we do an airstrike the first thing they're going to cry is, 'Airstrike killed civilians' when the missile actually struck militant extremists we were targeting in the first place," Army First Lt. Nathan Perry, a military spokesman, told the Associated Press at the time.

Karzai ordered a government commission to investigate and it confirmed that the group was indeed a wedding party. Forty-seven people were killed, mostly children and women, including the bride. U.S. military officials retreated slightly. They said they regretted any civilian casualties and promised to conduct their own investigation. But they never publicized the findings.

A month later, another bungled military operation exacerbated Karzai's distrust. A combined force of U.S. and Afghan ground troops, a low-flying AC-130 gunship and a Reaper drone laid waste to the village of Azizabad in Herat province in western Afghanistan.

The U.S. military said the operation targeted a "high-value" Taliban leader and stated there were no civilian fatalities. But it soon became apparent that something had gone seriously wrong. Within a day, military officials backtracked and admitted that five civilians had died. Even that proved to be a horrible undercount.

Witnesses reported that as many as sixty children had died in the hours-long attack and were buried under rubble. The United Nations, Afghan government and an Afghan human-rights commission conducted separate investigations, drawing on photographs, videos and survivor statements. They concluded that between seventy-eight and ninety-two civilians—most of them children—had been killed.

A furious Karzai visited the area and blasted the U.S. government for disregarding Afghan life. "I have been working day and night in the past five years to prevent such incidents, but I haven't been successful," he said. "If I had succeeded, the people of Azizabad wouldn't be bathed in blood."

Still, U.S. military officials defended the operation and accused Afghan officials of spreading Taliban propaganda. The Pentagon conducted its own investigation. After several weeks, it concluded that twenty-two insurgents and thirty-three civilians were killed but justified the assault on the village, saying the attack was "in self-defense, necessary and proportional."

The U.S. investigation summarily dismissed evidence gathered by the Afghans and the United Nations as uncorroborated or tainted by people with "financial, political, and/or survival agendas." Yet the military based its own findings in part on video filmed by a Fox News crew—led by Oliver North of Iran–Contra fame—that had embedded with U.S. forces during the attack on Azizabad.*

In addition to the botched airstrikes, Karzai excoriated U.S. and NATO forces for conducting hundreds of intrusive night raids on Afghan homes as part of their insurgent-hunting operations. Like the

---

* The U.S. military kept the full investigative report a secret until *USA Today* sued the Defense Department in 2018 to obtain almost 1,000 pages of files. The newspaper published an exposé of the Azizabad attack in December 2019.

airstrikes, the night raids sometimes went awry and Special Operations forces killed the wrong targets.

In a Lessons Learned interview, an unnamed U.S. military officer said mistakes were so common that some Army units were "focused on consequence management, paying Afghans for damages and condolence payments." The officer, who served in Khost province in eastern Afghanistan in 2008, recalled an incident when Army Rangers erroneously raided the home of an Afghan army colonel, killing him and his wife, a schoolteacher. "We killed our allies," the U.S. officer said.

In public, Bush administration officials expressed regret over the civilian casualties. In private, they seethed over Karzai's blistering comments and pressed him to tone down his criticism.

But Karzai wanted to demonstrate his independence, in part because he was keenly aware that the Taliban mocked him as an American stooge. He spoke out more about other sensitive issues that the U.S. military had downplayed or ignored.

For example, he castigated Washington for taking a soft line with Pakistan and failing to eliminate the Taliban's havens across the border. The criticisms had validity but his public potshots left U.S. officials indignant.

"Every time we had a huge fight with Karzai or he blew up in public, in every single instance he had been talking to us for months in private about that problem," Gates said. "We didn't pay attention . . . Many of these things we could have prevented had we just been listening better."

On one hand, U.S. officials expected Karzai to be a self-reliant and resolute leader. On the other, they wanted a subservient partner to do their bidding. "I made this point time and again inside the administration," Gates added. "People were just dissing Karzai: 'He's a crackpot.' 'He depends on us for everything.' 'He is a terrible ally.' I'd say, 'We're not such a great ally, either. If we were, we'd be listening better, because he's been telling all of us about this forever.' "

By the time Obama moved into the White House, his administration had already decided to take a tough-love approach with the Afghan president.

In early January 2009, Vice President–elect Joe Biden visited Kabul and met with Karzai and his cabinet in the palace for dinner. Biden and other U.S. officials goaded Karzai about his questionable political appointments, runaway government corruption and his brother's underworld connections. Karzai pushed back about night raids and civilian casualties. At one point, Biden threw down his napkin and the evening ended in acrimony.

One month later, Holbrooke flew to Kabul and met with Karzai in his second-floor office at the palace. Instead of trying to smooth things over from Biden's quarrelsome dinner, Holbrooke hinted that the knives were out. Karzai vented his own resentments. As soon as Holbrooke left, Karzai called Kai Eide, the U.N. diplomat, to his office and told him: He wants to get rid of me and of you.

Holbrooke wasn't the only U.S. diplomat who thought Karzai was no longer up to the job. In July 2009, Karl Eikenberry, the new U.S. ambassador, sent a cable to Washington that presented "two contrasting portraits" of Karzai—both of which portended trouble. "The first is of a paranoid and weak individual unfamiliar with the basics of nation-building and overly self-conscious that his time in the spotlight of glowing reviews from the international community has passed," Eikenberry wrote. "The other is that of an ever-shrewd politician who sees himself as a nationalist hero."

The bubbling feud soon boiled over. On August 20, 2009, Afghans returned to the polls for the second presidential election in the country's history. But turnout plummeted and the credibility of the vote sank into doubt right away. Within hours, reports spread that Karzai's supporters were systematically stuffing ballot boxes. Violence broke out across the country and more than two dozen civilians were killed.

On the day after the election, Holbrooke met with Karzai and suggested a runoff would be necessary even before the results were counted. Karzai accused Holbrooke of undermining him and walked out.

Two months passed before the Afghan elections commission released a final vote count. Karzai led the field with 49.67 percent of the vote—just shy of the 50 percent threshold necessary to avoid a runoff.

Few people believed the numbers. Karzai claimed he had won a majority and resisted a runoff. His opponents accused him of industrial-level fraud. U.S. officials desperately tried to negotiate a way out of the crisis. Eventually, Karzai was declared the winner, by default, after his chief rival withdrew.

But the hard feelings persisted.

Prior to his inauguration in November, Karzai invited PBS into the palace for a television interview. He accused the United States of abandoning Afghanistan after the Soviet withdrawal in 1989 and said he was worried it might happen again. "We keep hearing assurances from the United States, but we are, like, once bitten, twice shy. We have to watch and be careful."

Around the same time, Eikenberry sent a cable to Hillary Clinton that raised further doubts about the wisdom of counting on Karzai as a strategic partner. "It strains credulity to expect Karzai to change fundamentally this late in his life and in our relationship," Eikenberry wrote. Though the cable was classified, someone leaked it to *The New York Times*.

Karzai's public criticisms became increasingly inflammatory and conspiratorial. In a speech in April 2010, he blamed the fraud-ridden presidential election on "foreigners," whom he accused of trying to discredit him. A few days later, in a meeting with Afghan lawmakers, he threatened to join the Taliban if outsiders didn't stop pressuring him.

Marc Grossman, who served as the U.S. special representative to Afghanistan and Pakistan from 2011 to 2012, said Karzai's outbursts served his own narrow interests, but drove the Obama administration up a wall. "He used erratic behavior as a technique," Grossman said in a diplomatic oral-history interview. "It is how he kept everybody else off balance. He was extremely effective at it, even though there were times when we'd be tearing our hair out."

CHAPTER FIFTEEN

Consumed by Corruption

Hamid Karzai's fraudulent reelection worsened a deluge of corruption that engulfed Afghanistan in 2009 and 2010. Dark money cascaded over the country. Money launderers lugged suitcases loaded with $1 million, or more, on flights leaving Kabul so crooked businessmen and politicians could stash their ill-gotten fortunes offshore. Much of the money landed in the emirate of Dubai, where Afghans could pay cash for Persian Gulf luxury villas with few questions asked.

Back home, mansions known as "poppy palaces" rose from Kabul's rubble to house opium kingpins and warlords. The garish estates featured pink granite, lime marble, rooftop fountains and heated indoor pools. Architects concealed wet bars in basements to avoid detection by judgmental mullahs. Some poppy palaces rented for $12,000 a month—an incomprehensible sum to impoverished Afghans who lived hand-to-mouth.

In August 2010, Afghanistan's largest private bank liquefied into a cesspool of fraud. Nearly $1 billion in falsified loans—equivalent to one-twelfth of the country's economic output that year—disappeared into the pockets of politically connected investors who had run the bank as a pyramid scheme. Panic ensued as ordinary Afghans mobbed bank branches to withdraw their savings.

Washington had worried for years about corruption's hold on Afghanistan. But as the graft spread, Obama administration officials feared it would jeopardize their war strategy at the worst possible time—while American troops surged into Afghanistan. In public, U.S. officials promised to stamp out the affliction and hold Afghan leaders accountable.

"I want to be clear: We cannot turn a blind eye to the corruption that causes Afghans to lose faith in their own leaders," Obama declared in March 2009 when he announced an expansion of the war. "We will seek a new compact with the Afghan government that cracks down on corrupt behavior."

A few days later, Secretary of State Hillary Clinton said, "Corruption is a cancer as dangerous to long-term success as the Taliban or al-Qaeda."

In August 2009, Army Gen. Stanley McChrystal warned: "Malign actions of power brokers, widespread corruption and abuse of power . . . have given Afghans little reason to support their government."

But the rhetoric proved hollow. U.S. officials backed off and looked away while the thievery became more entrenched than ever. They tolerated the worst offenders—politicians, warlords, drug traffickers, defense contractors—because they were allies of the United States. Ultimately, they judged that Afghanistan's entire power structure was so dirty that cleaning it up was mission impossible.

Like the Bush White House, the Obama administration failed to confront a more distressing reality. Since the 2001 invasion, the United States had fueled the corruption by dispensing vast sums of money to protect and rebuild Afghanistan with no regard for the consequences. Limitless opportunities for bribery and fraud arose because U.S. spending on aid and defense contracts far exceeded what indigent Afghanistan could digest.

"The basic assumption was that corruption is an Afghan problem and we are the solution," Barnett Rubin, the State Department adviser, said in a Lessons Learned interview. "But there is one indispensable ingredient for corruption—money—and we were the ones who had the money."

Ryan Crocker, who served as the top U.S. diplomat in Kabul under both Bush and Obama, said the gusher of contracts to support U.S.

and NATO troops in Afghanistan virtually guaranteed that extortion, bribery and kickbacks would take root. He said corruption became so widespread that it presented a bigger threat to the U.S. mission than the Taliban.

"Our biggest single project, sadly and inadvertently, of course, may have been the development of mass corruption," Crocker said in a Lessons Learned interview. He called it "the ultimate point of failure for our efforts."

Americans found it easy to blame the Afghans for being on the take, but U.S. officials had soiled hands as well. As soon as the war started in 2001, they embraced bribery as a tactic when it suited their purposes.

To purchase loyalty and information, the CIA funneled cash to warlords, governors, parliamentarians, even religious leaders. The U.S. military and other agencies also abetted corruption by doling out payments or contracts to unsavory Afghan power brokers in a misguided quest for stability.

In 2002 and 2003, when Afghan leaders convened a traditional assembly to write a new constitution, the U.S. government gave "nice packages"—stacks of currency—to delegates who supported Washington's preferred stance on human rights and women's rights, according to an unnamed German official who served in Kabul at the time. "The perception that was started in that period: If you were going to vote for a position that [Washington] favored, you'd be stupid not to get a package for doing it," the German official said in a Lessons Learned interview.

By the time Afghanistan held elections in 2005 to choose 352 members of parliament, that perception had hardened. Lawmakers realized their votes could be worth thousands of dollars to the Americans, even for legislation they would have backed anyway, the German official said.

"People would tell each other, so-and-so has just been to the U.S. Embassy and got this money. They said, 'Okay now I need to go,'" the German official said. "So from the beginning, their experience with democracy was one in which money was deeply embedded."

By 2006, the Afghan government had "self-organized into a kleptocracy" under which people in power could plunder the economy without restraint, according to Christopher Kolenda, an Army colonel who advised several U.S. commanders during the war.

"The kleptocracy got stronger over time, to the point that the priority of the Afghan government became not good governance but sustaining this kleptocracy," Kolenda said in a Lessons Learned interview. "It was·through sheer naivete, and maybe carelessness, that we helped to create the system."

Kolenda said U.S. officials failed to recognize the lethal threat that corruption posed to their war strategy. "I like to use a cancer analogy," he said. "Petty corruption is like skin cancer; there are ways to deal with it and you'll probably be just fine. Corruption within ministries, higher level, is like colon cancer; it's worse, but if you catch it in time, you're probably okay. Kleptocracy, however, is like brain cancer; it's fatal."

By allowing corruption to fester, the United States helped destroy the legitimacy of the wobbly Afghan government they were fighting to prop up. With judges and police chiefs and bureaucrats extorting bribes, many Afghans soured on democracy and turned to the Taliban to enforce order.

In 2009, U.S. military commanders belatedly started a campaign to root out corruption and clean up the Afghan government as part of the Pentagon's enhanced counterinsurgency strategy. The awakening frustrated many U.S. civilian officials who felt the uniformed brass had downplayed the problem since the start of the war.

"It was like they just discovered something new about the pernicious effects of corruption," an unnamed former National Security Council staffer said in a Lessons Learned interview. For years, "people in the field would be moaning and groaning over the compromises made by the military on working with corrupt actors but they would be shut down."

The U.S. government mobilized a small army of anti-corruption lawyers, advisers, investigators and auditors to go to Kabul. What they found overwhelmed them.

The single biggest generator of corruption was the U.S. military's sprawling supply chain. The Pentagon paid Afghan and international contractors to deliver between 6,000 and 8,000 truckloads of fuel, water, ammunition, food and other supplies to the war zone each month.

Transportation costs were exorbitant. Most convoys had to travel about 900 miles from the nearest seaport at Karachi, Pakistan, to reach the main Khyber Pass border crossing at Torkham. Then they had to cross patches of hostile Afghan territory to reach U.S. bases scattered throughout the country.

A convoy of 300 trucks typically required 500 armed guards as basic protection. On top of that, trucking companies paid fat bribes to warlords, police chiefs and Taliban commanders to guarantee safe passage through their turf. A 2010 congressional report called the system "a vast protection racket" that was underwritten by U.S. taxpayers.

Gert Berthold, a forensic accountant who served on a military task force in Afghanistan from 2010 to 2012, helped analyze 3,000 Defense Department contracts worth $106 billion to see who was benefiting. The task force concluded that about 18 percent of the money went to the Taliban and other insurgent groups. "And it was often a higher percent," Berthold said in a Lessons Learned interview. "We talked with many former [Afghan] ministers, and they told us, 'You're under-estimating it.'"

The task force estimated that corrupt Afghan officials and criminal syndicates skimmed off another 15 percent. Berthold said the evidence was so damning that few U.S. officials wanted to hear about it. "No one wanted accountability," he said. "If you're going to do anti-corruption, someone has got to own it . . . No one is willing to own it."

Thomas Creal, another forensic accountant on the military task force, said U.S. agencies hesitated to take action for different reasons. The CIA didn't want to antagonize Afghan contractors or strongmen who were on the spy agency's payroll. Military commanders had mixed feelings about picking fights with crooked Afghan allies.

Creal said he brought cases to the U.S. embassy in Kabul to see if the Justice Department could initiate civil court proceedings to seize assets from corrupt defense contractors, but rarely got anywhere. "We got visibility on the flow of money, then the question was, what do we do with that?" he said in a Lessons Learned interview. "The political world gets in the way."

Even attempts to mildly punish those involved ran into resistance.

One year during Obama's first term in office, diplomats drew up a blacklist of "Afghan malign actors" and proposed to disinvite them from the annual Fourth of July party at the U.S. embassy. But other officials pushed back. There was "always a reason as to why someone couldn't be put on the list," an unnamed U.S. official said in a Lessons Learned interview. In the end, the embassy excluded only one person from the party.

"It was too late, the system was too entrenched," an unnamed senior U.S. diplomat said in a separate Lessons Learned interview.

*   *   *

In January 2010, Afghan anti-corruption agents trained by the United States raided the headquarters of the New Ansari Money Exchange, one of the country's largest financial institutions, and carted away tens of thousands of documents.

U.S. officials suspected the politically connected network was laundering money for narcotics traffickers and insurgents by transporting piles of cash to Dubai and other foreign destinations. Investigators calculated that New Ansari couriers moved as much as $2.78 billion out of the country between 2007 and 2010.

According to Army Lt. Gen. Michael Flynn, the U.S. and NATO military intelligence chief in Afghanistan at the time, U.S. forces played a pivotal role in the raid and pored over the seized documents and data.

"We literally went there and surrounded the bank and had a standoff. We took all of the data," Flynn said in a 2015 Lessons Learned interview. "It was huge. I thought it was a huge success. We conducted that raid and in three days, we did a lot of exploitation. We brought in like forty-five people from around the country very quietly."

"New Ansari was just incredibly corrupt," he said. "It had double books and people were just stealing us blind."

U.S. officials assumed that the huge cache of incriminating evidence would lead to prosecutions. But the Afghan criminal investigation soon hit a wall. "Was anyone held accountable?" Flynn asked. "No, no one was held accountable." *

The wall was inside the presidential palace.

Months after the raid, investigators wiretapped a conversation in which a senior aide to Karzai allegedly agreed to block the New Ansari probe in exchange for a bribe. Afghan law-enforcement agents arrested the aide, Mohammad Zia Salehi, in July 2010. Within hours, however, Karzai personally intervened and ordered Salehi's release from jail, declaring that investigators had overstepped their authority. The Afghan government later dropped all charges. Once again, the Obama administration backed down while the U.S.-driven anti-corruption campaign faltered.

"The pivot point was the Salehi case," an unnamed Justice Department official based in Kabul at the time said in a Lessons Learned interview. He said the arrest provoked "a hornet reaction" by the presidential palace, which ordered Afghan law enforcement agents to stop cooperating with the Americans. Gert Berthold, the forensic accountant, added, "The interest and enthusiasm seemed to be lost after Salehi."

The Afghan president posed a bigger problem. Karzai resented the U.S. anti-corruption push and saw it as foreign meddling. After his reelection fight, he was in no mood to appease the Americans. The Afghan attorney general, appointed by Karzai, blocked numerous public corruption investigations.

Some U.S. officials fumed and said it was time for a reckoning. Others argued that it was more important to mollify Karzai and maintain his waning support for U.S. and NATO military operations.

---

* Flynn retired from the Army in 2014 and later became known for his brief, legally troubled stint as President Trump's first national security adviser and for expressing extremist political views. Flynn pleaded guilty to lying to the FBI after Trump's victory in the 2016 presidential campaign. Trump pardoned Flynn in November 2020.

Colonel Kolenda said some Obama administration officials regarded corruption as "annoying" and less of a concern than the need to strengthen the Afghan security forces and degrade the Taliban. But soon after Salehi's catch and release, an even bigger scandal tested the Obama administration's equivocal stance on corruption.

One day that summer, a world-class poker player named Sherkhan Farnood paid a clandestine visit to the U.S. embassy in Kabul. In addition to his gambling talents, Farnood was the chairman of Kabul Bank, the largest private financial institution in the country. The 49-year-old had started the company six years earlier when Afghanistan was a banking desert, with no regulated lenders.

Kabul Bank grew swiftly thanks to a brilliant marketing campaign. Instead of paying interest, the bank handed out lottery tickets. Customers who deposited $100 received a one-time chance to win prizes ranging from clothes washers to new cars and apartments. The monthly lottery became a roaring success and Kabul Bank opened branches throughout Afghanistan.

The banking business turned Farnood into a tycoon. He splurged on real estate in Dubai, acquired a private Afghan airline and became a fixture at casinos in Las Vegas, London and Macau. "What I'm doing is not proper, not exactly what I should do. But this is Afghanistan," he once bragged to a *Washington Post* reporter.

But when Farnood entered the U.S. embassy compound in July 2010, he carried a cache of documents that exposed Kabul Bank as a teetering house of cards. A small group of Kabul Bank shareholders—including Farnood—had loaned themselves hundreds of millions of dollars by tapping deposits belonging to their lottery-crazed customers. Most of the money had disappeared and the bank was about to go under. Farnood had become enmeshed in a power struggle with the bank's co-owners. He told U.S. diplomats that he wanted to blow the whistle on the whole operation.

U.S. officials panicked over Farnood's revelations. If the bank failed, the losses could capsize the Afghan financial system and ignite a popular revolt. Kabul Bank served as the payroll agent for the Afghan government by handling accounts for 250,000 soldiers, police officers and civil servants. Many stood to lose their savings.

There was also the risk of a political meltdown. Farnood's documents underscored the degree to which the Karzai family and other Afghan elites were deeply entwined in Kabul Bank's operations and ownership structure.

Kabul Bank's third biggest shareholder was Mahmoud Karzai, the president's older brother. Another major shareholder was Haseen Fahim, the brother of Gen. Mohammed Fahim Khan, the Tajik warlord and Karzai's running mate as vice president.*

Farnood accused both men of conspiring with him to plunder the bank's assets. On top of that, he claimed that the bank had given $20 million to Karzai's reelection campaign.

"On a scale of one to ten, it was a twenty here," an unnamed senior U.S. Treasury Department official said in a Lessons Learned interview. "It had elements that you could put into a spy novel, and the connections between people who owned Kabul Bank and those who run the country."

Within weeks, Farnood and Kabul Bank's chief executive were forced to resign. News reports questioning the firm's solvency prompted a run on the bank. Tens of thousands of Afghans mobbed Kabul Bank branches to rescue their savings.

President Karzai held a news conference and tried to calm the panic. He declared his government would fully guarantee all Kabul Bank deposits as the central bank took control of its operations. Behind the scenes, however, the government scrambled to find enough cash to make good on Karzai's promise. Afghan officials made emergency arrangements to fly in $300 million in U.S. currency from a German bank in Frankfurt to alleviate the crisis.

---

* Mahmoud Karzai and Haseen Fahim denied wrongdoing. Neither was prosecuted, though the Afghan government later found that they failed to pay back millions of dollars in loans. In an email to the author, Mahmoud Karzai blamed Kabul Bank's management, U.S. officials and the International Monetary Fund for the bank's "destruction."

At first, in public and in private, the Obama administration leaned on Karzai to fully investigate the Kabul Bank scandal—not only to recover the stolen money but also to demonstrate to the Afghan people that no one was above the law. U.S. officials viewed the episode as a pivotal moment in the anti-corruption campaign and in the war itself.

"There were a million things we were trying to do, and all of it depended on the Karzai regime as an effective partner," an unnamed former senior U.S. official said in a Lessons Learned interview. "But if this [Kabul Bank scandal] was allowed to continue, is the rest of this kind of moot? There was a lot of personal anger and disgust. Feeling we cannot have this."

The scandal also embarrassed the U.S. government, which had deployed legions of financial advisers and consultants to Kabul to help Afghan banking officials regulate their nascent financial industry, yet overlooked a giant Ponzi scheme under their noses.

The warning signs were hard to miss. In October 2009, the U.S. embassy sent a cable to the State Department reporting that cash couriers were transporting large sums of money to Dubai on Farnood's airline. U.S. spy agencies knew about illicit activities inside Kabul Bank about a year before the meltdown, an unnamed senior U.S. official said in a Lessons Learned interview. American intelligence officials had tracked money flows from the bank to the Taliban and other insurgents, and shared the information with their counterparts in Afghan intelligence, he said. But none of the intelligence agencies alerted law enforcement, "because it wasn't in their mandate," he added.

In February 2010, U.S. and Afghan officials realized they needed to act after *The Post* published its interview with Farnood in a report on the bank's dodgy operations. The article's findings shocked Abdul Qadeer Fitrat, the governor of Afghanistan's central bank. Because Afghan regulators had limited power and resources, he asked U.S. Treasury officials to conduct a forensic audit of Kabul Bank.

The Americans said they needed Karzai to approve the request. But Karzai refused for months to meet with the central bank governor to discuss the issue, saying he was too busy. By the time the Afghan president consented to the audit, it was too late.

The U.S. government missed the extent of Kabul Bank's fraud even though it had hired numerous private-sector consultants to embed with Afghanistan's central bank as advisers.

A second unnamed Treasury Department official said that soon after he arrived in Afghanistan in the summer of 2010, he met with an American who had worked on contract with the central bank for at least three years. The Treasury Department official wanted to know more about Kabul Bank. Neither of them had any inkling it was on the verge of failure.

"We had an hour-long conversation," the second Treasury official said in a Lessons Learned interview. "I asked him, do you think this is a financially sound bank? He said, 'Yes.' And literally thirty days afterward, the whole house of cards came down. This was one of the biggest misses in my career. A $1 billion bank collapsed, and the U.S. adviser swore to me it was financially sound."

The Afghan government's takeover of the bank sparked a war of recriminations between regulators and the firm's politically connected investors. Meetings to untangle the bank's finances erupted into violence as participants threw dishes and chairs. Fitrat, the central bank governor, said his office had to stop serving hot tea so the combatants wouldn't scald one another.

In April 2011, Fitrat told the Afghan parliament that Kabul Bank's bad loans totaled almost $1 billion. He testified that many lawmakers and cabinet officials had pocketed questionable payments from the bank, but that Afghan law-enforcement officials had refused to prosecute. He also announced that the central bank would try to freeze the assets of Kabul Bank shareholders.

Afghan power brokers rebelled at attempts to retrieve the missing money. Two months later, fearing for his life, Fitrat fled to the United States. In a memoir, he wrote that Afghanistan was "hostage to a group of mafia-controlled politicians who were looting precious international assistance intended for improving the lives of the people."

For about a year after the scandal became public, the U.S. embassy in Kabul, led by Ambassador Karl Eikenberry, prioritized the case and pressed Karzai to take action, three former U.S. officials said in Lessons Learned interviews. But they said the embassy backed off after Ryan Crocker replaced Eikenberry in July 2011.

"It was a case study of how fragile and precarious U.S. policy can be. Literally overnight our entire policy changed," the second Treasury Department official said. Crocker's "attitude was to make the issue go away, bury it as deep as possible, and silence any voices within the embassy that wanted to make this an issue."

Crocker, Gen. David Petraeus and other Obama administration officials did not want to risk further offending Karzai because they needed his support at the height of the surge with 100,000 U.S. troops in the country. Crocker and his allies also did not want Congress or international donors to use the bank scandal as an excuse to cut off aid to Kabul.

"The United States started easing up its pressure due to the change-over in leadership at the embassy," an unnamed former International Monetary Fund official said in a Lessons Learned interview. "I saw the tide turn when the going got tough."

In a Lessons Learned interview, Crocker said he agreed corruption was an enormous problem that had sabotaged the war. But by the time the Kabul Bank scandal struck, he said it was too late. He also said he was sympathetic to a counterargument from the Afghan president, who spread the blame for the wave of corruption more broadly.

"I was struck by something Karzai said and repeated a number of times during my tenure, which is that the West, led by the U.S., in his clear view, had a significant responsibility to bear for the whole corruption issue," Crocker said.

After Karzai left office in 2014, his successor, Ashraf Ghani, reopened an inquiry into the Kabul Bank scandal. The investigation found that $633 million in improper loans still had not been repaid.

Farnood, the poker-playing founder of the bank, was sentenced to fifteen years. He died in prison in 2018.

Few others faced justice. The bank's chief executive also received a fifteen-year sentence, but it was loosely enforced; the government allowed him to leave his prison daily to tend to a large real-estate investment project. Nine other defendants paid fines or served less than a year in jail.

PART FIVE

THINGS FALL APART

2011—2016

CHAPTER SIXTEEN

At War with the Truth

Leon Panetta fingered a string of rosary beads as he sat in a CIA conference room in Langley, Virginia, his 73-year-old eyes glued to a secure video link that showed U.S. helicopters flying in the darkness over Pakistani terrain. At Mass that morning—May 1, 2011— Panetta prayed to God that the daring, secret mission he had hatched would work.

A former congressman and White House chief of staff, Panetta had served in government long enough to know that his job and reputation were at stake. As CIA director for the past two years, he had overseen the faltering hunt for Osama bin Laden, the most-wanted terrorist in the world. He had just asked for presidential approval to send two dozen Special Operations forces deep into Pakistan—a prickly nuclear power—based on the CIA's guess that a recluse living behind the walls of a $1 million compound in the city of Abbottabad was actually bin Laden. If the operation failed, the fallout would be impossible to contain.

Panetta watched two of the helicopters land at the compound via a live video feed transmitted by stealth drones circling over Abbottabad. But the airborne cameras could not see inside the compound walls. When a team of Navy SEALs barged into the building, all Panetta could do was listen and wait. After an interminable fifteen minutes, the team radioed back: They had found the target and killed him.

The spymaster resisted the urge to celebrate until the Special Operations forces returned safely to their staging base in Afghanistan and confirmed bin Laden's identity. Panetta smiled and thought of his old friend Ted Balestreri, a restauranteur in Monterey, California, who had once promised to open the most prized possession in his wine cellar—an 1870 Chateau Lafite Rothschild—if Leon ever caught the 9/11 mastermind. Panetta phoned his wife, Sylvia, at their home. Call Ted and tell him to turn on CNN, Panetta said, he owes me a bottle of wine.

Bin Laden's death appeared to mark a genuine turning point in the star-crossed war in Afghanistan. The whole purpose had been to eliminate bin Laden and his network. As long as the al-Qaeda leader remained free, no president could realistically consider ending U.S. military operations in Afghanistan. Now, after ten long years, the United States had finally won vengeance for 9/11 and an opportunity seemed at hand.

Two months later, Panetta traveled to Kabul. President Obama had just appointed him secretary of defense and this was his first overseas trip to meet the troops. He had good news to share.

Obama had decided to start bringing U.S. troops home. From a peak of 100,000, the number of troops would drop to 90,000 by the end of the year and shrink to 67,000 by the summer of 2012. On the surface, the U.S. war strategy looked like it might pan out. Panetta felt relaxed and loose.

Unlike his predecessors, who weighed every spoken word for their blowback potential, Panetta demonstrated a flair for blunt, unscripted comments during his visit to Afghanistan and the region. He blabbed away about the CIA's clandestine presence in Afghanistan, called bin Laden a "son of a bitch" and marveled to the troops at every stop how improbable it was for him—a part-time walnut farmer from California and the son of poor Italian immigrants—to end up in charge of the most powerful military in the world.

In a more serious-minded discussion with reporters traveling with him, Panetta characterized bin Laden's death as the beginning of the end of the so-called war on terror. Thanks to an unrelenting CIA drone strike campaign, Panetta estimated al-Qaeda had only ten to twenty "key leaders" still alive in Pakistan, Somalia, North Africa and the Arabian Peninsula. None was left in Afghanistan, where U.S. military officials guessed al-Qaeda could only draw on fifty to one hundred low-level fighters. "We're within reach of strategically defeating al-Qaeda," Panetta said. "I think now is the moment . . . We can really cripple al-Qaeda as a threat to this country."

The success of the bin Laden raid gave Obama a huge political lift. But it also raised the public's expectations and intensified pressure to show that his policies in Afghanistan were working. Obama had promised to turn around the war when he first ran for the White House. He would face the judgment of the voters the following year.

"We take comfort in knowing that the tide of war is receding," Obama declared in June 2011, when he announced the troop reduction. Under his withdrawal timetable, 33,000 troops would come home by August 2012, three months before Election Day.

The reputations of his senior military commanders were also on the line. They had sold their counterinsurgency strategy to the president and the American people two years earlier. Ever confident, they continued to predict success.

"We've made a lot of progress," Adm. Mike Mullen, the chairman of the Joint Chiefs of Staff, told television talk show host Charlie Rose in June 2011. "From a strategy standpoint it really appears to have worked as we had hoped."

But the upbeat, reassuring rhetoric obscured the truth: Despite massive investments, Obama's war strategy was failing. The United States and its allies could not fix some fundamental problems. The Afghan security forces showed little sign they could ever safeguard their own country. Taliban leaders slept soundly in their sanctuaries in Pakistan, biding their time until the foreign forces decided to leave. Corruption deepened its grip on the Afghan government, alienating and angering the people it supposedly served.

U.S. officials wanted to pull out but feared the Afghan state would collapse if they did. Bin Laden had hoped for this exact scenario when he planned 9/11: to lure the U.S. superpower into an unwinnable guerrilla conflict that would deplete its national treasury and diminish its global influence.

"After the killing of Osama bin Laden, I said that Osama was probably laughing in his watery grave considering how much we have spent on Afghanistan," Jeffrey Eggers, the Navy officer who served as a National Security Council staffer for Bush and Obama, said in a Lessons Learned interview.

To paper over the problems, U.S. officials repeatedly downplayed bad news from the front, sometimes twisting it to the point of absurdity.

In September 2011, a cloud of bleak headlines trailed Panetta when he went to Capitol Hill to testify before a Senate committee. An assassin had killed a former Afghan president in charge of peace overtures. The Taliban also had carried out a rash of suicide bombings and coordinated assaults on high-profile targets in Kabul—supposedly the most protected part of the country—including the U.S. embassy and NATO headquarters.

But even the blunt-spoken Panetta had to uphold the illusion of success. He drew a mostly sunny picture for lawmakers, citing "undeniable progress" and saying the war was "headed in the right direction." He called the assassination and suicide attacks "a sign of weakness of the insurgency," arguing that the Taliban resorted to such tactics only because it was losing territory to U.S. forces.

When Panetta returned to Afghanistan for a visit in March 2012, another string of public-relations disasters followed. Moments after the defense secretary's Air Force C-17 landed at a NATO base in Helmand province, an Afghan assailant drove a stolen truck onto the tarmac and tried to run over a U.S. Marine general and others in Panetta's welcoming party. The attacker set himself on fire and crashed the truck, later dying of his injuries. Panetta had not yet disembarked from his plane and no one else was hurt, but it was a close brush with catastrophe.

Just as they had five years earlier when a suicide bomber targeted Vice President Cheney at a different base in Afghanistan, U.S. military officials tried to cover up the incident. For ten hours, they withheld news of the attack from reporters who were traveling on the same plane with Panetta, releasing sketchy information only after British news media broke the story.

At first, Panetta and other officials suggested the timing of the attack was a coincidence and said they had no reason to believe it was aimed at him. But they subsequently acknowledged that if the attack had occurred five minutes later, the speeding truck could have struck Panetta as he walked off the plane.

During his trip, Panetta also had to deal with the fallout from one of the worst atrocities of the war. A few days before his arrival, a lone U.S. soldier, Staff Sgt. Robert Bales, strode into two Afghan villages in Kandahar province in the middle of the night and inexplicably massacred sixteen sleeping villagers, most of them women and children. The mass murder inflamed Afghans and the Taliban exploited it as propaganda fodder.

Despite all that, Panetta called his visit "very encouraging" and said the United States was "very close to accomplishing" its mission. "The campaign, as I've pointed out before, I think has made significant progress," he told reporters in Kabul. "We're on the right path. I'm absolutely convinced of that."

To reinforce the message, Obama administration officials touted statistics that distorted what was really happening on the ground. The Bush administration had done the same, but Obama staffers in the White House, the Pentagon and the State Department took it to a new level, hyping figures that were misleading, spurious or downright false.

"We have broken the Taliban's momentum," Secretary of State Hillary Clinton told a Senate committee in June 2011. As evidence, she quoted an array of metrics: Afghan schools had enrolled 7.1 million students, a seven-fold increase since the fall of the Taliban; infant mortality had decreased by 22 percent; opium production was down; hundreds of thousands of farmers had been "trained and equipped with new seeds and other techniques"; and Afghan women had received more than 100,000 micro-finance loans.

"Now, what do these numbers and others that I could quote tell us?" Clinton said. "Life is better for most Afghans."

But years later, U.S. government auditors would conclude that the Obama administration had based many of its statistics regarding infant mortality, life expectancy and school enrollment on inaccurate or unverified data.

John Sopko, the special inspector general for Afghanistan reconstruction, told Congress in January 2020 that U.S. officials "knew the data was bad" yet bragged about the numbers anyway. He said the lies were part of "an odor of mendacity" that permeated the government's portrayal of the war.

In Lessons Learned interviews, U.S. military officials and advisers described explicit and sustained efforts to deliberately mislead the public. They said it was common in the field, at military headquarters in Kabul, at the Pentagon and at the White House to skew statistics to make it appear the United States was winning the war when that was not the case.

"Every data point was altered to present the best picture possible," Bob Crowley, an Army colonel who served as a senior counterinsurgency adviser to U.S. commanders in 2013 and 2014, said in a Lessons Learned interview. "Surveys, for instance, were totally unreliable but reinforced that everything we were doing was right and we became a self-licking ice cream cone."

At military headquarters, "truth was rarely welcome" and "bad news was often stifled," Crowley said. "There was more freedom to share bad news if it was small—we're running over kids with our MRAPS [armored vehicles]—because those things could be changed with policy directives. But when we tried to air larger strategic concerns about the willingness, capacity or corruption of the Afghan government, it was clear it wasn't welcome."

John Garofano, a Naval War College strategist who advised Marines in Helmand province in 2011, said military officials in the field devoted an inordinate amount of resources to churning out color-coded charts that heralded positive results. "They had a really expensive machine that would print the really large pieces of paper like in a print shop," he said in a Lessons Learned interview. "There would be a caveat that these are not actually scientific figures, or this is not a scientific process behind this."

But Garofano said nobody dared ask whether the charts or numbers were credible or meaningful. "There was not a willingness to answer questions such as, what is the meaning of this number of schools that you have built? How has that progressed you toward your goal?" he said. "How do you show this as evidence of success and not just evidence of effort or evidence of just doing a good thing?"

Military officers and diplomats hesitated to pass negative assessments up the chain of command for another reason: careerism. Nobody wanted the blame for problems or failings on their watch. As a result, regardless of conditions, they claimed they were making progress.

"From the ambassadors down to the low level, [they all say] we are doing a great job," Lt. Gen. Michael Flynn, who oversaw military intelligence during Obama's troop surge, said in a Lessons Learned interview. "Really? So if we are doing such a great job, why does it feel like we are losing?"

For the duration of the war, U.S. Army brigade and battalion commanders were given the same basic mission upon their arrival in Afghanistan: to protect the population and defeat the enemy. "So they all went in for whatever their rotation was, nine months or six months, and were given that mission, accepted that mission and executed that mission," Flynn said. "Then they all said, when they left, they accomplished that mission. Every single commander. Not one commander is going to leave Afghanistan . . . and say, 'You know what, we didn't accomplish our mission.'"

The data regarding bombings, attacks and other violent encounters grew bleaker every time Bush or Obama conducted another review of the war strategy. It was impossible to square the negative trends with the optimistic public messaging about progress, so U.S. officials kept the complete datasets confidential.

"Every time data is shared it showed that everything was getting worse, especially with these strategic reviews," an unnamed senior U.S. official who served under Bush and Obama said in a Lessons Learned interview.

In another Lessons Learned interview, an unnamed National Security Council staff member said the Obama White House and Pentagon pressured the bureaucracy to produce figures to show that the troop surge of 2009 to 2011 was working, despite hard evidence to the contrary.

"It was impossible to create good metrics. We tried using troop numbers trained, violence levels, control of territory and none of it painted an accurate picture," the National Security Council staff member said. "The metrics were always manipulated for the duration of the war."

Even when casualty counts and other figures looked bad, the White House and Pentagon would spin them in their favor. They portrayed suicide bombings in Kabul as a sign that the insurgents were too weak to engage in direct combat. They said a rise in U.S. troop deaths proved that American forces were taking the fight to the enemy.

"It was their explanations," the White House staff member said. "For example, attacks are getting worse? 'That's because there are more targets for them to fire at, so more attacks are a false indicator of instability.' Then, three months later, attacks are still getting worse? 'It's because the Taliban are getting desperate, so it's actually an indicator that we're winning.'"

U.S. military officials tossed out so many different types of statistics and metrics that the public had no idea which ones really mattered.

Lawmakers also wondered. During a Senate Armed Services Committee hearing in April 2009, Sen. Susan Collins (R-Maine) asked Michèle Flournoy, the undersecretary of defense for policy, how the Obama administration would know if the troop surge was successful.

"How will we know if we're winning?" Collins said. "How will you know whether or not this new strategy is working? It seems to me that you need a set of clear benchmarks, clear metrics going in."

Flournoy gave a muddled answer. "There are a whole host—much more developed set of inherited metrics, given that we've been conducting these operations for a long time," she said. "What we're trying to do is sort through these more carefully. Some of them are more input related. And what we're really trying to focus on is outcomes and actual impacts. So we aren't starting with a blank sheet, but we are in the process of refining the metrics that have been used in Afghanistan."

As troops surged into the war zone, military commanders refined the art of cherry-picking statistics to make the case that their strategy was working.

At a July 2010 news briefing with reporters at the Pentagon, Army Maj. Gen. John Campbell, the commanding general of U.S. forces in eastern Afghanistan, said the Taliban had carried out 12 percent more attacks during the first half of the year compared to the first six months of 2009.

Aware that might sound bad, Campbell quickly added that "the effectiveness of those attacks have gone down about 6 percent." He did not explain how the military measured "effectiveness" with such precision. But he reassured reporters that the war was going well.

"Winning is achieving progress, and I think every single day we are achieving progress," he said.

In March 2011, the House Armed Services Committee summoned General Petraeus to provide an update on the war. He bombarded lawmakers with a fusillade of disjointed figures. Petraeus cited "a fourfold increase" in weapons and explosives caches "turned in and found." He said U.S. and Afghan commandos were killing or capturing "some 360 targeted insurgent leaders" in a "typical ninety-day period." In Marja, a town in Helmand province that had been pried loose from Taliban control, 75 percent of registered voters had cast ballots in a community council election. Throughout Afghanistan, the number of surveillance blimps and towers had increased from 114 to 184 since August.

"In closing," Petraeus said, "the past eight months have seen important but hard-fought progress."

Military officers in the field knew the blizzard of numbers meant little. "Unfortunately, with numbers you can spin them any way you want," Army Maj. John Martin, a self-described "staff bubba" who served as a planner at Bagram Air Base, said in an Army oral-history interview. "For example, if last year there were 100 attacks and this year there were 150, does that mean the situation has gotten worse because there have been more attacks?" Martin added. "Or does that mean now you have more guys going to more places and finding more bad guys, so there are more attacks, but you're making the situation better because you are finding more bad guys?"

Other senior officials said they placed great importance on one statistic in particular, albeit one that the U.S. government rarely mentioned in public. "I do think that the key benchmark is the one I've suggested, which is how many Afghans are getting killed," James Dobbins, the U.S. diplomat, told a Senate panel in 2009. "If the number's going up, you're losing. If the number's going down, you're winning. It's as simple as that."

Up to that point, however, nobody had bothered to reliably track Afghan casualties. For the Pentagon, the subject was a touchy one. Defense officials didn't like to answer questions about civilian deaths, much less talk about who was responsible. Tracking the number of wells dug and schools built was easier and generated more favorable publicity.

In a Lessons Learned interview, an unnamed senior NATO official said the alliance started to track civilian casualties in 2005 and set up "what was supposed to be the mother of all databases." But the program was dropped for unspecified reasons. "It should be a standard operating procedure from the start to record civilian casualties, but it wasn't," the senior NATO official said.

In 2009, the United Nations expanded a campaign to count civilian deaths and injuries in Afghanistan. The U.N. program became the first comprehensive tally of civilian casualties, but the numbers were discouraging and growing worse. On average, dozens of people were dying each week.

As U.S. troops surged into Afghanistan between 2009 and 2011, the annual number of civilian deaths rose from 2,412 to 3,133. The total dipped in 2012, but increased in 2013 and kept rising, reaching 3,701 deaths in 2014.

That meant the number of Afghan civilians getting killed had soared 53 percent over five years. Under Dobbins's simple rule, the United States and its allies were losing badly.

The United Nations survey blamed insurgents for most of the deaths. But regardless of who was responsible, the casualty figures showed that Afghanistan was growing more unstable and insecure—the exact opposite of what the U.S. counterinsurgency strategy was supposed to accomplish.

U.S. intelligence assessments also cast doubt on the war's progress. Intelligence analysts in the CIA and the military prepared reports that were far more pessimistic than the pronouncements from commanding generals in the field. But intelligence officials rarely spoke in public and their reports remained classified.

Once a year, Congress summoned senior intelligence officials to testify in open session about global threats to U.S. national security. They spoke in monotones and jargon, but their comments about Afghanistan were uniformly dour.

In February 2012, Army Lt. Gen. Ronald Burgess, the director of the Defense Intelligence Agency, gave a brief but dreary assessment to the Senate Armed Services Committee. He said Obama's troop surge and war strategy had done little to deter the insurgency.

He said the Afghan government was plagued by "endemic corruption" and that the Afghan army and police were riddled with "persistent qualitative deficiencies." In comparison, he described the Taliban as "resilient" and said it had been able to withstand losses inflicted by U.S. troops.

"From its Pakistani safe havens, the Taliban leadership remains confident of eventual victory," Burgess added.

At the same hearing, lawmakers asked Director of National Intelligence James Clapper to explain why U.S. intelligence agencies held such a negative view while military commanders were so optimistic. Clapper replied that the same disconnect emerged during the Vietnam War when intelligence officials knew the U.S. military was stuck in a quagmire but the generals didn't want to admit it in public.

"If you'll forgive a little history," Clapper said, "I served as an analyst briefer for General [William] Westmoreland in Vietnam in 1966. I kinda lost my professional innocence a little bit then when I found out that operational commanders sometimes don't agree with [intelligence officials about] their view of the success of their campaign."

Indeed, when it was their turn to testify one month later, U.S. military commanders remained resolute: They were making progress.

"The progress is real and, importantly, it's sustainable," Marine Gen. John Allen, the commander of U.S. and NATO forces, told the Senate Armed Services Committee in March 2012. "We have severely degraded the insurgency."

Senator Collins, the Maine Republican, pointed out that Allen and other generals had been singing the same refrain for years. "I recall that I've heard very similar assessments from our commanders for ten years now, that we're making progress," she said. "Why are you optimistic that ultimately we will be successful and prevail?"

"Ma'am, if I didn't think it was doable, I would tell you," Allen replied. "And I'd tell you very quickly, because I wouldn't want to spend another life in this fight if it wasn't doable."

The false narrative of progress became harder to maintain as more American troops withdrew. In 2013, the number of U.S. forces in Afghanistan dipped below 50,000 for the first time in four years. The Afghan army and police struggled to fill the void left by the Americans. The Taliban revived its forces and spread into new territory.

But the generals doubled down on their talking points. They also embraced a word they once avoided: *winning*.

When General Allen completed his nineteen-month stint as commander of U.S. and NATO forces in February 2013, he sounded more buoyant than ever. He said the Afghan security forces had improved and that the Afghan government was ready to take responsibility for its own security.

"This is victory," he said at his change-of-command ceremony in Kabul. "This is what winning looks like. And we should not shrink from using these words. This campaign is, and always has been, about the Afghan people and about winning."

Until that moment, commanders rarely promised outright victory. But other generals soon adopted Allen's language and bravado.

"I talk a lot about winning these days and I firmly believe that we're on a path to win," Marine Gen. Joseph Dunford Jr., Allen's successor, said at a military ceremony in Kabul in May 2013.

Dunford's deputy, Army Lt. Gen. Mark Milley, echoed his boss at the same ceremony when he addressed Afghan troops on the parade ground. "You will win this war and we will be there with you every step of the way," Milley said. He proclaimed that they were "on the road to victory, on the road to winning, on the road to creating a stable Afghanistan."

The Enemy Within

The team of U.S. Army soldiers peered through thermal-imaging scopes over the edge of their makeshift observation post, looking down into the barren valley for signs of the enemy. They thought they were safe behind their three-foot-high berm of sandbags, hidden underneath camouflage cover and the dark September sky.

About 1 a.m., gunfire erupted directly behind them. Afghan fighters carrying AK-47s, who had snuck up from the rear, ambushed the soldiers at close range.

Sgt. Sapuro Nena, 25, a guitar-playing Pacific Islander, was shot several times in the back. Private First Class Jon Townsend, newly married at age 19, was hit in the upper chest. Specialist Joshua Nelson, 22, a signals intelligence analyst from eastern North Carolina, took a barrage of gunfire in both legs. Private First Class Genaro Bedoy, a 20-year-old Texan with a baby daughter back home in Amarillo, was shot in his face. None of the four soldiers survived.

The killers were not strangers. They had enlisted in the Afghan National Police and worked alongside U.S. troops for weeks in Zabul province, a gateway for insurgents crossing between southern and eastern Afghanistan. What prompted the Afghan police officers to open fire on their American allies was not clear, but the murders escalated an alarming trend.

The act of treachery on September 16, 2012, capped a brutal two-month period during which uniformed Afghan security forces carried out sixteen fratricidal attacks, killing twenty-two U.S. and NATO personnel and wounding twenty-nine others.

Such assaults from within rarely occurred during the early years of the war. But as the Obama administration accelerated its efforts to train the Afghan army and police forces, the insider-threat phenomenon exploded. The number of publicly reported attacks by uniformed Afghans against their foreign allies rose from two in 2008 to forty-five in 2012, causing the deaths of at least 116 U.S. and NATO personnel during that period. The incidents became so common, it seemed as if U.S. troops were training the enemy.*

In some of the attacks, members of the Taliban infiltrated the Afghan army or police with the specific intent of inciting mayhem from within. In other cases, Afghan soldiers or police with no known connections to the insurgency took revenge on foreign troops for personal or ideological reasons. Often, the motives never became clear.

The burst of insider attacks jeopardized the U.S. and NATO mission. To win the war, the Western allies needed to expand and transform the Afghan army and police into a competent fighting force that could defeat the Taliban with minimal foreign help and stabilize the country in the years to come.

U.S. forces trained, equipped and mentored Afghan soldiers and police in close proximity around the clock. During joint operations, commanders exhorted Americans and Afghans to work "shoulder-to-shoulder"—*shohna ba shohna* in Dari. The system hinged on trust, so it risked collapse if the Americans had to worry that their Afghan partners might shoot them in the back.

But U.S. troops also committed acts that destabilized and undermined the coalition. In January 2012, a video that showed Marines

---

* Foreign troops were not the only targets. An Afghan police commander shot two Associated Press journalists while they were reporting in Khost province in April 2014, killing photographer Anja Niedringhaus and wounding correspondent Kathy Gannon.

urinating on Taliban corpses went viral online. In February, U.S. personnel at Bagram Air Base inadvertently burned copies of the Koran in a trash pile, sparking public protests. In March, tensions hit a peak when an Army staff sergeant massacred sixteen villagers in Kandahar province.

The insider attacks threatened the Obama administration's drawdown schedule. The U.S. military planned to gradually cede responsibility, district by district, to the Afghan security forces by the end of 2014. At that point, the Afghans would take charge of the fight throughout the country, with U.S. and NATO forces playing an advisory role.

By September 2012, the U.S. military had reduced its presence to 77,000 troops, down from a peak of 100,000. As Obama campaigned for reelection that fall, he promised to end the war entirely if voters elected him to a second term.

But the deaths that month of the four soldiers in Zabul forced the U.S. military to hit the brakes. Three days after the attack, Marine Gen. John Allen, the commander of U.S. and NATO forces, ordered a temporary halt to joint operations. Practically and symbolically, it was a major setback.

Normally a reserved, soft-spoken optimist, Allen expressed fury at the Afghan security forces' inability to stop the fratricidal killings. "I'm mad as hell about them," he told the CBS News program 60 Minutes. "We're willing to sacrifice a lot for this campaign, but we're not willing to be murdered for it."

The two sides resumed joint operations within ten days. But the concept of working together as brothers in arms never recovered. U.S. and NATO officials demanded that the Afghans re-screen the backgrounds of their soldiers and police. They also instituted a "guardian angel" program that assigned U.S. and NATO soldiers to keep a constant lookout for traitorous Afghans.

Army Maj. Christopher Sebastian, a signals officer who mentored the Afghan army from 2011 to 2012, recalled attending a graduation ceremony for the Afghans at a training academy in Kandahar. An infiltrator had placed a small bomb under the seat of an Australian colonel. When the officer stood up to shake hands with the graduates, the device detonated. Amazingly, no one was hurt. But Sebastian said the incident shattered everyone's nerves and solidified doubts that the U.S.–Afghan partnership would ever work.

"There was always a persistent feeling of dread as you went about your daily duties just because you always had to be looking over your shoulder," Sebastian said in an Army oral-history interview. "So, to expect that we are ever going to reach what the American army would consider success, I don't think that jives with reality."

The insider attacks generated waves of negative news coverage in the United States, Canada and Europe questioning whether the Afghans were trustworthy allies or deserving of support. Afraid that public opinion would turn decisively against the war, the U.S. military dusted off an old tactic: It buried the extent of the problem.

Military spokesmen deemphasized the attacks as "isolated incidents," a description at odds with the Pentagon's own assessments. In 2011, a U.S. Army behavioral scientist based in Kabul conducted an internal study titled "A Crisis of Trust and Cultural Incompatibility" that concluded insider attacks "are no longer isolated; they reflect a growing systemic threat."

To further minimize the issue in public, officials at military headquarters in Kabul routinely failed to disclose insider attacks in which troops were only wounded or escaped unhurt. And even in fatal cases, officials released brief, perfunctory statements that shed little light on what happened, or why.

After the four U.S. soldiers were killed in Zabul in 2012, the U.S. and NATO joint command in Kabul issued a press release consisting of three sparsely worded sentences. Details of the soldiers' deaths would never have become public had it not been for Adam Ashton, a reporter for *The News Tribune* of Tacoma, Washington.

Ashton had embedded in Afghanistan with another part of the soldiers' brigade from Joint Base Lewis–McChord, near Tacoma. For more than fifteen months, he wrote a series of articles that pieced together what happened. He interviewed Army contacts and used the Freedom of Information Act to pry loose a heavily redacted copy of the official investigation into the killings.

His stories revealed that there were six assailants—all members of the Afghanistan National Police. The Afghans had accompanied six U.S. soldiers to the observation post for a forty-eight-hour shift to look for Taliban fighters who had been launching mortars at a nearby U.S. base, Combat Outpost Mizan.

The turncoat police killed four of the U.S. soldiers and wounded the other two. One of them, Specialist David Matakaiongo, 26, another newlywed with a baby son, barely survived after AK-47 rounds shattered his legs and ribs.

Matakaiongo later said he sensed bad vibes from the Afghans and admitted the attack didn't come entirely as a surprise. "We knew what they were capable of," he said in an interview with Ashton. "I'm looking at these guys and thinking, 'You're going to shoot me.'"

Another survivor, Specialist Devin Wallace, miraculously avoided major injury. He played dead until the shooters ran off, then radioed for help. He told investigators he had been suspicious of the Afghans too and that they had turned noticeably sullen before the attack.

The Army investigation disclosed that the Afghans shot and killed a seventh person—a fellow Afghan policeman. Investigators believed he was targeted because he had befriended the Americans and refused to join in the attack.

The shooters escaped, vanishing into the valley. The investigation uncovered evidence of their ties to insurgents and found that Afghan police officials in Zabul had vouched for their reliability when they enlisted. But the Army redacted details of those findings from the report, leaving important questions unanswered.

The outbreak of fratricidal attacks jangled the nerves of U.S. troops throughout Afghanistan. Maj. Jamie Towery, an Army officer who served as a liaison to a NATO police training command in Mazar-e-Sharif from 2010 to 2011, said he constantly worried that an Afghan officer—even a trusted one—might suddenly go rogue.

He recalled an incident in August 2010 when an Afghan driver fatally shot two Spanish police officers who had worked closely with the driver for six months. "Really the most stressful place or time while I was there was when we would go to the range with students," Towery said in an Army oral-history interview. "We'd just never know when they might turn on you."

*   *   *

The insider attacks were just one of many systemic problems that continued to grip the Afghan army and police. Even after a decade of handholding by the United States and NATO, the Afghan armed forces struggled to operate independently.

The national army accounted for about two-thirds of the Afghan security forces. It reported to the Defense Ministry and included the Afghan air force, commando units and other troops.

The national police reported to the Interior Ministry. More of a paramilitary force than a crime-fighting agency, the police guarded the border, staffed checkpoints and held territory that the army had cleared of insurgents.

The Afghan forces grew in poorly planned spurts. After initially trying to cap their numbers at 50,000, the Bush administration set a long-term goal in 2008 to field 134,000 soldiers and 82,000 police. But when Obama took office the following year, his administration decided those ambitious targets were still insufficient to meet the rising Taliban threat. General McChrystal, the commander at the time, recommended a near-doubling of the Afghan army and police to 400,000 personnel combined. Obama and Congress settled on a slightly lower total of 352,000.

At that size, the Afghan army and police forces looked robust on paper. But a large percentage materialized as ghost billets, or no-show jobs. Afghan commanders inflated the numbers so they could pocket millions of dollars in salaries—paid by U.S. taxpayers—for imaginary personnel, according to U.S. government audits.

By the end of Obama's second term in office, U.S. officials determined that at least 30,000 Afghan soldiers didn't exist and removed their positions from the army payroll. A year later, the Afghan government erased an additional 30,000 ghost police officers from the ranks.

The United States eventually insisted that the Afghan government collect biometric data, including fingerprints and face scans, to verify the existence of people in uniform. But it took years to get the checks in place and they failed to eliminate the problem entirely.

The quality of recruits continued to pose an existential challenge. Jack Kem, a retired Army colonel, served as deputy to the U.S. general in charge of training the Afghan security forces from 2009 to 2011. He estimated that only 2 to 5 percent of Afghan recruits could read at a third-grade level despite efforts by the United States to enroll millions of Afghan children in school over the previous decade.

"The literacy was just insurmountable," Kem said in an Army oral-history interview. Some Afghans also had to be taught how to count. "I mean, you'd ask an Afghan soldier how many brothers and sisters they had, and they couldn't tell you it was four. They could tell you their names, but they couldn't go 'one, two, three, four.'"

Recruiters had a herculean job because of the high rate of attrition. When Kem arrived in Kabul in 2009, the Afghan army and police forces were shrinking because so many personnel were going AWOL. Despite intensive efforts to stanch losses, the problem persisted. In 2013, about 30,000 soldiers deserted from the Afghan army, roughly one-sixth of the force.

Those who stayed faced high odds of death. The casualty rate for Afghan soldiers and police became so bad that the Afghan government kept the exact numbers a secret to avoid destroying morale. By November 2019, researchers calculated that more than 64,000 Afghans in uniform had been killed over the course of the war—roughly eighteen times the number of U.S. and NATO troops who lost their lives.

Some U.S. officials blamed White House and Pentagon policies for the fiasco. "Thinking we could build the military that fast and that well was insane," an unnamed former senior State Department official said in a Lessons Learned interview. "We can't even stand up a sustainable local police unit in the U.S. in eighteen months. How could we expect to set up hundreds of them across Afghanistan in that time frame?"

The colossal training program did not suffer for want of money. At the peak of the war in 2011, Washington set aside nearly $11 billion in annual security assistance for Afghanistan—about $3 billion more than what neighboring Pakistan, which had a stockpile of nuclear weapons and a far more capable army, spent that year on its military.

Lt. Gen. Douglas Lute, the White House's war czar, said Congress appropriated so much money for the Afghan army and police that the Defense Department didn't know how to spend it all. "We can't just shovel one-year money at this problem," he said in a Lessons Learned interview. "You can't possibly build the [Afghan security forces] that fast."

In public, however, U.S. military commanders exuded confidence about what they were building. They repeatedly proclaimed that the Afghan security forces were improving and that U.S. troops soon would no longer need to serve in combat.

In a September 2012 briefing with reporters at the Pentagon, Army Lt. Gen. James Terry, the bootlegger's grandson who had returned to Afghanistan to become deputy commander of U.S. forces, sidestepped a barrage of questions about insider attacks and described the Afghan army and police as on the verge of taking over the fight. "There is progress over here in the campaign. We have momentum," he said. "And the Afghan national security forces, again, are steadily moving out into the lead."

As U.S. troops gradually withdrew and handed over responsibility to the Afghans, however, the Taliban took advantage. Insurgents expanded their spheres of control in southern and eastern Afghanistan, knocking Afghan forces back time and again.

The Pentagon's senior brass downplayed the reversals and continued to issue glowing report cards to their Afghan partners. In September 2013, Army Lt. Gen. Mark Milley, the new deputy commander of U.S. forces, boasted that "the conditions are set for winning this war."

"This army and this police force have been very, very effective in combat against the insurgents every single day," he said in a press briefing from Kabul. "Have there been one or two outposts that have been overrun? Yes. But you're talking about 3,000 or 4,000 outposts that are in the country. So the bottom line is, the Afghans have successfully defended the majority of the population of this country."

The truth was, Afghans abandoned their outposts with alarming frequency. American generals liked to pretend otherwise, but their troops in the field described many of the Afghan forces as incompetent, unmotivated and corrupt.

Maj. Greg Escobar, an Army infantry officer, spent 2011 trying to straighten out a dysfunctional Afghan army unit in Paktika province near the eastern border. The first Afghan battalion commander Escobar mentored lost his job after he was charged with raping one of his male soldiers. The commander's replacement, in turn, was killed by his own men.

Escobar said he came to realize the whole exercise was futile because the U.S. military was pushing too fast and the Afghans were not responding to what was, in the end, a foreign experiment. "Nothing we do is going to help," he said in an Army oral-history interview. "Until the Afghan government can positively affect the people there, we're wasting our time."

Army Maj. Michael Capps, a military police officer, trained the Afghan police at border areas along the Khyber Pass for a year. When he returned to the United States in 2009, people asked him: Can we win there?

"My answer would be, 'You could be at double-arm interval over every square meter of Afghanistan and still lose,'" he said in an Army oral-history interview, referring to military formations in which soldiers stand two arm-lengths apart. "You could lose that place covering every inch of ground. It's so porous, it's so different, it's so backward."

Other Army officers who trained the Afghans recounted scenes of mayhem and chaos that bode poorly for how they would perform on the battlefield. Maj. Mark Glaspell, an Army engineer with the 101st

Airborne Division who served as a mentor to Afghan forces from 2010 to 2011, said even simple exercises went haywire. In an Army oral-history interview, he recalled trying to teach an Afghan platoon in the eastern city of Gardez how to exit a CH-47 Chinook, a heavy-lift helicopter used to transport troops and supplies. They lacked an actual Chinook to practice on, so he lined up rows of folding chairs instead and instructed the Afghans how they would safely disembark.

"We were working on that and it was going pretty good and all of a sudden this Afghan soldier walks up and he and one of the guys in the class started to get into an argument," Glaspell said. Then a third Afghan soldier picked up a folding chair and pounded the first guy over the head.

"Well, then it was a brawl; it was on," Glaspell added. He let the Afghans duke it out until they got tired. "My interpreter actually looked at me, shook his head and said, 'This is why we'll never be successful,' and he walked away."

Maj. Charles Wagenblast, an Army Reservist who deployed to eastern Afghanistan for a year as an intelligence officer, said he learned the hard way that American logic did not always mesh with Afghan thinking. In fall 2010, he and other U.S. officers reminded their Afghan soldiers that winter was coming and suggested they might want to prepare, given that they had no fixed source of heat in their barracks.

"It was getting cold, 'Have you guys thought about getting some firewood?' That's how they heat stuff there. They say, 'No, it's not cold yet.'"

"But it will be cold, I'm pretty sure," Wagenblast replied. Yet the Afghans refused to take his word that the weather was destined to turn frigid. "And they'd say, 'Yeah, but how do you know that?' Wow. How do you argue with that? 'You guys need coats.' 'No, it's not cold yet. We'll get coats when it's cold.'"

Meanwhile, corruption coursed through the Afghan army and police from top to bottom. Government ministers parceled out generalships and command assignments in exchange for cash or as part of patronage rackets. Commanders in turn hogged a cut of their troops' salaries. Front-line soldiers and police lined their pockets by extorting the citizenry.

Over time, the Afghan public became so disgusted that many debated who represented the bigger evil—the Taliban or the Afghan government.

Shahmahmood Miakhel, a senior official in the Afghan defense ministry, said he once got an earful from district tribal leaders who could not stand either side.

"I asked that why is it possible that a large number of about 500 security forces cannot defeat about twenty or thirty Taliban. The community elders replied that the security people are not there to defend the people and fight the Taliban, they are there to make money" by selling their U.S.-supplied weapons or fuel, Miakhel recalled in a Lessons Learned interview.

He said he told the tribal elders, "'Okay, the government is not protecting you, but you are about 30,000 people in the district. If you don't like the Taliban then you must fight against them.' Their response was that we don't want this corrupt government to come and we don't want Taliban either, so we are waiting to see who is going to win."

In Lessons Learned interviews, U.S. officials complained incessantly about the Afghan police, saying they performed even worse than the Afghan army and did not care about protecting the population.

Thomas Johnson, an Afghanistan expert and Naval Postgraduate School professor who served as a counterinsurgency adviser in Kandahar province, said Afghans viewed the police as predatory bandits, calling them "the most hated institution" in Afghanistan. An unnamed Norwegian official estimated that 30 percent of Afghan police recruits deserted with their government-issued weapons so they could "set up their own private checkpoints" and rob people.

Ryan Crocker, the U.S. ambassador from 2011 to 2012, said in a Lessons Learned interview that the Afghan police were ineffective "not because they're out-gunned or out-manned. It's because they are useless as a security force and they're useless as a security force because they are corrupt down to the patrol level."

Maj. Robert Rodock, a military policeman in the U.S. Army who served as a liaison to the Afghan police, said they functioned more like a private militia serving as muscle for a warlord or tribal chief. He had to teach them basic concepts of public service and law enforcement.

"It was, 'Here's what handcuffing is,'" Rodock said in an Army oral-history interview. "'You can't walk down the middle of the market and steal something because you believe it's yours.' It's at that level."

Army Lt. Col. Scott Cunningham, a National Guard officer who served in Laghman province from 2009 to 2010, said many Afghan police officers spent their days idling in shipping containers that they set up as checkpoints—or "cop in a box" as the Americans called them. "There was no patrolling, there was no crime-solving, there was nothing," he said.

One day the Afghan police did a good thing: They pulled over a dump truck loaded with several tons of homemade explosives. Cunningham estimated the cargo might have had the same blast power as the truck bomb that blew up the nine-story Alfred P. Murrah Federal Building in Oklahoma City in 1995, killing 168 people.

But Cunningham grew anxious when the policemen insisted on hauling the truck away and disposing of the explosives themselves. "We didn't trust them with it one bit," he said. A standoff ensued, so a U.S. soldier took matters into his own hands. He grabbed an explosive charge with a time fuse and—in full view of the Afghan police—tossed it onto the back of the truck. "They had nothing to do but run," Cunningham recalled. The blast echoed for miles but nobody got hurt.

In Lessons Learned interviews, U.S. officials heaped special scorn on units known as the Afghan Local Police, a separate entity from the national police force. With about 30,000 personnel, they were militias organized at the local level and established in 2010 at the behest of the United States. The U.S. military trained the local police but the Afghan officers quickly earned a reputation for brutality and drew complaints from human rights groups.

One unidentified U.S. soldier said Special Forces teams "hated" the Afghan Local Police, calling them "awful—the bottom of the barrel in the country that is already at the bottom of the barrel." In a separate interview, an unnamed U.S. military officer estimated that one-third of local police recruits were "drug addicts or Taliban."

Scott Mann, an Army lieutenant colonel, said in a Lessons Learned interview that the local police training expanded too rapidly between 2011 and 2013. "If you use surrogates or take shortcuts, you get what you pay for," Mann said. "You get unaccountable militias that prey on the population."

Capt. Andrew Boissonneau, an Army civil-affairs officer, worked alongside Afghan Local Police units in Helmand province in 2012 and 2013. In an Army oral-history interview, he recalled one Afghan commander who suffered from a case of post-traumatic stress disorder so severe that he led his forces into combat with imaginary enemies.

"He held the checkpoint that was the closest to the Helmand River and every once in a while he would get in firefights with the Helmand River—meaning, he was seeing attacks that no one else was seeing and would order his guys to return fire," Boissonneau said.

Somehow, U.S. troops had to find a way to train such haunted souls and mold them into a proficient force that could defeat the rising insurgency and take control of their shell-shocked country. It was mission impossible.

CHAPTER EIGHTEEN

The Grand Illusion

President Obama had promised to end the war, so on December 28, 2014, U.S. and NATO officials held a ceremony at their headquarters in Kabul to mark the occasion. A multinational color guard paraded around as music played. A four-star general gave a speech and solemnly cased the green flag of the U.S.-led international force that had flown since the beginning of the conflict.

In his remarks, Obama called the day "a milestone for our country" and said the United States was safer and more secure after thirteen years of war. "Thanks to the extraordinary sacrifices of our men and women in uniform, our combat mission in Afghanistan is ending, and the longest war in American history is coming to a responsible conclusion," he declared.

Army Gen. John Campbell, the 57-year-old commander of U.S. and NATO forces, also hailed the purported end of the "combat mission" and embellished some of its achievements. Since the start of the war, he asserted, life expectancy for the average Afghan had increased by twenty-one years. "You times that by about 35 million Afghans represented here in the country, that gives you 741 million years of life," he added, crediting U.S., NATO and Afghan forces for what sounded like a remarkable improvement.*

But for such a historical day, the event seemed strange and underwhelming. The president didn't actually attend; Obama issued his remarks in a written statement from Hawaii while he relaxed on vacation. The military ceremony took place in a gymnasium, where several dozen people sat on folding chairs. There was little mention of the enemy, let alone an instrument of surrender. Nobody cheered.

In fact, the war was nowhere near a conclusion, "responsible" or otherwise, and U.S. troops would fight and die in combat in Afghanistan for many years to come. The bald-faced claims to the contrary ranked among the most egregious deceptions and lies that U.S. leaders spread during two decades of warfare.

Obama had scaled back military operations over the previous three years but he failed to pull the United States out of the quagmire. At the time of the ceremony, about 10,800 U.S. troops remained in Afghanistan, a decrease of almost 90 percent from the surge's high-water mark. Obama promised to withdraw the rest of the troops by the end of 2016, coinciding with the end of his term in office, save for a residual force at the U.S. embassy.

He knew most Americans had lost patience. Only 38 percent of the public said the war had been worth fighting, according to a December 2014 *Washington Post*–ABC News poll, compared to 90 percent who supported the war at the start of the conflict.

Yet the president faced countervailing pressures to stay put from the Pentagon and hawks in Congress. Obama had tried a similar staged approach to end the war in Iraq, where the U.S. military ceased combat operations in 2010 and exited entirely a year later. But those moves soon backfired.

---

* Like many statistics that U.S. officials touted as evidence of progress, Campbell's extrapolations were grossly exaggerated. A 2017 SIGAR audit discredited the life-expectancy figures as based on spurious data. Instead of twenty-one years, the World Health Organization estimated a six-year increase in life expectancy for Afghan males and an eight-year increase for Afghan females.

In the absence of U.S. troops, the Islamic State—an al-Qaeda offshoot—swept through the country and seized several major cities as the U.S.-trained Iraqi army put up scant resistance. To counter the Islamic State and prevent Iraq from falling apart, Obama reluctantly ordered U.S. forces to return, starting with a campaign of airstrikes in August 2014 and followed by 3,100 personnel on the ground. They would remain stuck there for years.

Obama wanted to avoid the same fate in Afghanistan, but he needed to buy more time for U.S. forces to build up the shaky Afghan army so it would not collapse like the Iraqi forces had. He also wanted to create leverage for the government in Kabul to persuade the Taliban to negotiate an end to the conflict.

To make it all work, Obama conjured up an illusion. His administration unveiled a messaging campaign to make Americans think that U.S. troops still in Afghanistan would stay out of the fight, with duties that relegated them to the sidelines. As the flag came down during the December 2014 ceremony in Kabul, Obama's commanders emphasized that the Afghan army and police would take full responsibility for their country's security from that point forward, with U.S. and NATO forces restricted to "non-combat" roles as trainers and advisers.

But the Pentagon carved out numerous exceptions that, in practice, made the distinctions almost meaningless. In the skies, U.S. fighters, bombers, helicopters and drones continued to fly air combat missions against Taliban forces. In 2015 and 2016, the U.S. military launched missiles and bombs on 2,284 occasions, a decline from previous years, but still an average of more than three times a day.

On the ground, the Pentagon created another combat exception for troops carrying out "counterterrorism operations," or raids on specific targets. Those rules of engagement permitted Special Operations forces to capture or kill members of al-Qaeda and "associated forces," a vague term that could also apply to the Taliban or other insurgents. The rules also allowed U.S. troops to come to the aid of Afghan forces to prevent the fall of a major city or in other circumstances. In other words, the U.S. military would continue to play an indispensable role and remain in the fight.

Still, after thirteen years of lackluster results, many U.S. leaders harbored doubts about what they had really accomplished and whether Obama's new approach could work any better than his previous one had. In a Lessons Learned interview, a senior U.S. official who served as a civilian in Afghanistan said it was fast becoming obvious that Obama's surge strategy had been a mistake. Instead of flooding the country with 100,000 U.S. troops for eighteen months, he said it would have been better to send one-tenth the number—but leave them in Afghanistan until 2030.

"You can create stability with boots and money, but the question is, will it hold when you leave?" he said. "Given our desire to ramp up quickly and leave quickly, there was no reasonable threshold we could reach where we could leave behind good governance."

When Richard Boucher, the senior U.S. diplomat who oversaw South Asia policy during the Bush administration, sat down for a Lessons Learned interview in 2015, he found a succinct way to illustrate the failure of the biggest nation-building project in U.S. history.

"If you look at it after fifteen years, we could have taken a thousand [Afghan] schoolchildren in first grade—well, not quite first, but fifth grade—and taken them to get educated and trained in Indian schools and colleges," he said. "Then we could have brought them back on an airplane by now and said, 'Okay, you guys run Afghanistan.' . . . Better than having a bunch of Americans going in and saying, 'We can build it for you.'"

Obama had based his aspirations for ending the war on a rickety political calendar. Given the unlikelihood of a Taliban surrender, he needed the Afghan government to commit to take over the fight so U.S. forces could leave.

After Karzai cheated his way to reelection in 2009, U.S. diplomats lobbied the Afghan president's aides to slip a line in his inauguration speech about accepting responsibility for the country's security on a specific timetable. The text promised that Afghan forces would take the lead "in ensuring security and stability across the country" within five years—by the end of Karzai's second term in office.

But the old warmth and trust in Karzai's relationship with the Americans dried up. Instead of working with the Obama administration to smooth the transition, Karzai impeded negotiations over a U.S.–Afghan security agreement that would have authorized the United States to keep troops in Afghanistan after 2014.

Washington wanted to maintain a small force so it could continue to train and equip the Afghan army and conduct counterterrorism strikes against al-Qaeda. But Karzai wanted to bar U.S. soldiers from raiding Afghan homes, a longstanding sore point. He also objected to a provision that immunized U.S. forces from prosecution under Afghan law.

The Obama administration refused to budge on either demand. Assuming Karzai would fold, U.S. officials threatened to close their bases and pull out entirely if he didn't sign the agreement by the end of 2013. But Karzai held firm and called Obama's bluff, guessing the Americans didn't really mean it.

He was right. U.S. officials backed off and had to wait until Karzai left office. His successor, Ashraf Ghani, signed the agreement in September 2014.

James Dobbins, the diplomat who helped run the Bonn conference in 2001, came back to serve as Obama's special representative to Afghanistan and Pakistan from 2013 to 2014. He said the spat over the security agreement exemplified a paradox that Obama never resolved. The president wanted the Afghans to think the United States was a steadfast ally that would not abandon them against the Taliban. Yet he was simultaneously telling war-weary Americans that it was time to leave. "There was a continuous tension in both our messaging and our actual behavior," Dobbins said in a Lessons Learned interview.

To maintain the "end of combat" fantasy for Americans at home, the Pentagon continued to deliver upbeat reports from the front.

In February 2015, Ashton Carter, a longtime Defense Department official appointed to serve as Obama's fourth defense secretary, visited Afghanistan for the first time in his new job. He kicked off his trip by repeating some of the same lines that his predecessors had recited since the start of the war. "A lot has changed here, so much of it for the better," Carter said in Kabul at a press conference with Ghani, the Afghan president. "Our priority now is to make sure this progress sticks."

But during a visit to Kandahar Air Field, he briefly wandered off script and admitted that the Afghans had been woeful and inept until recently—contradicting the glossy assessments U.S. officials had presented to the public for more than a decade.

"It's not that the Afghans aren't good at fighting. They are. But just a few years ago there really was no Afghan National Security Force at all," Carter said. "They're getting on their feet now, and they're beginning to do the things alone that we used to do for them."

For a few months, the Obama administration's tenuous plans seemed to hold. News from Afghanistan quieted down and U.S. troops stayed out of the spotlight. But as the Afghan security forces labored to hold their own against the Taliban, Americans resumed paying with their lives.

In April 2015, Specialist John Dawson, a 22-year-old Army medic from the village of Whitinsville, Massachusetts, died in an insider attack in Jalalabad. An Afghan soldier opened fire on coalition troops at a government compound, killing Dawson and wounding eight others.

Two months later, Krissie Davis, a 54-year-old civilian with the Defense Logistics Agency, died in a rocket attack on Bagram Air Base.

In August, First Sgt. Andrew McKenna, a 35-year-old Green Beret on his fifth deployment to Afghanistan, was killed in a firefight when Taliban fighters attacked a Special Operations forces camp in Kabul. The insurgents blew their way past the gate with a car bomb, killed eight Afghan guards and critically wounded another U.S. soldier. McKenna was posthumously awarded the Silver Star—the military's third-highest decoration for valor in combat—for helping to repel the attack while he was mortally wounded.

Nineteen days later, Air Force Cpt. Matthew Roland, 27, and Staff Sgt. Forrest Sibley, 31, were killed in another insider attack at an Afghan police checkpoint in Helmand province. Roland was posthumously awarded the Silver Star for sacrificing his life to save other Special Operations forces in the ambush.

In late September, the illusion that U.S. troops were no longer serving in combat disappeared entirely. After a long siege, insurgent forces seized Kunduz, Afghanistan's sixth biggest city, about 200 miles north of Kabul. The fall of Kunduz shocked the country; it was the first time since 2001 that the Taliban controlled a major urban area. U.S. Special Forces teams rushed to Kunduz to help the Afghan army retake the city over several days of heavy fighting.

In the early morning darkness of October 3, 2015, a U.S. Air Force AC-130 gunship—with the call sign "Hammer"—repeatedly strafed a Kunduz hospital with cannon fire, killing forty-two people. The hospital was run by the humanitarian group Doctors Without Borders. In an attempt to safeguard the trauma center, the group had provided U.S. and Afghan forces with the GPS coordinates of the site several days earlier, so there was no excuse for the attack.

Obama and other U.S. officials apologized for the catastrophe. A U.S. military investigation subsequently blamed the "fog of war," human error and equipment failures for what it called the "unintentional" destruction of the hospital. The Pentagon said sixteen U.S. service members received administrative punishments for their role in the attack. None faced criminal charges.

But instead of curtailing U.S. military operations, Obama dug in deeper. Twelve days after the Kunduz debacle, Obama ordered a halt to the slow withdrawal of U.S. troops and extended their mission indefinitely to prevent the Taliban from overrunning more cities. Breaking his promise to end the war, he said at least 5,500 troops would remain in Afghanistan after he left office in January 2017.

"I do not support the idea of endless war and I have repeatedly argued against marching into open-ended military conflicts," Obama announced from the Roosevelt Room in the White House. "Yet given what's at stake in Afghanistan . . . I am firmly convinced that we should make this extra effort."

Despite the enormous advantages that the Afghan military held in manpower, equipment and training, U.S. officials feared their allies would lose to the Taliban if the Americans left the battlefield. In a fleeting moment of candor, Obama conceded that "Afghan forces are still not as strong as they need to be."

To make the endless war more palatable to the public, Obama perpetuated the fiction that U.S. troops were only bystanders in the fight. In his remarks from the Roosevelt Room, he again insisted the combat mission was "over," though he qualified his statement slightly by specifying that Americans were not engaged in "major ground combat against the Taliban."

To the troops, the distinction made no difference. To them, Afghanistan was a combat zone. They all carried weapons. They all earned combat pay. Many were awarded combat decorations. More would die.

*   *   *

As 2015 drew to a close, the insurgency gained power and U.S. military leaders began to reveal rare flashes of pessimism.

During a return visit to Afghanistan in December, Ashton Carter damned the Afghan security forces with faint praise. In remarks to U.S. troops at a base near Jalalabad, he said the Afghan army and police "are getting there," but suggested he had limited confidence in the Pentagon's proxy force.

"If you'd have asked me to bet on it five years ago, I don't know. I'd maybe give you even odds on it or something," he said. "But it's coming together."

In a news briefing with reporters at Bagram that same day, General Campbell sounded even gloomier. "We just went through a very, very tough fighting season," he said. "We knew it was going to be a tough year, the Afghans knew it was going to be a tough year."

Three days later, on December 21, a suicide bomber carrying explosives on a motorcycle killed six U.S. Air Force security personnel on foot patrol near Bagram. Among the fatalities: Maj. Adrianna

Vorderbruggen, 36, an Air Force Academy graduate who had pushed for the 2011 repeal of the military's Don't Ask, Don't Tell prohibition on openly gay servicemembers. Vorderbruggen was posthumously awarded three combat decorations: the Bronze Star Medal, the Purple Heart and the Air Force Combat Action Medal. She left behind her wife, Heather, a military veteran, and their four-year-old son, Jacob.

As the war entered its fifteenth year, the United States faced a new combatant in Afghanistan and old fault lines began to shift.

The Islamic State, the fast-growing terrorist network in Iraq and Syria, expanded into Afghanistan and Pakistan. By early 2016, U.S. military officials estimated the local affiliate of the group had between 1,000 and 3,000 fighters, mostly former members of the Taliban.

Their emergence widened and complicated the war. In January 2016, the White House approved new rules of engagement authorizing the Pentagon to attack Islamic State in Afghanistan. That led to a surge in U.S. airstrikes against the group, which centered its operations in Nangahar and Kunar provinces in eastern Afghanistan, along the Pakistani border.

By that point, the U.S. military acknowledged that its original nemesis in the war—al-Qaeda—had all but disappeared from Afghanistan.

"By themselves, we don't think that they pose a real threat, a real significant threat to the government of Afghanistan," Army Brig. Gen. Charles Cleveland, a spokesman for U.S. forces in Afghanistan, told Pentagon reporters in May 2016. He offered what he called a SWAG—a military acronym for "scientific, wild-assed guess"—that about 100 to 300 al-Qaeda personnel maintained "some type of presence" in Afghanistan. Five years after the death of bin Laden, his network barely registered in the fight.

Meanwhile, the U.S. military put the Taliban into a nebulous new category. It was still a hostile force, but not necessarily the enemy. Obama administration officials had concluded that the only way to end the war and to stabilize Afghanistan was for the Afghan government to negotiate a peace deal with the Taliban. Previous attempts to start a reconciliation process had gone nowhere. U.S. officials wanted to try again and decided to treat the Taliban differently in hopes of persuading its leaders to come to the table.

As a result, the Pentagon imposed new rules of engagement under which U.S. forces could freely attack the Islamic State and the remnants of al-Qaeda. But they could only fight the Taliban in self-defense or if the Afghan security forces were on the verge of getting wiped out.

Even U.S. lawmakers were confused by the new approach. At a Senate Armed Services Committee hearing in February 2016, Sen. Lindsey Graham (R-S.C.) pushed General Campbell to explain.

"Is the Taliban an enemy of this country?" Graham asked.

"I didn't hear the question," Campbell replied.

"Is the Taliban an enemy of the United States?" Graham repeated.

Campbell stammered. "The Taliban, as far as helping al-Qaeda, and Haqqani, and other insurgent groups, the Taliban has been responsible for . . ."

Graham interrupted and asked multiple times if the U.S. military was permitted to go on the offense and attack Taliban forces or kill its senior leaders.

"Sir, again, I don't go into the rules of engagement authorities in open hearing," Campbell said, ducking the questions. "What I would tell you is that our country has made the decision that we are not at war with the Taliban."

But the Taliban was still very much at war with the United States and the Afghan government, and as far as the Taliban's leaders were concerned, the fight was going well. In 2016, insurgent forces overran Kunduz again, repeatedly bombed Kabul, and seized control of most of Helmand province, the heart of Afghanistan's lucrative opium-poppy belt.

In Washington, fears rose that the Afghan government was at risk of a political breakdown. Calling the situation "precarious," Obama reversed himself again in July 2016. Instead of drawing down to 5,500 troops as planned, he ordered U.S. forces to stay in Afghanistan. By the time he left the White House in January 2017, about 8,400 troops remained.

The next month, Army Gen. John Nicholson Jr., Campbell's successor as commanding general, appeared before the Senate Armed Services Committee. Asked if the United States was winning or losing, he replied: "I believe we're in a stalemate."

In his testimony, however, Nicholson foreshadowed what was in store under the new president, Donald Trump. "Offensive capability is what will break the stalemate in Afghanistan," Nicholson said.

In military jargon, that meant more troops and more weapons.

PART SIX

STALEMATE

2017—2021

CHAPTER NINETEEN

Trump's Turn

Nearly eight years had elapsed since the previous commander in chief delivered a prime-time, nationally televised speech in front of the troops to announce his new strategy for the war in Afghanistan. Now, on August 21, 2017, it was Donald Trump's turn.

Just as Obama did at West Point, Trump entered Conmy Hall at Fort Myer, Virginia, under dimmed lights as an Army band played "Hail to the Chief." He narrowed his eyebrows and pressed his lips into a serious expression as he theatrically ascended the stage, then motioned for the soldiers, airmen, sailors and Marines in the audience to stop standing at attention and sit down.

As Trump read from the teleprompter, some of his lines sounded like a replay of Obama's West Point address. Like Obama, Trump acknowledged that Americans were "weary of war." But after conducting yet another "comprehensive review" of the U.S. war strategy, Trump had decided to send more troops and expand military operations—just like his predecessor.

Trump said the Afghan government needed more time and help to strengthen its own security forces. He parroted Obama by cautioning that "our support is not a blank check" and added, "we are not nation-building again." He accused Pakistan of sheltering the insurgents and threatened to withhold aid if it didn't change its policies.

Americans had heard these promises many times before. But then Trump escalated the rhetoric as only he could. He vowed not just to end the sixteen-year-old war, but to win it—once and for all.

"We are killing terrorists," he said. "Our troops will fight to win. We will fight to win. From now on, victory will have a clear definition."

Trump's boastful pledge marked a surprising about-face for him on Afghanistan. Before he won the 2016 presidential election, the real-estate mogul and reality TV star had complained loudly about the war's expense and demanded that Obama pull out. In keeping with his slogan, "Make America Great Again," he denounced any foreign-aid programs that resembled nation-building.

"Afghanistan is a complete waste. Time to come home!" he tweeted in 2012.

"We have wasted an enormous amount of blood and treasure in Afghanistan. Their government has zero appreciation. Let's get out!" he tweeted in 2013.

"A suicide bomber has just killed U.S. troops in Afghanistan. When will our leaders get tough and smart. We are being led to slaughter!" he tweeted in 2015.

But once Trump moved into the Oval Office in January 2017, he ran into resistance. Trump's Cabinet and the Pentagon brass told him it could be cataclysmic to withdraw abruptly. If the Afghan government collapsed or the war spilled over to nuclear-armed Pakistan, he would own the problem. They urged him to carefully review the war strategy first and consider all the ramifications. Then he could act.

Trump agreed. But unlike other presidents, he had scant respect for the generals running the war and no patience for detailed policy deliberations.

Above all, Trump hated any hint of weakness or defeat. His defense secretary, James Mattis, had committed the grievous error of suggesting just that in June when he told the Senate Armed Services Committee that "we are not winning in Afghanistan right now." Gen. Joseph Dunford Jr., the chairman of the Joint Chiefs of Staff, made the same mistake six days later when he confessed during an appearance at the

National Press Club in Washington that "Afghanistan is not where we want it to be."

One month before Trump's speech at Fort Myer, Mattis invited the president to the Pentagon for a wide-ranging discussion about the importance of NATO and other military alliances. Mattis and the Joint Chiefs wanted to give him a special briefing in "The Tank," a secure conference room where the leaders of the Army, Navy, Air Force, Marine Corps and National Guard reviewed war plans and debated sensitive issues.

Mattis and Dunford thought Trump would be impressed by the gravitas of The Tank, located in the Pentagon's outer ring. Dignified oil portraits of four-star admirals and generals dating to the 1950s adorned the hallway outside the conference room. Maybe the setting would help sway the new president—who, like Obama, had never served in the armed forces—and bring him around to their way of thinking about Afghanistan and other global hotspots.

Trump agreed to attend the session, but quickly became fed up with the lecture. In particular, he blew his stack when Mattis and Dunford talked about Afghanistan. Trump called it a "loser war." He trashed the commanding general in Kabul, Army Gen. John Nicholson Jr., saying: "I don't think he knows how to win."

"I want to win," Trump said, according to an account of the meeting by *Washington Post* journalists Philip Rucker and Carol Leonnig. "You're a bunch of dopes and babies."

Trump's language and demeanor floored Mattis, Dunford and the chiefs. They had invested much of their careers in Afghanistan and worried Trump might try to pull the plug on the war before they could finish the strategy review.

Before becoming defense secretary, Mattis had served in the Marines for forty-four years. He deployed to Afghanistan in 2001 as a one-star general and became a four-star combatant commander under Obama. Dunford, a fellow Marine, had commanded U.S. and NATO forces in Afghanistan from 2013 to 2014.

Army Lt. Gen. H.R. McMaster, the White House national security adviser, had spent months working with Mattis and Dunford on the

Afghanistan strategy review. McMaster was also personally invested in the war. He had served a twenty-month stint at military headquarters in Kabul during Obama's troop surge.

Like Mattis and Dunford, McMaster thought the war had gone off the rails. He disdained Obama for withdrawing too many forces too quickly. McMaster favored sending several thousand soldiers back to Afghanistan—on top of the 8,400 troops still there—and maintaining those force levels indefinitely.

Even though his plan would cost $45 billion a year, McMaster believed the expense was worth it to prevent Afghanistan from disintegrating. The Afghan security forces were already doing most of the fighting. Only twenty U.S. troops had died in Afghanistan during the previous twelve months—a fraction of the casualty rate during the height of the war.

But McMaster, Mattis and Dunford needed to tread carefully to get Trump on board. After the president's explosion in The Tank, McMaster organized another high-level national security meeting on August 18, 2017, at Camp David, the presidential retreat in the Catoctin Mountains in Maryland, to discuss the results of the Afghanistan strategy review.

Leading up to the session, McMaster refined his pitch. He warned Trump that if he followed through on his tweets and withdrew all U.S. troops, al-Qaeda might return to Afghanistan and launch another attack on the U.S. homeland. McMaster also told Trump that twenty different terrorist groups were active in the region. In reality, al-Qaeda had shrunk to a shell of its former self and the other groups had limited reach. But no president wanted to risk another 9/11 happening on his watch.

At Camp David, the generals told Trump that they needed more forces and firepower in Afghanistan to break the stalemate. But they framed their proposed escalation as an antidote to Obama's handling of the war. They argued that Obama had bungled his troop surge by announcing that it would only last for eighteen months. The Taliban had just laid low and waited him out. Don't be like Obama and tip your hand to the enemy, they advised the president.

The criticism of Obama was catnip to Trump, who detested his predecessor. He approved sending several thousand more forces to Afghanistan. He also agreed to keep the troop increase open-ended.

In his speech three days later at Fort Myer, Trump unveiled the new strategy, yet made clear that he was skeptical of it. "My original instinct was to pull out. And historically, I like following my instincts," he said. "But one way or another, these problems will be solved. I'm a problem-solver. And in the end, we will win."

Trump declared he would fight the war differently than Obama in another respect: His administration would become more secretive.

"We will not talk about numbers of troops or our plans for further military activities," he said. Trump kept details of his decision to deploy more troops under wraps, even though anonymous U.S. officials had already leaked that 3,900 additional soldiers would go.

The president justified the enhanced secrecy as a tactic to keep the enemy guessing. But the policy shift had another purpose: It would leave Americans in the dark. The less visible the war, the less likely people would criticize Trump or his generals if it deteriorated further.

The Pentagon took advantage. Within three months, U.S. troop levels in Afghanistan rose to 14,000—an increase of 5,600 from when Obama left office. Other than the extra troops and added secrecy, however, Trump administration officials struggled to articulate what was different about their new strategy.

In an appearance before the House Armed Services Committee in October 2017, Mattis labeled the new strategy "R4+S." He said the acronym stood for "regionalize it, realign it, reinforce it and reconciliation, coupled with sustaining it." But the description was such a mouthful that Mattis and other U.S. officials rarely repeated it after that.

What became clear to the generals was that as long as Trump was president, they would have to speak more forcefully and boast that his war strategy was destined to succeed.

In a press briefing from Kabul on November 20, 2017, a newly confident General Nicholson—the war commander whom Trump had ripped in The Tank—said the Taliban was running out of options. "Our message to the enemy is that you cannot win the war. It's time to lay down your arms," he blustered. "If they don't, they're going to be confined to irrelevance . . . or death. And so these are the choices they face."

Eight days later, Nicholson held another press briefing. He went out of his way to heap praise on Trump's strategy, calling it "fundamentally different" and "a game changer." Though Nicholson had previously described the war as being locked in a stalemate, he insisted he no longer saw it that way. "The president has left no doubt in terms of our will to win," Nicholson said. "We will be here until the job is done . . . We are on our way to a win."

In the most substantive change in the war strategy, Trump authorized the military to intensify the bombing campaign.

Obama had imposed restrictions that prevented the U.S. military from conducting airstrikes except to protect U.S. troops, carry out counterterrorism operations or prevent Afghan forces from being overrun. By the end of his term, U.S. warplanes were launching fewer than one hundred bombs and missiles per month.

But at the Pentagon's request, Trump cast off the restraints and renewed the air assault on the Taliban with a fury. In 2017, the U.S. military doubled the number of airstrikes and more than tripled the munitions it dropped from the skies.

Then the military intensified the airstrikes even more. In 2018, U.S. aircraft released 7,362 bombs and missiles—a third more than any previous year in the war. They kept up the blistering pace in 2019 and in 2020.

While the fighting had become much less visible to Americans at home, the violence inflicted new levels of mayhem on the ground, killing and wounding record numbers of Afghan civilians. During Trump's first three years in office, U.S., NATO and Afghan airstrikes killed an estimated 1,134 civilians a year—double the annual average of the previous decade, according to an analysis by the Costs of War Project at Brown University.

Trump hoped the bombings would pressure the Taliban into negotiations. But the brute force tactics also suited the president's style.

In April 2017, the Air Force dropped a 21,600-pound bomb—the biggest ever used in the war in Afghanistan—on a network of Islamic State bunkers and tunnels in Nangahar province. The Pentagon's official name for the thirty-foot-long weapon was the Massive Ordnance Air Blast, or MOAB. But troops nicknamed it the Mother Of All Bombs.

U.S. military officials said the MOAB killed scores of Islamic State fighters. News of the giant bomb generated news coverage around the world.

Trump proudly called the strike "another very, very successful mission" and said it showed he was doing a better job overseeing the war than Obama. "If you look at what has happened over the last eight weeks and compare that, really, to what has happened over the last eight years, you will see there has been a tremendous difference," he told reporters at the White House.

But the explosion turned out to be a one-day wonder and had no lasting impact on the war. The Pentagon did not drop any more MOABs during Trump's term in office.

In contrast with the publicity around the bomb, the U.S. military started to hide important indicators that the war was backsliding. In September 2017, the Pentagon stopped releasing data on casualties suffered by the Afghan security forces. U.S. officials said they agreed to classify the figures at the request of the Afghan government.

The truth was that Afghan officials feared the high mortality rates were hurting recruiting and morale. Casualty figures had spiked as the Afghan security forces replaced U.S. and NATO forces on the front lines. By some estimates, thirty to forty Afghan soldiers and police were killed daily.

In comparison, the insurgents found it easy to recruit. By 2018, the Taliban's ranks had swollen to about 60,000 fighters, up from 25,000 seven years earlier, according to U.S. military estimates.

U.S. military commanders began to suppress other statistics they had once heralded. For years, they had closely tracked how much territory the Afghan government controlled compared to the Taliban.

Analysts surveyed each of the country's administrative districts and adjusted the figures by population density.

General Nicholson, the war commander, called it "the metric that's most telling in a counterinsurgency." During his back-to-back November 2017 news briefings, he said that about 64 percent of Afghanistan's population lived in districts controlled by the government, 24 percent lived in contested areas and 12 percent lived in the Taliban's zone.

Saying the war had "turned the corner," Nicholson predicted that the Afghan government would expand its control to 80 percent of the population within two years. At that juncture, he said, the Afghan government would secure "a critical mass" and "drive the enemy to irrelevance."

But the Afghan government got no closer to the mark. Instead, subsequent surveys showed the Taliban expanding its reach. Rather than confront the reality of what was happening, U.S. military leaders changed their minds about the value of the data and stopped tracking territorial control altogether by fall 2018.

In a July 2018 news conference in Kabul, Nicholson downplayed the relevance of the territory statistics—even though he had emphasized their importance just eight months earlier. He said the U.S. military had shifted its focus to another indicator: the willingness of the Taliban to engage in peace talks. "These were not the metrics you were talking about a year ago," he conceded, but called them "perhaps more important than some of these other measures that we traditionally use."

Other evidence piled up suggesting that the Taliban had gained the upper hand despite the massive U.S. bombing campaign. After agreeing to a partial, three-day ceasefire in June 2018, the Taliban rejected Afghan President Ashraf Ghani's request for another ceasefire in August. That month, the Taliban briefly seized control of the city of Ghazni and overran Afghan military bases in Faryab and Baghlan provinces.

The Trump administration endured another embarrassing moment in June when the Senate Armed Services Committee held a confirmation hearing for Army Gen. Scott Miller, the president's nominee to command U.S. forces in Afghanistan. A decorated commando, Miller had led the secretive Joint Special Operations Command and served in combat in Somalia, Bosnia and Iraq. He was also one of the first U.S. soldiers to deploy to Afghanistan after 9/11.

Downplaying the recent setbacks in Afghanistan, Miller painted a guardedly optimistic picture and repeated many of the talking points other generals had used over the years. "There is progress there," he said.

Sen. Elizabeth Warren, a Democrat from Massachusetts, challenged Miller, saying she had heard enough rosy talk. She ticked off example after example of military leaders saying the war had reached "a turning point"—dating back to 2010.

"General Miller, we've supposedly turned the corner so many times that it seems now we're going in circles," Warren said. "So let me just ask you: Do you envision turning another corner during your tenure as commander? After seventeen years of war, what are you going to do differently?"

Caught off guard, Miller struggled to give a coherent reply.

"Senator, first off, I—I acknowledge the seventeen years," he said. "I—I can't guarantee you a timeline or an end date. I know that going into this position or—or offer necessarily a turning point, unless there is—unless there's something to come back and—and report back that something has—something has changed. And that's where I anticipate— anticipate being."

From the witness table, Miller looked over his shoulder at an Army second lieutenant sitting behind him who had been a toddler when the war started. It was Miller's son, Austin. "This young guy sitting behind me, I never anticipated that this cohort would be in a position to deploy as I sat there in 2001 and—and looked at this," he said.

Despite Trump's promises of victory and his exhortations to fight to win, Miller and other U.S. military leaders kept trying to prod the Taliban into peace talks with the Afghan government. The Taliban, increasingly confident in their position, showed less interest. But the generals' optimism in public remained undimmed.

During a visit to Kabul in July 2018, Army Gen. Joseph Votel, the chief of U.S. Central Command, cited the recent limited, three-day ceasefire as cause for hope. He said the ceasefire "demonstrated the increased desire for peace, not only from the Afghan people, but from the belligerents of the conflict as well." Votel added, "I think our efforts here in Afghanistan are showing progress."

In September, Mattis told reporters at the Pentagon that he also had grown more hopeful that the Taliban would agree to talk. "For the first time, we have some semblance of strength to the reconciliation effort," he said. The war, he added, was "going in the right direction."

But the Taliban kept exposing the hollowness of the Americans' claims.

On October 18, several weeks after General Miller took command in Afghanistan, he visited Kandahar to confer with local leaders in the provincial governor's compound. As the late-afternoon meeting ended, Miller and the U.S. delegation walked outside, exchanged a few final words with their Afghan hosts and prepared to board helicopters to fly back to Kabul. Before they reached their aircraft, however, an Afghan soldier carrying a crate of pomegranates—a gift for the Americans—dropped the fruit and opened fire on the group with an AK-47.

The rogue soldier killed Gen. Abdul Raziq, a warlord who served as the provincial police commander, as well as the local intelligence chief, Abdul Mohim. The gunman also wounded Kandahar governor Zalmay Wesa, who had been walking alongside Miller.

Miller drew his pistol as he scrambled for cover, escaping injury.

Within seconds, the gunman was shot and killed. But the calamitous security breach rattled the whole country and strained U.S–Afghan relations. Afghan investigators determined the shooter had not been subjected to a background check when he enlisted as a guard for the Kandahar governor two months earlier.

The Taliban immediately claimed credit for the insider attack. As proof, they posted a video online of the gunman training with insurgents in Pakistan. Taliban officials said the plot was originally intended to kill General Raziq—a longtime foe—but that the infiltrator was also instructed to kill Miller once they learned he would be visiting the compound that day.

U.S. military officials downplayed the assertion that Miller was a target, saying he had just been caught in the crossfire. They also tried to cover up the fact that another senior officer, Army Brig. Gen. Jeffrey Smiley, the commander of U.S. forces in southern Afghanistan, had been shot and wounded in the attack. The U.S. military command in Kabul waited three days to disclose the information, doing so only after *The Washington Post* broke the news that Smiley had narrowly escaped death.

CHAPTER TWENTY

The Narco-State

In November 2017, military commanders in Afghanistan launched Operation Iron Tempest, a storm of airstrikes by some of the U.S. Air Force's most powerful warplanes. The main target: a clandestine network of opium-processing labs that U.S. officials said helped generate $200 million in drug money for the Taliban.

In a publicity blitz, the Pentagon released videos of long-range B-52 Stratofortress bombers—built to carry nuclear weapons—dropping 2,000-pound and 500-pound conventional munitions on suspected drug labs in Helmand province. F-22 Raptor stealth fighters pulverized targets with satellite-guided bombs after flying all the way from a U.S. Air Force base in the United Arab Emirates to join the attack.

U.S. commanders called the operation a turning point in the sixteen-year-long war, saying it was the first time they had deployed such fearsome airpower against Afghanistan's drug kingpins. After three weeks of strikes, they bragged they had eliminated twenty-five opium labs that otherwise would have cooked up $80 million in narcotics revenue to finance the insurgency.

"The new strategy highlights that this is a new war and that the gloves are off," Air Force Brig. Gen. Lance Bunch said during a press briefing from Kabul. "It's definitely been a game-changer and the Taliban is definitely feeling it." He added, "This will be a very long winter for the Taliban, as we will continue to disrupt their revenue sources again and again and again. . . . The war has changed."

But after several months, Operation Iron Tempest fizzled. An independent analysis by a British researcher found that many of the targets were abandoned, mud-walled compounds. Others were makeshift labs that typically processed small batches of opium worth thousands of dollars, not millions.

After more than 200 airstrikes, the Pentagon concluded that blowing up primitive targets with such devastating weapons was overkill and a waste of resources; the B-52s and F-22s each cost more than $32,000 to operate, per hour, not counting the expense of the munitions. After the initial rush of publicity, U.S. military officials gradually stopped talking about Iron Tempest and finally called it off. Public notification came in two paragraphs, buried in an eighty-four-page report to Congress.

The demise of Iron Tempest mirrored other oversold, high-dollar anti-drug campaigns in Afghanistan, including Operation River Dance, the Bush administration's 2006 attempt to eradicate fields of opium poppies in Helmand with tractors and weed whackers. In both instances, eleven years apart, U.S. and Afghan officials made a big show of marshaling their forces and promising victory, only to surrender quietly months later.

Of all the failures in Afghanistan, the war on opium ranked among the most feckless. During two decades, the United States spent more than $9 billion on a dizzying array of programs to deter Afghanistan from supplying the world with heroin. None of the measures worked. In many cases, they made things worse.

Between 2002 and 2017, Afghan farmers more than quadrupled the acreage devoted to growing opium poppies, according to estimates by the United Nations Office on Drugs and Crime. During the same period, the production of opium resin—the raw ingredient for heroin—nearly tripled, from 3,200 metric tons to 9,000. Harvests and production tailed off in 2018 and 2019, but the U.N. attributed the decreases to market factors and growing conditions instead of actions taken by U.S. or Afghan officials.

By then, the opium industry had emerged as the unrivaled winner of the longest war in American history. It suffocated other sectors of the Afghan economy, gained a stranglehold over the Afghan government and became indispensable to the insurgency.

"We stated that our goal is to establish a 'flourishing market economy,'" Lt. Gen. Douglas Lute, the White House war czar under Bush and Obama, said in a Lessons Learned interview. "I thought we should have specified a flourishing drug trade—that is the only part of the market that's working."

Arid, rural Helmand province—about the size of West Virginia—powered the drug economy more than any other part of Afghanistan. The more violent and unstable the province became, the more the opium industry thrived.

Besides their unmatched profitability, poppies were easier to cultivate than other crops amid all the fighting. Farmers and traffickers could store opium resin as long as necessary without it losing value. The product took up little space. Transportation was simple and inexpensive, making it ideal for smuggling. Demand stayed reliably strong.

Afghan elites in Kabul often looked down on Helmandi poppy farmers and traders as illiterate clodhoppers. But Air Force Maj. Matthew Brown, who served in the province in 2011, came away impressed by their ingenuity. Helmand "is dirty, filthy and hot," he said in an Army oral-history interview. But, he added, "these guys have a history of smuggling and growing drugs that's second to none. They're really, really good at it. I mean, our smugglers would probably be able to learn a thing or two from these guys."

Brown, who served on a team that tried to reintegrate former Taliban fighters into society, also said, "When someone says Afghanistan doesn't have the capacity to do something, I usually respond with, 'Well, they've got the capacity to provide the entire world's worth of opium.'"

Along with its NATO and Afghan allies, the U.S. government hatched all sorts of schemes to tackle the problem. But Afghan poppy farmers and drug traffickers outfoxed every attempt by Washington to coax, wheedle or compel them to stop.

The Bush and Trump administrations both wielded the stick. Under Bush, the State Department and Drug Enforcement Administration punished farmers by eradicating their fields of poppies, but that only encouraged them to side with the insurgency. Under Trump, the government ignored the farmers and bombed the opium processors, but new drug labs sprouted overnight and production continued unabated.

The Obama administration tried incentivizing farmers to switch crops, an approach that demanded more time and patience. That, too, fell flat.

Richard Holbrooke, the blustery diplomat who served as Obama's special envoy for Afghanistan and Pakistan, had publicly derided the Bush administration's tactics. Upon taking his post in 2009, he immediately brought poppy eradication to a halt.

"The Western policies against the opium crop, the poppy crop, have been a failure," he said during a conference on Afghanistan in Trieste, Italy, in June 2009. "They did not result in any damage to the Taliban, but they put farmers out of work and they alienated people and drove people into the arms of the Taliban."

The Obama administration shifted its focus and money to programs that tried to promote legal forms of agriculture. Holbrooke prodded the State Department, USAID and the Agriculture Department to send small armies of experts to persuade Afghan poppy farmers to switch to other crops, such as wheat, saffron, pistachios and pomegranates.

In Helmand, the U.S. government supplied farmers with seeds, fertilizer and small loans. They paid Afghan laborers to expand the province's network of canals and ditches so farmers could irrigate apple trees, grapevines and strawberry plants. They placed a huge emphasis on pomegranates and juice for export, even though the fruit required cold storage in a country with unreliable electricity.

For a while, it looked like the strategy might work. In 2009, opium poppy cultivation dropped to its lowest level in four years and stayed flat in 2010, according to the U.N.'s annual survey. Obama administration officials began to boast. "This is really paying off," Holbrooke told a House subcommittee in July 2010, referring to the inducements to grow legal crops. "This is our most successful program in the civilian side."

But the improvements were a mirage. In reality, other factors— including weather conditions and the fluctuating global demand for opium—had depressed the numbers. U.S. and European officials also knew the influential U.N. surveys could be unreliable. The surveys relied on sketchy data from satellite images and field inspections in one of the most unstable parts of the world. Officials had only a hazy idea of how many human beings lived in Helmand—estimates ranged from 900,000 to 2 million—so it was unrealistic to expect that they could calculate the acreage set aside for opium poppies each year with precision.

A former senior British official said the U.N. Office on Drugs and Crime privately admitted in 2010 that field workers had falsified its yield surveys for the previous two years. In a Lessons Learned interview, the British official criticized the U.N. for "ineptitude and lack of capacity," saying the errors were "unforgivable." But U.N. officials hid the mistakes from the public.

Sure enough, after dropping between 2008 and 2010, the U.N.'s poppy-growing figures resumed their rapid climb. Throughout the next four years, the U.N. estimated that poppy cultivation soared by more than 80 percent, reaching a new high.

Though well intentioned, many U.S. programs designed to nurture other forms of agriculture backfired. The refurbished canals and irrigation ditches in Helmand, intended to boost production of fruit and specialized crops, also made it easier and more profitable to grow poppies. And while U.S. subsidies induced Helmand farmers to start growing wheat, they often did it on the side and relocated their poppy fields to other parts of the province.

Some federal entities ignored the Obama administration's new approach and pushed to destroy poppy plants anyway. The State Department allocated tens of millions of dollars to a law-enforcement fund for Afghan governors, which they used to eradicate poppy fields on their own. In 2010, Marine Corps units in Helmand paid farmers near the town of Marja to stop growing poppies, an idea that had been discredited years earlier after British officials flubbed a similar program.

In a Lessons Learned interview, the former senior British official said his government, the State Department and Gen. David Petraeus—the war commander at the time—opposed eradication programs. "But no one could stop the Marines," the British official said. "It was generally understood that it wouldn't work but the program went ahead anyway."

Todd Greentree, a State Department official who served as a political adviser to the U.S. military from 2008 to 2012, said it proved impossible to develop a coherent strategy for all arms of the U.S. government. Opium served as the cornerstone of the economy in many rural areas. Drug revenue also oiled the political machinery across most of Afghanistan. As a result, any actions the Americans took to disrupt the opium trade risked undermining the military's counterinsurgency strategy.

"We were always debating and discussing it," Greentree said in a diplomatic oral-history interview. "But at the level of policy, it was a contradiction that was left unmanaged."

Dozens of counter-narcotics programs, many in competition with one another, existed within the State Department, the Pentagon, the Drug Enforcement Administration and other agencies. The Afghan government, NATO allies and the United Nations lobbied for their own ideas and operations. A consensus never emerged. Because no single person or agency was in charge, the problem festered.

Mohammed Ehsan Zia, a former Afghan cabinet minister in charge of rural development programs, said the United States and other NATO members just threw money at the opium problem. In a Lessons Learned interview, he said they constantly changed policies and relied on a carousel of consultants who knew nothing about Afghanistan.

As they did with other nation-building programs, Obama administration officials cared more about spending money quickly than they did about helping Afghans, Zia said. Small loans intended for farmers were wasted on overhead or ended up in the pockets of foreign agricultural advisers. The unintended message: "Reduce poppy now but disregard what needed to be done to reduce it."

"Foreigners read *Kite Runner* on [the] plane and believe they are an expert on Afghanistan and then never listen," Zia added, referring to the best-selling novel about an Afghan boy haunted by oppression and ethnic strife. "The only thing they are experts in is bureaucracy."

Some Obama administration officials said the failures represented another example of how the U.S. government fundamentally misunderstood Afghanistan. Unrelenting warfare since the Soviet invasion in 1979 had destroyed traditional agricultural practices, markets and trade routes. More than donated wheat seed and pomegranate-processing plants, Afghanistan needed peace so it could begin to repair the damage.

"Afghanistan is not an agricultural country; that's an optical illusion," Barnett Rubin, the academic expert who served as an adviser to Holbrooke, said in a Lessons Learned interview. The "largest industry is war, then drugs, then services." Agriculture, he added, "is down in fourth or fifth place."

In another Lessons Learned interview, an unnamed State Department official said it should have been obvious that none of the ideas to discourage Afghans from producing opium would succeed as long as the country remained unstable and global demand for the narcotic stayed high.

"When a country is at war, there is not much that can be achieved," the State Department official said.

*   *   *

Between 2002 and 2017, the U.S. government spent $4.5 billion on drug interdiction in Afghanistan—raids, seizures and other law-enforcement operations—with little to show for it.

The Obama administration more than doubled the number of interdiction operations in the country between 2010 and 2011. Finding opium was easy. The U.S. military and Afghan anti-narcotics officials, with the help of the DEA, confiscated or destroyed tens of thousands of kilos annually. But the seizures amounted to less than 2 percent of what Afghanistan produced each year.

Washington helped the Afghan government create a judicial system from scratch, building courthouses and prisons, training judges and prosecutors. Yet none of it could compete with Afghanistan's informal system of justice, which relied on political connections, tribal affiliations and rampant bribery.

Because drug money contaminated the political system, holding opium barons accountable was almost impossible. U.S. officials methodically compiled dossiers of evidence against suspected kingpins, only to watch their Afghan counterparts sit on the files.

"The issue is political will," an unnamed Justice Department official, who served in Kabul during the Obama years, said in a Lessons Learned interview. "After all how many major traffickers have actually been arrested let alone successfully prosecuted?"

Another senior U.S. official added: "If an Afghan got prosecuted for corruption he had to be incompetent or pissed a lot of people off."

The few who were prosecuted could buy their way out. In 2012, Afghan counter-narcotics agents captured Haji Lal Jan Ishaqzai, an opium trafficker who ran a network centered in Helmand and Kandahar provinces.

Ishaqzai had long operated under the protection of Ahmed Wali Karzai, the president's half-brother. The two men lived on the same street in Kandahar and played cards together. But Ishaqzai lost his security blanket in the summer of 2011 when Karzai was assassinated. Around the same time, the Obama administration officially designated Ishaqzai as a foreign narcotics kingpin, subjecting him to U.S. sanctions.

After Ishaqzai's arrest, an Afghan court in 2013 convicted and sentenced him to twenty years in prison. But Ishaqzai quickly worked the system. He allegedly bribed multiple judges with millions of dollars to approve his transfer from a prison in Kabul to another detention center in Kandahar. Once on his home turf, he persuaded local court officials to authorize his release in April 2014—nineteen years early. By the time authorities in Kabul found out, he had fled to Pakistan.

The Afghan government's unwillingness to punish influential traffickers infuriated U.S. officials, but there was not much they could do. The U.S. military could not legally target drug lords unless there was hard evidence that they represented a direct threat to Americans.

"In the terror model you kill the leader because he is against the government," an unnamed senior DEA official said in a Lessons Learned interview. But when it came to battling Afghan drug networks, "you can't kill the leader [because] he is part of the government patronage system."

Because Washington and Kabul lacked an extradition treaty, bringing opium bosses to the United States to stand trial was extremely difficult. In rare cases when kingpins did make appearances in a U.S. courtroom, things still went awry.

In 2008, U.S. officials lured an alleged Afghan trafficker, 54-year-old Haji Juma Khan, to Jakarta where Indonesian authorities arrested him and extradited him to New York. A federal grand jury indicted Khan, whose network was based in Helmand and Kandahar, on charges of selling massive amounts of heroin and morphine on international markets in support of the Taliban.

But the Justice Department's prosecution of Khan immediately ran into obstacles. The drug lord had served as a valuable paid informant for the CIA and the DEA. The agencies had secretly flown him to Washington for meetings two years earlier and allowed him to take a side trip to New York to go sightseeing and shopping.

When Khan's defense lawyer raised those connections in open court, a federal judge cut her off and warned her against disclosing classified information. The judge later sealed the legal proceedings, closing the case to the public.

The Obama administration designated Khan as a foreign drug kingpin in 2009, but his U.S. criminal charges vanished into a black hole. Though he was never convicted, he remained in federal custody for a decade. Federal prison records show he was released in April 2018. U.S. officials never explained their handling of his case.

As the U.S. military scaled back its presence in Afghanistan between 2011 and 2014, combating the opium trade became even harder. The Obama administration cut spending on agricultural programs and justice reform. Interest waned among U.S. ambassadors and generals, who saw the knotty drug problem as impossible to untie.

Constant staff turnover at the U.S. embassy in Kabul made matters more difficult. Mid and low-level officials assigned to tackle the issue often had little experience or knowledge of the opium trade. "We spent so much time swatting bad ideas down," an unnamed former legal attaché said in a Lessons Learned interview.

In 2016, new embassy staffers began to float some familiar-sounding ideas, like spraying herbicides on poppy fields and eradicating crops with tractors, according to an unnamed State Department contractor who had worked in Afghanistan for years on anti-narcotics programs. Because the war had dragged on for so long, the new staffers didn't realize those tactics had been tried before, to no avail.

Talking with the Taliban

Anastasia, a young blonde expatriate wearing a sleeveless black dress and stiletto heels, exhibited perfect posture as she played the baby grand piano. Her honeyed renditions of "Moon River" and "A Whole New World" drifted through the lobby of a five-star hotel in Qatar. Outside the lobby, overlooking the shoreline of the Persian Gulf, women in bikinis savored alcoholic drinks and flirted with bare-chested men in poolside cabanas. Back in Afghanistan, such licentiousness would have incurred the wrath of the mullahs.

But for two weeks in February and March 2019, a Taliban delegation to Qatar put aside its qualms and peacefully coexisted with the other guests at the Middle Eastern luxury resort. The ascetic Afghans tolerated Anastasia each afternoon when her piano tunes reverberated into their conference room, even though they had outlawed music when they held power and beaten offenders for daring to play such an instrument.

Inside the conference room, the social dynamics were no less awkward. A dozen bearded and turbaned Taliban leaders sat impassively behind one row of tables. On the other side of the room, their longtime enemies—the Americans—sat behind another row of tables and stared right back.

The man in the middle of the U.S. lineup was Army Gen. Scott Miller, whom the Taliban had tried to assassinate in Kandahar a few months earlier.

The Taliban negotiators bore their own personal grudges. Five of them had spent twelve years locked up at Guantánamo Bay, without trial, before the United States released them in a 2014 prisoner swap.

In the conference room, the Americans hoped both sides could set aside their accrued enmities and work out a deal to stop fighting. Just by meeting with the Taliban, U.S. officials had finally admitted the futility of the seventeen-and-a-half-year war.

Despite Trump's public promises to deliver a clear-cut victory, the president had ordered the State Department and the Pentagon to engage in formal, face-to-face negotiations with the Taliban and find a way to extricate U.S. troops from Afghanistan without making it seem like a humiliating defeat.

U.S. officials had said for a decade that brokering a political settlement between the Afghan government and the insurgents was the only feasible way to end the war. They knew a lasting military defeat of the Taliban was highly unlikely. Unlike al-Qaeda, whose shrinking membership consisted of a few Arabs and other foreign fighters, the Taliban was a Pashtun-led mass movement that represented a significant portion of the Afghan population and continued to gain strength.

"There has to be some reconciliation," Army Gen. David Petraeus said during a talk at Harvard University in 2009. "You cannot kill or capture your way out of an industrial-strength insurgency. The question is: How to do that?"

But the Bush and Obama administrations made only half-hearted attempts to find an answer. They squandered multiple opportunities to reach out to the Taliban when the United States and its allies held maximum leverage. They deferred to the Afghan government and allowed it to paralyze the diplomatic process. They unsuccessfully tried to divide and conquer the Taliban leadership, and insisted on unrealistic conditions for talks.

The United States missed its first chance to talk peace with the Taliban in 2001, weeks after the war began. The Bush administration, its allies in the Northern Alliance, and the United Nations, excluded

SIGAR | Office of the Special Inspector General for Afghanistan Reconstruction

LESSONS LEARNED RECORD OF INTERVIEW

Project Title and Code:	
LL-07 – Stabilization in Afghanistan	
Interview Title:	
GEN Edward Reeder	
Interview Code:	
LL 07 71	
Date/Time:	
Location:	
Fayetteville, NC	
Purpose:	
Interviewees:(Either list interviewees below, attach sign-in sheet to this document or hyperlink to a file)	
SIGAR Attendees:	
David Young, Paul Kane	

Sourcing Conditions (On the Record/On Background/etc.):				
Recorded:		Yes		No X
Recording File Record Number (if recorded):				
Prepared By: (Name, title and date)				
Paul Kane				
Reviewed By: (Name, title and date)				
David Young				

Key Topics:
Village Stability Operations

Origins of VSO

This was before my deployment when I was the XO for Admiral Olson at SOCOM. At the time, I was looking at Afghanistan and I was thinking that there has to be more to solving this problem than killing people, because that's what we were doing and every time I went back security was worse. So, I decided that I would have to take a completely different approach, to better understand the tribes and how the Taliban does what they do.

(b)(1) - 1.4(D) "Tell me why they fight, tell me why there is a fighting season, tell me why there are so many problems in Helmand and Kandahar" and they described the influence of poppy and fruit harvests, and how that dictated the seasonal patterns. But they also described how the

In the Lessons Learned interviews, senior U.S. officials admitted that their war strategy was fatally flawed and that they deliberately misled the public with rosy accounts and constant talk of progress. In this interview, Army Maj. Gen. Edward Reeder Jr., a Special Operations Commander who served six tours in Afghanistan, acknowledged that "every time I went back security was worse."

2

Marine Cpl. Burness Britt is lifted aboard a medevac helicopter flight in Helmand province in June 2011. Britt was wounded by a bomb that insurgents planted near the town of Sangin. He was severely injured but survived.

3

Gen. Abdul Rashid Dostum, a powerful Uzbek warlord from northern Afghanistan, arrives at Kabul International Airport in July 2018. Dostum was accused of war crimes by human-rights groups but maintained a close relationship with the U.S. government. One U.S. diplomat called him "a babyface Stalinesque Tito."

Vice President Joe Biden, President Barack Obama, Secretary of State Hillary Clinton, Defense Secretary Robert Gates and other national security officials gather in the White House Situation Room on May 1, 2011, to watch a live video feed of the mission that killed Osama bin Laden in Abbottabad, Pakistan.

U.S. soldiers lift weights in a makeshift outdoor gym at Observation Post Mustang in Kunar province in September 2011. The mountainous outpost in northeastern Afghanistan was near a major route that Taliban fighters used to infiltrate the country from Pakistan.

Army Gen. David Petraeus, the commander of U.S. and NATO forces in Afghanistan, exercises in his quarters at military headquarters in Kabul in July 2011.

Female officers in the Afghan National Army attend their September 2011 graduation ceremony in Kabul. The U.S. war strategy hinged on training and equipping Afghan security forces that could defend the country on their own. But the Afghan army and police forces became plagued by corruption and ethnic tensions.

Afghan Army Sgt. Masiullah Hamdard takes his first steps using his new prosthetic legs and arm at a Red Cross orthopedic rehabilitation center in Kabul in October 2013. Hamdard lost both of his legs and left forearm in an explosion in Kandahar province.

U.S. soldiers at Fort Campbell, Kentucky, board a plane to deploy to Afghanistan in November 2014. The next month, President Obama declared an end to the U.S. combat mission in Afghanistan, but several thousand troops remained in the country—and continued to fight and die in combat.

A gunner looks out of an Afghan army helicopter as it flies over Kabul in December 2019.

A group of Taliban fighters displays their weapons in Marawara district in Kunar province in July 2020. The small district—near the Pakistani border—was a Taliban stronghold for several years. Despite peace talks between the Taliban and the Afghan government, the fighters said they would continue to battle for control of the country.

the Taliban from the Bonn conference that drew up plans for a new Afghan government and constitution.

Another opportunity presented itself three years later, when Afghanistan held its first democratic presidential election and more than eight million Afghans turned out to cast ballots. Karzai won easily and the Taliban looked weak after its threats to derail the vote fell flat. But Karzai and the Bush administration failed to press their political advantage and made no concerted effort to reach out to the Taliban leadership.

Maj. Gen. Eric Olson, the commander of the Twenty-Fifth Infantry Division at the time, said U.S. officials recognized the moment as a strategic turning point for the Afghan government because the Taliban was "on the ropes." But they vacillated over what to do.

"We never figured out, I don't think, how to use military forces to support the reconciliation effort with the Taliban. In the end, that's got to be the national government who actually does it," Olson said in an Army oral-history interview. "I don't ever think we gave the Karzai government either the lead that they needed, or the support that they needed, to make reconciliation go."

Maj. Gen. Peter Gilchrist, a British officer who served as the deputy commander of coalition forces from 2004 to 2005, said the military set up a program to entice Taliban fighters to switch sides. But it struggled to obtain guidance from the State Department and approval from Afghanistan's many political factions.

"It was an interesting bit of spaghetti to untangle," Gilchrist said in an Army oral-history interview. "There was no point in doing something that was good with the Pashtuns and not good with the Tajiks or Hazarans."

Just coming up with a name for the program was tricky. Afghan officials were allergic to the term "reconciliation" because communists had used it during Soviet times. Eventually, they named it the Strengthening Peace Program. Gilchrist said about 1,000 insurgents enrolled, but the process was painstaking and failed to attract any "of the really key players."

After Obama took office, the president said the United States would try again to reach out to the Taliban. "There will also be no peace without reconciliation among former enemies," he said in a speech in March 2009.

But the Obama administration defined "reconciliation" narrowly. It created a new version of the Strengthening Peace Program with the Afghan government but limited eligibility to low-level fighters. U.S. officials pointedly excluded Taliban commanders and mullahs, labeling them as "irreconcilables" and saying they had no options except to surrender or die.

Pentagon officials felt confident taking a hardline approach because Obama and Washington's NATO allies had agreed to flood the war zone with more troops. They assumed their superior forces would give them the upper hand.

"As we regain the initiative, we will support an Afghan-led reconciliation process that's designed to essentially flip the foot soldiers, to bring low- and mid-level leaders to the side of the government," Michèle Flournoy, the undersecretary of defense for policy, told the Senate Armed Services Committee in April 2009. "If this process is successful, the senior leaders, the irreconcilables, should be more easily isolated and we should be better able to target them."

As Obama's troop surge unfolded, military commanders ratcheted up the tough talk.

"We're going to have to break them, irreconcilable from reconcilable," Marine Gen. James Mattis told the Senate Armed Services Committee in July 2010. "If they're irreconcilable, we will neutralize them. If they're reconcilable, if they'll put down their weapons, if they'll work with the government and work within the constitution, then there's going to be a home for them. All wars come to an end, and we've got to make sure we give them a way to end early."

U.S. military officials showed little understanding—or curiosity—about what motivated the Taliban to fight. In her congressional testimony, Flournoy asserted that the insurgency was rooted in "socio-economic crises" and predicted the rebellion would fade as the Afghan government became more established.

Many Afghans despised the Taliban for their brutal tactics. But a substantial percentage of the population—especially among the Pashtuns, Afghanistan's largest ethnic group—sympathized with or actively supported their jihad against the foreign soldiers from the United States and Europe. Their affinity was based more on shared ethnicity, religious beliefs and tribal allegiances than "socio-economic" factors. Unlike the Afghan security forces, which were beset by desertion and corruption, the Taliban had no trouble recruiting fighters who believed in the insurgents' cause.

A few Obama administration officials wanted to push harder for genuine peace talks with the Taliban. Among them were Richard Holbrooke, the State Department envoy, and Barnett Rubin, the academic expert on Afghanistan who maintained unofficial contacts with Taliban figures.

"Our argument was that we only have the insurgency because we don't have a political settlement. And if we don't address it, the military won't be able to," Rubin said in a Lessons Learned interview. But he said officials at the Pentagon and the CIA saw little reason to negotiate with the Taliban and defined reconciliation as "we'll be nice to people who surrender."

Secretary of State Hillary Clinton also resisted pursuing talks with the Taliban. Clinton feared that any attempt to bring the Taliban back into the fold could jeopardize the progress the Afghan government had made on human rights—women's rights in particular. According to Rubin, Clinton didn't want to be seen as soft on the Taliban as she contemplated another run for the presidency.

"Women are [a] very important constituency for her and she couldn't sell making a bargain with the Taliban," Rubin said. "If you want to be the first woman president you cannot leave any hint or doubt that you're not the toughest person on national security."

But Clinton and other heavyweights in Obama's cabinet had other reservations. They viewed the Taliban and al-Qaeda as inseparable and doubted the Taliban would ever cut all ties with bin Laden's network.

*   *   *

In public, the Obama administration portrayed their reconciliation programs for Taliban foot soldiers as methodical and productive. But Army officers who were directly involved described them as slapdash and ill-conceived.

Army Maj. Ulf Rota, a planning officer who served at U.S. and NATO headquarters in Kabul from 2010 to 2011, said a military bureaucracy called the Force Reintegration Cell oversaw the process. The cell was supposed to provide job training to former insurgents in exchange for promises never to take up arms against the government again. But he said program organizers rarely followed through.

The main feature was "a formal reintegration ceremony, where they said, 'I hereby renounce evil al-Qaeda, blah blah blah,'" Rota said in an Army oral-history interview. Most of those who reconciled were "just paid dudes that have nothing else to do. Sometimes they want to give it up and become part of the system again rather than get dragged off . . . and thrown in jail."

Air Force Maj. Matthew Brown, who worked on a reintegration team in Helmand province in 2011, said the program was short-sighted and superficial. He said historical experience showed that most armed insurgencies were grinding conflicts that lasted for twenty to forty years, so expecting large numbers of Taliban fighters to suddenly change their allegiance made no sense.

"It doesn't matter how smart you are, it doesn't matter how much money you spend, it doesn't matter how little you sleep every night, you're not going to substantively change the environment you're operating in in the short term," Brown said in an Army oral-history interview. "It's like society will push back against you the harder you push."

Brown said he remained skeptical that the fighters who offered to reconcile "were the real deal." Tribal leaders and Afghan government officials sometimes manipulated the system and funneled people through the reintegration program just to ingratiate themselves with the Americans.

"There's so many power brokers in Afghanistan that it could be as simple as the governor saying, 'Hey, I'm getting a lot of heat from the coalition. I need you to cough up six bodies.' Some guy's like, 'All right. If I do that will you do this for me?' The guy's like, 'Yes. Please just get these guys off my back for a month.' Miraculously six bodies get coughed up and it's a huge win for reintegration in Helmand."

Karzai established an Afghan High Peace Council in 2010 to coordinate overtures with senior Taliban figures. The Obama administration didn't want to undermine the Afghan government's authority, so it shied away from reaching out to the Taliban without Karzai's blessing.

But the Afghan-led diplomatic track moved at a glacial pace. Karzai and the warlords in his government had little incentive to agree to negotiations that might tacitly recognize the Taliban as a political movement or weaken their own hold on power. The Taliban likewise did not want to lend legitimacy to Karzai, whom they viewed as a foreign puppet. They refused to negotiate until foreign troops agreed to leave the country.

The Obama administration said it supported a dialogue between the Afghan government and the Taliban, but drew up its own list of demands: that the Taliban break ties with al-Qaeda, end violence and support equal rights for Afghan minorities and women.

When glimmers of progress did emerge, extremists on both sides tried to sabotage the process.

In September 2011, Burhanuddin Rabbani, a 71-year-old former Afghan president who led the peace council, received an emissary in his home who claimed he had a message to deliver from the Taliban leadership. When the messenger leaned in to greet Rabbani, he detonated a bomb hidden in his turban. Rabbani and the bomber were both killed. Two other members of the peace council were badly wounded.

U.S. diplomats nevertheless kept trying to nurture back-channel contacts. In January 2012, with Washington's backing, the government of Qatar granted the Taliban permission to open a political office in the country.

The intent was to provide insurgent leaders a protected location in a neutral country where they could meet with U.S. or Afghan government negotiators. But before they could open the political office, the Taliban suspended preliminary talks with U.S. representatives, accusing the Americans of reneging on a deal to release Taliban prisoners from Guantanamo Bay.

The Afghan government distrusted the Qatari back-channel because it feared losing control over negotiations. Ryan Crocker, who served as U.S. ambassador to Afghanistan from 2011 to 2012, said he warned State Department officials that they risked alienating Karzai by endorsing the Taliban's presence in Qatar, but they didn't listen.

"Hamid Karzai was just incensed over that whole thing," he said in a Lessons Learned interview. "We paid lip-service to the notion that this would have to be an Afghan-led, Afghan-managed process."

An attempt by U.S. officials to restart talks the following year blew up again before they got very far. In June 2013, the Taliban finally opened their office in Qatar. But the group also raised a flag and banner advertising the premises as the home of the Islamic Emirate of Afghanistan—the old name of the Taliban government.

The action antagonized Karzai, who saw it as an in-your-face attempt by the Taliban to win diplomatic recognition. He halted the nascent negotiations with the Taliban and refused to sign a bilateral security agreement with the United States that the Obama administration had been pushing.

With the number of U.S. troops in Afghanistan dwindling, the Taliban felt less urgency to rekindle talks unless the terms suited them.

James Dobbins, the career diplomat who returned to the State Department to serve as Obama's envoy to Afghanistan and Pakistan from 2013 to 2014, said the troop withdrawal timetable "was on balance probably unhelpful with respect to incentivizing the Taliban to enter into negotiations." But he said there were other obstacles, "most notably Karzai's deep ambivalence about whether or not he really wanted to do that and under what conditions."

The Taliban held another advantage: a U.S. prisoner of war. In 2009, insurgents captured Army Sgt. Bowe Bergdahl after he wandered away from a U.S. military base in eastern Afghanistan. The Pentagon had been trying to get him back for years, but the Taliban was driving a hard bargain. It demanded the release of Taliban leaders from Guantanamo.

After painstaking negotiations brokered by Qatar, in May 2014, the Obama administration finally agreed to release five Guantánamo inmates who had held senior roles in the Afghan government during the years of Taliban rule. In exchange, the Taliban freed Bergdahl in a carefully orchestrated handover with U.S. Special Forces at a remote rendezvous in eastern Afghanistan.

At first, the Obama administration celebrated the deal as a diplomatic breakthrough and hoped it might lead to further talks with the Taliban. But Republicans in Congress blasted the release of the Taliban prisoners and accused Obama of endangering U.S. national security.

Sen. Lindsey Graham of South Carolina labeled the inmates the "Taliban Dream Team" and said they "have American blood on their hands." Sen. John McCain of Arizona called them "the hardest of the hard core." Trump, then known chiefly as a reality TV show host, piled on with a tweet: "President Obama created a VERY BAD precedent by handing over five Taliban prisoners in exchange for Sgt. Bowe Bergdahl. Another U.S. loss!"

The political backlash killed off any chance of a further rapprochement for the rest of Obama's tenure. For the next four years, unabated warfare consumed Afghanistan and crushed the tepid attempts to make peace.

*   *   *

By 2018, the fighting seemed as senseless as ever. Civilian casualties soared as violence intensified between the Afghan security forces and the insurgents, with U.S. warplanes dropping record-levels of bombs from above.

The first sign of a diplomatic opening surfaced in February 2018, when Afghan President Ashraf Ghani offered to hold unconditional peace talks and said he'd be willing to recognize the Taliban as a political party. The Taliban refused. Its leaders continued to insist on negotiating directly with the Americans and on a complete withdrawal of foreign troops.

Four months later, however, the Taliban relented. After Ghani declared that the Afghan government would observe a unilateral cease-fire to mark the end of the holy month of Ramadan, the Taliban agreed to a three-day truce. For the first time since 2001, combatants from both sides put down their weapons and a brief euphoria took hold in a nation exhausted by war. The fighting resumed after seventy-two hours, but it became apparent that even many of the Taliban's front-line soldiers hungered for peace.

The Trump administration attempted to take advantage of the moment. For the first time, it authorized direct, high-level talks with the Taliban. In July 2018, a senior U.S. diplomat, Alice Wells, held a preliminary meeting with Taliban leaders in Qatar. In a major conces-sion to the insurgents, officials from Ghani's government were excluded from the meeting.

Soon after, the Trump administration called Zalmay Khalilzad, the veteran Afghan-American diplomat, back into public service to lead the negotiations with the Taliban. Khalilzad dove in. He met with the Taliban in Qatar in October. Days later, he persuaded the government of Pakistan to release the Taliban's deputy emir, Mullah Abdul Ghani Baradar, from prison.

Over several months, the two sides held multiple rounds of talks, many taking place in the fancy luxury resort in Qatar. Within a year, a deal appeared close. Under the terms, the United States would with-draw the remainder of its 14,000 troops and the Taliban would agree to negotiate a lasting settlement with the Afghan government and to forsake ties with al-Qaeda.

But in September 2019, the tentative accord unraveled in spectacular fashion. Trump had secretly invited Taliban leaders to Camp David to sign the deal, with Ghani as a witness. But both Ghani and the Taliban balked at the idea of traveling to the United States to join Trump for a photo op. When word leaked that the White House had invited leaders of a terrorist group to Camp David, members of Congress reacted with disbelief. Trump canceled the invitation and declared talks with the Taliban "dead."

After the uproar faded, Khalilzad resumed negotiations with the Taliban in Doha. On February 29, 2020, the two sides signed a complex agreement to wind down the war.

The Trump administration pledged to withdraw U.S. troops in stages, with all forces leaving by May 2021, and to press for the release of 5,000 Taliban prisoners held by the Afghan government. The Taliban promised to begin direct negotiations with Ghani's regime and provided assurances that Afghanistan would not be used to launch attacks on the United States.

But the accord was fraught with gray areas, contingencies and unresolved issues.

After dragging their feet for several months, representatives of the Afghan government and the Taliban finally met in September 2020 in Qatar for official talks. But fighting continued apace as the Taliban pressed for military advantage.

Pentagon officials lobbied Trump to slow down or postpone the U.S. troop withdrawal. But after Trump lost his bid for reelection, he ordered the military to reduce the number of U.S. forces in Afghanistan to 2,500 by the end of his term in January 2021.

That marked the smallest U.S. troop presence since December 2001, back when Afghanistan seemed like a manageable, short-term challenge. At the time, the Taliban had surrendered its last stronghold in Kandahar, U.S. troops had bin Laden pinned down in Tora Bora, and most Americans thought they had decisively won a brief war in a far-away land. For the next two decades, as the conflict degenerated and the quagmire deepened, their leaders lied about what was happening and kept insisting they were making progress.

Like Bush and Obama, Trump failed to make good on his promise to prevail in Afghanistan or to bring what he mocked as "the forever war" to completion. Instead, he handed the unfinished campaign to his political rival, Joseph Biden, the fourth commander in chief to oversee the longest armed conflict in American history.

Biden had closely tracked the arc of the war for two decades, having first traveled to Afghanistan in early 2002 as a U.S. senator. During the Bush administration, he called for sending more troops and resources to Afghanistan to stabilize the country. But by the time he became Obama's vice president in 2009, Biden had grown skeptical of what the United States could accomplish there.

During internal deliberations at the White House, Biden urged Obama to reject the expensive counterinsurgency strategy that expanded the war, pushing instead for a slimmed-down version of the troop surge. In 2011, he counseled Obama against sending the Navy SEALs into Pakistan to hunt down Osama bin Laden, arguing that the mission was too risky. In both instances, his advice went unheeded.

As soon as he became president in January 2021, Biden faced the same conundrum that had bedeviled Bush, Obama and Trump: how to end an unwinnable war? If he brought the remaining U.S. troops home, the Taliban stood an excellent chance of regaining power and the United States risked becoming the second superpower in a generation to leave Afghanistan in defeat. The alternative was to renege on Trump's agreement with the insurgents and keep U.S. forces there indefinitely to prop up the ineffectual and corrupt government in Kabul.

For three months, Biden searched for another way. His administration prodded the Taliban and the Afghan government to accelerate their stalled negotiations and to hold a summit with regional powers. But the efforts held little promise and gained no traction.

On April 14, Biden announced his decision. In a speech from the Treaty Room of the White House, he promised to withdraw all U.S. troops from Afghanistan by September 11, 2021—the twentieth anniversary of the 9/11 attacks.

Unlike his predecessors, Biden gave a sobering assessment of two decades of warfare. He did not try to frame the outcome as a victory. Instead, he said the United States had achieved its original objective long ago by destroying al-Qaeda's stronghold in Afghanistan. He suggested that U.S. troops should have left after they killed Osama bin Laden in May 2011. "That was ten years ago. Think about that," he said.

Ever since, he added, Washington's rationale for staying in Afghanistan had become "increasingly unclear" as it strove to "create ideal conditions" for ending the war. He recalled how military commanders had insisted seven years earlier—during his second term as vice president—that the Afghan army and police were ready to take full responsibility for their country's security, an assessment that proved to be feeble and foolish.

"So when will it be the right moment to leave? One more year, two more years, ten more years? What conditions must be met to depart?" Biden asked. "I'm not hearing any good answers to those questions. And if you can't answer them, in my view, we should not stay."

After his remarks at the White House, Biden crossed the Potomac River and visited Arlington National Cemetery to pay respects to the fallen. Carrying a furled black umbrella under overcast skies, he paced slowly through Section 60 of the cemetery, where veterans of the Afghanistan and Iraq wars are buried. Standing in front of a memorial wreath, he gave the sign of the cross and offered a salute. Then he gazed into the distance, surveying row upon row of white marble gravestones.

"Hard to believe," he murmured. "Look at them all."

Epilogue

Two months after he announced his intention to withdraw all U.S. troops, Biden welcomed Afghan President Ashraf Ghani to the White House. On June 25, 2021, they met in the Oval Office, seated in armchairs under the gaze of oil portraits of Abraham Lincoln and Thomas Jefferson. From an American perspective, the dapper-looking and English-speaking Ghani appeared to be the ideal person to lead Afghanistan. A former Fulbright Scholar and dual U.S.-Afghan citizen, he held a doctorate from Columbia University and enjoyed giving high-minded speeches at the Council on Foreign Relations and other think tanks about state-building and social transformation.

Though Ghani had an unmatched record as a technocrat, he had proven inept as a political leader. Official corruption and cronyism continued to flourish under his watch, and his government failed to make headway in negotiations with the increasingly confident Taliban. During their meeting, Biden promised Ghani ongoing financial and diplomatic support, but reiterated that he would have to find a way to survive without the U.S. military. "Afghans are going to have to decide their future, what they want," Biden said when reporters were ushered into the Oval Office for a photo op. "The senseless violence has to stop."

Ghani tried to put on a good face for the cameras. "President Biden's decision has been historic. It has made everybody recalculate and reconsider," he said. "We are here to respect it and support it." When journalists asked Ghani later in the day about leaked U.S. intelligence assessments predicting that his government could fall to the Taliban within six to twenty-four months, the Afghan president forced a smile. "There have been many such predictions and they have all proven, turned out, false," he replied.

Though the long-term prospects for Ghani's rule seemed dim, the drawdown of U.S. and NATO troops proceeded rapidly. Expectations rose that the allies would all vacate their bases in Afghanistan several weeks before Biden's deadline of September 11.

The German military pulled its final contingent of 570 soldiers from Afghanistan on June 29, when four transport aircraft departed the northern city of Mazar-e-Sharif. Germany had deployed 150,000 troops over two decades, fighting the country's first ground battles since World War II. Fifty-nine German soldiers died during the conflict, and the mission cost German taxpayers about $15 billion.

Other European countries completed their troop withdrawals around the same time. Italy, North Macedonia and Poland also departed Afghanistan on June 29, days after Belgium, Denmark, Estonia, Finland, Georgia, the Netherlands, Norway and Romania had done the same.

On July 2, the U.S. military abruptly abandoned Bagram Air Base, its largest military installation in Afghanistan, leaving in the middle of the night and turning off the electricity without notifying local Afghan army commanders. U.S. troops took their heavy weaponry with them but left behind more than 3 million items of marginal value: doors, windows, telephones, water bottles and packaged rations. Looters broke into the base and made off with some of the booty before Afghan government forces discovered the Americans had vanished.

By then, only several hundred U.S. soldiers remained in the country, and their primary task was to protect the U.S. embassy in Kabul. Britain pulled out most of its remaining troops a few days later. Any doubts as to whether the foreign troops, who had been a fixture of the Afghan landscape for twenty years, would actually leave had evaporated.

Other than a handful of defense hawks and retired generals, few people in the United States or Europe objected to the withdrawal. Most had long ago grown tired of what felt like a forever war, or had stopped paying attention. But as soon as the foreign troops packed up, the Taliban moved to fill the vacuum.

Taliban leaders had methodically planned for the moment. Their fighters imposed checkpoints on highways that connected the country's urban areas. Cities such as Kabul, Herat, Kandahar and Kunduz became increasingly isolated. With the roads in enemy hands, the Afghan army and police had to resupply their scattered network of bases and outposts with airdrops, a logistical nightmare. Many Afghan units surrendered to the Taliban after they ran out of ammunition and food.

As they consolidated their hold on the countryside, seizing about 100 districts over several weeks, the insurgents massed in preparation for attacks on vulnerable provincial capitals. After years of upbeat pronouncements, U.S. military officials sounded dour about Afghanistan's prospects. "The security situation is not good right now," General Scott Miller, the four-star commander of U.S. forces, told reporters at the end of June. "Civil war is certainly a path that can be visualized if this continues the trajectory it's on."

On July 8, Biden's national security team briefed the president about deteriorating conditions in Afghanistan. As he took questions from reporters later that day, Biden downplayed the possibility that Ghani's regime might collapse, saying the Afghans just needed more political resolve. "They clearly have the capacity to sustain the government in place. The question is: will they generate the kind of cohesion to do it?" he said. "They have the capacity. They have the forces. They have the equipment."

Biden bristled when asked if the U.S. withdrawal from Afghanistan might resemble the chaotic evacuation from Vietnam in 1975, when helicopters took off from the roof of the U.S. embassy in Saigon as crowds of panicked Vietnamese desperately tried to escape the communist advance. "There's going to be no circumstance where you see people being lifted off the roof of an embassy, of the United States from Afghanistan," he said. "The likelihood there's going to be Taliban overrunning everything and owning the whole country is highly unlikely."

Biden's remarks demonstrated how—even after twenty years of intensive warfare and diplomacy—the U.S. government remained blind to the fundamental realities on the ground in Afghanistan. That ignorance would haunt the United States and its allies until the very end.

Like his predecessors in the White House, Biden saw the reports of the Taliban's increasing grip on the country as a perception problem that could be managed with public-relations gestures. In a telephone call to Ghani on July 23, Biden urged the Afghan leader to hold a news conference to announce a new military strategy with the backing of an assortment of aging potentates, including former President Hamid Karzai and General Abdul Rashid Dostum, the whiskey-loving warlord.

"The perception around the world and in parts of Afghanistan, I believe, is that things aren't going well in terms of the fight against the Taliban," Biden said, according to a transcript of the fourteen-minute call obtained by the Reuters news agency. "And there's a need, whether it is true or not, there is a need to project a different picture."

Ghani complained that his government was facing "a full-scale invasion" composed of Taliban fighters and "international terrorists" with Pakistani backing. He also pleaded for the U.S. Air Force to conduct more airstrikes against the Taliban, even though the combat aircraft would have to fly from U.S. bases in the Persian Gulf because the Pentagon had closed its bases in Afghanistan. Biden agreed to the request but put the onus back on Ghani. "Look, close air support works only if there is a military strategy on the ground to support," he said before hanging up.

Two weeks later, the Taliban did exactly what Biden had predicted was "highly unlikely"—they began overrunning everything. On August 6, they seized a provincial capital—the city of Zaranj, near the border with Iran—for the first time as Afghan government forces fled without a fight. The next day, they took control of Sheberghan, Dostum's hometown. The day after that, they rolled into Kunduz and two other provincial capitals in the north while facing virtually no resistance from the Afghan army and police. In Kunduz, the most strategic prize, hundreds of Afghan troops fled the city and soon surrendered.

Still, U.S. officials were slow to grasp the severity of the situation. On August 10, U.S. intelligence agencies updated their assessments and predicted the Afghan government could collapse sooner than expected, perhaps within thirty to ninety days. Once again, however, they failed to understand what was unfolding in plain sight. Over the next three days, the Taliban juggernaut overran Afghanistan's second- and third-biggest cities—Kandahar and Herat—and seized Lashkar Gah, the capital of Helmand.

Belatedly, the Biden administration realized that Ghani's government would last for only a few more hours, not for months. The Pentagon and State Department faced a scenario for which they were wholly unprepared: a large-scale, rapid evacuation of U.S. diplomats and citizens, plus tens of thousands of Afghans who had aided the United States during the war and had been promised refuge. As Taliban fighters reached the outskirts of Kabul, the Pentagon announced that it would send 5,000 troops back to the capital to lead the evacuation.

On August 14, Ghani delivered a brief televised address and sounded like a passive actor in a drama swirling around him. "Our dear country Afghanistan is in serious danger of instability due to the war imposed on us," he said.

The next day, long-haired Taliban fighters rode into Kabul on motorbikes, meeting no resistance. Fearing for his life, Ghani climbed aboard a helicopter at the presidential palace and fled the country without informing most of his ministers or his American allies. By late afternoon, the Taliban occupied the palace and posed for photographs in Ghani's office.

Nine days after Taliban had seized its first provincial capital, it had taken control of the entire country.

With no combat airpower of its own and minimal resources, the scraggly collection of insurgents had overwhelmed a well-armed Afghan proxy force that Washington had spent more than $85 billion to train and equip. As the Afghan government imploded, the United States' nation-building project in Afghanistan went up in smoke and the Taliban celebrated their improbable victory against a global superpower.

Meanwhile, the exact scene that Biden predicted would never happen played out at the U.S. embassy in Kabul: an airborne caravan of military helicopters ferried hundreds of anxious staffers to Hamid Karzai International Airport. Embassy personnel rushed to burn documents and destroy computers before the Taliban could enter the capital's diplomatic quarter.

Over the next seventeen days, amid a tenuous truce with the Taliban, the United States and its European allies carried out the largest evacuation airlift in history. More than 124,000 people fled Afghanistan on flights from the Kabul airport. U.S. military aircraft transported 79,000 civilians, including 6,000 U.S. citizens. Another 40,000 people escaped on flights operated by other NATO members or on commercial aircraft.

In many ways, the fall of Kabul mirrored the fall of Saigon forty-six years earlier. As the airlift began, thousands of desperate Afghans swarmed the single runway at the airport. Video clips showed thick crowds of Afghan men sprinting alongside a gray U.S. Air Force C-17 Globemaster III transport plane as it taxied for takeoff. Several managed to cling to the outside of the giant aircraft. After the C-17 rose into the sky, two people plummeted to their deaths over Kabul. Crushed portions of human remains were later found in the plane's wheel well.

U.S. troops resecured the airfield, but for the next two weeks, refugees mobbed the gates. Families had to brave gauntlets of Taliban fighters just to reach the outside of the airport, where they waited for hours under a broiling sun in hopes that they might somehow talk their way in. Insurgents opened fire sporadically and administered beatings as U.S. and European officials gave confusing directions on who was allowed to enter the airport and what documents were necessary to do so.

U.S. officials worried that the exposed masses of refugees and military personnel had become an easy target for terrorists intent on causing further mayhem. On August 26, their fears were realized when a suicide bomber recruited by the Islamic State made his way to one of the airport gates and detonated his belt of explosives, killing 13 U.S. troops and 170 Afghan civilians.

Speaking from the White House, Biden promised to avenge their deaths but warned that the threat of similar attacks remained high as long as the airlift continued. While scouring Kabul for more bombers, the U.S. military fired a missile from a drone at a car on August 29, killing the driver and several bystanders.

At first, Pentagon officials claimed that they had disrupted another suicide mission; Army Gen. Mark Milley, the chairman of the Joint Chiefs of Staff, called it "a righteous strike." But journalists soon discovered that the driver of the car was in fact an Afghan humanitarian aid worker, Zamairi Ahmadi, and that nine members of his family, including seven children, had been killed. After the evacuation concluded on August 30, the Pentagon admitted it had committed "a tragic mistake."

Up until the very end of twenty years of war, the United States still could not tell the good guys from the bad guys.

Acknowledgments

Emblazoned on a wall in *The Washington Post*'s newsroom is a quotation—"Journalism is the first rough draft of history"—from Philip L. Graham, who served as the newspaper's publisher from 1946 to 1961. To put it less succinctly, news reporting is an initial attempt to define and interpret noteworthy events: a preliminary step in a never-ending effort to understand and interpret the past.

This book is a work of journalism, yet it doesn't quite match Phil Graham's definition; it more resembles a second, or even a third, draft of history. For the most part, *The Afghanistan Papers* reassesses events that occurred years ago and have already started to fade from memory. But the primary sources that provide the foundation for this book bring a new perspective on what went wrong and why the conflict persisted for so long. The Lessons Learned interviews, oral histories and snowflakes reveal for the first time, in blunt and incontrovertible terms, that U.S. leaders knew their war strategy was dysfunctional and privately doubted they could attain their objectives. Yet they confidently told the public year after year that they were making progress and that victory—winning—was just over the horizon.

This knowledge only came to light because the leadership of *The Washington Post*, my professional home for the past 23 years, made an institutional commitment to uncover the truth about the longest war in American history. When SIGAR repeatedly stonewalled my public-records requests, *The Post* faced a decision: back down and move on to an easier story, or else, sue the federal agency under the Freedom of Information Act (FOIA).

Hauling the federal government into court is not for the faint-hearted. FOIA lawsuits are almost always expensive and time-consuming—words that no editor wants to hear—and there is no guarantee a case will go your way. So I will be forever grateful to *The Post's* leadership for their resolve and dedication. Jeff Leen and David Fallis, my editors on the Investigative Desk, expertly managed the project from the start and gave me the time and space to dig. When I needed legal help and high-level support, Executive Editor Marty Baron, Managing Editor Cameron Barr and Publisher Fred Ryan didn't hesitate or flinch. They recognized the potential importance of the Lessons Learned interviews and cleared the way to file not just one but two lawsuits against SIGAR to force the government to comply with the open-records law. Reporters can't tackle difficult stories unless their bosses have their backs, and this group had mine.

Special credit goes to *The Post's* formidable legal department, especially James McLaughlin and Jay Kennedy, and three sharpshooter attorneys from the law firm Ballard Spahr—Charles Tobin, Maxwell Mishkin and Matthew Kelley—who represented *The Post* in federal court. They spent untold hours preparing and refining our FOIA cases, tangling with government attorneys and humoring my attempts at armchair lawyering. Without them, the trove of Lessons Learned documents would still be concealed from the public.

As SIGAR grudgingly began releasing the documents in drips and drabs after repeated delays, it became clear the interviews were not just newsworthy but showed that senior U.S. officials had lied to the public. *The Post's* editors decided that we would aim high with a multi-part series and present all the documents and audio recordings online so readers could see and hear for themselves. The newsroom leadership assembled a talented team of project developers, graphic designers, database whizzes and copy editors, as well as photo, video and audio producers. To ensure that word of our exclusive reporting didn't leak out prematurely, we operated on a need-to-know basis and code-named the project Avocado.

My everlasting thanks to the charter members of the Avocado team: Julie Vitkovskaya, Leslie Shapiro, Armand Emamdjomeh, Danielle Rindler, Jake Crump, Matt Callahan, Nick Kirkpatrick, Joyce Lee, Ted Muldoon, JJ Evans and Annabeth Carlson. Their talents are unmatched and they proved themselves worthy of the top-secret clearance. Former Kabul bureau chiefs Joshua Partlow and Griff Witte, two exceptionally smart and collegial correspondents, provided critical feedback on the story drafts through a separate back channel.

When deadline approached, the team expanded. Managing Editor Emilio Garcia-Ruiz, another strong backer of the project, cracked wise that half the newsroom was busy working on Avocado. Important contributions were made by Martine Powers, Madhulika Sikka, Michael Johnson, Tom LeGro, Brian Cleveland, Laris Karklis, Jenn Abelson, Meryl Kornfield, Alex Horton, Susannah George, Sharif Hassan, Sayed Salahuddin, Jennifer Amur, Eva Rodriguez, Doug Jehl, Julie Tate, Tim Curran, Greg Manifold, MaryAnne Golon, Robert Miller, Tim Meko, Chiqui Esteban, Jason Bernert, Courtney Kan, Brian Gross, Joanne Lee, William Neff, María Sánchez Díez, Kanyakrit Vongkiatkajorn, Ric Sanchez, Jennifer Hassan, Travis Lyles, T.J. Ortenzi, Tessa Muggeridge, Robert Davis, Kenisha Malcolm, Emily Tsao, Molly Gannon, Aja Hill, Diyana Howell, Coleen O'Lear, Steven Bohner, Amy Cavanaile, Mia Torres, John Taylor, Chris Barber, Eric Reyna, Charity Brown, Greg Barber, Danielle Newman, Iris Long and Mike Hamilton.

After the series was published, we heard from hundreds of readers who urged us to expand our reporting into a book. Marty Baron encouraged me to make it happen as a *Post* project. My literary agent, Christy Fletcher of Fletcher & Company, provided her usual wise guidance and played a critical role in transforming an idea into reality. Thanks also to Todd Shuster at Aevitas Creative Management and to *Post* managing editors Tracy Grant, Kat Downs Mulder and Krissah Thompson.

I am exceptionally grateful to the team at Simon & Schuster for recognizing the narrative potential in these historical documents and for devoting so much energy and resources to this book. Thanks in particular to Priscilla Painton, vice president and editorial director for Simon & Schuster's nonfiction program. Her spot-on insights, inspirational feedback and laser-precise edits improved every chapter. I can't wait to work together on our next book. Thanks also to the indispensable Hana Park for shepherding the project, to Kate Lapin for her proficient copyediting, and to John Pelosi for his careful legal review. It has also been a pleasure to work with a marketing and publicity dream team: Kirstin Berndt and Elise Ringo of Simon & Schuster and Kathleen Floyd of *The Post*.

This book would have been impossible to write had I not been able to tap into several other troves of documents. The National Security Archive at George Washington University provides an irreplaceable public service by prying loose records from federal agencies that prefer to operate in the dark. Enormous thanks go to Thomas Blanton, the Archive's director, and FOIA guru Nate Jones for suing the Defense Department under FOIA to obtain Donald Rumsfeld's snowflakes and for allowing me to sift through the entire 50,000-page avalanche. The Archive also shared a valuable batch of declassified diplomatic cables.

For more than a decade, the U.S. Army's Combat Studies Institute at Fort Leavenworth, Kansas, had the foresight to conduct oral-history interviews with veterans of the war in Afghanistan as part of its Operational Leadership Experience project. I owe a large debt to the project organizers for their methodical work. Thanks to Don Wright, the deputy director of Army University Press, for patiently answering my questions. Thanks also to Andrew Ba Tran of *The Post* for gathering thousands of the transcripts and making them easily accessible for my research.

I extend a special salute to the Miller Center at the University of Virginia, which fortuitously made dozens of transcripts from its George W. Bush Oral History Project publicly available just as I began writing this book. Thanks to Russell Riley, co-chair of the Miller Center's Presidential Oral History Program, for cheerfully fielding my many queries and going beyond the call of duty to triple-check the original audio recording of General Peter Pace's interview to make sure a colorful quotation was correct.

A special shout-out goes to Candace Rondeaux, a journalist and analyst who covered the war in Afghanistan for years. Thanks also to the Association for Diplomatic Studies & Training and its invaluable Foreign Affairs Oral History Program. Charles Stuart Kennedy, the program director since its inception in 1985, has personally interviewed more than one thousand retired American diplomats and the transcripts are always illuminating to read.

Several *Post* colleagues played essential roles in bringing this book to life, and I can't thank them enough for their hard work and expertise. Nick Kirkpatrick reviewed tens of thousands of photographs of the war in Afghanistan and curated a remarkable selection of images. The beautiful map inside the cover is the result of Laris Karklis's cartographic artistry. Julie Tate rigorously fact-checked the manuscript and helped compile the source citations. Needless to say, any errors or omissions are my responsibility alone.

It has been my greatest pleasure to collaborate with David Fallis, the front-line editor of this book and my longtime *Post* colleague and friend. We first teamed up on an investigative project more than two decades ago; his enthusiasm, drive and determination to get it right are unparalleled. A bulldog of a journalist, he belongs to that rare breed whose reporting and editing skills are equally of the highest caliber.

Finally, and most meaningfully, a heartfelt thank-you to my wife, Jennifer Toth, and our son, Kyle Whitlock. Jenny is a far more talented author and writer than me, and I cannot express how much I have depended on, and benefited from, her advice, love and steadfast support. Like many Americans, 9/11 reshaped our lives in unpredictable ways. Soon after we celebrated Kyle's first birthday in 2001, *The Post* sent me to Pakistan to help cover the war, the start of a journey that ultimately took our family all over the world. The past two decades have been an adventure, but none of it would have been possible, or worthwhile, without them.

—Craig Whitlock
Silver Spring, Maryland
March 1, 2021

Note on Sources

This book is based almost exclusively on public documents: notes of interviews with more than 1,000 people who played a direct role in the U.S. war in Afghanistan, as well as hundreds of Defense Department memos, State Department cables and other government reports.

The Washington Post obtained the Lessons Learned interview documents from the Special Inspector General for Afghanistan Reconstruction (SIGAR) after filing multiple public-records requests beginning in 2016, and two Freedom of Information Act (FOIA) lawsuits.

The Post's lawsuits eventually compelled SIGAR to release more than 2,000 pages of unpublished notes and transcripts from 428 interviews, as well as several audio recordings. SIGAR staffers conducted the Lessons Learned interviews between 2014 and 2018. Almost all the interviews focused on events that occurred during the Bush and Obama administrations. About thirty of the interview records are transcribed, word-for-word accounts. The rest are typed summaries consisting of notes and quotations. SIGAR has stipulated in court that all the material it released was independently verified by the agency.

Most of the people interviewed by SIGAR were Americans. SIGAR analysts also traveled to Europe and Canada to interview dozens of foreign officials from NATO countries. In addition, they visited Kabul to interview current and former Afghan government officials, aid workers and development consultants.

SIGAR redacted the names of most—about 85 percent—of the people it interviewed, citing a variety of FOIA privacy exemptions. In legal briefs, the agency categorized those individuals as whistleblowers and informants who might face harassment or embarrassment if their names became public.

The Post asked a federal judge to force SIGAR to disclose the names of everyone the agency interviewed for the Lessons Learned project, arguing that the public has a right to know the identities of officials who criticized the war and admitted that the U.S. government's policies were flawed. *The Post* further argued that those individuals were not whistleblowers or informants because SIGAR interviewed them for the purpose of publishing a series of public reports, not as part of a law-enforcement investigation. As of the time of this writing, the drawn-out FOIA litigation is unresolved.

Separately, by cross-referencing dates and other details from the documents, *The Post* independently identified thirty-four of the people interviewed by SIGAR, including former ambassadors, military officers and White House officials.

The Post sought additional comment from individuals whom it was able to identify as having given an interview to SIGAR. Responses from those who are quoted by name are included in the endnotes.

This book describes the positions held by unnamed Lessons Learned interview subjects—such as "senior State Department official" or "former White House staffer"—based on information provided by SIGAR in response to *The Post*'s FOIA requests as well as the context of the interviews.

Besides withholding names, SIGAR redacted portions of the interview documents, including information that was subsequently classified by the State Department, Defense Department and the Drug Enforcement Administration.

The Rumsfeld snowflake memos were shared with *The Post* by the National Security Archive, a nonprofit research organization affiliated with George Washington University.

Most of the Army oral-history interviews were conducted by the Operational Leadership Experience project, part of the Combat Studies Institute at Fort Leavenworth, Kansas. The Combat Studies Institute interviewed more than 600 service members between 2005 and 2015 upon their return from Afghanistan. Most were mid-career Army officers enrolled in professional military education courses at Fort Leavenworth, but the number includes some enlisted soldiers and personnel from other branches of the armed forces. The Army oral-history interviews are unclassified, publicly available, word-for-word transcriptions based on audio recordings. This book identifies military personnel by the rank they held at the time of their oral-history interviews. Many served multiple tours of duty in Afghanistan.

This book also cites a small number of oral-history interviews that the U.S. Army Center of Military History in Washington, D.C., conducted with senior officers in 2006 and 2007. Those interviews deal with events in the war from 2003 to 2005.

The University of Virginia oral-history interviews with senior members of the Bush administration were conducted by the Miller Center, a nonpartisan affiliate of the university that specializes in presidential scholarship. The Miller Center opened a portion of its George W. Bush oral-history collection to the public in November 2019. The lengthy interview transcripts are based on audio recordings.

Finally, this book draws on several diplomatic oral-history interviews that were conducted by the nonprofit Association for Diplomatic Studies and Training. The ADST's extensive, publicly available oral-history collection features interviews with U.S. diplomats about their experiences in the field during the past eight decades.

Endnotes

FOREWORD

xix *"There was no campaign plan":* Gen. Dan McNeill interview, undated, Lessons Learned Project, Special Inspector General for Afghanistan Reconstruction (SIGAR).

xix *"no coherent long-term strategy":* Gen. David Richards interview, September 26, 2017, Lessons Learned Project, SIGAR.

xix *"We did not know what we were doing":* Ambassador Richard Boucher interview, October 15, 2015, Lessons Learned Project, SIGAR.

xix *"We didn't have the foggiest notion":* Lt. Gen. Douglas Lute interview, February 20, 2015, Lessons Learned Project, SIGAR.

xx *"magnitude of this dysfunction":* Ibid.

xxi *"I have no visibility":* Donald Rumsfeld memo to Steven Cambone, September 8, 2003, National Security Archive, George Washington University.

xxiii *"this is about decades":* Gen. Peter Pace interview, January 19, 2016, George W. Bush Oral History Project, Miller Center, University of Virginia.

CHAPTER ONE: A MUDDLED MISSION

5 *"I may be impatient":* Donald Rumsfeld memo to Doug Feith, Paul Wolfowitz, Gen. Dick Myers and Gen. Pete Pace, April 17, 2002, the National Security Archive, George Washington University. The document was partially declassified by the Defense Department on September 22, 2010.

5 *"The only thing you can do":* Donald Rumsfeld interview with MSNBC, March 28, 2002.

5 the "most confident man" in America: Ibid.

6 "I am getting concerned": Donald Rumsfeld memo to Larry Di Rita and Col. Steven Bucci, March 28, 2002, the National Security Archive, George Washington University.

7 "If I were to write a book": Former senior State Department official interview, October 8, 2014, Lessons Learned Project, SIGAR. Name redacted by SIGAR.

7 "What were we actually doing": U.S. official interview, February 10, 2015, Lessons Learned Project, SIGAR. Name redacted by SIGAR.

7 "If there was ever a notion": Boucher interview, October 15, 2015, Lessons Learned Project, SIGAR.

8 "a systematic government": Ibid.

8 "We received some general guidance": Lt. Cmdr. Philip Kapusta interview, May 1, 2006, Operational Leadership Experiences project, Combat Studies Institute, Fort Leavenworth, Kansas.

8 The secret, six-page document: Unsigned memo, "U.S. Strategy in Afghanistan," October 16, 2001, the National Security Archive, George Washington University. Originally labeled as "draft for discussion," a handwritten note on the document states that the strategy was approved at a National Security Council meeting on October 16, 2001. In an October 30, 2001 snowflake attached to the memo, Rumsfeld called it "a pretty good paper" and added: "It seems to me that it is useful to update this from time to time." The document was declassified in full by the Defense Department on July 20, 2010.

8 "The U.S. should not commit": Ibid.

9 "we wanted to avoid the big footprint": Douglas Feith interview, March 22–23, 2012, George W. Bush Oral History Project, Miller Center, University of Virginia.

9 four hours to get it done: Ibid.

9 sat in front of his computer: Ibid.

10 "the fucking stupidest guy on the face of the earth": Woodward, Plan of Attack, p. 281. In his own book, published after Woodward's, Franks described Feith as "the dumbest fucking guy on the planet." Tommy Franks, American Soldier (New York: Regan Books, 2004), p. 362.

10 "He was always right": Gen. George Casey interview, September 25, 2014, George W. Bush Oral History Project, Miller Center, University of Virginia.

10 Feith got along well with Pace: Pace interview, Miller Center.

10 "I turned around to Pace": Feith interview, Miller Center.

10 some obvious questions: Ibid.

10 "One of the guys actually said": Kapusta interview, Combat Studies Institute.

10 *"Around November we were wondering"*: Pace interview, Miller Center.

11 *"they needed a bath"*: Maj. Jeremy Smith interview, January 9, 2012, Operational Leadership Experiences project, Combat Studies Institute, Fort Leavenworth, Kansas.

12 *"Even before the plane stopped"*: Ibid.

12 *guarding the 2002 Winter Olympics*: Vice Adm. Ed Giambastiani memo to Donald Rumsfeld, January 30, 2002, the National Security Archive, George Washington University.

12 *"There was one shower"*: Maj. David King interview, October 6, 2005, Operational Leadership Experiences project, Combat Studies Institute, Fort Leavenworth, Kansas.

13 *"It was moon dust"*: Maj. Glen Helberg interview, December 7, 2009, Operational Leadership Experiences project, Combat Studies Institute, Fort Leavenworth, Kansas.

13 *"Afghanistan's done"*: Maj. Lance Baker interview, February 24, 2006, Operational Leadership Experiences project, Combat Studies Institute, Fort Leavenworth, Kansas.

13 *"The guys just played video games"*: Maj. Andrew Steadman interview, March 15, 2011, Operational Leadership Experiences project, Combat Studies Institute, Fort Leavenworth, Kansas.

13 *"It was actually very boring"*: Maj. Steven Wallace interview, October 6, 2010, Operational Leadership Experiences project, Combat Studies Institute, Fort Leavenworth, Kansas.

14 *"We originally said that we don't do nation-building"*: Stephen Hadley interview, September 16, 2015, Lessons Learned Project, SIGAR.

14 *"everybody was talking about a year or two"*: Ambassador Robert Finn interview, October 22, 2015, Lessons Learned Project, SIGAR.

15 *"How many more attacks have there been"*: Gen. Tommy Franks interview, October 22, 2014, George W. Bush Oral History Project, Miller Center, University of Virginia.

15 *"Now, we created other problems"*: Ibid.

15 *"There was no campaign plan in the early days"*: McNeill interview, Lessons Learned Project.

15 *"'Who is General McNeill?'"*: Donald Rumsfeld memo, October 21, 2002, the National Security Archive, George Washington University. The name of the memo recipient was redacted by the Defense Department.

CHAPTER TWO: "WHO ARE THE BAD GUYS?"

17 *"Greetings from scenic Kandahar"*: Roger Pardo-Maurer letter from Kandahar, August 11–15, 2002, the National Security Archive, George Washington University. In a September 13, 2002, snowflake, Rumsfeld

asked his aide, Larry Di Rita, to obtain a copy of the Pardo-Maurer letter for him to read.

17 *"a quasi-Venusian sub-Martian environment"*: Ibid.

18 *"If there is a landscape less welcoming"*: Ibid.

18 *"a formidable pack"*: Ibid.

18 *"crude vainglorious chumps"*: Ibid.

18 *"quite likely the deadliest bunch in town"*: Ibid.

18 *"Time is of the essence here"*: Ibid.

19 *"we didn't know jack shit about al-Qaeda"*: Robert Gates interview, July 9, 2013, George W. Bush Oral History Project, Miller Center, University of Virginia.

20 *"The complexities will take a long time to unravel"*: Jeffrey Eggers interview, August 25, 2015, Lessons Learned Project, SIGAR.

20 *"Why, if we were focused on al-Qaeda, were we talking about the Taliban?"*: Ibid.

21 *"basically getting stoned at the time as a hippie"*: Michael Metrinko interview, October 6, 2003, Foreign Affairs Oral History Project, Association for Diplomatic Studies and Training.

21 *"Much of what we call Taliban activity was really tribal"*: Ibid.

22 *"ran around in beards and funny clothes"*: Ibid.

22 *his unit's mission was to capture and kill "anti-coalition militia"*: Maj. Stuart Farris interview, December 6, 2007, Operational Leadership Experiences project, Combat Studies Institute, Fort Leavenworth, Kansas.

22 *"We had to figure out who the bad guys were"*: Ibid.

22 *"how the hell do you know it's the Taliban?"*: Maj. Thomas Clinton interview, March 12, 2007, Operational Leadership Experiences project, Fort Leavenworth, Kansas.

22 *just "hillbillies" from small towns*: Maj. Gen. Eric Olson interview, July 23, 2007, U.S. Army Center of Military History, Washington, D.C.

23 *"They thought I was going to come to them with a map"*: Special Forces combat adviser interview, December 15, 2017, Lessons Learned Project, SIGAR. Name redacted by SIGAR.

23 *"I have no visibility into who the bad guys are"*: Donald Rumsfeld memo to Steve Cambone, September 8, 2003, the National Security Archive, George Washington University.

23 *a critical mass of intelligence reports*: "Tora Bora Revisited: How We Failed to get Bin Laden and Why It Matters Today," Report to the U.S. Senate Committee on Foreign Relations, November 30, 2009.

24 *"You say, 'Why didn't you?'"*: Franks interview, Miller Center.

24 *Yet nobody had asked for that many troops*: "Tora Bora Revisited," Report to the U.S. Senate Committee on Foreign Relations, November 30, 2009.

24 *During the apex of the fighting:* Maj. William Rodebaugh interview, February 23, 2010, Operational Leadership Experiences project, Combat Studies Institute, Fort Leavenworth, Kansas.

24 *"We were ready if they asked us":* Ibid.

24 *In response to criticism:* "Tora Bora Revisited," Report to the U.S. Senate Committee on Foreign Relations, November 30, 2009.

25 *"Mr. bin Laden was never within our grasp":* Tommy Franks, "War of Words," *The New York Times,* October 19, 2004.

25 *a dubious set of talking points:* "U.S. Department of Defense Talking Points—Bin Laden Tora Bora," October 26, 2004, the National Security Archive, George Washington University.

25 *"'Tora Bora is the deal, Franks. He's in Tora Bora'":* Franks interview, Miller Center.

26 *The hotel assured its guests that it had removed pork from the menu:* Dobbins, *After the Taliban,* p. 82.

26 *"A major mistake we made":* Barnett Rubin interview, August 27, 2015, Lessons Learned Project, SIGAR.

27 *"Everyone wanted the Taliban to disappear":* Barnett Rubin interview, January 20, 2015, Lessons Learned Project, SIGAR.

27 *"we violated the Afghan way of war":* Todd Greentree interview, May 13, 2014, Foreign Affairs Oral History Project, Association for Diplomatic Studies and Training.

27 *"the original sin":* "An Interview with Lakhdar Brahimi," *Journal of International Affairs,* Vol. 58, No. 1, Fall 2004.

27 *"there was a missed opportunity":* Ambassador James Dobbins interview, January 11, 2016, Lessons Learned Project, SIGAR.

28 *"Maybe we were not agile or wise enough":* Ambassador Zalmay Khalilzad interview, December 7, 2016, Lessons Learned Project, SIGAR.

CHAPTER THREE: THE NATION-BUILDING PROJECT

29 *they found overflowing toilets:* Franks interview, Miller Center.

29 *a thick haze of smoke:* Metrinko interview, Association for Diplomatic Studies and Training.

29 *"mile after mile of basically lifeless lug":* Ambassador Ryan Crocker interview, January 11, 2016, Lessons Learned Project, SIGAR.

29 *one hundred Marine guards had to share a single toilet:* Metrinko interview, Association for Diplomatic Studies and Training.

30 *"no real authority and nothing to work with":* Crocker interview, January 11, 2016, SIGAR.

30 *allocating $143 billion for reconstruction:* "Quarterly Report to the United States Congress," January 30, 2021, SIGAR, p. 25.

31 *"the writing is on the wall now":* Michael Callen interview, October 22, 2015, Lessons Learned Project, SIGAR.

31 *"pretty hard to justify and defend":* Crocker interview, January 11, 2016, SIGAR.

32 *no banks and no legal tender:* Senior USAID official interview, June 3, 2015, Lessons Learned Project, SIGAR. Name redacted by SIGAR.

32 *"It's hard to explain to people":* Ibid.

32 *Thirty people crowded around the table:* Boucher interview, SIGAR.

32 *"It was just like the American cabinet":* Ibid.

32 *"This huge banquet with piles of rice and dead goats":* Ibid.

33 *"We released the furies and then went home":* Hadley interview, SIGAR.

34 *"Nation-building was not high on the agenda":* U.S. official interview, September 23, 2014, Lessons Learned Project, SIGAR. Name redacted by SIGAR.

34 *the policy had "changed from anti– to pro–nation-building":* U.S. official interview, December 4, 2015, Lessons Learned Project, SIGAR. Name redacted by SIGAR.

34 *"There was a profound sense of a lack of possibility":* Richard Haass interview, October 23, 2015, Lessons Learned Project, SIGAR.

34 *"There was just not any appetite":* Ibid. In an email to the author in December 2019, Haass added: "There was no enthusiasm—as contrasted with Iraq, where there was altogether too much enthusiasm."

34 *"what is our theory and objectives?":* Senior Bush administration official interview, June 1, 2005, Lessons Learned Project, SIGAR. Name redacted by SIGAR.

34 *He summarized Rumsfeld's mindset this way:* Ambassador Ryan Crocker interview, December 1, 2016, Lessons Learned Project, SIGAR.

35 *"There was no way the State Department":* Dobbins interview, SIGAR.

35 *"the critical problem in Afghanistan is not really a security problem":* Donald Rumsfeld memo to President George W. Bush, August 20, 2002, the National Security Archive, George Washington University.

35 *"we could run the risk of ending up being as hated as the Soviets were":* Ibid.

36 *"a misunderstood figure":* Marin Strmecki interview, October 19, 2015, Lessons Learned Project, SIGAR.

36 *"It is often easier to do stuff ourselves":* Ibid.

36 *"We originally said that we won't do nation-building":* Hadley interview, SIGAR. In an email to the author in December 2019, Hadley added: "There is a good reason we do not have a stabilization model that works. The United States has rightly invested heavily and consistently in our military—and produced the finest military the world has ever known. But the United States has underinvested in those civilian tools

and capabilities of diplomacy, economic and social development, democratic governance, infrastructure development, and civilian institution building that are essential for any post-conflict stabilization effort to succeed. Even so, a lot positive was accomplished in Afghanistan."

37 *"In hindsight the worst decision was to centralize power":* European Union official interview, February 4, 2015, Lessons Learned Project, SIGAR. Name redacted by SIGAR.

37 *"it was thought that we needed a president right away":* Senior German official interview, February 2, 2015, Lessons Learned Project, SIGAR. Name redacted by SIGAR.

37 *"You'd think they've never worked overseas":* Senior U.S. official interview, October 18, 2016, Lessons Learned Project, SIGAR. Name redacted by SIGAR.

37 *"our policy was to create a strong central government, which was idiotic":* Senior U.S. diplomat interview, July 10, 2015, Lessons Learned Project, SIGAR. Name redacted by SIGAR.

37 *"a floating pool of tribes and warlords":* Boucher interview, SIGAR.

38 *"they're remote people":* Col. Terry Sellers interview, February 21, 2007, U.S. Army Center of Military History, Washington, D.C.

38 *his unit handed out posters of Karzai:* Col. David Paschal interview, July 18, 2006, Operational Leadership Experiences project, Combat Studies Institute, Fort Leavenworth, Kansas.

38 *"We did it the exact opposite in Afghanistan":* Ibid.

39 *"The Afghans think Americans have money coming out of their butts":* Thomas Clinton interview, Combat Studies Institute.

39 *"They have a very long history of being loyal":* Lt. Col. Todd Guggisberg interview, July 17, 2006, Operational Leadership Experiences project, Combat Studies Institute, Fort Leavenworth, Kansas.

39 *"It reminds me of a Monty Python movie":* Ibid.

CHAPTER FOUR: AFGHANISTAN BECOMES AN AFTERTHOUGHT

44 *"We used to laugh":* Lt. Col. Mark Schmidt interview, February 10, 2009, Operational Leadership Experiences project, Combat Studies Institute, Fort Leavenworth, Kansas.

45 *"There was still a lot of combat action going on":* Col. Thomas Snukis interview, March 1, 2007, U.S. Army Center of Military History, Washington, D.C.

45 *"Washington had probably lost a little bit of interest":* Col. Tucker Mansager interview, April 20, 2007, U.S. Army Center of Military History, Washington, D.C.

45 *"invade only one country at a time":* Dobbins interview, SIGAR.

45 *"If you look at the Clinton administration"*: Ibid.

46 *"The president wants to see you in Crawford"*: Franks interview, Miller Center.

46 *"So this idea of people taking their eye off the ball"*: Ibid.

46 *"the Bush administration had already concluded Afghanistan was done"*: Philip Zelikow interview, July 28, 2010, George W. Bush Oral History Project, Miller Center, University of Virginia.

47 *"nuisance bandits up in the mountains"*: Finn interview, SIGAR.

47 *"Before we left, my soldiers wanted to know"*: Maj. Gregory Trahan interview, February 5, 2007, Operational Leadership Experiences project, Combat Studies Institute, Fort Leavenworth, Kansas.

47 *"that just pulled all the focus"*: Maj. Phil Bergeron interview, December 8, 2010, Operational Leadership Experiences project, Combat Studies Institute, Fort Leavenworth, Kansas.

47 *"Either materially or politically, it all seemed to be about Iraq"*: U.S. official interview, October 21, 2014, Lessons Learned Project, SIGAR. Name redacted by SIGAR.

48 *"The whole effort in Afghanistan was in a bit of a sideways drift"*: Lt. Gen. David Barno interview, November 21, 2006, U.S. Army Center of Military History, Washington, D.C.

48 *he occupied a half-trailer:* Ibid.

49 *"The Army was unhelpful, to be generous"*: Ibid.

49 *"people who were kind of at the end of the pipeline"*: Ibid.

49 *"We had no U.S. military doctrine whatsoever at that point"*: Ibid.

49 *a provocative question:* Donald Rumsfeld memo to Gen. Dick Myers, Paul Wolfowitz, Gen. Pete Pace and Doug Feith, October 16, 2003, the National Security Archive, George Washington University.

50 *"it will be a long, hard slog"*: Ibid.

51 *"Given the stakes involved, we must remain committed"*: Zalmay Khalil-zad, "Afghanistan's Milestone," *The Washington Post*, January 6, 2004.

51 *twenty people had teamed up to write Khalilzad's column:* Thomas Hutson interview, April 23, 2004, Foreign Affairs Oral History Project, Association for Diplomatic Studies and Training.

51 *"I said, 'check with my grandson'"*: Ibid.

52 *"The two secretaries would kind of get nipping at each other's shorts"*: Pace interview, Miller Center.

52 *Condoleezza Rice would have to step into the fray:* Ibid.

52 *Though the defense secretary kept it a secret:* Ibid.

52 *"When you see leadership that is divisive and caustic"*: Lt. Gen. Douglas Lute interview, August 3, 2015, George W. Bush Oral History Project, Miller Center, University of Virginia.

52 *couldn't stand Rumsfeld at first:* Franks interview, Miller Center.

53 *"Don Rumsfeld is not the easiest guy in the world":* Ibid.
53 *the defense secretary's renewed interest ignited panic:* Maj. Gen. Peter Gilchrist interview, January 24, 2007, U.S. Army Center of Military History, Washington, D.C.
53 *"This was a real cultural shock for me":* Ibid.
53 *"very contentious, painful, difficult and tribulating":* Barno interview, U.S. Army Center of Military History.
54 *"The secretary was beating us up":* Mansager interview, U.S. Army Center of Military History.

CHAPTER FIVE: RAISING AN ARMY FROM THE ASHES

55 *they could earn about $2.50 a day:* Paul Watson, "Losing Its Few Good Men; Many of those who signed up to be trained for Afghanistan's fledgling army have quit, saying the pay isn't worth the risk," *Los Angeles Times*, November 27, 2003.
55 *riddled with potholes:* Lt. Gen. Karl Eikenberry interview, November 27, 2006, Operational Leadership Experiences project, Combat Studies Institute, Fort Leavenworth, Kansas.
55 *On 9/11, he narrowly escaped death:* "Pentagon 9/11," Defense Studies Series, Historical Office, Office of the Secretary of Defense, 2007.
55 *the hardscrabble scene reminded him of the suffering:* Eikenberry interview, Combat Studies Institute.
56 *"Everyone was having some pretty rough nights":* Ibid.
56 *He named it Task Force Phoenix:* Ibid.
56 *"a highly professional, multi-ethnic force":* "Talking Points—Afghanistan Progress," October 8, 2004, Office of Public Affairs, U.S. Department of Defense.
57 *"We got the [Afghan forces] we deserve":* Lute interview, SIGAR.
57 *the troops did a lot of talking with their hands:* Master Sgt. Michael Threatt interview, September 20, 2006, Operational Leadership Experiences project, Combat Studies Institute, Fort Leavenworth, Kansas.
57 *"there's going to be a thing there called a helicopter":* Maj. Bradd Schultz interview, August 6, 2012, Operational Leadership Experiences project, Combat Studies Institute, Fort Leavenworth, Kansas.
58 *"Tides? What are tides?":* Maj. Brian Doyle interview, March 13, 2008, Operational Leadership Experiences project, Combat Studies Institute, Fort Leavenworth, Kansas.
58 *"ludicrously modest":* Gates interview, Miller Center.
58 *"We kept changing guys who were in charge":* Ibid.
58 *blasted as "crazy":* Donald Rumsfeld memo to Gen. Richard Myers, January 28, 2002, the National Security Archive, George Washington University.

58 *"We are spending a fortune every day":* Donald Rumsfeld memo to Colin Powell, April 8, 2002, the National Security Archive, George Washington University.

58 *"naturally sympathetic":* Colin Powell memo to Donald Rumsfeld, April 16, 2002, the National Security Archive, George Washington University.

59 *the single biggest expense:* Quarterly Report to the United States Congress, October 30, 2020, SIGAR.

59 *"The way it gets resolved":* Strmecki interview, SIGAR.

59 *held the training program "hostage":* Khalilzad interview, SIGAR.

59 *"Now we're talking about God knows what":* Ibid.

59 *"You wouldn't invent how to do infantry operations":* Strmecki interview, SIGAR.

60 *"Our inability to keep up":* Eikenberry interview, Combat Studies Institute.

60 *"You're in country and like, 'What do we do now?'":* Staff Sgt. Anton Berendsen interview, February 8, 2015, Operational Leadership Experiences project, Combat Studies Institute, Fort Leavenworth, Kansas.

60 *he tripled the number of enlisted recruits:* Maj. Rick Rabe interview, May 18, 2007, Operational Leadership Experiences project, Combat Studies Institute, Fort Leavenworth, Kansas.

60 *"You couldn't fail basic training":* Ibid.

61 *"these guys couldn't hit the broad side of a barn":* Maj. Christopher Plummer interview, June 6, 2006, Operational Leadership Experiences project, Combat Studies Institute, Fort Leavenworth, Kansas.

61 *Afghan soldiers often wasted all their ammunition:* Maj. Gerd Schroeder interview, April 20, 2007, Operational Leadership Experiences project, Combat Studies Institute, Fort Leavenworth, Kansas.

61 *"'Okay, Mr. Afghan Soldier, shoot that watermelon'":* Ibid.

61 *"Before that they had no comprehension of marksmanship at all":* Ibid.

61 *when bullets started to fly:* Lt. Col. Michael Slusher interview, February 16, 2007, Operational Leadership Experiences project, Combat Studies Institute, Fort Leavenworth, Kansas.

62 *"They go out and they run right into the fire":* Ibid.

62 *"crack outfit":* Maj. John Bates interview, March 5, 2007, Operational Leadership Experiences project, Combat Studies Institute, Fort Leavenworth, Kansas.

62 *"We actually wrote their names on the weapons":* Ibid.

62 *"the sole of the boots come completely off":* Ibid.

62 *"It was all either full gas or full brake":* Command Master Sgt. Jeff Janke interview, February 16, 2007, Operational Leadership Experiences project, Combat Studies Institute, Fort Leavenworth, Kansas.

63 *they practiced turns on an oval dirt track:* Maj. Dan Williamson interview, December 7, 2007, Operational Leadership Experiences project, Combat Studies Institute, Fort Leavenworth, Kansas.

63 *"These guys were a menace to society":* Ibid.

63 *mistook urinals as drinking fountains:* U.S. military official interview, October 28, 2016, Lessons Learned Project, SIGAR. Name redacted by SIGAR.

63 *"the commodes were being broken":* Maj. Kevin Lovell interview, August 24, 2007, Operational Leadership Experiences project, Combat Studies Institute, Fort Leavenworth, Kansas.

63 *"a little bit less hubris".* Ibid.

63 *"They stand there in their bare feet and they use a giant spoon":* Maj. Matthew Little interview, May 15, 2008, Operational Leadership Experiences project, Combat Studies Institute, Fort Leavenworth, Kansas.

64 *"The entire kitchen would fill up with smoke":* Ibid.

64 *"just have it wash downstream":* Ibid.

64 *he decided to ask low-ranking Afghan soldiers:* Maj. Charles Abeyawardena interview, July 26, 2012, Operational Leadership Experiences project, Combat Studies Institute, Fort Leavenworth, Kansas.

64 *"They were going to go back and grow opium or marijuana":* Ibid.

65 *"the police will show up and rob your house a second time":* Maj. Del Saam interview, August 20, 2009, Operational Leadership Experiences project, Combat Studies Institute, Fort Leavenworth, Kansas.

65 *"ANP Horror Stories":* Donald Rumsfeld memo to Condoleezza Rice, February 23, 2005, National Security Archive, George Washington University.

65 *"written in as graceful and noninflammatory a way as is humanly possible":* Ibid.

66 *" 'Give me some goats or sheep or we'll have you shot on sight' ":* Saam interview, Combat Studies Institute.

66 *"They have a hard time picturing what we're trying to do":* Ibid.

CHAPTER SIX: ISLAM FOR DUMMIES

67 *"I felt like a dork":* Maj. Louis Frias interview, September 16, 2008, Operational Leadership Experiences project, Combat Studies Institute, Fort Leavenworth, Kansas.

68 *The idea came from a soldier Frias met in the chow hall:* Ibid.

68 *"soccer is such a big thing":* Ibid.

68 *"the wise old man would come in":* Ibid.

68 *the kids provided "good feedback":* Ibid.

68 *"Everybody wanted to have their say in it":* Ibid.

68 *distributed more than 1,000 soccer balls:* Maj. Gen. Jason Kamiya interview, January 23, 2007, U.S. Army Center of Military History, Washington, D.C.

68 *he rolled out one of the soccer balls:* Ibid.

69 *"Our job in Afghanistan is not to train the next Afghan Olympic soccer team":* Ibid.

69 *"an insult in any Muslim country":* Alastair Leithead, "Anger over 'blasphemous balls,'" BBC News, August 26, 2007.

70 *"Oh, Iraq, Afghanistan. It's the same thing":* Maj. Daniel Lovett interview, March 19, 2010, Operational Leadership Experiences project, Combat Studies Institute, Fort Leavenworth, Kansas.

70 *"Our mission was all about cultural awareness":* Ibid.

70 *tried to teach his class Arabic:* Maj. James Reese interview, April 18, 2007, Operational Leadership Experiences project, Combat Studies Institute, Fort Leavenworth, Kansas.

70 *the pre-deployment tactical training was foolish:* Maj. Christian Anderson interview, November 10, 2010, Operational Leadership Experiences project, Combat Studies Institute, Fort Leavenworth, Kansas.

70 *"Afghanistan has a lot of mountains, right?":* Ibid.

71 *He had to sit through classes on surviving nuclear:* Maj. Brent Novak interview, December 14, 2006, Operational Leadership Experiences project, Combat Studies Institute, Fort Leavenworth, Kansas.

71 *"'Geez, are these kids flipping me off?'":* Ibid.

71 *"We'd come in like gangbusters":* Maj. Rich Garey interview, December 5, 2007, Operational Leadership Experiences project, Combat Studies Institute, Fort Leavenworth, Kansas.

71 *he needed to work at the Afghans' pace:* Maj. Nikolai Andresky interview, September 27, 2007, Operational Leadership Experiences project, Combat Studies Institute, Fort Leavenworth, Kansas.

71 *"there wasn't such a thing as a one-hour meeting in Afghanistan":* Ibid.

72 *"Time to Americans is very important":* Maj. William Woodring interview, December 12, 2006, Operational Leadership Experiences project, Combat Studies Institute, Fort Leavenworth, Kansas.

72 *"Theirs is a culture of dishonesty and corruption":* Plummer interview, Combat Studies Institute.

72 *"In the Islamic world, it's either my way or death":* John Davis interview, November 21, 2008, Operational Leadership Experiences project, Combat Studies Institute, Fort Leavenworth, Kansas.

72 *"They're just like any other religion in America":* Thomas Clinton interview, Combat Studies Institute.

73 *"The embassy itself was a very, very small, very junior organization":* Barno interview, U.S. Army Center of Military History.

73 *"we might as well have been aliens":* Maj. Clint Cox interview, November 8, 2006, Operational Leadership Experiences project, Combat Studies Institute, Fort Leavenworth, Kansas.

74 *"we look astonishingly like the stormtroopers from Star Wars":* Maj. Keller Durkin interview, March 3, 2008, Operational Leadership Experiences project, Combat Studies Institute, Fort Leavenworth, Kansas.

74 *"The kids looked at me like, 'Oh my God. What is that?' ":* Maj. Alvin Tilley interview, June 29, 2011, Operational Leadership Experiences project, Combat Studies Institute, Fort Leavenworth, Kansas.

74 *"you think you're going to see Moses walking down the street":* Ibid.

74 *It was common for young people to marry their first cousins:* Maj. William Burley interview, January 31, 2007, Operational Leadership Experiences project, Combat Studies Institute, Fort Leavenworth, Kansas.

74 *"I hate to say it, but there was a lot of inbreeding":* Ibid.

74 *"if you can grab the beard you can trust the guy":* Ibid.

75 *"For an American male, walking through town holding the hand of another man?":* Maj. Christian Anderson interview, November 10, 2010, Operational Leadership Experiences project, Combat Studies Institute, Fort Leavenworth, Kansas.

75 *man-love Thursday came as a shock:* Woodring interview, Combat Studies Institute.

75 *"You really have to put your feelings aside":* Ibid.

76 *an Afghan man approached a baby-faced male American soldier:* Maj. Randy James interview, October 8, 2008, Operational Leadership Experiences project, Combat Studies Institute, Fort Leavenworth, Kansas.

76 *"It didn't get out of hand; nothing bad happened":* Ibid.

CHAPTER SEVEN: PLAYING BOTH SIDES

77 *reading a book in his hooch:* Trahan interview, Combat Studies Institute.

78 *triple-strand concertina wire:* Gregory Trahan testimony, *U.S. v. Ibrahim Suleman Adnan Adam Harun Hausa*, March 8, 2017, United States District Court, Eastern District of New York.

78 *The captain put his book down:* Trahan interview, Combat Studies Institute.

78 *glimpsed the gunmen dressed in black:* Ibid.

78 *a patrol of about twenty U.S. soldiers and twenty allied fighters:* Trahan testimony, *U.S. v. Ibrahim Suleman Adnan Adam Harun Hausa.*

78 *"I was ready to pack it in":* Trahan interview, Combat Studies Institute.

78 *the patrol climbed the winding dirt track:* Trahan testimony, *U.S. v. Ibrahim Suleman Adnan Adam Harun Hausa.*

79 *canteens of water, burlap bags and a cache of 107mm rockets:* Trahan interview, Combat Studies Institute.

79 *AK-47s, grenades and at least one heavy machine gun:* Trahan testimony, *U.S. v. Ibrahim Suleman Adnan Adam Harun Hausa.*

79 *other soldiers saw a red mist spray out:* Sgt. First Class Conrad Reed testimony, *U.S. v. Ibrahim Suleman Adnan Adam Harun Hausa,* March 8, 2017, United States District Court, Eastern District of New York.

79 *U.S. troops radioed for help and requested howitzer fire:* Trahan interview, Combat Studies Institute.

79 *"I think the Pakistanis thought we were shooting at them":* Ibid.

80 *"the biggest challenge was getting timely, accurate intelligence":* Ibid.

80 *he abandoned a pocket-sized Koran:* press release, "Al Qaeda Operative Convicted of Multiple Terrorism Offenses Targeting Americans Overseas," March 16, 2017, Department of Justice.

82 *"If we are going to get the Paks to really fight":* Donald Rumsfeld memo to Doug Feith, June 25, 2002, the National Security Archive, George Washington University.

83 *"there was a failure to perceive the double game":* Strmecki interview, SIGAR.

83 *"Pakistan would continue to see the Taliban as a useful surrogate":* Dobbins interview, SIGAR.

84 *Everybody had a theory:* Olson interview, U.S. Army Center of Military History.

84 *"The American and Afghan perception":* Farris interview, Combat Studies Institute.

84 *"these well-educated Pakistani generals who were nicely dressed":* Ibid.

85 *"I think that's pretty speculative":* Lt. Gen. David Barno interview, January 4, 2005, National Public Radio.

85 *"are the Pakistanis playing a giant double-cross":* Gen. Barry McCaffrey memo to Col. Mike Meese and Col. Cindy Jebb, June 3, 2006, the National Security Archive, George Washington University. On June 15, Rumsfeld forwarded a copy of McCaffrey's memo to Gen. Peter Pace, the Joint Chiefs Chairman, calling it "an interesting report."

86 *"The web of paranoia and innuendo":* Ibid.

86 *Others disagreed:* Marin Strmecki, *Afghanistan at a Crossroads: Challenges, Opportunities and a Way Forward,* August 17, 2006, the National Security Archive, George Washington University. Strmecki's report was originally classified SECRET/NOFORN. It was declassified by the Defense Department on December 1, 2008.

86 *"Musharraf has not made the strategic choice to cooperate fully":* Ibid.

86 *Pakistani interlocutors habitually complained:* Crocker interview, December 1, 2016, SIGAR.

87 *"we're hedging our bets, you're right":* Ibid.

CHAPTER EIGHT: LIES AND SPIN

91 *in a Toyota Corolla:* Griff Witte, "Bombing Near Cheney Displays Boldness of Resurgent Taliban," *The Washington Post,* February 28, 2007.

92 *"The Taliban's claims":* Jason Straziuso, "Intelligence suggested threat of bombing in Bagram area before Cheney's visit, NATO says," Associated Press, February 28, 2007.

92 *word had leaked out about Cheney's presence:* Maj. Shawn Dalrymple interview, February 21, 2007, Operational Leadership Experiences project, Combat Studies Institute, Fort Leavenworth, Kansas.

92 *The bomber wasn't far off the mark:* Shawn Dalrymple interview with author, September 26, 2020.

92 *in a different convoy about thirty minutes later:* Ibid.

92 *"The insurgents knew this, it was all over the news":* Dalrymple interview, Combat Studies Institute.

92 *they originally set up a ruse:* Dalrymple interview with author.

93 *"You'd never expect him to ride in the gun truck":* Ibid.

95 *"You have all the clocks but we have all the time":* State Department cable, Kabul to Washington, "Afghan Supplemental," February 6, 2006. The cable was originally classified SECRET. It was partially declassified by the State Department in 2010 and released in response to a Freedom of Information Act request by the National Security Archive.

95 *stoked fear among U.S. officials:* Bush administration official interview, September 23, 2014, Lessons Learned Project, SIGAR. Name redacted by SIGAR.

95 *"we finally woke up to the fact that there was an insurgency":* Ibid.

95 *camping and riding horses and yaks:* Ambassador Ronald Neumann interview, June 19, 2012, Foreign Affairs Oral History Project, Association for Diplomatic Studies and Training.

95 *"it was going to get much bloodier, much worse":* Ibid.

95 *"Nobody ever said to me":* Ibid.

96 *"We thought the Taliban's capability was greatly reduced":* Brig. Gen. Bernard Champoux interview, January 9, 2007, U.S. Army Center of Military History, Washington, D.C.

96 *"we're going to allow these guys to keep us languishing here":* Capt. Paul Toolan interview, July 24, 2006, Operational Leadership Experiences project, Combat Studies Institute, Fort Leavenworth, Kansas.

96 *"It's a direct result of the progress that's being made":* Donald Rumsfeld interview, CNN, *Larry King Live,* December 19, 2005.

96 *"violence will rise through the next several months":* State Department cable, Kabul to Washington, "Policy on Track, But Violence Will Rise," February 21, 2006. The cable was originally classified SECRET. It was

partially declassified by the State Department on June 9, 2010, and released in response to a Freedom of Information Act request by the National Security Archive.

96 *Neumann expressed fear:* Ibid.

96 *"I thought it was important to try to prepare the American public":* Neumann interview, Association for Diplomatic Studies and Training.

97 *didn't sugarcoat his verdict:* McCaffrey memo, the National Security Archive.

98 *"very aggressive and smart in their tactics":* Ibid.

98 *"They are in a disastrous condition":* Ibid.

98 *"We will encounter some very unpleasant surprises":* Ibid.

98 *"It is not that the enemy is so strong but that the Afghan government is so weak":* Strmecki memo, National Security Archive.

98 *"We are not winning in Afghanistan":* State Department cable, Kabul to Washington, "Afghanistan: Where We Stand and What We Need," August 29, 2006. The cable was originally classified SECRET. It was partially declassified by the State Department on June 11, 2010, and released in response to a Freedom of Information Act request by the National Security Archive.

99 *"We are winning":* Terry Moran, "Battlefield Wilderness," ABC *Nightline,* September 11, 2006.

99 *a new set of talking points:* Office of the Secretary of Defense Writers Group, "Afghanistan: Five Years Later," October 6, 2006.

99 *"Five years on, there is a multitude of good news":* Ibid.

99 *"an excellent piece":* Donald Rumsfeld memo to Dorrance Smith, October 16, 2006, the National Security Archive, George Washington University.

99 *"about ten times worse":* Staff Sgt. John Bickford interview, February 23, 2007, Operational Leadership Experiences project, Combat Studies Institute, Fort Leavenworth, Kansas.

100 *"they were always in Pakistan and regrouping":* Ibid.

100 *"These are very smart people":* Ibid.

100 *"hardcore ideologues":* Toolan interview, Combat Studies Institute.

101 *"We'd ask the Afghans why":* Maj. Darryl Schroeder interview, November 26, 2007, Operational Leadership Experiences project, Combat Studies Institute, Fort Leavenworth, Kansas.

101 *one of his grandfathers was a farmer and the other a bootlegger:* Brig. Gen. James Terry interview, February 13, 2007, Operational Leadership Experiences project, Combat Studies Institute, Fort Leavenworth, Kansas.

101 *"So you'd think that I'd have an appreciation of clans":* Ibid.

101 *"'Tell me about the Taliban'":* Ibid.

101 *"There are three kinds":* Ibid.

CHAPTER NINE: AN INCOHERENT STRATEGY

103 *The veteran Cold War warrior woke up before 5 a.m.:* Gates, *Duty,* p. 5.

103 *white Dodge Durango:* Gates interview, Miller Center.

103 *Bush wanted to hide his visitor:* Ibid.

104 *They chatted for an hour:* Ibid.

104 *"our goals were too ambitious":* Ibid.

104 *"crush the Taliban":* Ibid.

104 *received a call from Joshua Bolten:* Ibid.

105 *"There was no coherent long-term strategy":* Richards interview, SIGAR.

106 *"just completely knocked the stuffing out of them":* Ibid.

106 *the Canadians "were knackered":* Ibid.

106 *"they were collectively exhausted":* Ibid.

106 *"And Rummy said, 'General what do you mean?'":* Ibid.

106 *it permitted them to enjoy copious amounts of alcohol:* Craig Whitlock, "German Supply Lines Flow with Beer in Afghanistan," *The Washington Post,* November 15, 2008.

107 *"We felt that we were giving it our all":* Ambassador Nicholas Burns interview, January 14, 2016, Lessons Learned Project, SIGAR.

107 *"a Frankenstein organization":* Maj. Brian Patterson interview, October 2, 2008, Operational Leadership Experiences project, Combat Studies Institute, Fort Leavenworth, Kansas.

108 *"to give better political shape":* Desmond Browne letter to Donald Rumsfeld, December 5, 2006, the National Security Archive, George Washington University.

108 *a "commendable" idea:* Donald Rumsfeld letter to Desmond Browne, December 13, 2006, the National Security Archive, George Washington University.

108 *"There was no center":* NATO official interview, February 18, 2015, Lessons Learned Project, SIGAR. Name redacted by SIGAR.

108 *"at that point I was 'out of Schlitz'":* Gates interview, Miller Center.

109 *"a lot of verbiage and talk, but no plan":* McNeill interview, SIGAR.

109 *"I tried to get someone to define for me what winning meant":* Ibid.

109 *"Iraq was sucking up all the resources":* Lt. Col. Richard Phillips interview, September 6, 2011, Operational Leadership Experiences project, Combat Studies Institute, Fort Leavenworth, Kansas.

109 *"just spinning our wheels":* Maj. Stephen Boesen interview, July 7, 2008, Operational Leadership Experiences project, Combat Studies Institute, Fort Leavenworth, Kansas.

110 *"my children will probably be doing the same mission":* Ibid.

110 *he spent 85 percent of his time:* Lute interview, SIGAR.

110 *"We were devoid of a fundamental understanding of Afghanistan":* Ibid.

110 *"It's really much worse than you think":* Ibid.
111 *"Is it alive and well now?":* Gwen Ifill, "Interview with Gen. Dan McNeill," PBS *Newshour with Jim Lehrer,* December 10, 2007.
111 *"Well, that statement didn't come from me":* Ibid.
112 *spaghetti-like chains-of-command:* Lute interview, Miller Center.
112 *"The left hand was not talking to the right hand":* Ibid.
112 *"raid a compound overnight":* Ibid.

CHAPTER TEN: THE WARLORDS

115 *publicly urged Afghanistan to confront its tumultuous past:* press release, "Afghanistan: Justice for War Criminals Essential to Peace," Human Rights Watch, December 12, 2006.
115 *paid a private visit to one of the most notorious figures on the list:* State Department cable, Kabul to Washington, "Meeting with General Dostum," December 23, 2006, WikiLeaks. The cable was classified CONFIDENTIAL.
116 *they found the warlord in a melancholy mood:* Ibid.
116 *"I've been called so many names":* Ibid.
116 *settled into an overstuffed chair and did his best to calm Dostum's "quasi-paranoia":* Ibid.
117 *"On the basis of the enemy of my enemy is my friend":* Sarah Chayes interview, May 26, 2015, Lessons Learned Project, SIGAR.
117 *the U.S. government took a "schizophrenic" approach:* Andre Hollis interview, May 16, 2016, Lessons Learned Project, SIGAR.
118 *Their deaths remained a secret:* Assessments and Documentation in Afghanistan, Physicians for Human Rights.
119 *no one was ever held accountable:* Cora Currier, "White House Closes Inquiry into Afghan Massacre—and will Release No Details," *ProPublica,* July 31, 2013.
119 *"Dear U.S. president, George W. Bush!":* Gen. Abdul Rashid Dostum letter to President George W. Bush, the National Security Archive, George Washington University. Dostum's letter is undated and it lists Bush's address as "1600 Pennsylvania Avenue, Washington, D.C."—with no zip code.
119 *"I wish your Excellency good health":* Ibid.
119 *the Pentagon took special care to deliver it:* Gen. Tommy Franks memo to Donald Rumsfeld, January 9, 2002, the National Security Archive, George Washington University.
119 *"He turned out to be quite a warfighter":* Donald Rumsfeld memo to Larry Di Rita, January 10, 2002, the National Security Archive, George Washington University.

119 *urged him to give Dostum more power:* State Department cable, Kabul to Washington, "Congressman Rohrabacher's April 16 Meeting With President Karzai," April 16, 2003, WikiLeaks. The cable was classified CONFIDENTIAL.

120 *Karzai was incredulous:* Ibid.

120 *"under the Taliban at least there was law and order":* Ibid.

120 *"a babyface Stalinesque Tito":* Hutson interview, Association for Diplomatic Studies and Training.

120 *floated an assortment of half-baked ideas:* Ibid.

120 *told Dostum he needed to think realistically:* Ibid.

120 *"Dostum had never heard of Aristide, or Haiti for that matter":* Ibid.

121 *U.S. military commanders ordered a B-1 bomber:* Khalilzad, *The Envoy*, p. 202–203.

121 *one of the warlord's aides placed a panicky phone call:* Joshua Partlow, "Dostum, a former warlord who was once America's man in Afghanistan, may be back," *The Washington Post*, April 23, 2014.

121 *Lamm thought about saying no:* Col. David Lamm interview, March 14, 2007, U.S. Army Center of Military History, Washington, D.C.

121 *"'We've got to treat a warlord at Walter Reed?'":* Ibid.

121 *thanked them for saving his life:* Ibid.

122 *The warlords "had thirty years of civil war behind them":* Finn interview, SIGAR.

122 *"a mortal threat to the legitimacy of the regime":* Strmecki interview, SIGAR.

122 *"people who diminish what was achieved in this phase are a little unfair":* Ibid.

123 *"a major threat to the country's future":* State Department cable, Kabul to Washington, "Confronting Afghanistan's Corruption Crisis," September 15, 2005. The cable was originally classified CONFIDENTIAL. It was declassified in full by the State Department on December 9, 2014, and released in response to a Freedom of Information Act request by the National Security Archive.

123 *Both men, however, were politically untouchable:* Partlow, *A Kingdom of Their Own*, p. 142–143.

123 *Boucher admired Sherzai:* Boucher interview, SIGAR.

123 *"I thought that was one of the funniest things I ever heard":* Ibid.

124 *it was better to funnel contracts to Afghans:* Ibid.

124 *"I want it to disappear in Afghanistan, rather than in the Beltway":* Ibid.

124 *"a benevolent asshole":* Nils Taxell interview, July 3, 2015, Lessons Learned Project, SIGAR. In a December 2019 email to *Washington Post* reporters, Taxell added: "I must admit that I don't recognize the specific language attributed to me by SIGAR, so the qualifier 'as recorded

by SIGAR' is rather pertinent. Furthermore, I want to be clear that in my line of reasoning I was not expressing my opinion on any particular individual."

124 *"There was always a question of corruption":* Lt. Col. Eugene Augustine interview, February 22, 2007, U.S. Army Center of Military History, Washington, D.C.

125 *"a simple-minded tyrant":* McNeill interview, SIGAR.

125 *"SMA was dirty":* Ibid.

125 *The black-bearded warlord had a tense history with Karzai:* Partlow, *A Kingdom of Their Own*, p. 54.

126 *the defense minister once blew his stack:* Russell Thaden interview, June 13, 2011, Operational Leadership Experiences project, Combat Studies Institute, Fort Leavenworth, Kansas.

126 *"Fahim Khan was really upset about it until he learned which drug lab":* Ibid.

126 *"He giggled while he related this":* Crocker interview, January 12, 2016, SIGAR.

127 *"I would have considered him capable of any iniquity":* Ibid.

127 *"as far as I know, he is still dead":* Ibid.

CHAPTER ELEVEN: A WAR ON OPIUM

129 *a fleet of Massey Ferguson farm tractors:* Lt. Col. Michael Winstead interview, November 7, 2013, Operational Leadership Experiences project, Combat Studies Institute, Fort Leavenworth, Kansas.

130 *"there will be no opium in this province":* Emmanuel Duparcq, "Opium-free in two months, vows governor of Afghanistan's top poppy province," *Agence France-Presse*, March 3, 2006.

130 *"that's just plain B.S.":* Lt. Col. Michael Slusher interview, February 16, 2007, Operational Leadership Experiences project, Combat Studies Institute, Fort Leavenworth, Kansas.

131 *he rushed to the scene and helped remove the bodies:* Winstead interview, Combat Studies Institute.

131 *a bag with $250,000 in cash:* Ibid.

131 *"We were really struggling":* Ibid.

131 *"deserted their posts":* State Department cable, Kabul to Washington, "Helmand Eradication Wrap Up," May 3, 2006, WikiLeaks. The cable was unclassified.

131 *the ranks of the eradicators had dwindled:* State Department cable, Kabul to Washington, "Helmand Governor Daud Voices Concerns About Security," May 15, 2006, Wikileaks. The cable was classified CONFIDENTIAL.

131 *To cover up the debacle:* Maj. Douglas Ross interview, June 23, 2008, Operational Leadership Experiences project, Combat Studies Institute, Fort Leavenworth, Kansas.

131 *only "a modest amount" of the poppy crop was destroyed:* State Department cable, "Helmand Eradication Wrap Up," Wikileaks.

131 *Yet the State Department certified the false numbers:* Winstead interview, Combat Studies Institute.

132 *"I had a number of villagers ask me":* Ibid.

132 *"very corrupt individuals":* State Department cable, "Helmand Eradication Wrap Up," WikiLeaks.

132 *"Believe me, my hair turned white":* Ross interview, Combat Studies Institute.

132 *"Ninety percent of the people's income":* Lt. Col. Dominic Cariello interview, February 16, 2007, Operational Leadership Experiences project, Combat Studies Institute, Fort Leavenworth, Kansas.

133 *"That drug dealer doesn't care":* Bates interview, Combat Studies Institute.

133 *"We were disgruntling the whole province":* Ibid.

133 *"The eradication campaign also appears":* State Department cable, "Helmand Eradication Wrap Up," WikiLeaks.

133 *"very bad and continuing to deteriorate":* State Department cable, "Helmand Governor Daud Voices Concerns About Security," WikiLeaks.

133 *"As soon as we handed it off to the British":* Slusher interview, Combat Studies Institute.

135 *"Mullah Omar could enforce it with his blind eye":* Tooryalai Wesa interview, January 7, 2017, Lessons Learned Project, SIGAR.

135 *"Everyone from Congress brought it up immediately":* Metrinko interview, Association for Diplomatic Studies and Training.

135 *"we don't have a functioning toilet here":* Ibid.

136 *They agreed to pay Afghan poppy farmers $700 an acre:* "Counternarcotics: Lessons from the U.S. Experience in Afghanistan," June 2018, SIGAR.

136 *"Afghans, like most other people, are quite willing to accept large sums of money":* Metrinko interview, Association for Diplomatic Studies and Training.

136 *"an appalling piece of complete raw naivete":* Anthony Fitzherbert interview, June 21, 2016, Lessons Learned Project, SIGAR. In a December 2019 email to a *Washington Post* reporter, Fitzherbert added: "The 'cash for poppies programme' was finally abandoned and cancelled when it became clear that it was not only not working, but that it was having negative consequences. I hasten to add here that I myself had no direct involvement with this programme in any form or capacity."

136 *INL posted just one employee to the U.S. embassy:* Barno interview, U.S. Army Center of Military History.

136 *"There was literally no coordination":* Gilchrist interview, U.S. Army Center of Military History.

137 *"no one's in charge":* Donald Rumsfeld memo to Doug Feith, November 29, 2004, the National Security Archive, George Washington University.

137 *"We somehow came up with the explanation that it was drugs":* Barnett Rubin interview, August 27, 2015, Lessons Learned Project, SIGAR.

137 *"She thinks it is important to act soon":* Donald Rumsfeld memo to Gen. Dick Myers, Paul Wolfowitz, Doug Feith and Tom O'Connell, October 19, 2004, the National Security Archive, George Washington University.

138 *"opium could strangle the legitimate Afghanistan state in its cradle":* State Department cable, "Confronting Afghanistan's Corruption Crisis," National Security Archive.

138 *"Uribe was a credible leader":* John Wood interview, June 17, 2015, Lessons Learned Project, SIGAR.

138 *"Karzai thought this would be seen by Afghans as chemical warfare":* Khalilzad interview, SIGAR.

139 *"to halt all U.S. economic activity west of the Mississippi":* Ambassador Ronald McMullen interview, August 1, 2012, Foreign Affairs Oral History Project, Association for Diplomatic Studies and Training.

139 *Wide-eyed congressmen saw poppies growing everywhere:* State Department cable, Kabul to Washington, "Codel Hoekstra Sees Poppy Problem First Hand," March 23, 2006, WikiLeaks. The cable was classified CONFIDENTIAL/NOFORN.

140 *"I would just say they were pretty flowers":* Boucher interview, SIGAR.

140 *"desperate pressure for short-term results":* Ambassador Ronald Neumann interview, June 18, 2015, Lessons Learned Project, SIGAR.

141 *"the single most ineffective program in the history of American foreign policy":* Richard Holbrooke, "Still Wrong in Afghanistan," *Washington Post,* January 23, 2008.

141 *"It actually strengthens the Taliban and al-Qaeda":* Ibid.

CHAPTER TWELVE: DOUBLING DOWN

147 *"We may have done too good of a job explaining how bad it is":* Maj. Fred Tanner interview, March 4, 2010, Operational Leadership Experiences project, Combat Studies Institute, Fort Leavenworth, Kansas.

147 *"He said it very professionally":* Ibid.

148 *"there has to be more to solving this problem than killing people":* Maj. Gen. Edward Reeder interview, October 26, 2017, Lessons Learned Project, SIGAR. In a December 2019 email to a *Washington Post* reporter,

Reeder added: "At the time of this quote in 2009, I was quite content with how General David McKiernan . . . was prosecuting the counter-insurgency campaign and had no issues with supporting his strategy. My point of the quote at the time I arrived in February 2009 as the commander of the Combined Forces Special Operations Command, I felt we need[ed] another alternative to attacking the Taliban . . . I thought we needed a grass roots, local defense initiative that would make the Taliban uncomfortable with fighting locals of the same ethnicity and shared tribal affiliation."

148 *"It was a lot more convoluted"*: Maj. George Lachicotte interview, November 1, 2011, Operational Leadership Experiences project, Combat Studies Institute, Fort Leavenworth, Kansas.

148 *"There wasn't a clear strategy"*: Ibid.

148 *"What does it look like when it comes time for us to leave?"*: Maj. Joseph Claburn interview, September 13, 2011, Operational Leadership Experiences project, Combat Studies Institute, Fort Leavenworth, Kansas.

149 *"He pushes himself mercilessly"*: Dexter Filkins, "Stanley McChrystal's Long War," *New York Times Magazine*, October 14, 2009.

149 *"drunk on their Iraq experience"*: Maj. John Popiak interview, March 15, 2011, Operational Leadership Experiences project, Combat Studies Institute, Fort Leavenworth, Kansas.

150 a *"properly resourced" counterinsurgency campaign*: "Commander's Initial Assessment," International Security Assistance Force, August 30, 2009. The report was originally classified CONFIDENTIAL. The Defense Department declassified most of the report on September 20, 2009, after *Washington Post* reporter Bob Woodward obtained a copy and informed Obama administration officials that *The Post* intended to publish it. *The Post* published the declassified version on September 21, 2009.

150 *"There are big implications with calling this a war"*: Senior NATO official interview, February 24, 2015, Lessons Learned Project, SIGAR. Name redacted by SIGAR.

150 *To paper over the problem*: Ibid.

151 *"the perception was that al-Qaeda was no longer a problem"*: Ibid.

151 *"we rarely tried to understand what the disease was"*: USAID official interview, October 18, 2016, Lessons Learned Project, SIGAR. Name redacted by SIGAR.

152 *"he knew he would get in trouble if he said that"*: Barnett Rubin interview, February 17, 2017, Lessons Learned Project, SIGAR.

152 *"Pakistan will remain the single greatest source of Afghan instability"*: State Department cable, Kabul to Washington, "COIN Strategy: Civilian Concerns," November 6, 2009.

152 *"dig us in more deeply"*: Department of State cable, Kabul to Washington, "Looking Beyond Counterinsurgency In Afghanistan," November 9, 2009. Both cables were classified SECRET. *The New York Times* obtained copies of the cables and published them online. Eric Schmitt, "U.S. Envoy's Cables Show Worries on Afghan Plans," *New York Times*, January 25, 2010.

153 *"The timeline was just sprung on us"*: Gen. David Petraeus interview, August 16, 2017, Lessons Learned Project, SIGAR.

153 *like Petraeus, he said he was "stupefied"*: Rubin interview, February 17, 2017, SIGAR.

153 *"there was a mismatch between deadline and strategy"*: Ibid. In a December 2019 email to the author, Rubin added: "I am surprised I said that. Maybe the notes are wrong. I always firmly believed that the audience for the timeline was the Pentagon, no one else. I understood why the president wanted to do that, but he did not take into account how it would be heard in the region."

154 *"I can't describe the smell"*: Smith interview, Combat Studies Institute.

154 *"Been there, done that"*: Ibid.

154 *"'Hey sir, why the hell are we doing this?'"*: Maj. Jason Liddell interview, April 15, 2011, Operational Leadership Experiences project, Combat Studies Institute, Fort Leavenworth, Kansas.

154 *"I have a difficult time answering"*: Ibid.

156 *a string of backbiting, catty remarks*: Michael Hastings, "The Runaway General," *Rolling Stone*, July 8, 2010.

CHAPTER THIRTEEN: "A DARK PIT OF ENDLESS MONEY"

159 *"It's like pouring a lot of water into a funnel"*: David Marsden interview, December 3, 2015, Lessons Learned Project, SIGAR. In a December 2019 email to a *Washington Post* reporter, Marsden added that "the most important issue that affected the outcome [of the war] was totally in our control: the one-year rotation of personnel. As a very rare person who worked on Afghanistan in and out of the country for eight years I learned the impact of that almost like an Afghan."

159 *"We lost objectivity"*: USAID official interview, October 7, 2016, Lessons Learned Project, SIGAR. Name redacted by SIGAR.

159 *Washington expected him to dole out roughly $3 million daily*: Aid contractor interview, August 15, 2016, Lessons Learned Project, SIGAR. Name redacted by SIGAR.

159 *"He said hell no"*: Ibid.

159 *lavished money on dams and highways*: Lute interview, SIGAR.

159 *"Can't we get a bit more rational about this?"*: Ibid.

159 *"in some God-forsaken province"*: Ibid.

160 *"The police chief couldn't even open the door"*: Ibid.

160 *"they wanted their kids out herding goats"*: Special Forces team adviser interview, December 14, 2017, Lessons Learned Project, SIGAR. Name redacted by SIGAR.

160 *"It blew my mind"*: Tim Graczewski interview, January 11, 2015, Lessons Learned Project, SIGAR.

161 *"Don't know who did it"*: Ibid.

161 *found it largely deserted:* "Shorandam Industrial Park: Poor Record-keeping and Lack of Electricity Prevented a Full Inspection of this $7.8 million Facility," SIGAR Inspection Report, April 2015.

162 *"Why did we think providing electricity"*: Senior USAID official interview, August 15, 2016, Lessons Learned Project, SIGAR. Name redacted by SIGAR.

162 *He had deep misgivings about the dam project:* Crocker interview, December 1, 2016, SIGAR.

162 *"I was sure it was never going to work"*: Ibid.

162 *"it was all nonsense"*: NATO official interview, February 24, 2015, Lessons Learned Project, SIGAR. Name redacted by SIGAR.

162 *spent $775 million on the dam:* "Afghanistan's Energy Sector," SIGAR 19-37 Audit Report, May 2019.

163 *he raised what he called the "bigger" question:* Eggers interview, SIGAR.

163 *"Why does the U.S. undertake actions that are beyond its abilities?"*: Ibid.

164 *"Petraeus was hell-bent on throwing money at the problem"*: U.S. military officer interview, July 18, 2016, Lessons Learned Project, SIGAR. Name redacted by SIGAR.

164 *"What drove spending was the need to solidify gains"*: Petraeus interview, SIGAR.

164 *Afghan farmers were a century behind the times:* Col. Brian Copes interview, January 25, 2011, Operational Leadership Experiences project, Combat Studies Institute, Fort Leavenworth, Kansas.

164 *"a certain elitist bias"*: Ibid.

164 *"We were always chasing the dragon"*: Senior USAID official interview, November 10, 2016, Lessons Learned Project, SIGAR. Name redacted by SIGAR.

165 *"the shit kicked out of me":* Former State Department official interview, August 15, 2016, Lessons Learned Project, SIGAR. Name redacted by SIGAR.

165 *"They started shouting, 'We have cleared Garmsir'"*: Barna Karimi interview, January 16, 2017, Lessons Learned Project, SIGAR.

165 *they paid little attention to who was benefiting:* Safiullah Baran interview, February 18, 2017, Lessons Learned Project, SIGAR.

165 *a brother who was in the local wing of the Taliban:* Ibid.

166 *"Afghans are some of the most jealous people I've ever met":* U.S. official interview, June 30, 2016, Lessons Learned Project, SIGAR. Name redacted by SIGAR.

166 *a giveaway that they were cut-and-pasted:* Army civil-affairs officer interview, July 12, 2016, Lessons Learned project, SIGAR. Name redacted by SIGAR.

166 *"the smartest thing to do is nothing":* Ibid.

167 *Likened the flood of aid to "crack cocaine":* Brian Copes interview, February 25, 2016, Lessons Learned Project, SIGAR.

167 *built a replacement greenhouse out of iron rebar:* Ibid.

167 *"Congress gives us money to spend":* Ibid.

167 *Despite its best efforts:* "Department of Defense Commanders' Emergency Response Program: Priorities and Spending in Afghanistan for Fiscal Years 2004–2014," SIGAR Office of Special Projects, April 2015.

167 *"nothing but walking-around money":* Ken Yamashita interview, December 15, 2015, Lessons Learned Project, SIGAR. In a December 2019 email to a *Washington Post* reporter, Yamashita added: "CERP is walking-around money in the sense that it was never meant to be used as long-term reconstruction funding. Some of the reconstruction was meant to rebuild after military engagement; at other times it was meant to provide support to community leaders. In this second purpose, it did serve a political purpose by supporting the leadership of the community."

167 *"a dark pit of endless money":* NATO official interview, February 24, 2015, Lessons Learned Project, SIGAR. Name redacted by SIGAR.

167 *"We wanted hard quantitative metrics":* U.S. Army officer interview, June 30, 2016, Lessons Learned Project, SIGAR. Name redacted by SIGAR.

168 *"It was an insult to the people":* Wesa interview, SIGAR.

168 *"all the schoolteachers quit their jobs":* Thomas Johnson interview, January 7, 2016, Lessons Learned Project, SIGAR. In a December 2019 email to the author, Johnson added: "Unbeknownst to the Canadians the village's few schoolteachers, who were making between $60–80 per month, immediately quit their jobs to dig irrigation canals at a higher salary and obviously disrupted the village's educational system. As soon as this fact was relayed to the Canadians, they raised the salaries of the schoolteachers and the problem was corrected."

168 *"There weren't enough teachers to fill them":* U.S. military officer interview, July 11, 2016, Lessons Learned Project, SIGAR. Name redacted by SIGAR.

CHAPTER FOURTEEN: FROM FRIEND TO FOE

170 *"He thought he was corrupt as hell"*: Rubin interview, January 20, 2015, SIGAR. In a December 2019 email to the author, Rubin added: "I tried to convince Holbrooke that he was blaming Karzai for problems whose source was the U.S. Given the system we had set up of off-the-books money for counterterrorism forces and militia leaders, Karzai could not compete politically without getting access to the same sources of money himself. The 'official' political system of elections and so on was a façade for the real power game. The former was supported by the State Department, the latter was run by CIA and the Defense Department."

171 *"The reason Karzai made deals with the warlords"*: Gates interview, Miller Center.

171 *he leaned over and whispered a message:* Ibid.

171 *"there was blatant foreign interference"*: Ibid.

172 *the spy agency encouraged him:* Partlow, *A Kingdom of Their Own*, p. 44–47.

172 *Pakistan's ISI spy agency first floated Karzai's name:* Ambassador James Dobbins interview, July 21, 2003, Foreign Affairs Oral History Project, Association for Diplomatic Studies and Training.

172 *"Karzai was telegenic and cooperative"*: Ibid.

172 *dove on top of Karzai:* Ian Shapira, "The CIA acknowledges the legendary spy who saved Hamid Karzai's life—and honors him by name," *Washington Post*, September 18, 2017.

172 *Karzai's satellite phone rang:* Lyse Doucet, "The Karzai years: From hope to recrimination," BBC News, July 11, 2014.

173 *"Hamid, what's your reaction?"*: Ibid.

173 *"Just a cold, drafty palace to try and preside over"*: Ambassador Ryan Crocker interview, September 9, 2010, George W. Bush Oral History Project, Miller Center, University of Virginia.

173 *Crocker jumped at the chance for a homemade meal:* Ibid.

173 *"We need a flag"*: Crocker interview, December 1, 2016, SIGAR.

173 *"That's up to you"*: Ibid.

174 *"Like I had a clue"*: Crocker interview, Miller Center.

174 *"It was a day I will never forget"*: Donald Rumsfeld memo to President George W. Bush, December 9, 2004, the National Security Archive, George Washington University.

175 *The menu rarely changed:* Khalilzad, *The Envoy*, p. 132–133.

175 *"When I went to Iraq, Karzai was so popular"*: Khalilzad interview, SIGAR.

175 *Karzai needed to spend hours talking:* Strmecki interview, SIGAR.

175 *accusing Ahmed Wali Karzai of controlling the drug trade:* Sami Yousafzai, "A Harvest of Treachery," *Newsweek*, January 8, 2006.

176 *"we have never had clear evidence that one could take to court"*: Department of State cable, Kabul to Washington, "Karzai Dissatisfied: Worries about Newsweek; Plans More War Against Narcotics," January 10, 2006, WikiLeaks. The cable was classified CONFIDENTIAL.

176 *For years, the agency paid him*: Dexter Filkins, Mark Mazzetti, and James Risen, "Brother of Afghan Leader Said to be Paid by C.I.A.," *The New York Times*, October 27, 2009.

176 *"By targeting him, we were damaging our relations"*: Greentree interview, Association for Diplomatic Studies and Training.

176 *"Karzai was never sold on democracy"*: Hadley interview, SIGAR.

177 *"Whenever we do an airstrike"*: Amir Shah and Jason Straziuso, "Afghan officials: US missiles killed 27 civilians," *Associated Press*, July 6, 2008.

178 *Witnesses reported that as many as sixty children died*: Letter to Secretary of Defense Robert Gates on U.S. Airstrikes in Azizabad, Afghanistan, Human Rights Watch, January 15, 2009.

178 *"in self-defense, necessary and proportional"*: Memorandum for Acting Commander, "Executive Summary of AR 15-6 Investigation," U.S. Central Command, October 1, 2008.

178 *"financial, political, and/or survival agendas"*: Ibid.

179 *"We killed our allies"*: U.S. military officer interview, January 8, 2015, Lessons Learned Project, SIGAR. Name redacted by SIGAR.

179 *"Every time we had a huge fight with Karzai"*: Gates interview, Miller Center.

179 *"People were just dissing Karzai"*: Ibid.

180 *Biden threw down his napkin*: Woodward, *Obama's Wars*, p. 70.

180 *He wants to get rid of me and of you*: Kai Eide, "Afghanistan and the U.S.: Between Partnership and Occupation," Peace Research Institute Oslo, 2014.

180 *"two contrasting portraits"*: State Department cable, Kabul to Washington, "Karzai on the State of U.S.–Afghan Relations," July 7, 2009, WikiLeaks. The cable was originally classified SECRET.

180 *"a paranoid and weak individual"*: Ibid.

180 *Karzai accused Holbrooke of undermining him*: Packer, *Our Man*, p. 484–486.

181 *"once bitten, twice shy"*: Margaret Warner, "Interview with Afghan President Hamid Karzai," *PBS Newshour with Jim Lehrer*, November 9, 2009.

181 *"It strains credulity to expect Karzai to change"*: State Department cable, "COIN Strategy: Civilian Concerns."

181 *"He used erratic behavior as a technique"*: Ambassador Marc Grossman interview, June 13, 2014, Foreign Affairs Oral History Project, Association for Diplomatic Studies and Training.

CHAPTER FIFTEEN: CONSUMED BY CORRUPTION

183 *Much of the money landed in the emirate of Dubai:* Andrew Higgins, "An Afghan exodus, of bank notes," *Washington Post*, February 25, 2010.

183 *mansions known as "poppy palaces" rose from Kabul's rubble:* Karin Brulliard, "Garish 'poppy palaces' lure affluent Afghans," *Washington Post*, June 6, 2010.

184 *"Malign actions of power brokers":* Commander's Initial Assessment, International Security Assistance Force, August 30, 2009.

184 *"The basic assumption was that corruption is an Afghan problem":* Rubin interview, January 20, 2015, SIGAR.

185 *"Our biggest single project, sadly and inadvertently":* Crocker interview, January 11, 2016, SIGAR.

185 *the U.S. government gave "nice packages":* German official interview, July 31, 2015, Lessons Learned Project, SIGAR. Name redacted by SIGAR.

185 *"you'd be stupid not to get a package":* Ibid.

185 *"so-and-so has just been to the U.S. Embassy and got this money":* Ibid.

185 *"self-organized into a kleptocracy":* Christopher Kolenda interview, April 5, 2016, Lessons Learned Project, SIGAR.

186 *"The kleptocracy got stronger over time":* Ibid.

186 *"Petty corruption is like skin cancer":* Ibid.

186 *"It was like they just discovered something new":* Former National Security Council official interview, April 22, 2015, Lessons Learned Project, SIGAR. Name redacted by SIGAR.

187 *between 6,000 and 8,000 truckloads:* "Warlord, Inc.: Extortion and Corruption Along the U.S. Supply Chain in Afghanistan," Report of the Majority Staff, Subcommittee on National Security and Foreign Affairs, House Committee on Oversight and Government Reform, June 2010.

187 *A convoy of 300 trucks typically required 500 armed guards:* Ibid.

187 *about 18 percent of the money went to the Taliban:* Gert Berthold interview, October 6, 2015, Lessons Learned Project, SIGAR.

187 *"And it was often a higher percent":* Ibid.

187 *corrupt Afghan officials and criminal syndicates skimmed off another 15 percent:* Ibid. In a December 2019 email to a *Washington Post* reporter, Berthold added: "Where we identified anomalies in the flow of procurement funds, we typically proved, through financial records, that 16–25% of funds (where anomalies were identified) went to bad actors. We were told that this percentage was low, some saying that it was more like 40%."

188 *"The political world gets in the way":* Thomas Creal interview, March 23, 2016, Lessons Learned Project, SIGAR.

188 *disinvite them from the annual Fourth of July party:* U.S. official interview, September 11, 2015, Lessons Learned Project, SIGAR. Name redacted by SIGAR.

188 *"the system was too entrenched":* Senior U.S. diplomat interview, August 28, 2015, Lessons Learned Project, SIGAR.

188 *"We literally went there and surrounded the bank":* Lt. Gen. Michael Flynn interview, November 10, 2015, Lessons Learned Project, SIGAR.

189 *"New Ansari was just incredibly corrupt":* Ibid.

189 *"No, no one was held accountable":* Ibid.

189 *"The pivot point was the Salehi case":* Justice Department official interview, April 12, 2016, Lessons Learned Project, SIGAR. Name redacted by SIGAR.

189 *"The interest and enthusiasm seemed to be lost":* Berthold interview, SIGAR.

190 *some Obama administration officials regarded corruption as "annoying":* Kolenda interview, SIGAR.

190 *"What I'm doing is not proper":* Andrew Higgins, "Banker feeds Afghan crony capitalism; Firm's founder has secured Dubai home loans for some in Karzai's inner circle," *Washington Post,* February 22, 2010.

190 *exposed Kabul Bank as a teetering house of cards:* Andrew Higgins, "Kabul Bank crisis followed U.S. push for cleanup," *Washington Post,* September 18, 2010.

190 *loaned themselves hundreds of millions of dollars:* "Report of the Public Inquiry into the Kabul Bank Crisis," Independent Joint Anti-Corruption Monitoring and Evaluation Committee, Government of Afghanistan, November 15, 2012.

190 *enmeshed in a power struggle:* U.S. official interview, March 1, 2016, Lessons Learned Project, SIGAR. Name redacted by SIGAR.

190 *Kabul Bank served as the payroll agent:* Joshua Partlow and Andrew Higgins, "U.S. and Afghans at odds over Kabul Bank reform," *Washington Post,* October 7, 2010.

191 *Kabul Bank's third biggest shareholder was Mahmoud Karzai:* Andrew Higgins, "Karzai's brother made nearly $1 million on Dubai deal funded by troubled Kabul Bank," *Washington Post,* September 8, 2010.

191 *"On a scale of one to ten":* Senior Treasury Department official interview, October 1, 2015, Lessons Learned Project, SIGAR. Name redacted by SIGAR.

191 *emergency arrangements to fly in $300 million:* Fitrat, *The Tragedy of Kabul Bank,* p. 170.

192 *"There were a million things we were trying to do":* Former senior U.S. official interview, December 12, 2015, Lessons Learned Project, SIGAR. Name redacted by SIGAR.

192 *U.S. spy agencies knew about illicit activities:* Senior U.S. official interview, March 1, 2016, Lessons Learned Project, SIGAR. Name redacted by SIGAR.

192 *none of the intelligence agencies alerted law enforcement:* "Report of the Public Inquiry into the Kabul Bank Crisis," Independent Joint Anti-Corruption Monitoring and Evaluation Committee.

192 *"it wasn't in their mandate":* Senior U.S. official interview, March 1, 2016, Lessons Learned Project, SIGAR. Name redacted by SIGAR.

192 *The article's findings shocked:* Fitrat, *The Tragedy of Kabul Bank,* p. 115.

192 *Karzai refused to meet with the central bank governor:* "Report of the Public Inquiry into the Kabul Bank Crisis," Independent Joint Anti-Corruption Monitoring and Evaluation Committee

193 *Neither of them had any inkling:* Treasury Department official interview, July 27, 2015, Lessons Learned Project, SIGAR. Name redacted by SIGAR.

193 *"the whole house of cards came down":* Ibid.

193 *his office had to stop serving hot tea:* Fitrat, *The Tragedy of Kabul Bank,* p. 202.

193 *"a group of mafia-controlled politicians":* Ibid, p. 192.

194 *"a case study of how fragile and precarious U.S. policy":* Treasury Department official interview, July 27, 2015, SIGAR.

194 *"I saw the tide turn when the going got tough":* International Monetary Fund official interview, February 25, 2016, Lessons Learned Project, SIGAR. Name redacted by SIGAR.

194 *sympathetic to a counterargument:* Crocker interview, January 11, 2016, SIGAR.

194 *"I was struck by something Karzai said":* Ibid.

CHAPTER SIXTEEN: AT WAR WITH THE TRUTH

199 *Panetta fingered a string of rosary beads:* Panetta, *Worthy Fights,* p. 320–321.

200 *Panetta smiled and thought of his old friend:* Panetta, *Worthy Fights,* p. 301 and p. 328.

200 *a flair for blunt, unscripted comments:* Craig Whitlock, "Panetta echoes Bush comments, linking Iraq invasion to war on al-Qaeda," *The Washington Post,* July 11, 2011.

202 *"Osama was probably laughing in his watery grave":* Eggers interview, SIGAR.

204 *U.S. government auditors would conclude:* Prepared Remarks of John F. Sopko, "SIGAR's Lessons Learned Program and Lessons from the

Long War," January 31, 2020, Project on Government Oversight retreat, Washington, D.C.

204 *"Every data point was altered"*: Bob Crowley interview, August 3, 2016, Lessons Learned Project, SIGAR.

204 *"truth was rarely welcome"*: Ibid.

204 *"They had a really expensive machine"*: John Garofano interview, October 15, 2015, Lessons Learned Project, SIGAR.

205 *"There was not a willingness to answer questions"*: Ibid. In a December 2019 email to a *Washington Post* reporter, Garofano added: "With the hindsight of eight years, I see things a bit differently: These guys were executing. But where was the strategic oversight? There was no independent body in the Congress or Pentagon that asked, What is working and what is not? Should we continue building Highway One? Can we build an economy that will sustain the nation and society we are trying to construct? Washington, no less than the operators on the ground, fought the war one year at a time. It was easier to provide just enough resources to prevent catastrophe than to reassess strategy and tactics. And reassessment will not occur on the ground any more than assembly line workers will redesign an automobile."

205 *"why does it feel like we are losing?"*: Flynn interview, SIGAR.

205 *"So they all went in for whatever their rotation was"*: Ibid.

205 *"it showed that everything was getting worse"*: Senior U.S. official interview, July 10, 2015, Lessons Learned Project, SIGAR. Name redacted by SIGAR.

206 *the Obama White House and Pentagon pressured the bureaucracy:* National Security Council staff member interview, September 16, 2016, Lessons Learned Project, SIGAR. Name redacted by SIGAR.

206 *"It was impossible to create good metrics"*: Ibid.

206 *the White House and Pentagon would spin them in their favor:* Ibid.

206 *"It was their explanations"*: Ibid.

207 *"with numbers you can spin them any way you want"*: Maj. John Martin interview, December 8, 2008, Operational Leadership Experiences project, Combat Studies Institute, Fort Leavenworth, Kansas.

207 *"does that mean the situation has gotten worse:"* Ibid.

208 *"the mother of all databases"*: Senior NATO official interview, February 18, 2015, Lessons Learned Project, SIGAR. Name redacted by SIGAR.

208 *"It should be a standard operating procedure"*: Ibid.

CHAPTER SEVENTEEN: THE ENEMY WITHIN

213 *looking down into the barren valley for signs of the enemy:* Adam Ashton, "Ambush, shootings a deadly betrayal by allies" (Tacoma, Washington) *News Tribune*, May 12, 2013. See also Adam Ashton, "The Cavalry at

Home: A soldier's wounds and a will to live," (Tacoma, Washington) *News Tribune*, December 14, 2013.

213 *gunfire erupted directly behind them:* Ibid.

213 *shot several times in the back:* Ibid.

214 *capped a brutal two-month period:* Bill Roggio and Lisa Lundquist, "Green-on-blue attacks in Afghanistan, the data," August 23, 2012, The Long War Journal.

215 *"I'm mad as hell":* Lara Logan, "Interview with Gen. John Allen," *60 Minutes*, September 30, 2012.

216 *placed a small bomb under the seat of an Australian colonel:* Maj. Christopher Sebastian interview, November 1, 2012, Operational Leadership Experiences project, Combat Studies Institute, Fort Leavenworth, Kansas.

216 *"a persistent feeling of dread":* Ibid.

216 *"they reflect a growing systemic threat":* Jeffrey Bordin, "A Crisis of Trust and Cultural Accountability," U.S. Forces–Afghanistan, May 12, 2011.

216 *he wrote a series of articles:* See Adam Ashton, "Ambush, shootings a deadly betrayal by allies," (Tacoma, Washington) *News Tribune*, May 12, 2013; Adam Ashton, "Report sheds light on 2012 'green-on-blue' attack," (Tacoma, Washington) *News-Tribune*, August 6, 2013; Adam Ashton, "The Cavalry at Home: A soldier's wounds and a will to live," (Tacoma, Washington) *News Tribune*, December 14, 2013.

217 *six assailants:* Ibid.

217 *"We knew what they were capable of":* Ashton, "The Cavalry at Home," *News-Tribune*.

217 *might suddenly go rogue:* Maj. Jamie Towery interview, December 17, 2012, Operational Leadership Experiences project, Combat Studies Institute, Fort Leavenworth, Kansas.

218 *"We'd just never know when they might turn on you":* Ibid.

219 *only 2 to 5 percent of Afghan recruits could read:* Jack Kem interview, April 23, 2014, Operational Leadership Experiences project, Combat Studies Institute, Fort Leavenworth, Kansas.

219 *"The literacy was just insurmountable":* Ibid.

219 *army and police forces were shrinking:* Ibid.

219 *more than 64,000 Afghans in uniform had been killed:* Neta C. Crawford and Catherine Lutz, "Costs of War Project," Watson Institute for International and Public Affairs, Brown University, November 13, 2019.

219 *"Thinking we could build the military that fast and that well was insane":* Former senior State Department official interview, August 15, 2016, Lessons Learned Project, SIGAR. Name redacted by SIGAR.

220 *"We can't just shovel one-year money at this problem":* Lute interview, SIGAR.

221 *killed by his own men:* Maj. Greg Escobar interview, July 24, 2012, Operational Leadership Experiences project, Combat Studies Institute, Fort Leavenworth, Kansas.

221 *"Nothing we do is going to help":* Ibid.

221 *Can we win there?:* Maj. Michael Capps interview, December 14, 2011, Operational Leadership Experiences project, Combat Studies Institute, Fort Leavenworth, Kansas.

221 *"You could lose that place covering every inch of ground":* Ibid.

222 *he lined up rows of folding chairs:* Maj. Mark Glaspell interview, November 2, 2012, Operational Leadership Experiences project, Combat Studies Institute, Fort Leavenworth, Kansas.

222 *"it was going pretty good":* Ibid.

222 *"Well, then it was a brawl":* Ibid.

222 *U.S. officers reminded their Afghan soldiers that winter was coming:* Maj. Charles Wagenblast interview, August 1, 2012, Operational Leadership Experiences project, Combat Studies Institute, Fort Leavenworth, Kansas.

222 *" 'No, it's not cold yet' ":* Ibid.

222 *"But it will be cold, I'm pretty sure":* Ibid.

223 *got an earful from district tribal leaders:* Shahmahmood Miakhel interview, February 7, 2017, Lessons Learned Project, SIGAR.

223 *"I asked that why is it possible":* Ibid.

223 *"the most hated institution":* Thomas Johnson interview, SIGAR.

223 *"set up their own private checkpoints":* Norwegian official interview, July 2, 2015, Lessons Learned Project, SIGAR. Name redacted by SIGAR.

223 *"they are useless as a security force":* Crocker interview, January 11, 2016, SIGAR.

224 *"It was, 'Here's what handcuffing is' ":* Maj. Robert Rodock interview, October 27, 2011, Operational Leadership Experiences project, Combat Studies Institute, Fort Leavenworth, Kansas.

224 *"cop in a box":* Lt. Col. Scott Cunningham interview, August 15, 2013, Operational Leadership Experiences project, Combat Studies Institute, Fort Leavenworth, Kansas.

224 *"We didn't trust them with it one bit":* Ibid.

224 *"the bottom of the barrel":* U.S. soldier interview, September 7, 2016, Lessons Learned Project, SIGAR. Name redacted by SIGAR.

224 *"drug addicts or Taliban":* U.S. military officer interview, October 20, 2016, Lessons Learned Project, SIGAR. Name redacted by SIGAR.

225 *"You get unaccountable militias that prey on the population":* Lt. Col. Scott Mann interview, August 5, 2016, Lessons Learned Project, SIGAR.

225 *he led his forces into combat with imaginary enemies:* Capt. Andrew Boissonneau interview, September 17, 2014, Operational Leadership Experiences project, Combat Studies Institute, Fort Leavenworth, Kansas.
225 *"he would get in firefights with the Helmand River":* Ibid.

CHAPTER EIGHTEEN: THE GRAND ILLUSION

228 *Only 38 percent of the public said the war had been worth fighting:* Washington Post–ABC News poll, December 11–14, 2014.
229 *the U.S. military launched missiles and bombs on 2,284 occasions:* Combined Forces Air Component Commander, "2013–2019 Airpower Statistics," February 29, 2020, U.S. Air Forces Central Command.
230 *Instead of flooding the country with 100,000 U.S. troops:* Senior U.S. official interview, September 13, 2016, Lessons Learned Project, SIGAR. Name redacted by SIGAR.
230 *"will it hold when you leave?":* Ibid.
230 *"we could have brought them back on an airplane by now":* Boucher interview, SIGAR.
230 *slip a line in his inauguration speech:* Lute interview, SIGAR.
231 *"There was a continuous tension":* Dobbins interview, SIGAR.
233 *with the call sign "Hammer":* Tim Craig, Missy Ryan and Thomas Gibbons-Neff, "By evening, a hospital. By morning, a war zone," *Washington Post,* October 10, 2015.
233 *GPS coordinates of the site:* "Initial MSF internal review: Attack on Kunduz Trauma Centre, Afghanistan," Médecins Sans Frontières, November 2015.

CHAPTER NINETEEN: TRUMP'S TURN

243 *Mattis and the Joint Chiefs wanted to give him a special briefing in "The Tank":* Rucker and Leonnig, *A Very Stable Genius,* p. 131–136.
243 *Trump called it a "loser war":* Ibid.
243 *"You're a bunch of dopes and babies":* Ibid.
244 *McMaster thought the war had gone off the rails:* McMaster, *Battlegrounds,* p. 212–214.
244 *McMaster believed the expense was worth it:* Ibid.
244 *Leading up to the session, McMaster refined his pitch:* Ibid.
246 *Then the military intensified the airstrikes even more:* "2013–2019 Airpower Statistics," U.S. Air Forces Central Command.
246 *U.S., NATO and Afghan airstrikes killed an estimated 1,134 civilians a year:* Neta C. Crawford, "Afghanistan's Rising Civilian Death Toll

Due to Airstrikes, 2017–2020," Costs of War project, Brown University, December 7, 2020.

247 *By some estimates, thirty to forty Afghan soldiers and police were killed daily:* Rod Nordland, "The Death Toll for Afghan Forces Is Secret: Here's Why," *The New York Times,* September 21, 2018.

250 *an Afghan soldier carrying a crate of pomegranates:* Mujib Mashal and Thomas Gibbons-Neff, "How a Taliban Assassin Got Close Enough to Kill a General," *The New York Times,* November 2, 2018.

250 *the shooter had . . . enlisted as a guard:* Ibid.

251 *Smiley had narrowly escaped death:* Dan Lamothe, "U.S. general wounded in attack in Afghanistan," *Washington Post,* October 21, 2018.

CHAPTER TWENTY: THE NARCO-STATE

254 *An independent analysis by a British researcher:* David Mansfield, "Bombing the Heroin Labs in Afghanistan: The Latest Act in the Theatre of Counternarcotics," January 2018, LSE International Drug Policy Unit.

255 *"we should have specified a flourishing drug trade":* Lute interview, SIGAR.

255 *"these guys have a history of smuggling":* Maj. Matthew Brown interview, July 30, 2012, Operational Leadership Experiences project, Combat Studies Institute, Fort Leavenworth, Kansas.

255 *"the entire world's worth of opium'":* Ibid.

256 *"The Western policies against the opium crop":* Phil Stewart and Daniel Flynn, "U.S. Reverses Afghan Drug Policy, eyes August Vote," *Reuters,* June 27, 2009.

257 *"ineptitude and lack of capacity":* Former senior British official interview, June 17, 2015, Lessons Learned Project, SIGAR. Name redacted by SIGAR.

258 *"no one could stop the Marines":* Ibid.

258 *"We were always debating and discussing it":* Greentree interview, Association for Diplomatic Studies and Training.

258 *just threw money at the opium problem:* Mohammed Ehsan Zia interview, April 12, 2016, Lessons Learned Project, SIGAR.

258 *"disregard what needed to be done":* Ibid.

259 *"The only thing they are experts in is bureaucracy":* Ibid.

259 *"that's an optical illusion":* Rubin interview, February 17, 2017, SIGAR. In a December 2019 email to the author, Rubin added: "The main problem is that opium cultivation is a livelihood strategy for a significant part of the population in the poorest country in Asia and one of the poorest in the world. You can't criminalize people's livelihood strategies and expect

them to support you. The global regime of criminalization of drugs cedes the production and sale of an addictive substance to organized crime and its protectors. The whole drug policy regime is a disaster, and we imported it into our Afghan policy."

259 *"When a country is at war, there is not much that can be achieved"*: State Department official interview, June 29, 2015, Lessons Learned Project, SIGAR. Name redacted by SIGAR.

260 *"The issue is political will"*: Justice Department official interview, April 12, 2016, Lessons Learned Project, SIGAR. Name redacted by SIGAR.

260 *"he had to be incompetent or pissed a lot of people off"*: Senior U.S. official interview, June 10, 2016, Lessons Learned Project, SIGAR. Name redacted by SIGAR.

260 *Ishaqzai had long operated under the protection of Ahmed Wali Karzai*: Joseph Goldstein, "Bribery Frees a Drug Kingpin in Afghanistan, Where Cash Often Overrules Justice," *The New York Times*, December 31, 2014.

260 *He allegedly bribed multiple judges:* Ibid.

261 *"In the terror model you kill the leader"*: Senior DEA official interview, November 3, 2016, Lessons Learned Project, SIGAR. Name redacted by SIGAR.

261 *allowed him to take a side trip to New York to go sightseeing and shopping:* James Risen, "Propping Up a Drug Lord, Then Arresting Him," *The New York Times*, December 11, 2010.

261 *When Khan's defense lawyer raised those connections:* Johnny Dwyer, "The U.S. Quietly Released Afghanistan's 'Biggest Drug Kingpin' from Prison. Did He Cut a Deal?" *The Intercept*, May 1, 2018.

262 *"We spent so much time swatting bad ideas down"*: Former legal attaché interview, June 27, 2016, Lessons Learned Project, SIGAR. Name redacted by SIGAR.

262 *some familiar-sounding ideas:* State Department contractor interview, September 16, 2016, Lessons Learned Project, SIGAR. Name redacted by SIGAR.

CHAPTER TWENTY-ONE: TALKING WITH THE TALIBAN

263 *Her honeyed renditions of "Moon River"*: David Harding, "Waiting for the Taliban," *Agence France-Presse*, March 19, 2009.

263 *The ascetic Afghans tolerated Anastasia each afternoon:* Ibid.

265 *the Taliban was "on the ropes"*: Olson interview, U.S. Army Center of Military History.

265 *"We never figured out"*: Ibid.

265 *"It was an interesting bit of spaghetti to untangle"*: Gilchrist interview, U.S. Army Center of Military History.

265 *because communists had used it:* Ibid.

267 *"if we don't address it, the military won't be able to":* Rubin interview, August 27, 2015, SIGAR. In a December 2019 email to the author, Rubin added: "During the 2009 policy review, we worked a lot to get the option of political negotiations with the Taliban (reconciliation, political settlement) on the table. Holbrooke said that those terms were too inflammatory. We finally settled on the term 'threat reduction' to describe a potential political track with the Taliban. The idea was that a political settlement by whatever name would lower the level of threat faced by the Afghan state and no longer require the totally unsustainable security forces that we were building. In the back of my mind was the certainty that one way or another somehow the U.S. was going to leave Afghanistan and we had to keep that in mind in everything we did."

267 *"we'll be nice to people who surrender":* Rubin interview, February 17, 2017, SIGAR. In a December 2019 email to the author, Rubin added: "They were not hardliners in the Obama administration. They were the members of the permanent national security establishment, the so-called 'deep state.' I don't use the term though because it implies a conspiracy, whereas it is just the normal inertia of a trillion-dollar bureaucracy."

267 *"she couldn't sell making a bargain with the Taliban":* Rubin interview, December 2, 2015, SIGAR. In a December 2019 email to the author, Rubin added: "[Hillary Clinton] had little or no faith that it would succeed. She understood the logic behind it, but did not see why she should take a political risk for something that would probably fail. Obama too did not want to take this political risk."

268 *it rarely followed through:* Maj. Ulf Rota interview, September 12, 2011, Operational Leadership Experiences project, Combat Studies Institute, Fort Leavenworth, Kansas.

268 *"'I hereby renounce evil al-Qaeda, blah blah blah'":* Ibid.

268 *"It doesn't matter how smart you are":* Brown interview, Combat Studies Institute.

269 *"Miraculously six bodies get coughed up":* Ibid.

270 *"Hamid Karzai was just incensed":* Crocker interview, January 11, 2016, SIGAR.

270 *"on balance probably unhelpful":* Dobbins interview, SIGAR.

Bibliography

Barfield, Thomas. *Afghanistan: A Cultural and Political History.* Princeton, N.J.: Princeton University Press, 2010.

Bergen, Peter L. *Manhunt: The Ten-Year Search for Bin Laden from 9/11 to Abbottabad.* New York: Crown Publishers, 2012.

Chandrasekaran, Rajiv. *Little America: The War Within the War for Afghanistan.* New York: Alfred A. Knopf, 2012.

Chayes, Sarah. *The Punishment of Virtue: Inside Afghanistan After the Taliban.* New York: The Penguin Press, 2006.

Coll, Steve. *Directorate S: The CIA and America's Secret Wars in Afghanistan and Pakistan.* New York: Penguin Press, 2018.

———. *Ghost Wars: The Secret History of the CIA, Afghanistan, and bin Laden, from the Soviet Invasion to September 10, 2001.* New York: Penguin Press, 2004.

Constable, Pamela. *Playing with Fire: Pakistan at War with Itself.* New York: Random House, 2011.

Dobbins, James. *After the Taliban: Nation-Building in Afghanistan.* Washington, D.C.: Potomac Books, 2008.

Eide, Kai. *Power Struggle over Afghanistan: An Inside Look at What Went Wrong and What We Can Do to Repair the Damage.* New York: Skyhorse Publishing, 2012.

Feith, Douglas J. *War and Decision: Inside the Pentagon at the Dawn of the War on Terrorism.* New York: Harper Collins, 2008.

Fitrat, Abdul Qadeer. *The Tragedy of Kabul Bank.* New York: Page Publishing, Inc., 2018.

Franks, Tommy. *American Soldier.* New York: Regan Books, 2004.

Gannon, Kathy. *I is for Infidel. From Holy War to Holy Terror: 18 Years Inside Afghanistan.* New York: PublicAffairs, 2005.

Gates, Robert M. *Duty: Memoirs of a Secretary at War.* New York: Alfred A. Knopf, 2014.

Graham, Bradley. *By His Own Rules: The Ambitions, Successes, and Ultimate Failures of Donald Rumsfeld.* New York: PublicAffairs, 2009.

Haqqani, Husain. *Pakistan: Between Mosque and Military.* Washington, D.C.: Carnegie Endowment for International Peace, 2005.

Jones, Seth G. *In the Graveyard of Empires: America's War in Afghanistan.* New York: W.W. Norton & Company, 2009.

Khalilzad, Zalmay. *The Envoy: From Kabul to the White House, My Journey Through a Turbulent World.* New York: St. Martin's Press, 2016.

McChrystal, Stanley. *My Share of the Task: A Memoir.* New York: Portfolio/ Penguin, 2013.

McMaster, H.R. *Battlegrounds: The Fight to Defend the Free World.* New York: Harper, 2020.

———. *Dereliction of Duty: Lyndon Johnson, Robert McNamara, the Joint Chiefs of Staff, and the Lies that Led to Vietnam.* New York: HarperCollins, 1997.

Neumann, Ronald E. *The Other War: Winning and Losing in Afghanistan.* Washington, D.C.: Potomac Books, Inc., 2009.

Packer, George. *Our Man: Richard Holbrooke and the End of the American Century.* New York: Alfred A. Knopf, 2019.

Panetta, Leon. *Worthy Fights: A Memoir of Leadership in War and Peace.* New York: Penguin Press, 2014.

Partlow, Joshua. *A Kingdom of Their Own: The Family Karzai and the Afghan Disaster.* New York: Alfred A. Knopf, 2016.

Rashid, Ahmed. *Descent into Chaos: The United States and the Future of Nation-Building in Pakistan, Afghanistan, and Central Asia.* New York: Viking, 2008.

———. *Taliban: Militant Islam, Oil and Fundamentalism in Central Asia.* New Haven, Conn.: Yale University Press, 2000.

Rubin, Barnett R. *Afghanistan from the Cold War Through the War on Terror.* New York: Oxford University Press, 2013.

Rucker, Philip and Carol Leonnig. *A Very Stable Genius: Donald J. Trump's Testing of America.* New York: Penguin Press, 2020.

Rudenstine, David. *The Day the Presses Stopped: A History of the Pentagon Papers Case.* Berkeley, Calif.: University of California Press, 1996.

Rumsfeld, Donald. *Known and Unknown: A Memoir.* New York: Sentinel, 2011.

Sheehan, Neil, Hedrick Smith, E.W. Kenworthy, and Fox Butterfield. *The Pentagon Papers. The Secret History of the Vietnam War.* New York: Quadrangle Books, Inc., 1971.

Warrick, Joby. *The Triple Agent: The al-Qaeda Mole Who Infiltrated the CIA.* New York: Doubleday, 2011.

Woodward, Bob. *Bush at War.* New York: Simon & Schuster, 2002.

———. *Obama's Wars.* New York: Simon & Schuster, 2010.

———. *Plan of Attack.* New York: Simon & Schuster, 2004.

Photo Credits

9. David Guttenfelder/AP
10. Moises Saman/Magnum Photos
11. Benjamin Lowy/Getty Images
12. Jonathan Newton/*The Washington Post*

INSERT 3

1. No Credit
2. Anja Niedringhaus/AP
3. Rahmat Gul/AP
4. Pete Souza/The White House/AP
5. John Moore/Getty Images
6. Charles Ommanney/Getty Images
7. Paula Bronstein /Getty Images
8. Javier Manzano for *The Washington Post*
9. Matt McClain/*The Washington Post*
10. Lorenzo Tugnoli for *The Washington Post*
11. Lorenzo Tugnoli for *The Washington Post*

Index

ABC News, 99
Abeyawardena, Charles, 64–65
Abu Ghraib prison, 54
Afghan army. *See also* Afghan security
   forces
   building up, 229
   compared with Taliban, 98
   as facsimile of the U.S. military, 57
   problems with, 221–222
   reasons for serving in, 64–65
   soldiers deserting from, 219
   training, 33, 55–57, 60–63
   warlord's loyalists in, 126
   weapons, 61, 62
   Western designs for bases and
      barracks for, 63–64
Afghan government. *See also* Afghan
   security forces; Karzai, Hamid
   constitution, 26, 36, 50–51, 185, 265
   corruption and, 123–124, 185–186,
      189–190
   dependence on the U.S., 36
   Kabul Bank and, 190–191, 193
   negotiations with Taliban, 235–236,
      272–273
   opium production/trade and, 131,
      132, 258, 259–260
   territories compared by, 247–248
   war crimes in the 1990s by, 115–116
   warlords and, 119–120, 121, 122
   weakness in, 98

Afghan High Peace Council, 269
Afghanistan
   civil war, 26, 115, 116, 118
   cultural awareness/training about,
      69–72
   elections. *See* election(s), in
      Afghanistan
   governance plan for, 13
   nation-building. *See* nation-building
   U.S. officials' lack of knowledge
      about, 20–21, 27, 66
Afghan National Security Forces
   (ANSF), 150. *See also* Afghan
   security forces
Afghan police force, 33, 98. *See also*
   Afghan security forces
   Afghan Local Police, 224–225
   Afghan National Police (ANP),
      65–66, 213, 218
   Germany and, 33
   ineffectiveness of, 223–224
   insider attacks, 213–214, 217
   poppy production and, 132
   responsibilities, 218
   Rumsfeld's report on, 65
   training of, 59, 65–66
Afghans. *See also* civilians
   at Bonn, Germany conference, 25–26
   cooking by, 63–64
   cultural disconnect with Americans,
      73–74

Afghans (*cont.*)
  identifying with Taliban, 151
  life expectancy, 204, 227–228
  role in 9/11 attacks, 19–20
Afghan security forces, xix. *See also*
  Afghan army; Afghan police force
  casualties of, 247
  compared with the Taliban, 209
  corruption, 209, 222–223
  deaths, 219, 247
  imaginary personnel, 218–219
  ineffectiveness of, 221–225
  insider attacks by, 213–218, 232–233
  Lessons Learned interviews on, 57,
    59, 63, 219–220, 223, 224–225
  McCaffrey's honest assessment of, 98
  misleading information about,
    56–57, 94, 155, 210, 220–221
  "non-combat" roles of U.S. troops
    and, 229–230
  quality of recruits, 219
  responsibility for country's security,
    229, 230–231, 275
  size/growth of, 218–219
  training, 57–60, 65, 214, 219–220
  U.S. spending on, 56, 58–59
Afghan warlords, 115–127
  Afghan government and, 119–120,
    121, 122
  corruption and, 122–123
  Dostum, Abdul Rashid, 115–122,
    171
  Fahim Khan, Mohammed Qasim,
    125–127, 171, 191
  Karzai, Hamid and, 120–121, 122,
    125–126, 171, 176
  opium industry and, 124–125, 126
  Taliban and, 117
  Tora Bora campaign, 23–25, 46, 70,
    273
  U.S. government and, 115, 116–117,
    118, 119, 122
  war crimes by, 115–116
Af-Pak border, 79–81
airfields, 12–13. *See also* Kandahar Air
  Field

airstrikes, 9, 177, 246
  against al-Qaeda in Tora Bora, 23–24
  civilian casualties and, 150, 177–178,
    246
  date of first, 6
  against Islamic State, 229, 235
  Obama's restrictions on, 246
  on opium labs, 253–254
  on Tora Bora, 23
  under Trump, 246–247
Akhundzada, Sher Mohammad,
  124–125
alcohol consumption, 26, 106–107, 263
al-Iraqi, Abdul Hadi, 80
Allen, John, 210, 215
Alliot-Marie, Michèle, 137–138
al-Qaeda. *See also* bin Laden, Osama
  airstrikes against in Tora Bora, 23–24
  death of key leaders, 200–201
  difficulties in identifying, 18–19
  in early part of war, 3–4
  Islamic State offshoot, 229
  McChrystal report and, 151
  mission and objectives for war in
    Afghanistan, 6, 7–8, 20
  Pakistan and, 20, 80–81, 82, 83, 147
  reconciliation program, 267–268
  September 11th terrorist attacks and,
    xvi
  Shkin ambush and, 80–81
  Taliban/Afghanistan and, 19–20, 26,
    267, 269
  threat of, after bin Laden's death,
    200–201, 235, 244
  Tora Bora bombing campaign, 23–24
  U.S.'s lack of knowledge about, 19
  in war strategy of McChrystal, 151
ambassadors, 48. *See also* Crocker,
  Ryan; Eikenberry, Karl; Finn,
  Robert; Khalilzad, Zalmay;
  Neumann, Ronald; U.S. embassy
  (Kabul)
American embassy. *See* U.S. embassy
  (Kabul)
American Enterprise Institute, 50, 108
Anderson, Christian, 70, 75

Andresky, Nikolai, 71–72
anti-Taliban warlords. *See* Northern
    Alliance
Arabic language/script, 69, 70
Ashton, Adam, 216–217
Association for Diplomatic Studies and
    Training, xxi
Augustine, Eugene, 124
Azizabad attack, 177–178

bacha bazi, 75
Baghdad, Iraq, 46, 48, 175
Bagram Air Base, 11–12, 24, 29, 154
    casualties at, 232, 234
    Combined Forces Command, 48
    Dostum, Abdul Rashid and, 121
    emergency landing in snowstorm
        (February 2008), 93
    growth of, 12
    psy-ops team, 68–69
    shower installed at, 11–12
    suicide bombing at, 91–92, 93
    U.S. personnel burning copies of the
        Koran at, 215
Baker, Lance, 13
Bales, Robert, 203
Balkans, the, 31, 45, 51
banks, 183, 190–195
Baradar, Mullah Abdul Ghani, 272
Baran, Safiullah, 165
Barno, David, 48–49, 53, 56, 73, 85, 136
Bates, John, 62, 133
beards, 21, 22, 74
Bedoy, Genaro, 213
Berendsen, Anton, 60
Bergdahl, Bowe, 270–271
Bergeron, Phil, 47
Berthold, Gert, 187, 189
Bickford, John, 99–100
Biden, Joseph, 93, 156, 180, 274–275
Binalshibh, Ramzi, 82
bin Laden, Osama
    Afghanistan/Taliban and, 19–20, 151,
        267
    al-Qaeda and, 235
    Biden on hunting down, 274, 275

death of, 199–200
in hiding, 4, 15, 23, 85
hunt for, 11
in Pakistan, 85
plan to lure U.S. in an unwinnable
    conflict, 201–202
Tora Bora campaign, 23–25, 46, 273
video of, 48
Boesen, Stephen, 109–110
Boissonneau, Andrew, 225
Bolten, Joshua, 104
Bonn Agreement, 26, 36, 45
Bonn conference, 13, 25–28, 35, 83, 172,
    265
Bosnia, 38, 45, 46, 249
Boucher, Richard, xix, 7–8, 32, 37,
    123–124, 140, 230
Brahimi, Lakhdar, 27
bribery, 184, 185, 186, 187, 189
British officials, 136, 139, 175, 257
British troops, 51, 101, 105–106, 126,
    133, 148
Browne, Desmond, 108
Brown, Matthew, 255, 268
Dunch, Lance, 253–254
Burgess, Ronald, 209
Burley, William, 74
Burns, Nicholas, 107
Bush, George W. (administration)
    on Afghan security forces, 218
    Afghan warlords and, 117, 119, 122, 125
    efforts to negotiate with Taliban,
        264–265
    General McNeill and, 15
    goals and objectives for War in
        Afghanistan, 8, 14
    on how long the war will last, 6–7, 14
    meeting with Robert Gates, 103–104
    misleading the public, 96–97, 108,
        111–112
    Mission Accomplished speech,
        43–44, 47
    nation-building under, 30–39, 31, 32
    on objectives and mission, 8, 14
    on opium production/trade, 129–133,
        135–136, 256

Bush, George W. (administration) (*cont.*)
  Pakistan and, 82
  public approval of, 4
  speech at USS *Abraham Lincoln*,
    43–44
  troop surge under, 94, 104
  U.S. spending under, 30, 95, 137, 158
  at Virginia Military Institute, 3, 4, 14
  war strategy, 105–106, 108–109

Callen, Michael, 31
Campbell, John, 207, 227–228, 234,
  236
Camp David, 244, 272–273
Canada/Canadians, 18, 105–106, 108,
  168, 216, 283
Capps, Michael, 221
car bombs, 232
Cariello, Dominic, 132
Carter, Ashton, 231–232, 234
Casey, George, 10
casualties, xx
  in 2007, 110
  in 2015, 232–233
  in 2017, 244
  by Afghan security forces, 213–218
  of Afghan security forces, 219, 247
  ambush near Shkin, 79, 81
  civilian, 110, 177–179, 208–209, 246
  in earlier part of the war, 4
  insider attacks, 213, 232–233
  Iraq War, 47
  under Obama administration (2010),
    155
  during Operation Medusa (2006),
    106
  summer 2003, 47
  total number of, xx
  of U.S. Air Force security personnel,
    234–235
ceasefire, 248–249
CERP (Commanders' Emergency
  Response Program), 166, 167
Champoux, Bernard, 96
Chayes, Sarah, 117
Chechens, 20

Cheney, Dick, 34, 91–93, 174, 202
Churchill, Winston, xv
CIA and CIA operatives, 9, 21, 22, 80,
  112, 261
  alliance with mujahedin, 116
  corruption and, 123, 185, 187
  criticism of, 18, 22
  drone strike campaign, 200–201
  funneling weapons to Afghan rebels,
    81–82, 116
  intelligence reports on war's
    progress, 209
  Karzai, Ahmed Wali and, 176
  Karzai, Hamid and, 172
  Pakistan spy agency teaming up with,
    81, 82
  Predator drone, 78
  Tora Bora campaign, 23–24
  warlords and, 116–117, 118, 121, 136
CIA contractors, 81
civilians. *See also* Afghans
  casualties, 110, 177–179, 208–209,
    246
  distinguishing Taliban from,
    18–19, 22
  massacred by Robert Bales, 203
  understanding of elections, 38–39
Claburn, Joseph, 148
Clapper, James, 209–210
Cleveland, Charles, 235
Clinton, Bill (Clinton administration),
    31, 45–46, 97
Clinton, Hillary, 151, 169, 181, 184, 203,
    267
Clinton, Thomas Jr., 22, 39, 72–73
Collins, Susan, 206, 210
Collins, Tom, 92
Combat Outpost Mizan, 217
Combat Studies Institute, xxii
Combined Forces Command, 48
comic books, 67–68
*Commander's Guide to Money as a
  Weapons System* (U.S. Army),
    163
congressional hearings, xxii, 56. *See
  also* Senate hearings

Conservative Political Action
    Conference, 111–112
constitution (Afghanistan), 26, 36,
    50–51, 185, 265
contractors, 159, 160, 186–188
cooking, by Afghans, 63–64
Copes, Brian, 164, 167
corruption, xix, 183–195
    Afghan government, 123–124,
        175–176, 185–186, 189–190
    Afghan security forces, 209, 222–223
    Afghan warlords and, 122–123
    contractors, 186–188
    defense contractors and, 187–188
    drug-related, 137–138
    Kabul Bank scandal, 190–195
    Karzai, Hamid and, 12, 170, 189, 194
    New Ansari investigation, 188–189
    Obama administration on, 183–185,
        190, 192
    opium production/trade and,
        137–138
    police, 65
    U.S. responsibility, 185–186
Costs of War Project, Brown University,
    246
counterinsurgency strategy, 49, 105
    Biden on, 274
    under Bush, 105–106
    Kajaki Dam project and, 161
    McChrystal's strategy and, 149, 150,
        151, 152
    under Obama, 149–150, 158, 201
    public-works projects and, 163
Creal, Thomas, 187–188
Crocker, Ryan, 29–30, 31, 34–35, 86,
    126–127, 162, 173–174, 184–185,
    194, 223, 270
Crowley, Bob, 204
cultural awareness and training, 69–72
cultural disconnect, between Afghans
    and U.S. troops, 73–74
cultural ignorance and
    misunderstandings, 67–69, 168
Cunningham, Scott, 224
currency, 32, 185, 191

Dalrymple, Shawn, 92, 93
Dari language, 21, 57, 67, 68, 70, 120, 214
Daud, Mohammed, 130
Davis, John, 72
Davis, Krissie, 232
Dawson, John, 232
defense contractors, 187–188
Defense Department, xv, xx, xxi, 17, 35,
    76, 167, 178, 220, 231
Defense Department contracts, 187
Delta Force, U.S. Army, 24, 112
democracy, 8, 36, 37, 38, 97, 109, 169,
    176, 186
Dennis, Jerod, 79
diplomacy. See also U.S. embassy
    (Kabul)
    Bonn conference, 25–26, 27
    negotiations with Taliban, 235–236,
        263–268, 269–270, 271–274
    under Obama, 147
    prisoner of war exchange, 270–271
    treatment of the Taliban and, 26–27
Dobbins, James, 27, 35, 45–46, 83, 172,
    208, 231, 270
Doctors Without Borders, 233
Dostum, Abdul Rashid, 115–122, 171
Doucet, Lyse, 172–173
Doyle, Brian, 57–58
driving, by Afghan forces, 62–63
drones, 78, 177–178, 199
Drug Enforcement Administration
    (DEA), 129, 137, 256, 258, 259, 261
drugs. See opium production/trade
Dubai, 13, 124, 183, 188, 190, 193
Dunford, Joseph Jr., 211, 242–244
Dunn, Michael, 9
Durbin, Robert, 94, 97
Durkin, Keller, 73–74

East Africa, bombing of U.S. embassies
    in, 19
education, 57, 160, 168
Eggers, Jeffrey, 20, 163, 202
Eide, Kai, 171, 180
Eikenberry, Karl, 55, 56, 60, 94, 95, 99,
    152, 180, 181, 194

election(s), in Afghanistan
  2004, 54, 174, 265
  2005, 185
  2009, 170, 171, 180–181
  community council, in Marja, 207
  understanding of, by civilians, 38–39
enemy. *See also* al-Qaeda; Taliban
  defining and identifying the, 22, 148,
    151
  insider attacks, 213–218, 232–233
  U.S. military's lack of understanding
    the, 20–21, 100, 101
  U.S. troops not understanding who
    was the, 23
Engel, Eliot, xxii
Escobar, Greg, 221
exit strategy, lack of a clear and
  realistic, 4, 7

Fahim, Haseen, 191
Fahim Khan, Mohammed Qasim,
  125–127, 171, 191
Farnood, Sherkhan, 190–191, 192, 194
Farris, Stuart, 22, 84–85
Feith, Douglas, 9–10, 82, 137
Finn, Robert, 14, 47, 122
Firebase Shkin, 77–81, 99
Firebase Tillman, 99
Fitrat, Abdul Qadeer, 192, 193
Fitzherbert, Anthony, 136
flag, Afghanistan, 173
Flournoy, Michèle, 154–155, 206–207,
  266
Flynn, Michael, 188, 189, 205
Force Reintegration Cell, 268–269
Foreign Service, xxi, 21, 27, 29, 35,
  73, 116, 176. *See also* oral-history
  interviews, Foreign Service
  officers/diplomatic
Fort Myer, Virginia, 241, 243, 245
Franks, Tommy, 10, 14–15, 119
  overseeing wars in both Afghanistan
    and Iraq at the same time, 46
  on Rumsfeld, Donald, 52–53
  Tora Bora campaign (December
    2001) and, 23, 24–25

fratricidal (insider) attacks, 213–218,
  232–233
Freakley, Benjamin, 94, 97, 130
Freedom of Information Act (FOIA),
  xviii, xxi, 217
Frias, Louis, 67–68
Fulbright Hearings, xviii
funding. *See* U.S. spending

Gannon, Kathy, 214
Garey, Rich, 71
Garofano, John, 204–205
Gates, Robert, 19, 58, 103–104, 108, 113,
  145–146, 147, 171, 179
  meeting with George Bush, 103–104
  priority of Iraq, 108
  replacing Rumsfeld as defense
    secretary, 104
Germany/Germans, ix, 13, 25–26, 33,
  56, 65, 106, 121, 172, 185, 191
Ghani, Ashraf, 194, 231, 248, 271, 272
Gilchrist, Peter, 53, 136–137, 265
Glaspell, Mark, 221–222
"Global War on Terror," xxii. *See also*
  War in Afghanistan
government. *See* Afghan government;
  U.S. government
Graczewski, Tim, 160–161
Graham, Lindsey, 236, 271
Green Berets, 17, 59, 67, 232
Greentree, Todd, 27, 176, 258
Grossman, Marc, 181
Guantánamo Bay, 82, 264, 270, 271
Guggisberg, Todd, 39

Haass, Richard, 34
Hadley, Stephen, 14, 33, 36, 110, 176
Haiti, 31, 45, 120
Harun, Ibrahim Suleiman Adnan, 80–81
Hazara warlords, 83
Helberg, Glen, 13
Helmand province, 105, 124–125, 129,
  130, 131–132, 133, 139, 148, 155,
  162, 202, 232, 236, 254, 255,
  256–257, 261, 268–269
Herat, Afghanistan, 10, 39, 177–178

HESCO barriers, 78
Hindu Kush mountains, 80
Hoekstra, Peter, 139
Holbrooke, Richard, 140–141, 152, 153, 156, 170, 171, 180, 256, 259, 267
Hollis, Andre, 117
homosexuality, 75
House Armed Services Committee, 154–155, 163, 207, 245
humanitarian assistance/groups, 13, 74, 233
human rights
    Afghan constitution and, 185
    Afghan police and, 224
    warlords and, 117
Human Rights Watch, 115, 116
Hussein, Saddam, 47
Hutson, Thomas, 51, 120
hydroelectric power station, 161–162

India, 26, 83, 171
industrial park project, 160–161
INL, 136, 137, 139
intelligence officials/reports
    from Afghanistan/Pakistan border, 80
    assessment on war's progress, 111, 209–210
    on bin Laden, 23, 25
    Kabul Bank scandal and, 192
    on strength of the Taliban, 94–95
International Security Assistance Force (ISAF), 107
interviews. See Lessons Learned interviews; oral-history interviews
Iran, xvi, 20, 21, 25, 26, 51, 134, 172
Iraq and Iraq War
    Bush and Robert Gates discussing, 104
    CERP projects cut-and-pasted from, 166
    fighting war in Afghanistan during the, 45–47
    Islamic State, 229, 235
    Khalilzad as ambassador to, 175
    Mission Accomplished speech (USS Abraham Lincoln), 43–44

Obama's approach to ending, 228–229
    prioritizing over Afghanistan, 15, 45, 47, 108, 109, 110, 112–113
    training Afghan army and, 60, 69, 70
    U.S. troops for, 45, 94
Iraqi army, 229
ISAF (International Security Assistance Force), 107
Ishaqzai, Haji Lal Jan, 260
ISI (Inter-Services Intelligence), 81–82, 86
Islam
    poppy cultivation and, 134
    views by U.S. soldiers on, 72–73
Islamabad, 77, 82, 83, 85, 86
Islam for Dummies, 67
Islamic Emirate of Afghanistan, 270
Islamic State, 229, 235, 236, 247

Jalalabad, Afghanistan, 10, 23, 123, 232, 234
James, Randy, 76
Jang-Ho, Yoon, 91
Janke, Jeff, 62
Johnson, Thomas, 168, 223
Jordanian embassy, 48

Kabul, Afghanistan, 10, 32, 36. See also Afghan government; U.S. embassy (Kabul)
    bombing of, 236
    nation-building and, 29–30
    suicide bombings in, 202
    U.S. and NATO ceremony in (2014), 227–228, 229
    U.S. dignitaries visiting in 2001, 30
Kabul Bank scandal, 190–195
Kabul Military Training Center, 55–56, 60–61
Kajaki Dam project, 161–162
Kamiya, Jason, 68–69
Kandahar (city), Afghanistan, 17, 25, 26, 101–102, 106, 112, 117, 123, 148, 160–162, 174, 250, 260, 263
Kandahar Air Field, 12, 13–14, 17–18, 160, 232

Kandahar province, 22, 27, 61, 73, 100, 105, 135, 147, 148, 155, 162, 165, 168, 171, 172, 203, 215, 223, 260, 261, 273
Kapusta, Philip, 8, 10
Karimi, Barna, 165
Karzai, Ahmed Wali, 123, 175, 176, 260
Karzai, Hamid
  assassination attempts, 174
  B-52 bomb dropped on camp of, 172
  Cheney's visit and, 91, 93
  corruption and, 123, 170, 189, 194
  Dostum, Abdul Rashid and, 119–120
  election of 2004, 54, 265
  election of 2009, 170, 171, 180–181
  handing out posters of, 38
  inauguration of (2009), 169
  as interim leader, 13, 26, 30, 172–173
  Kabul Bank scandal and, 191, 192–193
  as leader of new government, 13, 37
  lunch with U.S. diplomats (2002), 32
  negotiation efforts with Taliban, 265, 269, 270
  poppy cultivation and, 125, 138, 140
  relationship with U.S., 170–172, 173–181, 231
  Rumsfeld's press conference with, 44–45
  at State of the Union Address to Congress, 32–33
  taking responsibility for country's security, 230–231
  Taliban and, 172, 174
  U.S.-Afghan security agreement, 231
  warlords and, 120–121, 122, 125–126, 171, 176
  on war strategy, 151
Karzai, Mahmoud, 191
Kayani, Ashfaq, 86–87
Kem, Jack, 219
Khalilzad, Zalmay, 27–28, 50–51, 59, 73, 138–139, 174–175, 272, 273
Khan, Haji Juma, 261
Khost province, 164, 167, 179, 214
King, David, 12
King, Larry, 96

Kite Runner, 258–259
kleptocracy, 185–186
Known and Unknown (Rumsfeld), xxi
Kolenda, Christopher, 186, 190
Koran, 69, 80–81, 215
Kosovo, 25, 38, 45, 110
Kunar province, 235
Kunduz, Afghanistan, 118, 233, 236
Kunduz hospital, 233

Lachicotte, George, 148
Lamm, David, 121
language(s)
  Afghan army and, 57
  CIA operatives and Afghan, 22
  cultural training for U.S. military, 67, 69, 70
Lashkar Gah, Afghanistan, 133, 139
law enforcement. See Afghan police force
Leonnig, Carol, 243
Lessons Learned interviews
  on Afghan security forces, 57, 59, 63, 219–220, 223, 224–225
  on Afghan warlords, 117, 122, 126–127
  on bin Laden, 202
  on Bonn Agreement, 26, 27
  on civilian casualties, 179, 208
  on corruption, 123, 124, 125, 184–185, 186, 187–188, 189
  on diplomacy with Taliban, 27, 28
  on identifying the enemy, 20, 23
  on Iraq War, 45, 47
  on Kabul Bank scandal, 191, 192, 193, 194
  on Karzai, 170, 175, 176
  on lack of campaign plan, 15
  McChrystal's review, 150, 151, 152
  on misleading the public, 204–206
  on mission/objectives of the war, xix, 7–8, 14, 20, 110, 150
  on nation-building, 14, 30–37, 159, 160–161, 162, 163, 164–165, 166–168, 230
  on NATO-led coalition, 107, 108, 109

on negotiating with the Taliban, 267,
  270
on Obama's timeline, 153
on Pakistan, 82, 83, 86
Pentagon Papers compared with, xx
on poppy production/trade, 135, 136,
  137, 138–139, 140, 257, 258, 259,
  260, 261, 262
request for transcripts and audio
  recordings, xviii
on Rumsfeld, 106
by soldiers serving more than one
  combat tour, 148
on suicide attacks and roadside
  bombs, 95
on treating Taliban the same as
  al-Qaeda, 26
views by U.S. officials in, xviii–xx
on war strategy, 105, 108, 110, 152,
  230
Liddell, Jason, 154
life expectancy statistics, 204, 227–228
literacy, 31, 57, 65, 219
Little, Matthew, 63–64
Losano, Raymond, 79
Lovell, Kevin, 63
Lovett, Daniel, 70
loya jirga, 36, 50–51
Lute, Douglas, xix–xx, 52, 57, 110, 112,
  159, 160, 220, 255

Mann, Scott, 225
Mansager, Tucker, 45, 53, 54
Marines. See U.S. Marines
Marja, Afghanistan, 155, 207, 257
Marquez, Geraldine, 91
Marsden, David, 159
Marshall Plan, 30
Martin, John, 207–208
Massive Ordnance Air Blast (MOAB),
  247
Matakaiongo, David, 217
Mattis, James, 242–244, 245, 250, 266
Mazar-e-Sharif, Afghanistan, 10, 27, 39,
  50, 118, 120, 121, 217
McCaffrey, Barry, 85–86, 97–98

McCain, John, 155, 271
McChrystal, Stanley, 146, 149–150,
  151–152, 153–154, 155–156, 184,
  218
McKenna, Andrew, 232
McKiernan, David, 113–114, 145,
  146–147
McMaster, H.R., 243–244
McMullen, Ronald, 139
McNamara, Robert, xx
McNeill, Dan, xix, 15, 109, 111, 113, 125
meetings, cultural practices in
  Afghanistan, 71–72
Metrinko, Michael, 21–22, 135, 136
Miakhel, Shahmahmood, 223
military. See Afghan army; U.S. Army;
  U.S. troops
military operations. See also airstrikes;
  casualties; war strategy
at Afghanistan-Pakistan border,
  77–79, 81
Azizabad attack, 177–178
bombing of wedding party, 177
eradicating opium production,
  253–254
during Iraq War, 47–48
joint operations, 129, 214
at Kunduz, 233
major offensives in 2003, 50
night raids, 178–179
under Obama, 228, 233, 246
Operation Iron Tempest, 253
Operation Medusa, 105–106
Rumsfeld's press conference on
  ending of, 44–45
successes, in early phase of the war,
  3–4, 10–11
Tora Bora, capture of bin Laden at,
  23–25
under Trump administration,
  246–247
2015-2016, 229
U.S. lying to news media about, xv
Miller Center, xxiii. See also oral-history
  interviews, University of Virginia
Miller, Scott, 248–249, 250–251, 263

Milley, Mark, 211, 220–221
Mission Accomplished speech, 43–44
mission creep, 7–8
mission of War in Afghanistan. *See* objectives and goals of War in Afghanistan
Mohammed, Khalid Sheikh, 82
money laundering, 183, 188
MSNBC interview, 5
mujahedin, 116–117, 118, 123
Mullah Omar, Mohammed, 20, 27, 74, 134–135, 151
Mullen, Mike, 145, 146, 147, 201
Musharraf, Pervez, 82, 83–84, 85–86, 93–94

Nangahar province, 123, 177, 235, 247
narcotics, 100, 130, 138, 188, 253. *See also* opium production/trade
National Guard troops, 60, 164, 243
National Public Radio (NPR), 85, 152
National Security Council strategy paper, 8–9
nation-building, 14, 53, 241, 242. *See also* opium production/trade
    under Bush, 30–39
    Gates on, 104
    Lessons Learned interview illustrating failure of, 230
    under Obama, 158–168, 258
    one nation at a time, 45–46
    Rumsfeld on, 45
    security assistance expenses, 58–59
NATO and NATO-led coalition
    civilian death statistics, 208
    increase in troops, 153
    insider attacks on personnel of, 214, 215–216
    night raids, 178
    restricted to "non-combat" roles, 229
NATO (allies) and NATO-led coalition
    Article 5, xvi
    bureaucratic dysfunction, 107
    differences among troops, 106–107, 108
    Eikenberry's efforts to get support from, 94

mission statement of War in Afghanistan, 150–151
    Operation Medusa, 105–106
    poppy production programs, 258
    positive public reports about, 113
    responsibilities in Afghanistan, 105
    restricted to combat in self-defense, 150
    war on opium and, 133–134, 136, 137
    war strategy, 106, 108–109
NATO headquarters, Taliban suicide bombings/assaults on, 202
Navy SEALs, 18, 112, 199, 274
Nelson, Joshua, 213
Nena, Sapuro, 213
Netherlands, 105
Neumann, Ronald, 95–96, 98, 123, 132, 133, 138, 140, 175
New Ansari Money Exchange, 188–189
The News Tribune, 216
The New York Times, 25, 181
Nicholson, John, 147, 237, 243, 245–246, 248
Niedringhaus, Anja, 214
night raids, 178–180
9/11. *See* September 11th terrorist attacks
9/11 Commission, xvii
Norland, Richard, 115, 116, 176
North Atlantic Treaty Organization (NATO). *See* NATO and NATO-led coalition
Northern Alliance, 9, 10, 26, 83, 118–119, 125, 172, 264
Novak, Brent, 70–71

Obama, Barack (administration), xvii
    on Afghan security forces, 218, 219
    Biden's recommendations to, 274
    breaking promise to end the war, 233–234
    on corruption, 183–185, 190, 192
    counterinsurgency strategy, 149–150, 158, 201
    on "end" of the war, 227–228
    firing McChrystal, 156

on Iraq War, 228–229
military operations under, 228, 233, 246
misleading statistics/metrics by, 203–208
nation-building campaign under, 158–168
on opium production/trade, 256–257, 259, 261
prisoners of war and, 270–271
reconciliation efforts with Taliban, 266–268, 269, 270–271
speech at West Point (2009), 157–158
timeline imposed by, 153
troop surge strategy, 152–153, 157, 206–207, 209, 230, 244
troop withdrawal, 201, 228
Trump compared with, 241, 244–245
U.S.-Afghan security agreement, 231
U.S. spending under, 30, 158–163
war strategy, 17, 146, 147–149, 152–153, 158, 230
objectives and goals of War in Afghanistan. See also war strategy in Afghanistan, during Iraq War, 47
basic mission given to every commander, 205
Bush on, 8, 14
focus on al-Qaeda versus Taliban, 20
lack of, 7, 14–15, 109, 110
Lessons Learned interviews on, xix, 7–8, 14, 20, 110, 150
mission statement of U.S. and NATO, 150–151
for nation-building, 34
unclear, in 2008, 147–148
U.S. troops asking, 154
Office of the Special Inspector General for Afghanistan Reconstruction, xviii. See also Lessons Learned interviews
Olson, Eric, 22, 84, 265
Operation Avalanche, 50
Operation Bodyguard, xv
Operation Iraqi Freedom, 43–44
Operation Iron Tempest, 253–254

Operation Mountain Resolve, 50
Operation Mountain Viper, 50
Operation River Dance, 129, 130–132, 133, 137, 138, 139, 140, 254
opium production/trade, xix, 33, 110
aerial spraying program, 138–139, 140
Afghan warlords and, 124–125, 126
airstrikes on opium labs, 253–254
ban on, 134–135
Bush administration on, 129–133, 136–141, 256
cash-for-poppies program, 136
corruption and, 137–138
failure of programs to stop, 254–259, 261–262
increase in/success of, 129–130
Karzai, Ahmed Wali and, 175–176
law enforcement efforts, 259–261
Obama administration on, 256–257, 259, 261
Operation River Dance, 129, 130–132, 133, 140
opium, 134
success/growth of, 254–255, 257
switching crops, 256–257
Taliban and, 129–130, 132–133, 134, 137
Uruzgan province, 74
U.S. spending on war against, 137, 254, 259
oral-history interviews
Foreign Service officers/diplomatic, xxi, 21–22, 27, 51, 95, 96, 120, 135, 139, 172, 176, 181, 258
University of Virginia, xxiii, 9, 11, 15, 19, 24, 46, 52, 53, 104, 112, 171, 173
U.S. Army, xxii–xxiii, 8, 12, 13, 22, 24, 38, 47, 57, 60, 62, 65, 67, 70, 71, 72, 76, 78, 84, 92, 96, 100, 101, 109, 121, 126, 131, 132, 133, 137, 148, 150, 154, 216, 221–222, 225, 268

Pace, Peter, xxiii, 9, 10–11, 52
Pakistan/Pakistani border
al-Qaeda followers in, 20
Biden on Navy SEALS in, 274

Pakistan/Pakistani border (*cont.*)
  bin Laden in, 23, 24, 25
  bin Laden killed in, 199
  Bonn conference and, 26
  border sanctuaries, 93, 96, 110, 152, 201
  contractor transportation costs and, 187
  diplomatic efforts, 147
  insurgents and weapons from, 80
  Ishaqzai fleeing to, 260
  ISI (Inter-Services Intelligence), 81–82
  Islamic State in, 235
  Karzai and, 172, 174, 179
  McChrystal's war report on, 151–152
  military spending, 220
  negotiations and, 272
  operations at Pakistan-Afghanistan border, 77–78, 81
  playing both sides, 82–86
  Shkin ambush, 77–79, 80–81
  Taliban and, 82–83, 86–87, 93, 96, 100
Panetta, Leon, 199–201, 202–203
Panjwai district, 105, 106
Pardo-Maurer, Roger, 17–18
Partlow, Joshua, 121
Paschal, David, 38
Pashto language, 57, 67, 68, 70
Pashtuns/Pashtun tribes, 13, 19, 26, 74, 77, 83, 151, 172, 174, 264, 267
Patterson, Brian, 107
Paul, Rand, xxii
peace talks/negotiations, 235–236, 248, 249, 263–268, 267, 269–270, 271–274
Pentagon. *See also* U.S. Army
  Afghan police and, 65–66
  corruption and, 186–187
  lack of clarity in orders by (2001), 8
  misleading or false information from, 18, 203
  training a new Afghan army, 33
  Trump's meeting at, 243
Pentagon Papers, xx

Perry, Nathan, 177
Petraeus, David, 149, 153, 155, 156, 163–164, 194, 207, 258, 264
Phillips, Richard, 109
Plan Colombia, 138
Plummer, Christopher, 61, 72
police force. *See* Afghan police force; Afghan security forces
Popiak, John, 150
poppy. *See* opium production/trade
poppy palaces, 183
Powell, Colin, 32, 34, 51–52, 58
press conferences, 5, 11, 45, 47–48, 50, 113, 114, 147, 232
prisoners of war, 270–271
propaganda, soccer, 68–69
psychological operations (psy-ops), 67–68, 69, 100
public-health project, 168
public support for War in Afghanistan, xvi, 228

Qatar, 263, 269, 270, 271, 272, 273

Rabbani, Burhanuddin, 269
Rabe, Rick, 60
Raziq, Abdul, 250
Reed, Conrad, 81
Reeder, Edward Jr., 148
Reese, James, 70
religious codes of conduct/customs, 66
Rice, Condoleezza, 34, 52, 65
Richards, David, xix, 105–106, 109
roadside bombings, 93, 95
Rodebaugh, William, 24
Rodock, Robert, 223–224
Rodriguez, David, 93
Rohrabacher, Dana, 119–120
Roland, Matthew, 232–233
Ross, Douglas, 132
Rota, Ulf, 268
Rubin, Barnett, 26, 27, 137, 152, 153, 170, 184, 259, 267
Rucker, Philip, 243
Rumsfeld, Donald
  on Afghan army training, 58, 59

on "Afghanistan: Five Years Later"
        paper, 99
on Afghan police, 65
Dostum, Abdul Rashid and, 119
on escape of bin Laden, 25
Gates, Robert replacing, 104
health problems, 52
interview with Brian Williams, 5
on Iraq, 47–48
on Karzai, 174
lack of sympathy with general, 106
leadership traits, 52–54
meeting with Tommy Franks, 46
misleading the public about the
        war(s), 47–48, 49–50, 54, 96
MSNBC interview, 5
on nation-building, 34–36
on opium production/trade, 137–138
on Pakistan and Musharraf, 82, 85
Powell, Colin and, 51–52
press conference with Karzai, 44–45
private doubts and misgivings, 4, 5–6
snowflakes, xxi, xxii, xxiv, 4–5, 15, 23,
        49–50, 58, 65, 82, 99, 119, 137, 174
on telling lies during wartime,
        xv–xvi, 5
Tora Bora campaign and, 25
video conferences, 53–54
on a war strategy, 9, 11
on who the enemy was, 23
Russia/Russians, 26, 51, 61, 81, 103,
        118, 172. See also Soviet Union, in
        Afghanistan

Saam, Del, 65, 66
Salehi, Mohammad Zia, 189, 190
Samar, Sima, 33
Schloesser, Jeffrey, 113
Schmidt, Mark, 44
schools, 8, 39, 97, 113, 123, 158, 159,
        160, 166, 203, 205, 208
Schroeder, Darryl, 100–101
Schroeder, Gerd, 61
Schultz, Bradd, 57
Sebastian, Christopher, 215–216
Sellers, Terry, 38

Senate Armed Services Committee, 155,
        156, 206, 209, 210, 236, 237, 242,
        266
Senate Foreign Relations Committee,
        25, 93
Senate hearings, 110, 153, 155, 202, 203
September 11th terrorist attacks, xv,
        135
    bin Laden's death and, 200
    going to war following, xvi, 3
    mission of War in Afghanistan and,
        6, 7, 147
    Pakistan and, 82
    role of Afghans in, 19–20
    U.S. officials lying to the media after, xv
    withdrawing troops on twentieth
        anniversary of, 274
sex slaves, 75
Sharp, Walter, 56
Shea-Porter, Carol, 163
Sheberghan, Afghanistan, 118, 121
Sherzai, Gul Agha, 123–124
Shkin. See Firebase Shkin
Sibley, Forrest, 232
SIGAR, xviii. See also Lessons Learned
        interviews
Skelton, Ike, 155
Slusher, Michael, 61–62, 130, 133
Smiley, Jeffrey, 251
Smith, Jeremy, 11–12, 154
Snukis, Thomas, 45
soccer, 68–69, 158
Somalia, 10, 31, 45, 201, 249
Sopko, John, 204
Soviet Union, in Afghanistan
    avoiding mistakes of, 4, 9, 35
    weapons and, 19, 81
    withdrawal, 33, 86, 116, 181
Spann, Johnny Micheal, 118
Special Forces, 11, 22, 23, 44, 67, 74, 84,
        96, 100, 118, 119, 148, 160, 172, 174,
        224, 233, 271
Special Forces Village, 18
Special Operations Forces, 8, 9, 12,
        25, 70, 112, 146, 148, 149, 179,
        199–200, 229, 232–233, 249

State Department, xvi, 51, 158, 164
    Bureau of International Narcotics
        and Law Enforcement, 136
    central Afghan government and, 37
    misleading statistics, 203
    nation-building and, 34, 35
    negotiations and, 265, 270
    Operation River Dance and, 130–131
    poppy production/war on opium and,
        126, 136, 256, 257
    reopening of embassy, 21
    security forces training program, 56,
        58, 65
    strategy reviews, 112
State of the Union Address to Congress
    (2002), 32–33
statistics
    Lessons Learned interviews revealing
        distorted, xix
    life expectancy, 228
    misleading information about
        territorial control, 247–248
    misleading, under Obama
        administration, 203–208
Steadman, Andrew, 13
Strengthening Peace Program, 265, 266
Strmecki, Marin, 36, 59–60, 83, 86, 98,
    122, 175
Sudan, 19
suicide bombings/attacks, 91–93, 95,
    96, 110, 137, 202, 206, 242
Sunni Muslims, 72
Syria, 235

Tajik warlords, 83, 125, 171, 172, 191
Taliban
    Afghan general on three types of,
        101–102
    Afghan security forces and, 98, 104,
        214, 223
    Afghans identifying with, 151
    Afghan warlords and, 117
    al-Qaeda and, 19–20, 26, 267, 269
    assuming destruction of, 47
    Bonn Agreement and, 26
    control over Kunduz, 233

    corruption and, 186, 187
    countries holding diplomatic
        relations with, 82
    deaths from war crimes, 118–119
    Defense Department contracts and,
        187
    described by intelligence official, 209
    difficulties in identifying, 18–19, 22
    diplomatic efforts with, 25–28
    Dostum, Abdul Rashid and, 115, 116,
        118
    growth in, 247
    on homosexuality, 75
    intelligence reports indicating a
        danger from, 94–95
    Kabul Bank and, 192
    Karzai, Hamid and, 120, 172, 174,
        179, 181
    lack of understanding of, 100–102, 151
    made to be the enemy, 20
    misleading the public about strength
        of, 111
    nation-building projects and,
        161–162, 165, 167, 168
    negotiations with, 235–236, 263–
        268, 269–270, 271–274
    objectives for War in Afghanistan
        and, 7–8
    in Operation Medusa, 105–106
    opium cultivation/trade and, 129–
        130, 132–133, 134–135, 137
    Pakistan and, 80, 82–83, 85, 86–87,
        93, 96, 100
    peace talks, 248, 249
    poppy farmers joining the, 132–133
    reconciliation programs, 268–269
    regrouping and resurgence of, 50, 77,
        100, 111, 137, 210
    rules of engaging with (2016), 236
    Rumsfeld on, 5, 54
    suicide bombings, 91–93, 202
    territories controlled by, 247–248
    toppling government of, 3–4
    tribal rivalry/feuding, 21
    U.S. officials on threat from, 94–96,
        97–98, 207

U.S. troops urinating on corpses,
213–214
war crimes by Dostum, 115
warlords compared with, 117, 120
"The Tank," 243
Tanner, Fred, 147
Task Force Phoenix, 56, 57, 60, 62
Taxell, Nils, 124
tea boys (sex slaves), 75
teachers, 168
televised interviews/speeches, 6,
43–44, 99, 111, 157–158, 181, 201
terrorist groups, 235, 244. See also
al-Qaeda; Taliban
Terry, James, 101–102, 220
Thaden, Russell, 126
The Petersberg, Germany, 25
Tilley, Alvin, 74
Tillman, Pat, 99
Toolan, Paul, 96, 100
Tora Bora, Afghanistan, 23–25, 46, 70,
273
Towery, Jamie, 217–218
Townsend, Jon, 213
Trahan, Gregory, 47, 77–79, 80, 81
training
Afghan army, 33, 55–57, 60–63
Afghan security forces, 57–60, 65,
214, 219–220
cultural awareness, 69–72
police force, 59, 65–66
tribal codes of conduct, 66
Trump, Donald (administration), 237
Camp David meeting, 244
criticism of Obama, 244–245, 271
Flynn and, 189
Fort Myer speech (2017), 241–242
Khalilzad and, 28
misleading information and
deceptions by, 50, 247, 248–251
in national security meetings, 243,
244
negotiations with Taliban, 28, 264,
271–274
on opium production/trade, 256
war strategy, 241, 243–244, 245–247

United Nations
bombing of Baghdad headquarters, 48
Bonn, Germany conference, 13,
25–26, 264–265
civilian casualties count, 208–209
investigation of Azizabad attack, 178
nation building and, 31
opium poppy cultivation programs/
survey, 134, 135–136, 254, 256,
257, 258
United Nations Security Council, xvi
University of Virginia, xxiii. See also
oral-history interviews, University
of Virginia
Uruzgan province, 38, 74, 105
USAID, 34, 35, 51, 158, 159, 160, 161,
163–165, 166, 256
U.S. Air Force, 105–106, 172, 233, 234–235
U.S. Army. See also military operations;
U.S. troops
Operational Leadership Experience
project, xxii
oral-history interviews with soldiers,
xxii
U.S. Army Center of Military History,
xxii
U.S. Army Corps of Engineers, 63,
159–160
USA Today, 50, 178
U.S. Central Command, 8, 10, 11, 23, 24,
46, 119, 149, 249
U.S. diplomats, lack of experience in
Afghanistan, 73. See also oral-
history interviews, Foreign Service
officers/diplomatic
U.S. embassy (Kabul)
classified warnings from, 95, 96, 98
closing of, 20
Combined Forces Command moved
near, 48
corruption and, 187–188
cultural disconnect of ambassadors,
73
interviews with officials serving in.
See oral-history interviews, Foreign
Service officers/diplomatic

U.S. embassy (Kabul) (*cont.*)
Kabul Bank scandal and, 190, 192, 194
Karzai, Ahmed Wali and, 176
opium cultivation/war on opium and, 131, 133, 135, 136, 139, 140, 262
reopening, 21, 29–30
Taliban suicide bombings/assaults on, 202
U.S. government. *See also* Bush, George W. (administration); Obama, Barack (administration); U.S. military; U.S. officials
Afghan warlords and, 115, 116–117, 119, 122, 124, 126
Kabul Bank scandal and, 192–193, 194
training Afghan army, 57
U.S. Justice Department, 187, 261
U.S. Marines, 10, 24, 148, 165, 204, 214–215, 241, 243, 257–258
U.S. military. *See also* military operations; Pentagon; U.S. troops
Afghan army designed as facsimile of, 57
on attack on Panetta, 202–203
cultural awareness and training, 69–72
distortions and deceptions about the war by, 93
identifying the enemy, 22–23, 100–102, 148, 151
Kunduz hospital and, 233
misleading statistics/metrics by, 204, 206–208
nation-building projects and, 163–165, 166
on Pakistan/Pakistanis, 85–86
poppy production and, 136
on war's progress, 209–210
U.S. officials
corruption and, 186
covering up attack on Panetta, 202–203
on decision-making in early stages of the war, 7

Dostum, Abdul Rashid and, 120–121
honesty about progress in Afghanistan by, 113–114, 146–147
lack of knowledge about Afghanistan, 20–21, 27, 66
on lying during wartime, 5
military's assessments on war's progress, 209–211
negotiations with Taliban, 235–236, 263–268, 269–270, 271–274
U.S. officials, deceptions and misleading information by, xv–xvii, xviii–xix, xxi, xxiv. *See also* Lessons Learned interviews; oral-history interviews
in 2006, 94, 99–100
about Afghan security forces, 56–57, 94, 155, 210, 220–221
about "end" of the war, 227–228
about insider attacks, 216
about Iraq War, 47–48
about opium production/trade, 130
after bin Laden's death, 201–202
by Bush, George (administration), 96–97, 108, 111–112
in February 2007, 108
by General McNeill, 111, 113
Khalilzad's *Washington Post* op-ed, 50–51
Obama, Barack (administration), 154–156
statistics/metrics under Obama administration, 203–208
on Taliban threat and strength, 94–96, 97–98, 207, 209
on territory control statistics, 247–248
under Trump administration, 50, 247, 248–251
upbeat reports (2015), 231–232
USS *Cole*, 19
U.S. Special Forces. *See* Special Forces
U.S. Special Operations Command, 25
U.S. Special Operations Forces. *See* Special Operations forces
U.S. spending, xx. *See also* nation-building

bribing Afghan leaders and, 185
under Bush, 30, 95, 137, 158
corruption and, 184
on Kandahar dam and electrical
projects, 162
under Obama, 30, 158–163
on security assistance to Afghanistan,
56, 58–59, 220
for troops and resources in
Afghanistan (2006), 95
on war on opium, 137, 254, 259
U.S. troops. *See also* casualties; military
operations; U.S. military
alcohol consumption, 106–107
Biden on withdrawal of, 274–275
cultural disconnect between Afghans
and, 73–74
decrease in, 200, 215
deployed under Bush, 146
deployed under Obama, 152–153,
157
deployed under Trump, 244–245
in early part of the war, 4
efforts to limit, 9
email report from Kandahar, 17–18
at Firebase Shkin (April 2003), 77–79
general lamenting deaths of, xix–xx
having nothing to do, 13
insider attacks and, 213–317
for Iraq War, 45, 94
living conditions, 11–13
NATO-led coalition and, 106–107,
108
negotiations involving removal of,
272, 273
in "non-combat" roles, 229–230, 234
number in Afghanistan, xx, 12, 25,
111, 200, 228, 236
Obama's withdrawal timetable, 201
pledge to withdraw, 96, 153, 201, 228,
242, 272, 273, 274
rules of engagement, 229–230, 235,
236
sent to Afghanistan in 2008, 113
serving multiple tours in Afghanistan,
81, 148, 154

in strategy objective, October, 2001,
8–9
surge of, under Bush, 94, 104
surge of, under Obama, 152–153, 157,
206–207, 209, 230, 244
on Taliban threat, 99–100
views of Islam by, 72–73
women, 76
Uzbeks/Uzbekistan, 11–12, 20, 83, 115,
118, 171, 172

Vietnam War, xvi, xviii, xx, 6–7, 95, 139,
209–210
Virginia Military Institute, Bush's visit
to, 3, 14
Vogle, Greg "Spider," 172
Vorderbruggen, Adrianna, 234–235
Votel, Joseph, 249–250
voting, psy-op project on, 67–68. *See
also* election(s), in Afghanistan

Wallace, Devin, 217
Wallace, Steven, 13
Walter Reed Army Medical Center, 100,
121
Walters, John, 130
War in Afghanistan. *See also* military
operations
exit strategy, 4, 7
fighting Iraq War while in the, 45–47
Iraq War taking priority over, 15, 47,
108, 109, 110, 112–113
misleading the public about. *See* U.S.
officials, deceptions and misleading
information by
mission and objectives. *See* objectives
and goals of War in Afghanistan
warlords. *See* Afghan warlords
Warren, Elizabeth, 249
war strategy, 9–10. *See also*
counterinsurgency strategy;
military operations
under Bush, 105–106, 108–109
corruption and, 183–184, 186
lack of, xix, 105, 109–110
McChrystal's report on, 150–152

war strategy (*cont.*)
  misleading statistics/metrics and,
    206–207
  National Security Council strategy
    paper, 8–9
  under NATO-led coalition, 105–108,
    109
  under Obama, 17, 147–149, 152–153,
    158, 230
  reviews of, 112–113, 149, 150
  Robert Gates on, 104–105
  timeline under Obama, 153
  troop surge, under Bush, 94, 104
  troop surge, under Obama, 152–153,
    157, 206–207, 209, 230, 244
  Trump administration and, 241,
    243–244, 245–246
wartime, Rumsfeld on telling lies
    during, xv–xvi
Washington Post, xvii
  breaking news about Taliban insider
    attack, 251
  on Dostum payouts, 121
  Farnood interview, 192
  filing lawsuits against SIGAR, xviii
  Holbrooke's opinion column in,
    140–141
  Khalilzad op-ed, 50–51
  series of articles about Afghanistan,
    xxi–xxii
Washington Post–ABC News poll, 228

weapons
  Afghan army, 61, 62
  B-52 bombers, 253–254
  funneled to Afghan rebels fighting
    Soviet Union, 81, 116
  from Pakistan, 80
  of Taliban versus Afghan army, 98
weapons of mass destruction, 47
Wells, Alice, 272
Wesa, Tooryalai, 135, 168
Wesa, Zalmay, 250
West Point (U.S. Military Academy), 48,
    49, 57, 70, 110, 152, 153, 157, 163, 241
Williams, Brian, 5
Williamson, Dan, 62–63
Winstead, Mike, 131, 132
Winter Olympics, Salt Lake City (2002), 12
women and women's rights, 7, 75, 76,
    185, 203, 267
Wood, John, 138
Woodring, William, 72, 75
Wood, William, 140
World War II, xv, xvi, 25, 30

Yasini, Mirwais, 69
Yemen, 19

Zabul province, 213, 215, 216, 217
Zelikow, Philip, 46
Zia, Mohammed Ehsan, 258–259
Zizumbo, Daniel, 91

About the Author

Craig Whitlock is an investigative reporter for *The Washington Post.* He has covered the global war on terrorism for *The Post* since 2001 as a foreign correspondent, Pentagon reporter, and national security specialist. In 2019, his coverage of the war in Afghanistan won the George Polk Award for Military Reporting, the Scripps Howard Award for Investigative Reporting, the Investigative Reporters and Editors Freedom of Information Award, and the Robert F. Kennedy Journalism Award for international reporting. He has reported from more than sixty countries and is a three-time finalist for the Pulitzer Prize. He lives in Silver Spring, Maryland.